Psychology at W

Edited by Peter B. Warr

Penguin Books

Penguin Books Ltd, Harmondsworth, Middlesex, England
Penguin Books Inc., 7110 Ambassador Road, Baltimore,
Maryland 21207, USA
Penguin Books Australia Ltd, Ringwood, Victoria, Australia

—

First published 1971

—

—

Made and printed in Great Britain
by Cox & Wyman Ltd, London, Reading and Fakenham
Set in Monotype Times

Contents

To the memory of
Sir Frederic Bartlett

Introduction

This book represents an up-to-date record of psychologists' thinking and research into behaviour and experience at work. Students of industrial relations, business and management, students of the behavioural and social sciences generally, and members of educational, professional and trade-union study groups may all expect to find material which overlaps their interests. So too may the many managers and administrators who are not in a strict sense 'students' but who share a curiosity and concern for the developing science of psychology and for what it can offer them in their day-to-day work.

However, although the authors have had this wide readership in mind, they have selected their material and their style of presentation with one primary group of readers clearly before them – undergraduate and graduate students of psychology. We have a particular set of reasons for wishing to communicate with this group and their teachers, and it is to them that this Introduction is mainly addressed.

Over the past decades there has been a strong tendency for the work of academic psychologists to be appraised mainly in terms of its methodological rigour and its conceptual purity. These are most desirable characteristics, but in giving them emphasis we tend all too readily to forget about other qualities which should influence our evaluation. It is extremely easy (and correspondingly common) for academic teaching and research to become divorced from problems which are important outside the university environment. Inside the academic culture a sort of serious-minded game-playing has become valued as the norm, and those members of the psychological profession who have emerged with status and the power to influence have tended to be those who are not only skilled and energetic but also who adhere to the cultural norm.

Within the bounds of a university department of psychology this has often meant that the teachers who earn their students' respect are the ones who can generate research papers and ideas where methodology and predictions-based-on-theory are of greatest concern. Because these features are not so readily attained in real-life research, the able students within the cultural framework which rewards laboratory investigation tend to develop into able teachers in that same framework; and the selection and assessment of students is undertaken within a value-system which remains stable and reassuring.

Meanwhile, back in the world there are some 'applied' psychologists who are trying hard to tackle the pressing human problems of the day. These psychologists have many skills of an interpersonal kind but relative to their 'purer' counterparts they often lack methodological sophistication and theoretical incisiveness. They also lack status and influence within the profession so that they are rarely in a position to get at the root of this problem of imbalance – the teaching and the climate within university departments.

In brief, pure psychology is too pure and applied psychology is too applied; and much academic psychology is barricaded within its fortress of purity. Such a complaint is hardly new, but it is one which usually receives little more than lip-service and a shrug of the shoulder. Some isolated attempts have been made to bridge the gap – perhaps by persuading respected laboratory experimentalists to teach applied psychology or by importing non-academics to describe their subject. There are several reasons why these approaches usually fail, but the primary factor is that they are only minor deviations within a self-stabilizing cultural network. To change such a cultural system there has to be continuous application, both internal and external, of pressures of several kinds or of appreciable force. And as far as academic psychology is concerned there are many signs that these pressures are now building up more strongly than for a quarter of a century. Public and governmental opinion is becoming linked with professional dissatisfaction over theoretical sterility to generate a major potential for change.

In some respects psychology's present situation resembles that of the 1940s. Practical necessity and theoretical concern at that time led to marked changes in outlook and understanding. Particularly influential in the United Kingdom were the studies and opinions of the Professor of Experimental Psychology at Cambridge University. This was F. C. Bartlett, whose work has been of the profoundest significance to psychology in Britain and abroad. His career is well summarized in several tributes published after his death (e.g. Broadbent, 1970; Buzzard, 1971; Conrad, 1970), and it is to his memory that this book is dedicated.

Bartlett saw that the development of psychology rested upon its involvement in day-to-day problems. He argued forcibly that the major theoretical advances were likely to come from those research workers whose prime concern was with genuinely practical problems. The juxtaposition of 'theoretical' and 'practical' here is most important: Bartlett's notion was that we certainly need a theoretical structure but that this has to be built upon a foundation of practical reality rather than on the basis of what psychologists from their academic vantage-point may take to be reality.

This can be emphasized through a pair of quotations. The first comes from a symposium held in 1947, in which Bartlett asserted:

> No matter what 'kind' of psychologist a person is, he is a student of human behaviour. To my mind the history of psychology shows that if he shuts himself up narrowly in any particular small sphere of conduct inside or outside the laboratory (but specially inside), he will tend to get over-immersed in a terrific lot of detail about behaviour problems which he cleverly imagines for himself, and will approximate to a sort of puzzle solving which is often extremely interesting and, in a debating sense, intellectually attractive, but which leaves him revolving round and round his limited area. This works both ways, and if it is true that the general, or the laboratory psychologist must be prepared to keep his problems alive by going outside the study or beyond his immediate experimental settings, it is equally true that the field psychologist must seek his executive solution[1] with loyalty to that rigour of scientific method and that honest sense of evidence which only the study and the laboratory appear to instil. (Bartlett, 1947, pp. 215–16)

The second quotation comes from an appreciation written after Bartlett's death in 1969:

> He would sometimes say that no good psychologist should be interested only in psychology. This made him friends outside his own subject, and also guaranteed to his professional writings a realism and contact with life sometimes lacking in academic psychologists. His ideas concerning

1. In the context of the discussion from which this is taken an 'executive solution' was a set of practical activities to solve a problem. This was contrasted with a 'fundamental solution' – an explanation in terms of cause and effect.

psychology stemmed not from the criticism and development of abstract ideas, but from pondering on the mechanism which could produce an efficient stroke at cricket or explain why an African tribesman could remember perfectly the details of a number of cows sold a year previously. From a purely scientific point of view this made his ideas more original and more productive than those of the abstract theoretical schools; and from a worldly point of view he doubtless made psychology more acceptable to the representatives of other fields. (Broadbent, 1970, pp. 1–2)

Referring these quotations back to our discussion of contemporary academic psychology, we might argue that teachers and students should no longer concentrate so exclusively on the psychology of the published experiment. Bartlett's orientation would suggest that a shift away from problems arising out of the journal page would not only increase our practical value to society but that it would also advance and develop psychology as a theoretically oriented science. In the long term this second consequence is of course the important one.

The present volume is in a sense a contemporary assertion of Bartlett's philosophy. The authors have tried where possible to emphasize the links between general psychology and psychology at work, to show how there is nothing qualitatively different between the study of man in an organizational setting and the study of man as the psychology student is often taught to view him. We have also tried to show how investigations into people in their day-to-day work activities can be as intellectually stimulating and challenging as research into these same people in the laboratory. On more than one occasion an author has felt obliged to decry the overzealous application of a standard laboratory paradigm, but (as the first chapter convincingly argues) this is not the same as a general denunciation of laboratory psychology. Indeed several of the authors have themselves made notable and elegant contributions to laboratory research and they will no doubt continue to do so; here we may observe their recognition of its limitations.

One further general point should be made. The argument in this Introduction has focussed upon a single aspect of applied psychology, that which deals with people in their working environment. Much the same argument is applicable to other types of investigation: applied psychology in all its forms – educational, clinical, occupational or whatever – is too distantly related to psychology as an academic discipline. Applied psychologists draw too little from the general body of knowledge, and (more importantly) most of them contribute too little to it. However as we have seen, there are signs of change and the academic culture is slowly responding to internal and external pressures. The present book is written in the hope that Professor Bartlett's orientation will increasingly become the norm.

The authors have as their common theme the understanding of man in his complex day-to-day activities, but they naturally differ between themselves in their backgrounds and outlooks. The chapters are arranged in a sequence which roughly speaking moves from an emphasis on the individual through the study of groups to a stress on organizations as a whole. This sequence is conceptually an attractive one, but it is not necessarily the most suitable path for all readers to follow. Students of psychology should however make a point of commencing their journey at the first chapter; thereafter they may wend their way as it suits them. I hope however that no matter where they end up they will have a clearer appreciation of the excitement, the value and the limitations of psychological research into people in their working environment.

P.B.W.

References

BARTLETT, F. C. (1949), 'What is industrial psychology?', *Occupational Psychology*, vol. 23, pp. 212–18.

BROADBENT, D. E. (1970), 'Sir Frederic Bartlett: an appreciation', *Bulletin of the British Psychological Society*, vol. 23, pp. 1–3.

BUZZARD, R. B. (1971), 'Sir Frederic Bartlett, 1886–1969', *Occupational Psychology*, vol. 45, pp. 1–11.

CONRAD, R. (1970), 'Sir Frederic Bartlett, 1886–1969; a personal homage', *Ergonomics*, vol. 13, pp. 159–61.

1 Relation between Theory and Application in Psychology[1]

Donald Broadbent

A major theme of this book is that research psychologists are sometimes too loathe to leave their laboratories. Such an argument in no way denies the value of laboratory research itself but it does emphasize the need to draw problems, approaches and insights from situations which are of day-to-day significance to ordinary people. Dr Broadbent develops this theme to suggest that major theoretical advances are particularly likely to come from an applied perspective. His own research from this standpoint has been extremely fruitful in both theoretical and empirical terms, and in this chapter he includes examples from his own work as well as that of other people.

At the 1948 International Congress of Psychology an Evening Discourse was given by Sir Frederic Bartlett, the Professor under whom I myself was trained. One could sum up the theme of his discourse as being that the major theoretical advances in psychology were coming from those laboratories interested in practical and applied problems. Although many things have changed in the interval, I wish to present a new form of the same argument.

If I am going to do this successfully, the first step must of course be to recognize and examine the opposite argument, the reasons why some people feel that applied psychology is of no theoretical interest. There are a number of these reasons, each of which has some truth in it, and it is as well to admit these truths. First, it is perfectly true that those concerned with the future of the science should resist any pressure to work on problems solely because the general public or the government of their country regard them as important. To give way to such pressure can be disastrous: the community as a whole is not qualified to judge the probability that research in a given field will produce tangible results. There is no doubt that many problems, to which answers would be of great benefit to society in general, are sufficiently beyond the reach of current techniques that a large investment of effort in them would be a waste of valuable resources (Medawar, 1970). To put it bluntly

1. A version of this chapter was given as an Evening Discourse at the Nineteenth International Congress of Psychology, London, 1969.

and concretely, it would be of enormous value to the world at large if some psychological solution could be found to the problem of the persistent criminal. The probability of such a solution being obtained in the short-run is however extremely low, even if every psychologist in the world were to drop all other concerns and to concentrate upon that problem. On the other hand, the benefits of a slight increase in the speed with which letters can be sorted amount only to a few million pounds a year: but the probability that such a result can be achieved by the expenditure of a few thousand pounds on research is extremely high (Conrad, 1960). Thus even from an applied point of view it is irrational to drop all other interests and concentrate only upon those problems which have a colourful and emotional appeal to the community at large.

In any event, the immediate economic importance of a piece of applied research is not necessarily the main point; rather that the problem is drawn from real life. One of Professor Bartlett's main interests, for example, was the solution of certain psychological problems arising from observation of skilled performance in the game of cricket (Bartlett, 1951a). Answering these problems was at first of no economic importance – although the knowledge thus achieved has in the end turned out to be of some industrial significance (Poulton, 1970; Taylor, 1960). The reason why this research was in the tradition I favour, however, was not that it was of immediate economic benefit, but that the problem was drawn from a real and practical situation, in which human beings naturally perform. I must emphasize therefore that, in arguing for the theoretical importance of applied psychology, I am not supporting the view that psychologists should necessarily work on projects with an early financial return.

A second fear which academics sometimes have about applied psychology is that it may concentrate on the conduct of a number of specific experiments, each of which is of no general significance. (A caricature of the applied psychologist, from this point of view, might be the man who is endlessly concerned with the best diameter of cranks and handwheels, or the width of scale divisions on dials.) To this the answer must be that the best contribution to practical problems is to produce a general theory, which avoids the need for experiment in each specific situation. When a designer produces a new kind of helicopter, he would rather the psychologist could tell him the best methods of training for the pilot, by consulting a well-formulated theory of his functioning (Benjamin, 1970). He would certainly regard this as more practical than a need for comparison of several complete experimental training programmes before any decision could be reached. Thus the applied psychologist, of the kind I want to support, is always trying to understand how people work, and not simply to do an unintelligent experiment in the specific situation.

Thirdly, I do not really mean to deny all value to the research currently pursued by academics. When a real life situation, of economic importance or not, has raised some general theoretical problem, that problem will itself elaborate and raise numerous issues. Several generations of workers may need to pursue it, in separation from the mundane surroundings which gave it birth. Thus as psychology advances, many problems which arose in the real world have been taken up by workers in the ivory tower, sometimes to the point where their origins have been forgotten. In other sciences, this tendency is particularly noticeable, so that there may seem little in common between the theoretical physicist of the modern university and his applied forbears who were worried about problems of gunnery, navigation or bridge building. So equally there are psychologists working in cloistered academic departments on problems which now seem to be pursued for purely theoretical reasons, which nevertheless have some real and concrete origin. This is even more true now than it was at the time of Sir Frederic Bartlett's address twenty years ago, and I would therefore be perfectly happy to admit that there is much work of theoretical importance which is being done by psychologists other than applied ones.

I must admit all these points and recognize that applied psychology is open to serious dangers. It may divert to badly chosen problems because of social pressure, it may deteriorate into mere measurement on specific points instead of achievement of general understanding, and furthermore problems which have been raised from the field can quite properly be pursued from a purely theoretical point of view. After all these points have been admitted, however, I should still like to argue that the applied psychologist is more likely to make major theoretical contributions than is his academic colleague. One reason for this is the sense of realism which is forced upon the applied man: he cannot choose specially favourable conditions for testing his theories, but must expose them to the full range of circumstances that may apply in the field. There is nothing like a little acquaintance with the use of simulators in flying training, to show up the deficiencies of psychological theories of learning (Hammerton, 1967). Again, contact with practical situations forces on our attention major variables, which it is easy to neglect altogether if we pick our problems from articles in the academic literature. For example, we would hardly have thought from the psychological journals of 1930 to 1960 that a dominant feature of human beings was their tendency to lie down every twenty-four hours and become completely unresponsive for seven or eight hours. This is such a widespread phenomenon that we might imagine that it has a fairly basic importance in theories of behaviour. Applied psychologists have it borne in upon them fairly constantly (Colquhoun, Blake and Edwards, 1968). Furthermore, even if we have already chosen a field of work, by considering it in its applied context we may see all sorts of limitations in views which are generally accepted theoretically.

Perhaps this is the point at which to become more concrete and to give an example of the sort of thing I mean. Let us take the question of grouping in memory strings of letters or digits. It is a fairly universal truth in the academic literature that such strings are better recalled if they are presented grouped by threes, rather than in any other way (see for example Wickelgren, 1964). This fact has been used in the design of the British letter sorting code, or 'Zip Code' to use the American expression. Our code has six characters, not all digits because that would give an insufficient number of addresses in the country as a whole. On the other hand, six letters would give a code larger than is necessary, and digits are easier to copy and remember than letters are, by an amount which is enough to be important in practice. So the code has four letters and two digits, of which the two digits occur in the position in the sequence where errors are most probable, namely in the middle. The point to which I especially want to draw attention, however, is that the six items are presented always in two groups of three, so that our own code at the Applied Psychology Unit becomes CB2 2EF. Grouping by threes in this way is likely to give fewer errors than any other form of grouping.

But a new possibility is raised by using psychological information in this way to design codes. The telephone number of our Unit is 0223–55294. On the same principle, perhaps this ought to be presented in a different way, and should perhaps appear as 022–355–294. Such a revised form of grouping ought perhaps to be used on our notepaper, and possibly the Post Office should change the way in which numbers are set out in its directories. When however one thinks of other numbers which we frequently use, an important point emerges. The number of the Cambridge University Department of Psychology is 022–351–386. My own home telephone number is 022–354–232. In other words, the first four digits are the same for all Cambridge numbers, and in fact for numbers in the city itself the next digit is usually 5. The first five digits of the number therefore are always the same. When one calls another city, these five digits will be different, but it is clear that one cannot regard each telephone number as a random string of digits. There are subsections within the string, within each of which the transition probabilities are different from those which apply in other parts of the string.

The classic data on grouping were obtained with random strings of items. If now we consider the new situation of strings with non-homogeneous transition probabilities between items, is the classic and well-established advantage of grouping by threes really still true? The answer is that it is not. If we carry out an experiment in which large numbers of strings of digits are presented to the subject and in which certain combinations of digits recur frequently at the beginning of the list only, then the best size of group depends upon the number of initial digits which recur together in the same way as do the exchange digits in telephone numbers. When it is the first three of the string which represent the 'exchange', then grouping by threes is still preferable. If however the first five digits represent the 'exchange', then grouping by threes ceases to be so advantageous, and for any nine-digit string, a grouping by five and four may even be preferable.

The practical situation, then, has revealed in this case that a generalization thought to hold very widely does not in fact hold under all circumstances. Grouping by threes does not have any universally accepted theoretical explanation – which is itself rather a criticism of current theory. It does mean however that the impact of this particular result from applied work is less immediate in theory than would otherwise be the case, but when a satisfactory explanation of grouping is found, this fact will need to be included.

The illustration is drawn from the general field of engineering psychology, which happens to be the field of applied work in which I myself am concerned, and in which I know most examples. Before I go on to the main part of this paper, however, I ought to emphasize that I am not confining the importance of applied research solely to the field of applied experimental psychology. I should be the first to admit that work of great theoretical importance is carried out through studies on brain and behaviour, for which the practical impetus comes from the need for knowledge of the likely effects on human experience and behaviour when the brain is injured. Again, an applied field such as mechanical translation has given rise to a need for understanding grammar and syntax more thoroughly than was true in the past, and this has blossomed into a flourishing theoretical field of psycholinguistics. (In this case, a main conclusion of the work seems to have been that mechanical translation raises too many difficulties to be worthwhile, and the theory has been elaborated to the point where the applied interest is not immediately obvious to fresh inquirers, but it was there at the beginning all the same.) Educational psychology again raises problems of learning; the attempt to improve industrial relationships leads to theoretical studies of attitudes and the perception of other persons. A desire to change nutritional habits in the population may lead to academic studies of opinion change in small social groups; and so on. Many other fields of application have their corresponding theoretical contributions. In concentrating on engineering psychology and its impact on theory in experimental psychology, therefore, I am only choosing illustrations from a field I know.

Given these qualifications, what kind of contribution does applied psychology make to theory? I want to set out some instances of the kind of impact it has had in recent years, merely as examples to give some concrete content to my general thesis. Let us start by looking at some of the jobs which people actually do nowadays. The classic approach of the psychologist is to consider the reaction of a man to some single stimulus or pattern. Yet when we look at working situations, we often find that man is in fact faced with a large array of different possible sources of information, not with just one. The pilot of a modern airliner or the astronaut in his capsule are familiar examples (Voss, 1961). But the principle is a general one: the Victoria Line of the London underground system is very largely automatic in operation, the trains starting and stopping in obedience to signals controlled by punched tape. But the flow of trains does need to be monitored by human beings, to rectify accidental disturbances which might otherwise disrupt the system. This means that a relatively small number of men are watching displays which give the position of every train in the system, the departure of any from the timetable, the current state of the programme machines which control the signals, and so on (Raffle and Sell, 1970). Jobs of this kind are the rule rather than the exception, and they are very remote from the academic psychologists' concentration on a man faced with a single stimulus for perception.

When one looks at people doing jobs of this kind, the first point which emerges is that there are limits on their ability to cope with incoming information. The ability to react adequately to one of the things which are happening is to some extent incompatible with the ability to react efficiently to something else. There are of course some simple mechanical reasons for this, such as the difficulty of working switches with the same hand that is also dialling a telephone number, and the impossibility of pointing the eyes in two directions at once. But more analytic experiments, using tachistoscopic experiments or auditory stimulation, show that the limitation is not one of the senses, nor one of the responding limbs. There seems to be some central limit on the capacity of the nervous system for processing information.

This has immediate practical consequences in that it means that jobs such as signal regulation on the Victoria Line have to be arranged to take it into account. In that example, for instance, the designers of the task have arranged that human intervention need not take the form of altering each signal personally and directly, because that would mean that an intervention, even if rare, would involve many different actions at the same time. Rather, the regulator is able to take a decision, and to implement it by a few relatively simple operations; if he decides to reverse all trains reaching a certain point, this can be implemented by one action and then left to carry on automatically, thus saving time for handling other aspects of the problem.

In addition to its direct practical application, however, the idea of limits of processing capacity leads on to further analysis of performance. If there is a limit on capacity, it is likely that there will be some kind of mechanism inside the nervous system which protects that limited capacity by selecting only part of the surroundings for action. Indeed, experiment shows that this is so; and further shows that it is not merely due to efferent control of the sense organs. For example, it is possible to listen to one voice amongst a babble of sound, but this is not due to the brain adjusting the sensitivity of one ear relative to the other. The result can be shown experimentally with stereo presentation to the two ears, where each ear is receiving the desired voice embedded in enough sound to make it unintelligible if that ear alone is stimulated (Broadbent, 1954). When a man receives both presentations, however, with the relevant message leading by a few milliseconds in one ear, and the irrelevant sounds leading in the other ear, he is able to select the particular voice he wants. He cannot be doing so by switching off one ear. Again, one can demonstrate that attention may be directed to a particular feature of a visual event after stimulation has occurred, and not just in advance of the arrival of a particular stimulus (Sperling, 1960). Attention cannot therefore be simply a change in the sensitivity of the eye or ear alone. It must involve central processes which operate upon the stimulation received, and select some of it for further analysis.

We have thus reached the view that a man faced with an aircraft cockpit, or a display of underground trains, cannot deal with all the information which is available, but rather selects some part for decision. There are different mechanisms by which selection can operate. One very common one can be illustrated by the practical problem of finding a particular coin in a handful of change. Any visitor to London in 1969 would have noticed that we were using a system of coinage which was not decimal. However, in 1971 there came a change of currency, which psychological experiments show to be likely to produce fewer errors (Committee of Inquiry on Decimal Currency, 1963). This also involves a change of coinage and consequently experiments have been done on the speed with which one coin can be recognized amongst a group of others. The most usual cue for differentiating coins is size, but there are limits to the range of sizes that can be employed; usually therefore most countries use coins of at least two different kinds of metal, thus introducing a feature of colour. For our purposes, too few different coins could be produced using only two features, and a difference in shape was also introduced. The point to which I want to draw attention, however, is that the finding of certain desired items amongst the large array of other irrelevant ones is made much easier if all relevant items bear some one common physical feature, which is not possessed by any of the irrelevant ones (Wright, Hull and Conrad, 1969).

Another example of the same mechanism is the design of labels for drugs. The task of a nurse or dispenser looking for a particular dose of a particular drug is made very difficult by giving this information merely in a written description on the label. Most labels look very alike, and if all of them have to be read to decide that most of them are irrelevant, much time is taken. If however all labels of a certain type have a distinctive colour, the finding of the desired drug can be carried out much faster (Poulton, 1964). In general terms, if one is searching for a particular item on a complex display, then it is the number of items of the same colour as the target item which largely determines the time taken to find it, and other irrelevant items in different colours have rather little importance (Green and Anderson, 1956).

The nervous system likes therefore to make use of a strategy of discarding irrelevant parts of the surroundings merely by their failure to possess some one feature which all relevant parts possess. This process I have called 'filtering'; a knowledge of its existence is of considerable practical importance and also of some theoretical significance.

It is not however the only mechanism by which selective attention takes place. We may also have the case in which the desired and relevant aspects of the surroundings possess no single common feature which distinguishes them from other and quite irrelevant events of which no notice ought to be taken. Thus we may be looking for a coin which is both small and silver in colour, and some unwanted coins will be small although copper coloured, while others will be silver but too large. To take another example, the late Professor Fitts of Michigan conducted an important series of experiments on histogram patterns. The subject carried out a visual search amongst a series of such patterns in search of one particular pattern which matched the sample provided. No one feature of the target pattern distinguished it from the other irrelevant ones (Fitts and Leonard, 1957). As Fitts showed, the time taken to find the desired target depended upon the number of irrelevant items amongst which the search was to occur, as well as upon the difficulty of each individual comparison.

This line of work arose from a practical problem of detecting certain patterns on cathode ray tube displays. But the problem has recently risen into great prominence amongst academic psychologists, thanks to the important developments by Neisser of a similar task using words rather than patterns as the stimulus items (Neisser, 1967). The broad conclusion is that in this type of selection the irrelevant items are considered serially, one after another, and thus irrelevant items have much greater importance than they do if some single feature distinguishes them from the target item. On the other hand, it seems likely that the irrelevant items are not fully analysed, merely enough information being extracted from them to decide that they are indeed irrelevant. This can be inferred from the speed with which they are dealt with, from the effects of changes in the vocabulary of irrelevant items, and from the knowledge of those items which the searcher picks up incidentally.

When search of this kind is in progress, the economy of capacity in the nervous system is achieved in a rather different way from that found in filtering; in the latter strategy the man analyses very few features of the irrelevant events other than the single feature which shows that they are irrelevant. In the case we are now considering, this form of economy is impossible, but as we have said certain features of the input may not be fully analysed. In order to achieve efficient responses despite this limitation, the man may be biased towards or against the occurrence of certain percepts in such a way that a relatively large amount of sensory evidence is necessary to produce some reactions, while others will occur after very little such evidence. An important analysis of the effects of such biasses on the probability of correct reaction has been carried out in Michigan by the Electronics Defense Group, whose practical origins need no emphasis (e.g. Green and Swets, 1966). The point which they established beyond all question is that the probability of correct response may be greatly altered by changes in bias which give only small alterations in the probability of false response. Before their work this was not generally realized, and it is not going too far to say that their insight has revolutionized classical and academic psychophysics. They have demonstrated that the high probability of correct response achieved in cases where a certain stimulus is very probable may be attained, not by a complete and capacity-demanding analysis of the information from the senses, but rather because of the adoption of a very efficient strategy of perceiving the probable stimulus even if the evidence for its occurrence is relatively slight.

Other analyses have extended similar principles from psychophysical situations to the perception of words (Broadbent, 1967; Morton, 1968). A similar interpretation has been applied to studies of attention in hearing, where the listener may select a particular word because of its probability or meaning, even though the stimulus does not possess some single feature allowing filtering (Treisman, 1960; Moray, 1960). It seems clear that a second mechanism, in addition to filtering, must be recognized as existing, and as deciding which percepts occur selectively in the presence of a mass of external events. This second strategy of selective perception I call 'pigeon-holing'.

We have therefore a position, largely forced upon us from applied psychology, that a man is limited in his ability to process information; that this limit is a central one rather than one due to sensory or motor limitations; that as a result he selects only parts of his surroundings for response; and that this selection can take place through at least two different kinds of mechanism. The first of these I call 'filtering': selection for response of events which possess a distinguishing feature. The second I have called 'pigeon-holing': the occurrence of particular, favoured classes of response even when the evidence received by the brain is somewhat ambiguous. In each case, it has been practical situations which have forced upon us possibilities which might have been ignored in the laboratory.

I now want, however, to take a further step in the argument, bringing it up to date, by emphasizing that the mechanisms I have described are not passive mechanical operations which always occur regardless of situation. Rather, they are genuine strategies which a man adopts in appropriate situations but may depart from if the environment ceases to be one in which they are appropriate. One example of this is seen in Rabbitt's (1966) experiment on visual search. Whereas Neisser had found that search could proceed as rapidly for several targets as for one, Rabbitt showed that this depended upon the probability of a target being rather low. If targets were very frequent, Rabbitt found that the speed of search got slower if several targets were involved. We might say that irrelevant items were discarded with very little analysis if the probability was such that it was unlikely that anything more needed to be done about them. If the targets were numerous, and it was thus probable that a complete analysis of the stimulus would be necessary, even the irrelevant items were analysed fairly fully, sufficiently to distinguish one of the possible targets from another.

Another example is worth going into in more detail, as the applied connection is more obvious and the experiments are unpublished. In buying a ticket for the Victoria Line, the traveller experiences the difficulty of needing to buy a more expensive ticket if he is going further. Unfortunately, the London Underground is sufficiently large that it is not thought practical to introduce the flat-rate system common in cities with a less extensive network. One can simply go to the booking office and ask for a ticket of the correct value, but it would be faster and more efficient if more people could use the automatic machines to buy their tickets; consequently there is a problem of letting the passenger know the fare he needs for a particular destination from a particular station. There are two ways in which this can be done, and indeed is done. One is to mark each machine with a list of the stations which can be reached with a ticket of that value; the other is to present a complete alphabetical list of stations, giving the fare against each station. From the point of view of psychological theory, we have already seen that visual search amongst words seems to be carried out successively, so that the later the item appears in the list, the longer it seems to take to find. On this basis, one would expect that it would be more efficient to look at lists of stations classified by fare, rather than at a complete alphabetical list of all stations on the system. On the hypothesis of serial search, one would in the latter case need on average to examine half the station names on the system before reaching the one desired; of course the examination of each irrelevant name would be very brief, and consist in all probability of merely checking that it did not possess the correct initial letter. Nevertheless, some substantial time would be occupied in this way. When separate lists were presented for each fare value, however, a similar search through about half the list would be necessary for each fare, until a point in the list was reached at which it was clear that the desired name was not on the list. Only half the fares would need examination however, as well as only half the list for each fare; since on average the correct name would be found before going any further. Thus the serial examination of lists classified by fare as well as alphabetically should roughly halve the time needed to find the target name.

Experiment shows that this theory is completely incorrect. The examination of a series of lists, each separate for a particular fare value, is slower than the examination of a complete alphabetical list of all stations. When one looks at the time taken to find individual targets, one can see why this is so. In an alphabetically organized list, the assumption of serial search ceases to be tenable, because the time taken to find a target does not depend on position in the list. It is as fast to find the fare to Walthamstow as it is to Arnos Grove. What seems to happen rather is that the man approaches an alphabetically organized list with a general awareness of the approximate location in the list where his target must be, even though he has not seen this particular list before and does not know in detail where one letter leaves off and another begins. He thus searches at the very start in approximately the correct region of the list, and finds his target far more rapidly than would be possible with a serial search.

Once again, the applied situation has drawn our attention to a theoretical point which might have escaped notice if we were confined to the laboratory. The lesson one must draw is that the strategies of information processing are exceedingly flexible, and that our efforts to avoid undue pressure upon our own brains can take a variety of forms. One strategy will be used in one situation and another introduced when the circumstances change. In disentangling these aspects of higher control over the lower level strategies, we can hope to get still further into an understanding of our own nature.

Will such further understanding merely help us to press buttons faster, to understand speech better on the telephone, or to choose a right drug rather than a wrong one? Even if that were the only return, it would still be socially worthwhile. However, I believe that the understanding of human nature which we gain in this way can in the long run be of far wider significance. I would like therefore to close by changing fields altogether and by calling attention to recent work in social psychology, in which one can see the importance of the same principles of perception as those we have been discussing in abstract and mechanical situations.

The filtering mechanism, for example, represents a strategy of selecting information from one source and neglecting that from others. This cuts down conveniently amongst excessive amounts of data on a control console, but equally it can be seen at work in social situations, where again people are bombarded by vast quantities of information. To meet this problem, they read certain newspapers only, and may regard exactly the same article as more 'true' if it is attributed to the *Daily Telegraph* than to the *Daily Mirror* (Warr and Knapper, 1968). In schools or factories, they may listen to certain individuals and ignore others.

Equally, the pigeon-holing mechanism has broader implications. Just as a man can be biased in favour of seeing a faint light when he knows such a light is probable, so the occurrence of information of one kind about another man changes the probability of judgements of another kind being made about the same man. In concrete terms, if one is told that a man is 'impulsive', one tends to give him higher ratings for 'friendliness' than one would in the absence of information about his impulsiveness. Similarly, to be 'practical' apparently means that one has a lower chance of being judged 'intelligent', and it is sad to learn that being 'cynical' increases one's chances of being judged 'intelligent'. Here we have biasses in perceptual judgement, even in the absence of incoming information, produced by probabilities which the percipient thinks he has assessed (Warr and Knapper, 1968).

The mechanisms of filtering, pigeon-holing and other similar processes are to a large extent adaptive – they protect our relatively small brains from a massive overdose of incoming information. Yet they can be dangerous, because they can lead us to ignore important features of our surroundings, or to make confident responses when the evidence available really does not justify such action. In social situations there are certainly some beneficial effects of these strategies, but their harmful ones are only too evident. Consciousness of the factors which are biasing our perception and a better understanding of the ways in which this happens, are the first step towards eliminating these harmful side effects. I feel therefore that in the long run a sound theory of human information processing will turn out to have practical implications very much more valuable than the immediate gain in displays, controls, and the lay-out of work. Yet the latter are still important, because as we have seen it is in the study of such real and concrete situations that we find the theoretical principles which will ultimately bring us to a solution of more fundamental problems.

This then is my message: it is theoretically productive to get our ideas from applied work. I have chosen examples from engineering psychology because that is my field, and the practical situations which I have mentioned have tended to be British. My whole theoretical orientation has made use of ideas developed not only or especially in the United Kingdom, but also in the Soviet Union, in the United States, and in many other countries in Europe and elsewhere; I have not given specific reference to most of these, simply because they are so numerous. You may well feel therefore that what I have been saying is general and international psychology, rather than being particularly British, and that I have failed to indicate some particular national line of thought which makes a distinctive contribution to the world scene. Indeed, I hope that what I have said does reflect very much the influences of a wide variety of our colleagues throughout the world, and that this approach is open to influences from any other country. If therefore you feel that this approach is at the cross-roads of a number of different national influences, and ask me what I would regard as especially British about it, the answer would be 'That fact itself'.

SUMMARY

In this chapter, it is argued that applied psychology is the best basis for a genuine theory of human nature. As an example, we discuss experiments on the handling of large quantities of information in semi-automatic systems. Two mechanisms emerge: the 'filtering' type in which a man concentrates on information from some sources only, and the 'pigeon-holing' type which biasses the man towards certain probable responses and thus saves him from needing to analyse large amounts of information before making such responses. It is also important that the strategy employed depends upon the man's situation, and is not simply wired into the structure of his brain. Such mechanisms might be overlooked by purely theoretical psychologists, who can ignore the complex nature of most real-life situations. Once found, these principles are of use in understanding many other situations as well as the ones which gave rise to them; that is, they are 'theoretical' in the best sense.

FURTHER READING

The particular theoretical points raised in this chapter have been discussed at length by D. E. Broadbent in *Decision and Stress* (Academic Press, 1971).

From a theoretical point of view, U. Neisser (*Cognitive Psychology*, Appleton–Century–Crofts, 1967) is of interest; more in the applied tradition are A. T. Welford (*Fundamentals of Skill*, Methuen, 1968); and K. F. H. Murrell (*Ergonomics*, Chapman & Hall, 1965).

Attention as a separate function is considered by Neville Moray in *Listening and Attention* (Penguin, 1970).

A variety of features met in industrial situations are considered by David Legge in *Skills* (Penguin, 1970) and by D. H. Holding in *Experimental Psychology in Industry* (Penguin, 1970).

2
Hours of Work and the Twenty-Four-Hour Cycle of Rest and Activity

Robert Wilkinson

By the 1930s psychologists had already contributed significantly to studies of working conditions, fatigue and hours of employment. Since then their research has become progressively more sophisticated, and in this chapter Dr Wilkinson illustrates one particularly important line of development. He examines the biological and social consequences of different types of shift-work, setting these in the context of studies of circadian rhythms more generally. He describes some of his own work together with that of colleagues and other investigators, and on the basis of the accumulated evidence he is able to make some practical recommendations about optimal work schedules.

The National Board for Prices and Incomes has recently brought out a report on 'Hours of work, overtime, and shift working' (1970). One of the conclusions is that overtime and shiftwork are, on the whole, viewed with favour by both men and management. The men get the chance to augment their pay packet. Management can make greater use of existing manpower through overtime, while shiftworking allows fuller implementation of plant. Nevertheless the report calls for a more searching and less intuitive assessment of whether prevailing levels of overtime and shiftwork in fact represent the most efficient or even productive use of our resources. It also questions whether a satisfactory balance has been struck between the economic advantages and the social costs of shiftworking. These questions come opportunely for the nation, and for this chapter. If national interests of health, happiness and stability are to prevail over parochial ones of profit it is necessary that an objective and unbiassed authority should exert some influence on these matters, as, of course, the Prices and Incomes Board is trying to do. Its influence, however, can only be as powerful as the evidence it can bring to bear. Producing this is largely the job of the research scientist, and particularly in this context, of the applied psychologist. His role is twofold: first to unearth the facts about how well people work and live under various systems of working hours, and second, on the basis of this to seek explanatory laws which can be applied generally.

The root of many of the problems of the modern industrial state is that machines evolve much faster than men: they do not have to go back to square one as we do at the start of each new generation. In our present context the dilemma takes this form: the human adult is an animal whose body is tuned by evolution and training to go about its business during the hours of daylight and sleep during those of darkness. Ask it to work at night and sleep during the day and it does both rather badly. Yet this is what modern technological progress demands, first when machines are so complex that they must work day and night to repay their cost, and second when jet planes are so fast they can move people across several time zones in a few hours. The end result of both of these is that people have to work when they would normally be sleeping and either not sleep at all or sleep when their bodies are expecting to be up and about. This chapter is concerned with how much both performance and sleep are impaired by this, how swiftly the body can adapt to the change, and how best to arrange things so that as little harm as possible comes to people's health, happiness and ability to do the job.

Let us look more closely at the cause of the trouble, man's twenty-four-hour or 'circadian' cycle of rest and activity.

THE CIRCADIAN RHYTHM OF REST AND ACTIVITY IN MAN

According to Kleitman (1963) there is a fifty to sixty-minute rest/activity cycle in the human newborn infant, which soon couples with a three to four-hour gastric cycle. By about four months these have for the most part given way to the normal twenty-four-hour cycle which is reflected in the child's sleeping and waking behaviour and in the levels of various physiological and biochemical measures including body temperature and a number of other cardiovascular variables: activity of the adrenal cortex, urine flow, excretion of phosphate, sodium and potassium, blood constituents, and so on. What concerns us most at present is man's ability to adapt the phase of this circadian cycle; that is, to move his sleep/wakefulness cycle round the clock as he moves from one working shift to another, or from one country to another. First let us examine the twenty-four-hour cycle itself in terms of the two measures which will concern us most: a psychological one, working efficiency, and a physiological one, deep body temperature taken by a normal clinical thermometer.

Body temperature and performance

The circadian variation of body temperature has been studied since at least the middle of the nineteenth century. Recent data by Colquhoun, Blake and Edwards (1968a) are based on two-point rolling means and provide one of the clearest impressions of the shape of the curve (Figure 2.1). This function was derived from fifty-nine young men whose oral body temperatures were taken at

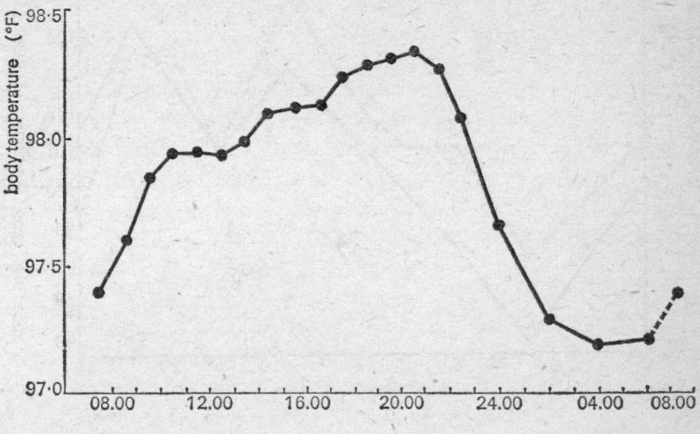

Figure 2.1 Oral body temperature of fifty-nine subjects at twenty points of the twenty-four-hour cycle. Note that the curve has been smoothed by taking 'rolling means', that is, each point of the curve is the average of two measurement points, 06.00 and 08.00, then 08.00 and 10.00, and so on. (From Colquhoun *et al.*, 1968a)

two-hour intervals throughout twenty-four hours on two separate occasions. The important points to note are the deep trough of temperature during the small hours of the morning and the gradual rise during the day to a peak which is in the mid-evening in these records but which can occur anywhere between noon and late evening as a function, among other things, of the individual's personality and social habits (Blake, 1967).

The circadian function of performance is more difficult to record on a twenty-four hour basis. People rarely work for twenty-four hours at a stretch, and if they did mounting fatigue would confuse the picture. What is needed is performance for shorter periods over a number of days and at different times of the day and night on successive days. This in fact is achieved, in the interests of a fair distribution of the unpleasant early morning watches, by a conventional naval three watch system of duties. (This system is described later on p. 38 under the name of Three Man System). Thus when the US Navy asked for this watch system to be compared

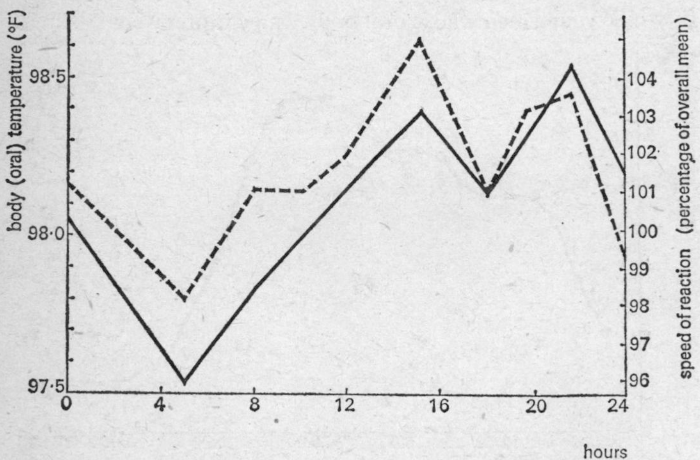

Figure 2.2 Co-variation or oral temperature and serial reaction time during the twenty-four hours. Speed of reaction is expressed as a percentage of the average over all subjects in all conditions. The solid line is oral temperature, the broken one reaction time score. (Data adapted from Kleitman, 1963, p. 157)

with others it provided an excellent opportunity for Kleitman and Jackson (1950) to record a composite performance curve with sections from all days, thus covering the whole twenty-four hours. Figure 2.2 shows this curve for one of the performance tests, choice serial reaction (colour naming) which was administered for about five minutes at roughly two-hour intervals when the men were on duty. The points are the average of nine subjects. Oral body temperature was recorded at the same time and is shown also. Clearly the two curves are very similar, and in fact the correlation between body temperature and speed of reaction was +0·89. This, together with earlier results covering a wider range of tests but during the hours of daylight only, persuaded Kleitman (1963) that 'most of the curves of performance can be brought into line with the known circadian body temperature curve, allowing for individual skewing of the curve towards an earlier or later, rather than mid-afternoon peak'. More recently further studies, particularly the exhaustive ones of Colquhoun, Blake and Edwards (1968a; 1968b; 1969) have supported the existence of a body temperature/performance relationship. Others, however, force us to make some comments and qualifications.

There is no doubt that under normal conditions performance, in some respects at least, is impaired at about the same point in the circadian cycle as body temperature is depressed. The obvious question, raised but rather clouded by Kleitman himself, is that of the causal relationship, if any, between the two measures. Kleitman and Jackson (1950) were at pains to refute the idea that it was the level of body temperature which directly caused that of performance to vary during the circadian cycle. Yet in his review (1963, p. 163) Kleitman considers the possibility of a direct effect of body temperature upon thought processes by influencing the level of metabolic activity in the cells of the cerebral cortex. Rutenfranz, Aschoff and Mann (1970) discount this in a recent study, similar to that of Kleitman and Jackson, in which they controlled for the effect of time of day by examining the temperature/performance correlation separately at each measurement point of the day or night. The correlation fell almost to zero. This indicates that it is not body temperature which is determining performance but some unknown factor, which varies in circadian fashion and carries body temperature and some aspects of performance along with it. Thus we can still measure body temperature in an attempt to determine working efficiency where this latter cannot easily be assessed but we cannot expect to change the circadian pattern of performance by artificially influencing the level of body temperature.

It should be remembered in this discussion that we are speaking of the body temperature/performance relationship in the context of circadian variations only. It is easy to forget that there are many other non-circadian influences which may enter to disrupt the measurement of the relationship especially when this is attempted outside the laboratory. One of these may be fatigue when tests are presented repeatedly during the day. This fatigue may produce lower levels of performance than would be expected on the basis of body temperature alone. Blake (1967) avoided this difficulty by presenting tests only once a day for five days, a different time being chosen each day. In most of his tests he found that peak performance occurred at 9 p.m., much later than Kleitman found. Would Kleitman's curves have shown this pattern if he had tested only once a day? If so, his body temperature/performance relationship would probably have been less satisfactory. Unfortunately no records of body temperatures are available for Blake's one-test-a-day study.

In his experiment Blake presented eight performance tests, the duration of which ranged from five to sixty minutes. He noted that on the whole the usual time of day effects were most marked in those tests which were long and repetitive; and a quick calculation from his data reveals a correlation of about +0·7 between the duration of the task and the degree to which its scores followed the usual rise in body temperature during the course of the day. This influence of task duration, plus the fact that incentive will reduce circadian performance variations (Chiles, Alluisi and Adams, 1968) especially in extraverts (Blake and Corcoran, 1970) makes the influence of low points of the circadian cycle look very similar to that of sleep deprivation (see Wilkinson, 1965). In support of this correspondence is the finding (Wilkinson, 1970) that the two interact; effects of loss of sleep are greater in the morning than later in the day, and are usually very marked during the night (Chiles, *et al.*, 1968). Now, although the term may lack as precise a scientific foundation as we would like, it may prove useful at this point to think in terms of the level of arousal of the body.[1] Sleep deprivation may be regarded as lowering arousal both physiologically (Ax and Luby, 1961) and psychologically (Wilkinson, 1965). The correspondence between the behavioural picture of loss of sleep and of that prevailing at the low points of the circadian cycle suggest that the latter too may be reflecting a state of low arousal. To the extent that we understand the effects of loss of sleep on performance (Wilkinson, 1965; 1970) this approach may have heuris-

1. This notion and the consequences of varying arousal level are further examined in chapter 3.

tic value in indicating those working situations in which we can expect body temperature to provide a reasonably accurate guide to the level of working efficiency.

The role of body temperature

We are concerned ultimately with the effects of the circadian cycle on performance, but of course there are many irrelevant factors which may influence working efficiency especially in the less controlled situations of real life. Also in the factory or other field settings it is often impractical to take measures of performance. In the light of this, our interest in the closeness and generality of the body temperature/performance relationship is obvious. To the extent that body temperature can reflect the circadian component of performance its adaptation to abnormal routines may be taken as an indication of the adaptation of working efficiency where the latter cannot be assessed directly in the field. With this in mind let us see what variations in the normal body temperature pattern are to be observed as people adapt or fail to adapt to abnormal patterns of work and rest.

ADAPTATION OF THE CIRCADIAN RHYTHM OF BODY TEMPERATURE AND PERFORMANCE

This question can be examined both in the laboratory and in the field. We will take the laboratory first, and pay particular attention to those studies in which performance as well as body temperature was measured, thus allowing the two to be correlated.

Adaptation in the laboratory

Perhaps the most comprehensive group of studies of this kind are those undertaken between 1960 and 1967 by a group of workers at the MRC Applied Psychology Unit in Cambridge. These were designed to examine various patterns of shift working in the laboratory and assess their relative efficiency.

The first of these (Wilkinson and Edwards, 1968) compared the traditional Naval System of rotating four-hour watches requiring three men per station with a proposed one in which two men worked stabilized five or seven-hour shifts. Figure 2.3 shows the hours of work involved. In the rotating system the hours move round the clock usually by four hours each day in order to share the unpopular night watches fairly among the three men. As a result no man works the same hours on successive days. In the stabilized system they retain the same hours throughout, one man handling predominantly day and the other the night watches. The stabilized two-man system yielded a level of performance rather *better* than the rotating one requiring three men. This was due partly to the stabilization of the hours of work and partly to the fact that in the two-man system the men alternated work on three tasks throughout a shift, whereas with the three-man system a given job was continued throughout a given shift. Our particular

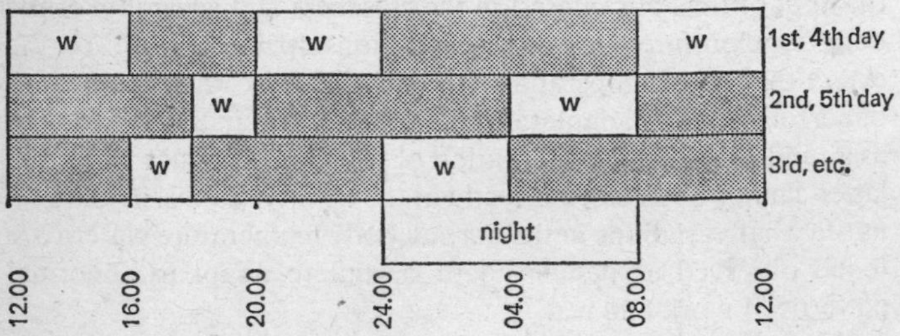

Figure 2.3 Plan of work (w) and rest periods (hatched area) in Naval rotating three watch system. (From Wilkinson and Edwards, 1968)

concern here however is with the adaptation of body temperature and performance in the group of men who carried out the 'night' version of the two-man stabilized system, which called for work between the hours of noon and 5 p.m. and midnight and 7 a.m. This programme was carried out for twelve days, sleep being taken between 8 a.m. and noon and in the early evening. Figure 2.4 shows the adaptation of body temperature and performance from first to fourth three-day period. A complete inversion of body temperature was not obtained. The change is better described as a flattening of the normal curve involving a definite raising of the level during the hours of night work. Performance of the three tasks, vigilance, adding and complex decision-making, also adapted only partially to the reversal routine. In terms of the speed of adaptation, changes in the relative levels of day and night performance were becoming apparent by the sixth day but even after twelve days nothing like a complete inversion of the circadian cycle of either body temperature or performance could be claimed.

Further experiments were carried out by Colquhoun, Blake and

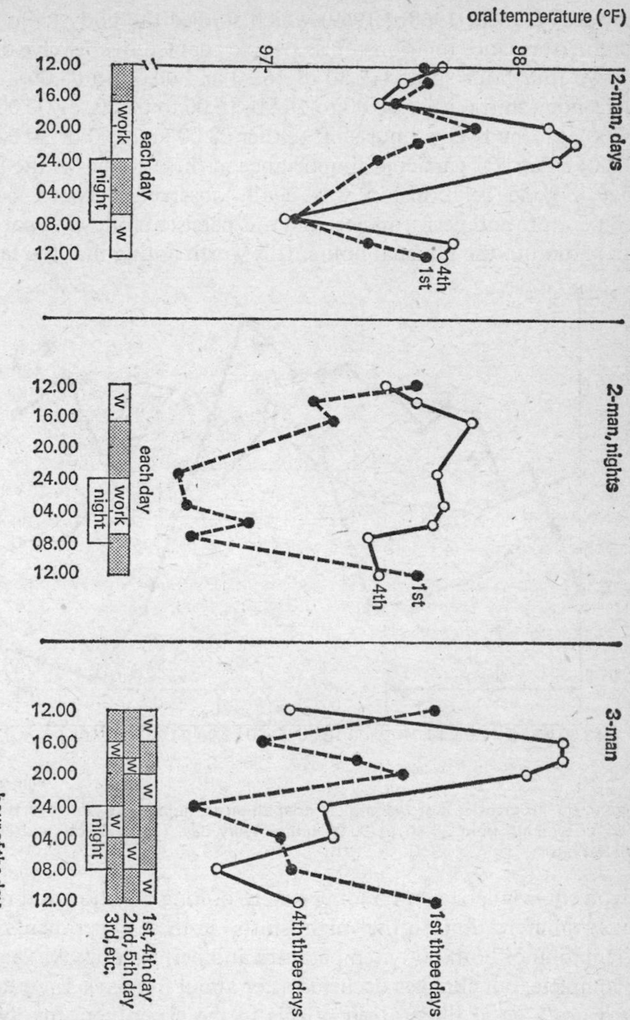

Figure 2.4 Adaptation of body temperature from first (dotted line) to fourth (full line) three-day period in a twelve-day programme of work on a stabilized two-man Naval watch system or a rotating three-man one. (From Wilkinson and Edwards, 1968)

Edwards (1968a; 1968b; 1969) which studied the body temperature/performance relationship as people adapted over twelve days to two four-hour shifts (12.30 to 16.30 and 00.00 to 08.00), one eight-hour shift (either 08.00 to 16.00, 16.00 to 00.00, or 00.00 to 08.00), or one twelve-hour shift (either 08.00 to 20.00 or 20.00 to 08.00) a day. Of particular importance in these studies is the fact that a good relationship was again observed between body temperature and performance, and this persisted following partial adaptation to the unusual hours. It is worth noting that the tasks

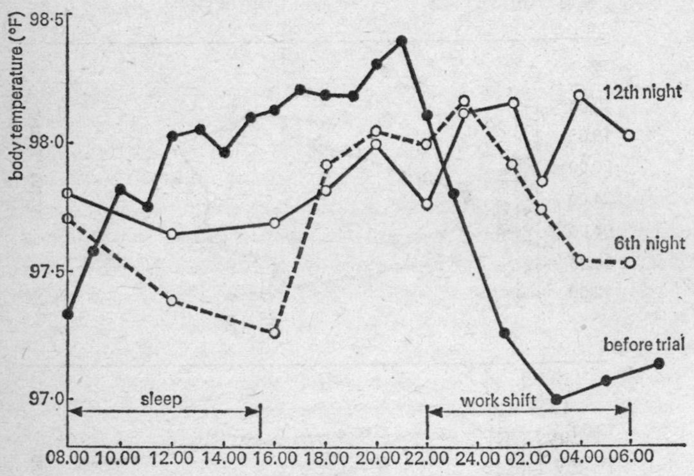

Figure 2.5 Progressive but incomplete adaptation to night shift working: twelve days of working from 22.00 to 06.00 hours every day. (From Colquhoun *et al.*, 1968b)

involved – vigilance and adding – were of long duration and relatively uninteresting. In the 'night shifts' in these experiments the adaptation of both body temperature and performance was again incomplete, but changes occurred after about five days. Figure 2.5 provides a good illustration of this in the experiment involving eight-hour shifts.

The failure to produce a complete circadian reversal was, presumably, because the men were surrounded by life going on as usual to the normal routine, as indeed most shift workers are.

Would isolation from the world have allowed complete inversion, and if so, how soon would it have been achieved? Answers to these questions have been provided by Aschoff and his colleagues (1969) using sound-proof, light-proof underground shelters to confine their subjects. From a wide range of studies, including free-running rhythms and rhythms entrained to 26·7 or 22·7-hour days, what concerns us here is that Aschoff was able to achieve a complete phase shift of the normal circadian body temperature and sleep/wakefulness cycles 'immediately or after a very few days' under these conditions.

Time zone transition

Essentially the same situation occurs when people are transported rapidly from one part of the world to another, changing to a life up to twelve hours out of phase with the one they have just left. Here, conditions for adaptation are ideal, the surroundings being completely and naturally at one with the new rhythm that has to be adopted. How rapid is adaptation under these circumstances? There have been a number of scientific studies of this situation; a good example is that of Klein *et al.* (1970). Twelve experienced pilots carried out twelve-minute flights on a flight simulator at two hour intervals throughout the day and night from 9 a.m. to 9 a.m. the following day. These twenty-four hour test periods were repeated on two days in Germany and then, following a flight to USA, on days 1, 3 ,5, and 8 in the new time zone eight hours behind the one they had left. After seventeen days they returned to Germany and carried out the same routine. Figure 2.6 shows deviation from average flying performance on the simulator (+ve equals impaired) during the various points of the experiment. The first point to note is the clarity of the normal circadian cycle of performance. The test was one of moderate duration but it was operated many times during the course of the study so that it qualifies as a long duration exercise, which the pilots would find complex but also repetitive and relatively uninteresting. With such curves it is easy to see how at first the new external cycle battles with the old internal one producing a curve which is a resultant of the two influences. This continues until the performance pattern finally snaps almost totally into the new rhythm, although vestiges of the European cycle were still present after eight days in the USA. On

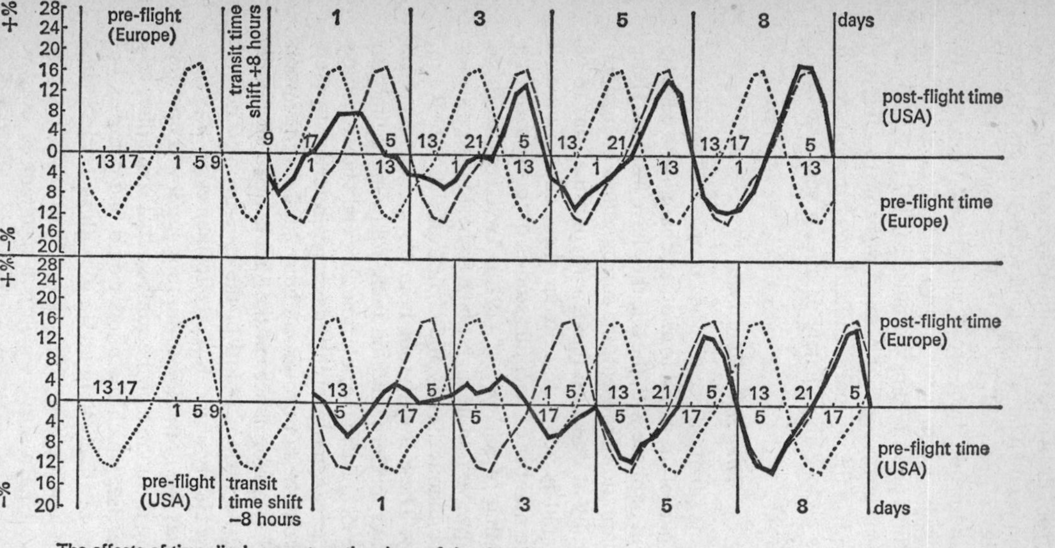

Figure 2.6 Adaptation of pilots' simulator performance to phase shift following a flight from Germany to U S A (top half) and back (bottom half). The heavy line represents true measurements; the dotted line shows where the normal (pre-flight) rhythm would have fallen had it continued during the post-flight days. (From Klein *et al.*, 1970)

the return much the same happened and the now entrained USA rhythm had to revert to the European one eight hours ahead; however, the disorganization of the cycle was more marked and lasted longer before performance snapped back to the original cycle. This reflects the general finding that West to East flights produce more disorganization than those from East to West. Klein *et al.* point out that this is probably because the West-East trips, being night ones, involve loss of sleep, because in catching up eight hours the night is truncated and sleep is difficult as one lands at the start of a European day. The answer would seem to lie in commencing West-East flights early in the day so that even with the loss of eight hours it will be sleeping time when passengers land, even if they are not quite ready for sleep.

Adaptation in industry

As a preamble to this section we must consider at least the main dimensions along which shift systems vary in industry. There is a very wide variety of shift systems at present in operation; we could not possibly go into all or even a number of the common ones here. Fuller details can be found in Murrell's book (1968, ch. 19), and in the supplement to the recent PIB report (1970).

There are four main dimensions of shift systems:

1. *Two Shift* systems use a Morning (often 06.00–14.00) and an Afternoon (often 14.00–22.00) shift only. *Three Shift* systems incorporate an additional Night shift (often 22.00–06.00).

2. *Continuous* systems work throughout the seven days of the week. *Discontinuous* systems have a break for all men and plant usually over the weekend.

3. Continuous systems, as a rule, may have *Stabilized* shifts, when a particular shift always works the same time each day (e.g. seven days on 'Mornings'), or they may have *Rotating* shifts (of which the Naval Three Man System is an example, see pp. 34–5 and 37–8). Here the times of work 'rotate' around the clock each day or at intervals of very few days, so that each day or each few days a man works different hours.

4. Discontinuous systems, as a rule, may have *Alternating* shifts where people change at regular intervals, often of one week, from one stabilized shift (say 'Mornings') to another (say 'Nights') the

weekend break intervening. *Permanent* shifts involve people remaining permanently on one of the two or three stabilized shifts, either, for example, 'Mornings', 'Afternoons', or 'Nights'.

In the previous section I described the work of Colquhoun and his associates in the laboratory. Let us now follow them into the field to see whether the body temperatures of miners adapt to their particular system of shifts. At Linby Colliery in Nottinghamshire, they found a standard Discontinuous, Stabilized, Weekly Alternating, Three Shift system in operation. In other words, the men worked from Monday to Friday, had the weekend off, and changed shifts each week. The question was whether body temperature, taken orally, would reveal adaptation to the abnormal hours of work within the five weekdays that each shift was worked. In the two shifts calling for abnormal sleeping times, the Morning and the Night, some evidence for adaptation appeared and was more pronounced for the older workers. On the Night shift the modification, as in the laboratory, took the form of a flattening of the normal curve rather than an inversion. Colquhoun and Edwards were careful to point out the inadequacies of measurement in this setting due to unpredictable changes in the manning of particular shifts selected for measurement and unavoidable variation in the times of measurement. They rightly call for more studies of the same kind involving larger numbers of men and different shift systems. Would men on permanent nights, for example, spend so much of their working hours with body temperatures lower than normal, or would some degree of permanent adaptation have occurred? An answer to this question has been provided, in a different setting, by van Loon (1963). He recorded body temperatures of three young men producing parts for typewriters. Normally they worked a day shift from 8.00 a.m. to 5.15 p.m., but were asked to work a night shift for thirteen weeks to clear arrears. The hours were 10.30 p.m. to 7.30 a.m. on the five weekdays. The three men all showed short-term adaptation to the night routine during the week, only to lose it when they returned to normal life during their weekend off. There was thus little evidence of long-term adaptation to the 'permanent' night routine, simply because it was not permanent.

Under certain conditions, however, it appears that truly permanent night work can exist. Lobban (1965) was able to examine the potassium excretion level of permanent night shift workers in the mines of Longyearbyen, Spitzbergen, North Norway. Here there is continual darkness during the months of November, December and January, and continuous daylight during the summer months. Potassium excretion, which shows a normal circadian fluctuation similar to that of body temperature, was 'perfectly entrained to the activity pattern, being reversed in relation to normal working time, throughout the year'. Presumably this adaptation was achieved because the inverted pattern of life penetrated into the leisure hours and activities of the night shift, due to the lack of any light/dark cycle for much of the year.

Comment

Laboratory, time zone and field studies combine to show that within a week or less people can adapt almost completely to a phase shift in the circadian cycle, if the external surroundings change in step, as happens when we travel across time zone boundaries. If surroundings remain locked in the old rhythm, however, as in shift working, the adaptation even over two weeks is only partial. Whether this adaptation would become more complete with time is an important but as yet unanswered question.

The foregoing analysis of laboratory and field studies suggests that under present shift systems, most, if not all, night work is being carried out by people whose psychological levels are ill-adapted to an inverted routine and who are therefore working well below their normal levels of efficiency. Laboratory work also predicts that their sleep cannot be very good either. Webb and Agnew (1967) have shown that sleep during the day is physiologically different from that taken at night. It is shorter and contains fewer of the EEG patterns which normally characterize sleep which is remembered as good (Rechtschaffen, Hauri and Zeitlin, 1966). Thus sleep may be inadequate in both quality and quantity. Loss of sleep is another factor which can impair working efficiency even when sleep is reduced by as little as one third on two nights (Wilkinson, 1969). More important, the impact of loss of sleep is particularly marked when work is repetitive (Wilkinson, 1965), is carried on for prolonged periods (Wilkinson, 1958), is lacking in incentive (Wilkinson, 1961), and takes place during the low points of the circadian cycle (Wilkinson, 1970). Shift working with high overtime in heavily automated production lines appears to present a coalescence of much that can be unfortunate for working efficiency. Both the soil and the seed of fatigue are there. On scientific evidence, limited though it is then, most of today's shift systems should be thoroughly bad for the health of the worker and his output.

Let us see if it really is as bad as this in practice when we ask the people concerned and examine records of health and output.

SHIFT SYSTEMS IN PRACTICE

Non-permanent shift systems

As a result of a questionnaire-based study of nearly 1800 workers embracing a number of industrial units in the Netherlands, Dirken (1966) concluded that 'for subjective well-being in both its somatic and psychological aspects shift work can in general probably hardly be called a problem'. The questionnaire consisted of fifty-eight questions of a Yes/No type about complaints, the items resembling those of the Cornell Medical Health Questionnaire and of neuroticism inventories. It was filled out by 614 shift and 1168 non-shift workers. Whether the former term included all kinds or simply those on alternating shifts is not clear. Nevertheless, the result is surprising in light of what laboratory findings predict. Dirken offers the explanation that some of the adverse effects of shift work may be veiled by self-selection: those who are unable to stand it will have returned to day work so that to some extent shift workers may represent an élite in terms both of their health and of their efficiency on the job. Wedderburn (1967) asked 174 manual workers in a steel works the direct question, 'On the whole, how do you feel about working shifts?' Fifty-four per cent liked them mainly because they provided more time off, but also possibly because they earned more money. Thirty-three per cent had no preference. Thirteen per cent did not like working shifts. The main reason for their dislike was the interference with their social activities particularly at the weekend. The shifts they preferred were the ones which offended least in this respect, namely discontinuous rather than continuous ones, rapidly rather than slowly alternating ones, and the morning and night rather than the afternoon shift (which prevented going out in the evening). These preferences constitute almost a conspiracy against the adaptation to night work, so necessary on biological grounds if inefficiency at night is to be avoided. However, it might be argued that, since adaptation can only be achieved by a permanently inverted routine permeating both work and leisure activities, and since this only seems obtainable in the northern reaches of Norway, perhaps it is best biologically as well as in terms of the workers' preference to adopt the other extreme, namely a rapid alternation of shifts with weekends free where possible. As this system does not give people time to adapt to night work it spares them the trouble of losing their adaptation when they return to days!

There have been a number of studies of sickness records among shift workers. A typical finding is that of Taylor (1967) who found that continuous weekly alternating three shift workers had a significantly *lower* rate of sickness than day workers doing similar jobs. This may possibly be due to a form of medical selection following the drop-out rate of those shift workers who found the routine too much for them. Taylor, however, places more emphasis on another explanation: he found that shift workers regard themselves as a rather special group of people more involved in their work than day workers, and operating in smaller well-knit social groups providing both a sense of security and high level of morale. While this is probably true, it makes it very difficult to make valid comparisons of the health of shift and non-shift workers.

The problem may be approached obliquely by studying the sleep of shift workers; fortunately most questionnaires contain items on this point and are surprisingly unanimous to the effect that the sleep of shift workers is frequently reported as inferior in both quality and quantity to that of people working during the day, although a negative report by Tune (1967) provides a striking exception to this. A clue may be provided by a particularly important report by Thiis-Evensen (1958) who compared the housing conditions of the people he approached. Those who owned their own houses supported Tune's finding of no important differences, but among those in poor housing 73 per cent of shift workers as compared with 18 per cent of day workers reported insomnia as a problem. On the basis of this finding Thiis-Evensen labels noise during the day as one of the root problems of shift working and calls for sympathetic design of accommodation to ensure that the sleep of shift workers during the day shall be protected from interruption as far as possible.

Working efficiency is difficult to assess under factory conditions. Full records of output are difficult to obtain, and when they are available it is difficult to distinguish the influence of shift systems from the many other factors which can cause production to vary. What information we have, however, supports the laboratory prediction of reduced efficiency when work is being carried out at night. Bjerner, Holm and Swenssen (1955) have carried out the most comprehensive study. They gained access to the logging records in a gas works covering the years 1912 to 1931. The shift system was the conventional Discontinuous, Weekly Alternating, Three Shift one. Figure 2.7 shows the number of errors made in logging during the course of the three eight-hour shifts, Morning, Afternoon and Night, in three separate establishments. Efficiency during the night shift was reduced by between about 10 per cent and 40 per cent. In a shorter but basically similar study by Browne (1949) the delay in answering calls on the part of the teleprinter switchboard operators was about 50 per cent greater during the night shift. Lastly, in a study of rapidly alternating (two-day) shift workers Gavrilescu *et al.* (1966) administered performance tests before, during and after each shift. Again people were less efficient during the night and, to a lesser extent, the afternoon shifts.

Unfortunately none of these studies allows direct comparison of the output of shift and day workers: they merely provide comparisons of night and day shifts within shift workers. The superiority of the day shifts in the comparison, however, may perhaps be regarded as the best indication that, were it possible to keep other things equal, working conditions, health, ability, and so on, a comparison of day with alternating shift workers would favour the non-shift men as regards their ability to work efficiently.

On the other hand, the study of attitudes towards alternating shift systems reveals, surprisingly, that on the whole people like them, providing evenings and weekends are not interfered with too much. This is not what the laboratory forebodings of low efficiency, lost sleep and ill health would predict, unless, of course, these considerations are not uppermost in the minds of either workers or management when they contemplate the undoubted short-term advantages of shift working: higher earnings, more free time, and for management lower fixed costs.

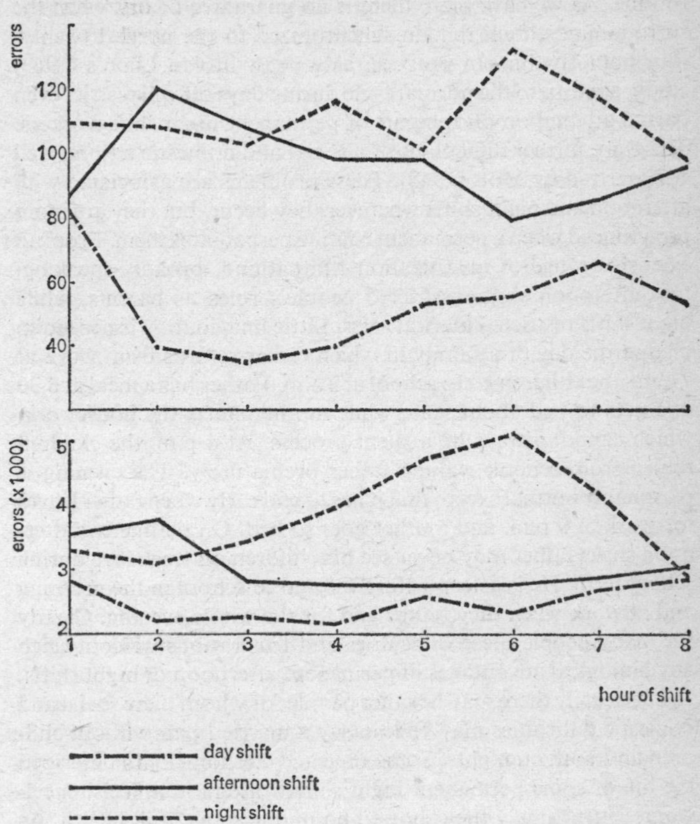

Figure 2.7 Total logging errors made in each hour on three shifts in a paper mill (above) and gas works (below). (Data adapted from Murrell, 1965)

Stabilized (permanent) shift systems

The scientist condemns alternating shift systems because they do not allow the body to adapt to a stable sleep/work/play cycle either of a normal or inverted kind. Grant this adaptation and biological objections disappear. In theory permanent shift systems should achieve this, since whatever shift is worked, the morning, the afternoon or the night, the body will eventually adapt to the changed routine. As we have seen, there is no guarantee of this when the surrounding stimuli remain synchronized to the normal twenty-four hour rhythm. In practice, as we saw in van Loon's (1963) study, a return to the normal cycle during days off will restrict even partial adaptation on the part of permanent night shift workers. There are further difficulties of a social and domestic nature, well summarized by Mott (1965). These problems are associated with afternoon and night shifts wherever they occur, but they are more pronounced when a permanent routine perpetuates them. From an extensive range of investigation Mott found, broadly speaking, that afternoon shifts restricted people's roles as parents, while night shifts restricted marital roles. Little imagination is needed to picture the day of a family in which father returns from work at 7 a.m., the children go to school at 8 a.m. Father has a meal at 8.30 and gets to bed about 9.30, while mother starts the housework, which cannot always be a silent process. At 4 p.m. the children return from school, waking father prematurely. The evening is reasonably normal except that it has to end early when father leaves for work at 9 p.m. and mother goes to bed. On permanent afternoon shifts father may never see his children on weekdays during school term. He is asleep before they go to school in the morning and at work when they return and for the whole evening. Clearly for many people these difficulties and frustrations will outweigh any biological advantages of permanent afternoon or night shifts.

But equally there may be other people for whom these social and domestic difficulties may be less, say a married pair without children and both on nights. Some time ago Vernon (1940) described the life of some permanent night shift workers in a Welsh steelworks; surprisingly they showed no undue signs of ill health. As regards output, both Bonjer (1960) and Bjerner, Holm and Swensson (1955) report that permanent night shift workers do rather better than those on other shifts. All these suggestions, however, are vulnerable to attack on the grounds that night workers may be a self-selected and superior group, the less robust and the less efficient having dropped out. This argument is difficult to counter without records from the same individuals before, during and after a period of permanent night work, and such records appear difficult to find. Questionnaire studies of social and domestic life are less subject to these weaknesses, and two good examples are those of Brown (1957) and Mott (1965). Both suggest that neither the social integration nor the sleeping ability are as disturbed on permanent night work as on alternating shifts.

One of the most convincing indications of people's attitudes is what they do when left free to make a choice. De la Mare and Walker (1968) found this situation among a group of telegraph operators who had a considerable degree of choice as to which

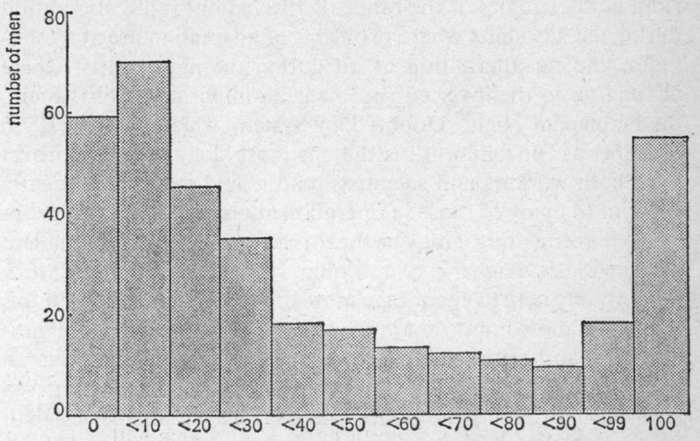

Figure 2.8 The effect of allowing men to exchange shifts in an alternating three shift system: distribution of the population in terms of the percentage time spent working nights (which equalled 35 per cent for everyone before any exchanges). (From de la Mare and Walker, 1968)

shift (in a discontinuous weekly alternating, three shift system) they wished to work each week. This degree of choice was achieved by allowing the workers to exchange shifts so that, for example, if a man wished to work all nights he could trade his afternoon and his morning shifts with other people's 'nights'. The histogram in Figure 2.8 shows the numbers of men electing to spend various percentages of their time on night work. Many people rejected the alternating system in favour of a stabilized one, working either all days or all nights. The important point here is that there does seem to be a considerable proportion of the workers who are quite prepared to work nights on a permanent basis. Given enough to man the whole night shift, the problems of twenty-four-hour working might be greatly reduced. As de la Mare and Walker point out, if the night work is manned by a permanent night shift, then the two day shifts can be handled by an alternating system so that no one has to work the unpopular afternoon shift, with its loss of evening activity, for more than, say, two days at a time. This compromise samples from both extremes of the range of alternation: rapid alternation during the day shifts where problems of adaptation are at a minimum, and no alternation at all during the night shifts, where adaptation to the inverted routine is all-important. This system, the Permanent Night, Double Day System, which Walker (1970) describes as 'uncommon', is the one most likely to win approval from both workers and scientists, and would seem to be greatly superior to many of those in operation at present. The main problem in implementing it may be that of recruiting enough permanent night workers. Higher pay and more relaxed conditions of work can certainly help to encourage more of the population to join this group, but more important in the long term may be the willingness of public authorities to regard permanent night workers as an important growing section of the community who must be catered for as such. Probably the greatest need is for sympathetic design of accommodation. If they are to sleep adequately by day, it is important that these people should be insulated from the noises of the day, especially in crowded urban environments. Second, the marked group consciousness of permanent night workers should be encouraged by the provision of appropriate social clubs, and community facilities, which would of course be open (including the weekend) at the times most convenient for them.

To remain competitive a modern technological state may have to accept an increasing degree of twenty-four hour working of men and machines. If this is to be done efficiently it seems very likely that there will be increasing dependence upon the permanent night shift workers. It behoves government and local authorities to recognize the growing importance of these people and provide appropriately for them.

SUMMARY

The problem is that man has evolved and been trained to a twenty-four-hour cycle of work during the day and sleep during the night, whereas modern technological systems increasingly demand that machines be manned throughout the twenty-four hours. Are the current ways of organizing this round-the-clock working the best from the point of view of the health, happiness and stability of the population, as well as its working efficiency? The twenty-four-hour rhythm of body temperature and performance are described with reference to both laboratory and field studies, and the degree and speed with which both of them adapt to night work or other abnormal routines is assessed. Much depends upon the world around and whether it is geared to the new time routine (as when one crosses a time zone, flying from Europe to USA) or not (as in night shift work). As regards performance, the kind of work and its duration are also important, suggesting that loss of sleep may be at least as influential as body rhythms in causing ill effects through abnormal working hours. The correlation between performance and body temperature is assessed with a view to using the latter as a guide to working efficiency in the field where the effects of different shift systems cannot be assessed directly by measuring output.

On the whole the message from the biological studies is that many of the shift systems currently in use are bad for output and for health, particularly in terms of the amount of sleep lost. Examining the attitudes of workers and such records as can be obtained the impression is that these shifts are not so bad in practice. However, this may be because shift workers comprise a self-selected élite, thus distorting comparisons between them and non-shiftworkers based on records of output, sickness, absenteeism and accidents. Overall the view is taken that, although alternating shift systems are accepted (probably because they provide more pay and more free time), the effects of these routines upon health and efficiency may still be harmful. Stabilized shift systems, where people remain permanently on one shift, are more satisfactory, particularly the permanent night shift. A system of rapidly alternating morning and afternoon shifts combined with a permanent night shift is supported. The problem of obtaining sufficient permanent night-shift workers could be eased by two moves: first, and most important, reduce the ill-effects of disturbed sleep during the day by providing housing with better sound insulation in the bedroom. Second, provide appropriate round-the-clock community and entertainment facilities for permanent night workers to encourage them to follow their inverted routine even during their days off.

FURTHER READING

The Prices and Incomes Board's 'Hours of work, overtime, and shift working' (HMSO, 1970) is a good source of further detail on the general problems imposed by shiftworking in the United Kingdom. The scene in the USA is covered by P. E. Mott in *Shift Work – The Social, Psychological and Physical Consequences* (University of Michigan Press, 1965); this monograph also describes a study which in conception and scale provides perhaps the best model for future research. A briefer, but more accessible review of shiftworking is provided by K. F. H. Murrell in his general text on *Ergonomics* (Chapman & Hall, 1965).

For those who can find them, the old Industrial Fatigue (later Health) Research Board Reports make instructive reading. Sponsored by the Medical Research Council and published by Her Majesty's Stationery Office between 1917 and 1937, these reports throw light on the very direct methods of the applied psychologist of those days. The most relevant reports are numbers 1, 2, 6, 24, 47. Together with many other studies they are summarized in R. Sergean's *Managing Shiftwork* (Gower Press, 1971).

3
Skilled Performance and Stress

Christopher Poulton

The great majority of our activities are to some degree skilled, and the nature of skilled performance has been extensively studied. Dr Poulton here examines its main characteristics in the framework of a model whose main features are working memory, long-term memory, computer and input and output selectors. He shows how a person's performance is critically affected by the level of his arousal, and evidence is presented about the effects of stress or arousal level. Stresses which are considered include personal threat, noise loss of sleep and drugs. In addition to examining these separately, Dr Poulton shows how they may combine together to affect performance. As an applied experimental psychologist he has published widely on these topics and in related areas.

This chapter concerns much that happens in everyday life. Most of a person's activities have been well practised, and so are skilled. When a person is active, he is often under stress. The stress may be imposed upon him by his employer, who expects him to work hard to earn his pay. The stress may be self imposed. People have standards of performance which they try hard to uphold in the jobs they do. Or the environment may impose the stress. It may be too noisy or too hot. Skilled performances are often carried out under stress.

TWO KINDS OF SKILL

Every activity can be said to involve deciding what to do and then doing it. In studying activities such as talking or typewriting, the principal emphasis is generally put on selecting the response. The talker has to decide which words to use; the typist has to decide which keys to press. Talking and typing require skill for their execution. The talker has to speak so that he can be understood. The typist has to hit the correct key sufficiently hard to type the letter, and not so hard that the typeface perforates the paper. But the activities are usually studied as decisions. The person's choice of a word or of a key is related to the other choices which he or she could have made.

In studying activities such as reaching for an object or steering a car, the principal emphasis is generally put on the execution of the response. In reaching for an object, the person has to move his hand the correct distance in the correct direction. The car driver has to turn his steering wheel through the correct angle at the correct time. Reaching and steering require decisions before they are carried out – the person has to decide what to reach for; the driver has to decide where he wants the car to go to. But the activities are usually assessed in terms of the speed and precision of the movement, not in terms of the choice of movement.

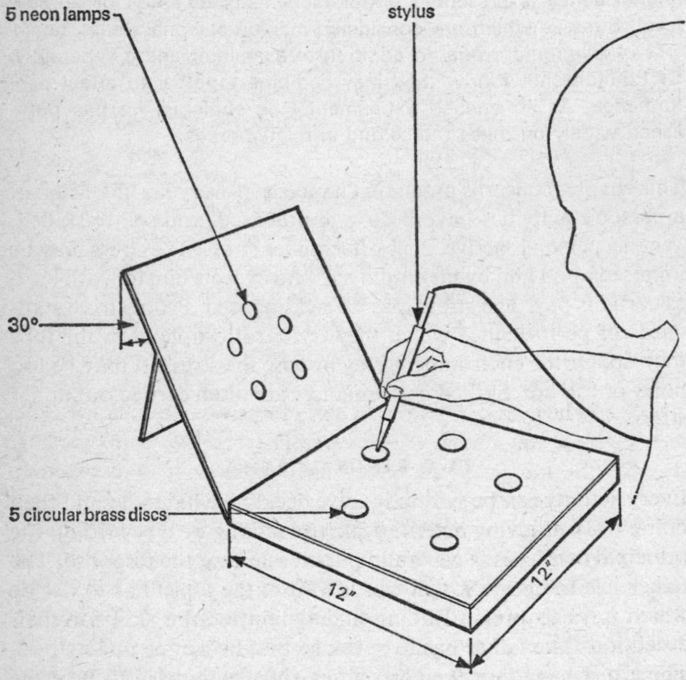

Figure 3.1 The 5-choice task. (After Leonard, 1959)

Any one of a number of tasks can be used to study the way people *choose* the responses which they make. An example is the five-choice task of Figure 3.1. One of the five lamps on the left lights up. The man has to touch the corresponding brass disc with his stylus as quickly as he can. As soon as he touches a disc, the lamp goes off and another lamp comes on. Unpractised people usually average about one tap per second. After a lot of practice the quickest people sometimes average almost two taps per second.

If the subject touches the correct disc, his response is automatically recorded as correct. If he touches one of the other four discs, his response is recorded as an error. If he does not respond for 1·5 seconds the apparatus waits until he does respond, but it automatically records a gap in his sequence of responses. Slow responding produces both gaps and also a relatively small total number of correct responses.

Tracking is the only task which has been used extensively to study the way people *execute* responses. Tracking is usually studied in the laboratory with electronic apparatus. The subject has to try to keep a moving marker superimposed upon a target marker which may or may not move (Poulton, 1966).

A SIMPLE THEORETICAL MODEL FOR SKILLED PERFORMANCE

Figure 3.2 illustrates a simple theoretical model which shows what the brain does during skilled performances. The inputs on the left of the figure are from the eyes and ears and from the sense organs scattered throughout the body. A number of arrows are shown leading from the box labelled inputs to the working memory. This is because the eyes can take in a complete scene at a glance. The ears can receive a number of sounds simultaneously, as in listening to orchestral music. At the same time there may be inputs from a number of other sense organs.

The outputs on the right of the figure are to the muscles. A number of arrows are shown leading from the output selector to the box labelled outputs. This is because when a person moves his hand or says something, a large number of muscles are used. The rest of the connections between the boxes are by single arrows. This is to indicate the bottleneck in the brain through which all messages have to pass.

Working memory and rehearsal

The box in Figure 3.2 labelled working memory holds a representation of what the person is looking at, or listening to, or thinking about. The representation fades beyond recall in a few seconds unless it is maintained in some way. In looking at a scene, the inputs from the eyes keep the sensory representation in the working memory. When the eyes move to another scene, the sensory representation of the previous scene disappears almost at once (Sperling, 1960). Try it and see.

Anything which remains in the working memory after half a second or so must have been rehearsed. Rehearsal means selecting items from the scene. In the model of Figure 3.2, the input selector

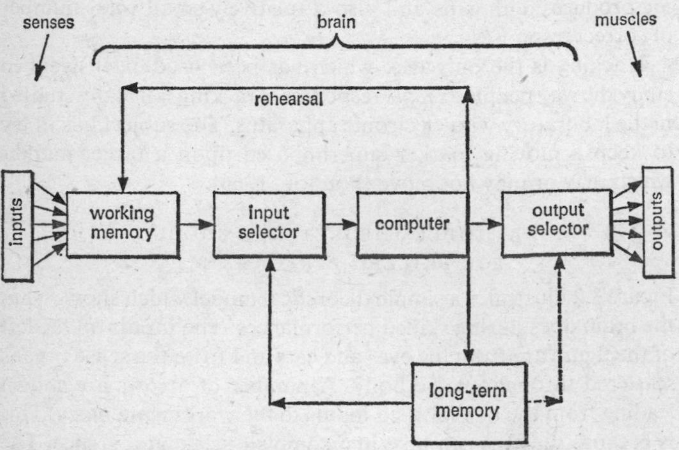

Figure 3.2 A simple theoretical model which shows what the brain does. (Modified from Broadbent, 1958, Figure 7)

passes the items through the box labelled computer and round the rehearsal loop back to the working memory. It is not quite as simple as this, because the items are usually given names while they are being rehearsed. It is the name, not the visual image of the item, which is usually stored. Naming involves obtaining the name from the long-term memory. If items in the visual scene do not have familiar names, fewer of them can be rehearsed and stored (Eriksen and Lappin, 1967).

In listening to somebody speaking, the inputs from the ears change all the time. There is no constant sensory representation in the working memory as there can be in looking at a scene. Probably for this reason, unrehearsed sounds do not disappear from the working memory quite as quickly as visual impressions do when they are not rehearsed before the eyes move to another scene. If words are not rehearsed, it may be several seconds before they disappear completely from the working memory (Broadbent, 1957b, Experiment 2).

Computer of limited capacity

The box labelled computer in Figure 3.2 is not like a modern high-speed digital computer. It works relatively slowly. When a task is difficult, the computer takes quite a time to carry it out. A learner driver may practise pressing the brake with his foot each time a red lamp comes on in front of him. When he is expecting the red light, he may be able to start pressing the brake pedal in about 0·2 second. Less than half this time is taken up by the message travelling to the brain from the eyes along the visual nerves, and by the messages travelling from the brain along the nerves to the muscles of the leg and foot. More than half of the time is taken by the computer in Figure 3.2. If there are several possible signals, each of which requires a different response, the computer may take 0·5 second, or longer to select the appropriate response. The extra time to react produces the 'thinking distance' which is travelled by a car before it can be stopped. It is illustrated on the back cover of The Highway Code (Ministry of Transport, 1968).

The computer's task is made more difficult if the signals are difficult to perceive, or difficult to discriminate from each other. Reaction time increases as a result. The computer's task is also more difficult if responses have to be made with great precision, as in using a slide rule, or in repairing the inside of a wrist watch. In order to achieve the extra precision, a longer average time is needed (Fitts, 1954).

The amount which can be held in the working memory is limited by the time the computer takes to rehearse. Each item in the working memory has to be rehearsed before it fades beyond recall. While items are being rehearsed, the remaining items are fading rapidly. The average person has a maximum memory span of about eight random letters or digits. If he is given more than this to remember, some are forgotten before they can be rehearsed. Try it on yourself. Undergraduates may have a maximum memory span of ten or eleven random digits.

Single-channel input selector

In Figure 3.2 there are a number of arrows leading from the box labelled inputs to the working memory. But only one arrow connects the working memory to the input selector, and there is a single arrow connecting the input selector to the computer. This is to indicate that only one message at a time can be selected and fed into the computer. While the computer is dealing with one message, other messages have to wait. Chapter 1 describes strategies which are used to select messages, or parts of messages.

A person may be told to make a quick hand movement each time he hears a bell. Each time he hears a buzz, he has to make a different quick movement. After practice, he takes about 0·2 second to respond to the bell. When the buzz sounds during his reaction time to the bell, his response to the buzz takes about 0·35 second, instead of the expected 0·2 second (Poulton, 1970, Figure 5). The extra delay is not caused by having to make a second response with the same hand, because the 2 responses can involve different hands (Davis, 1957).

The period of time during the reaction to the first signal has been called the psychological refractory period. It is similar to the refractory period of the single nerve fibre, but it lasts a good deal longer. The input selector of Figure 3.2 feeds the first signal into the computer. While the computer is dealing with the first signal, the second signal has to wait in the working memory (Welford, 1967).

The delay in responding to the second signal may sometimes last one second or longer if the man is not expecting the second signal (Poulton, 1970, p. 13). The input selector may not be set to select a second signal. Instead it may be set to select the sensory consequences of the first response. The person may be readjusting his hand. Or he may be waiting for the experimenter to tell him how long he took to respond. The second signal then has to capture the input selector, before it can reach the computer.

Long-term memory and the automation of skill

Each rehearsal of material in the working memory helps to establish it in the long-term memory, which is illustrated at the bottom of Figure 3.2. Once material has become established in the long-term memory, it remains available or partly available for hours or days. The long duration of the storage contrasts with the duration of only a few seconds in the working memory.

In talking, and in carrying out other practised movements, the input selector draws upon material in the long-term memory. The material is passed through the computer to the output selector. It also passes along the rehearsal loop to the working memory. This mechanism supplies the person with a running memory of what he is doing. He can draw upon this information when he wants to know where he has got to in his talking or his movements. If he is talking, he also receives feedback to his working memory through his ears. If he is moving, he obtains feedback from the moving parts of his body. He can also look and see what he is doing. Thus in talking and in moving the input selector and computer use in turn information from the long-term and working memories.

When a skill has become highly practised, it needs less computer time. Something like a template has been constructed in the long-term memory. The input selector has only to select the template and to pass the information through the computer to the output selector. The highly practised skill can then be carried out without involving the input selector and computer. This is indicated in Figure 3.2 by the broken arrow connecting the boxes labelled long-term memory and output selector. The input selector and computer are required only when it is necessary to check on how the skill is being carried out, or to change templates. Between whiles they are available for some other activity (Bahrick, Noble and Fitts, 1954).

The gradual automation of skill can be observed in teaching someone to drive a car. In the very early stages, practically the whole of the learner's attention is occupied by his control movements. A signal for action, perhaps from the road ahead, is fed by the input selector of Figure 3.2 into the computer. The appropriate rudimentary template has then to be found in the long-term memory. Information from the template is fed by the input selector through the computer to the output selector. It leads to a control movement.

The learner driver has then to check that he has done the right thing. He needs sensory information fed back through the input selector to the computer from his hands and feet as to what movements were made, to check whether they were correct or not. Later he needs sensory information from his eyes about the behaviour of the car. Errors are corrected by the input selector choosing a somewhat different template from the long-term memory. Information from this template is then fed through the computer to the output selector.

While the learner driver is doing all this, he may have little or no idea of what is happening in the road ahead. His computer capacity is fully occupied in attempting to control the car. At this early stage driving instructors report that they have to keep a lookout on the road ahead, to see that the car does not hit anything.

At a later stage of practice the learner driver does not need to monitor every aspect of his control movements so carefully. Appropriate templates have still to be found in the long-term memory. The information from them has still to be fed through the input selector and computer to the output selector. But once this has been done, the long-term memory and output selector can communicate directly along the broken arrow in Figure 3.2. The man does not need to keep a close check upon his control movements. This leaves his input selector and computer free to deal with other aspects of driving, such as what is happening in the road ahead.

At a still later stage the driver may have computer time in reserve whenever the amount of relevant information coming from the road ahead is not too great. The surplus computer time can be measured. The driver is given questions to listen to and to answer orally when he can. His score on the questions reflects the amount of unused computer time (Brown and Poulton, 1961). The scores of learner drivers have been found to increase with the number of days of training on the road (Brown, 1966b).

THE OPTIMUM LEVEL OF AROUSAL

The computer of Figure 3.2 works most efficiently when a person is alert or moderately aroused. The computer works less well when arousal is low and the person finds it difficult to keep awake. The computer also works less well when arousal is too high and the person is over-excited or over-anxious. The theoretical relationship between arousal and the efficiency of performance is illustrated by the unbroken curve in Figure 3.3. The level of arousal may increase from A_1 to the optimum at A_2 on the abscissa. The efficiency of performance on the ordinate rises from P_1 to P_2.

Arousal may continue to increase beyond A_2 as far as A_3. The efficiency of performance then starts to fall. It drops from P_2 to P_3.

The changes in arousal illustrated in the figure are accompanied by physiological changes. When a person is over-excited, he may feel his heart beating more obviously, he may sweat and his muscles may be more tense.

The position of the optimum level of arousal depends upon the nature of the task. A complex task does not require such a high level of arousal as a simple task does. You may find you can dig

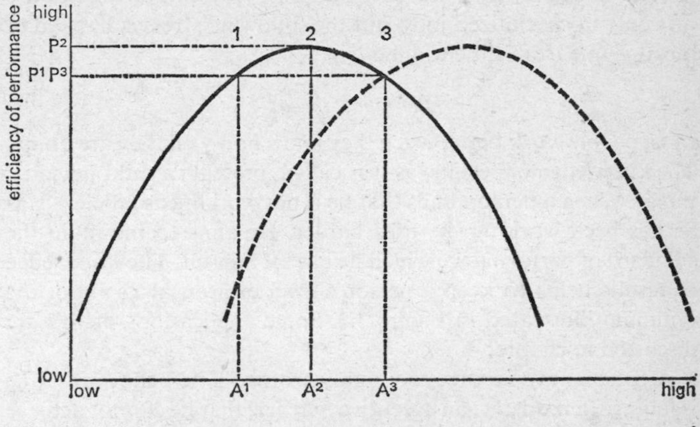

Figure 3.3 Theoretical inverted U curves showing the relationship between arousal and the efficiency of performance. (After Corcoran, 1965)

over the vegetable patch in your garden more quickly when you are highly aroused. But the solution to a difficult problem is more likely to come when you are not too highly aroused. It may come only when you are beginning to relax in a warm bath or in bed. For the simple task of digging, the inverted U lies further to the right, like the dotted curve in the figure. The unbroken inverted U might represent performance on the complex task of solving a difficult problem.

The point A_1 on the abscissa represents a relatively low level of arousal. Here increasing the level of arousal increases efficiency on both simple and complex tasks. The point A_3 represents a relatively high level of arousal. Here the dotted function is rising while the unbroken function is falling. Increasing the level of arousal from this point increases efficiency on the simple task. But it reduces efficiency on the complex task. This paradox is sometimes called the Yerkes–Dodson law. One of the effects of practice is to make a task more simple for the practised man. With practice the inverted U is also shifted to the right.

COMMON KINDS OF STRESS

A person's alertness can be influenced by stress. There are many stresses in the modern world (Poulton, 1970). Some stresses are met only in specialized jobs, but the following stresses happen to most people from time to time.

Personal threat

Most people work better when they know how well they are doing. The knowledge of results, as it is called, presents a mild personal threat. When a person finds that he is not working as efficiently as he has been working, he tries harder. He aims to maintain the standard of performance which he has set himself. The knowledge of results helps to keep a person's level of arousal at about the optimum illustrated in Figure 3.3. Some applications of this are discussed in chapter 4.

A person may become too highly aroused if he believes that he is failing. In industry, an executive may feel that he cannot achieve what is expected of him. An experimenter in the laboratory may give his victim false knowledge of results, so that the victim is told that he is performing badly, when he is trying hard to do his best (Lazarus, Deese and Osler, 1952). The level of arousal in Figure 3.3 may then be well beyond the optimum. If so, the more aroused the person becomes, the worse he is likely to do. Very severe personal threats may be met by people imprisoned for political reasons in police states (Sargant, 1957).

Too much to do at once

An executive in industry may be expected to keep track of a number of things at once. He may be in the middle of a serious discussion, when he has to answer a number of difficult questions over the telephone. Talking or telephoning while driving is another example of doing two tasks simultaneously. Each task may require the full capacity of the computer of Figure 3.2 from time to time. When some of the capacity is tied up with the other task, the man will not work as efficiently as he can do when he has only the one task to deal with. He is likely to work more slowly. If he continues to work at the same speed, he is likely to make mistakes.

A person who finds himself in this predicament may realize that he is not working as well as he usually does. If so, he may become too highly aroused and do still worse.

Noise

Jobs near machinery are often noisy. Noise is also met around busy airports and near crowded streets in cities. In large offices the noise may be too loud for the jobs which people have to do in them. Noise makes it difficult to hear what a person is saying. A sudden noise is distracting. A person switches his attention for an instant to the noise and loses track of what he is doing. Continuous loud noise increases a person's alertness or level of arousal. It may make him work faster. But complex work is likely to be done less accurately (Broadbent, 1957a).

Insufficient loss of heat

The human body produces heat. If the heat cannot be got rid of, the body temperature rises. This can happen near furnaces, and in the sun in hot countries. Too many clothes can also prevent the body from losing sufficient heat. When a person first enters a hot damp atmosphere, the heat as it were hits him in the face. This is likely to increase his alertness or level of arousal for a time (Poulton and Kerslake, 1965). As the person's body begins to warm up, his level of arousal falls below normal and his brain performs inefficiently. Eventually he becomes uncomfortably hot and over-excited (Wilkinson, Fox, Goldsmith, Hampton and Lewis, 1964). If he is unable to escape from the heat at this stage, he may soon collapse.

Loss of sleep

People may miss sleep when they work on night shift. When a person is sleepy, he has a low level of arousal and works inefficiently. He may have brief lapses of consciousness if he has to sit still listening or reading. You can sometimes notice a brief lapse in the afternoon round a committee table or at a lecture. A person's eyes almost close for a second, and his head may droop. Then he suddenly wakes up again. A sleep debt of five hours is enough to produce a reliable deterioration in performance on a prolonged inspection task (Wilkinson, 1969). Loss of sleep is one of the topics discussed in chapter 2.

Drugs which increase or reduce arousal

Tea and coffee contain caffeine, which increases arousal. The amphetamine drugs benzedrine and dexedrine also increase arousal. If a person is feeling sleepy, these stimulants can increase his arousal to nearer the normal level. The person may then work more efficiently. The risk is that the person may unexpectedly be subjected to some stress which itself increases arousal. The person may then become too highly aroused and make a stupid error, perhaps a fatal error. It can happen to a student if he takes a stimulant just before a stressful examination.

Sleeping tablets, tranquillizers and the more effective remedies for hay fever, reduce arousal. The person who takes them behaves like someone who has lost sleep.

DETERIORATION OF SKILL UNDER STRESS

A stress may either increase or decrease arousal from the optimum in Figure 3.3. When this happens, the computer of Figure 3.2 functions less efficiently. It cannot deal as adequately with a task which requires its full capacity. When arousal falls below the optimum, the computer works more slowly and makes more errors. When arousal rises above the optimum, the computer again makes more errors. If it works faster, it makes still more errors. We have seen that a rather similar effect can be produced by overloading the computer when it is working normally, by giving the person too much to do at once.

The simple picture of an overloaded computer may be complicated by strategies which are adopted to deal with the effects of the overload. The person may attempt to compensate for the fall in his efficiency by changing the strategy of the input selector of Figure 3.2. He may concentrate upon what he considers to be the more important aspects of the task, at the expense of the less important aspects. These effects of stress will be outlined in greater detail.

Decisions degraded by high workload

We have seen that it is not possible to make two decisions at the same time. But a routine well-practised skill can be performed while doing something else as well. The two different effects of doing two tasks at once are illustrated in an experiment carried out by Brown, Tickner and Simmonds (1969). Each of twenty-four drivers had to answer questions over a radiotelephone while deciding whether or not a gap ahead between two obstacles was just wide enough to drive the car through. Brown and his colleagues found that the driver made reliably more wrong decisions while driving and answering questions, than in a control condition while driving without questions. The driver also answered the questions reliably less correctly, and took reliably longer to do so, when he answered the questions while driving, than in a control condition when he answered the questions while the car was stationary.

The computer of Figure 3.2 could not make a decision about the width of the gap in the road ahead while it was occupied with answering a question. The decision about the width of the gap was a difficult one. It probably took several seconds to arrive at the best bet. Answering a question received over the radiotelephone during this period interfered with the decision. If the driver delayed his decision for too long, he had to drive through the gap whether he liked it or not, because he was not allowed to stop or swerve sharply. If the driver delayed dealing with the question until after he had decided whether or not to accept the gap, there was a chance that he had partly forgotten the question. If so, his answer could be wrong as well as late.

Routine overlearnt skills less affected

Once the driver had decided to accept a narrow gap, his skill in steering the car through the gap was not reliably degraded by having to answer questions at the same time. This is because steering the car had become pretty automatic. The result is in line with the results of laboratory experiments on tracking. Practised people can track almost as well when they have to carry out an additional task which involves listening and speaking as they can without the additional task (Garvey and Taylor, 1959). After sufficient practice, the computer of Figure 3.2 has only to initiate actions. Once practised actions have been initiated, they can be executed using the path between the long-term memory and the output selector which is indicated by the broken arrow. The computer is then freed temporarily for the other task. As long as the eyes are still looking at the tracking display, a critical change in the display can capture the input selector. The input selector will then switch the computer back to the tracking task.

It is additional visual tasks which degrade tracking (Garvey, 1960; Fuchs, 1962). This is because a person cannot look in two places at once. While a driver is looking in his rear mirror, he cannot see his errors in steering. Thus they cannot attract his attention.

Decisions degraded by other stresses

An experimenter can present a subject with an unfamiliar task for the first time while he is under stress. This is a useful method of detecting the effect of a small amount of stress. An unfamiliar task is likely to be difficult. The subject has to understand what he has to do. He has to decide on the best strategy to use. The unbroken function in Figure 3.3 shows that an increase to only a moderately high level of arousal may reduce the person's efficiency if his arousal was previously at the relatively low optimum level required for a difficult task. Under the stress he may decide on a relatively poor strategy. He may resort to a routine overlearnt programme of behaviour which is not the most appropriate one. Unfamiliar tasks have yielded measurable changes in performance at relatively low levels of stress. The levels often lie below those at which changes in performance have been reported for practised tasks (Poulton, 1965).

Compensation by restricting attention

When a person is highly aroused and finds that he is performing badly, he may attempt to compensate by concentrating on the most important aspects of the task. Hockey (1970b) gave sixteen young sailors a tracking task to represent steering a car in traffic. The subject was told to give the task top priority.

He had also to extinguish each of six lamps whenever one came on by pressing the corresponding one of six buttons with his left hand. The lamps were arranged in a semicircle. When he was looking at the tracking display directly in front of him, the six lamps subtended the angles to his line of sight which are shown at the bottom of Figure 3.4. The two lamps twenty degrees out from his line of sight each came on an average of twice per minute at irregular intervals of time. The four lamps further out each came on an average of once every two minutes. This is indicated at the top of the figure. Lamps coming on might correspond to the movements of other road users, or of pedestrians stepping off the pavement into the road.

After practice in quiet, the sailors had to perform the combined task for forty minutes, once in noise of 100 decibels and once in quiet. The average performance of both tasks was equally proficient but the averages concealed differences in the actual scores. In quiet, the average time for which the tracking task was performed accurately decreased from the first ten minutes of the task to the last ten minutes. In noise there was if anything a slight improvement over the forty minutes.

The effect of the noise on the average time taken to extinguish the lamps is illustrated in Figure 3.4. The lamps close to the man's line of sight as he looked at the tracking display were always extinguished more quickly on average than the lamps further towards the side. But in noise the difference was exaggerated. The sailors concentrated harder on the two nearer lamps which came on most frequently, at the expense of the four further lamps which did not come on so often.

The results can be interpreted as an attempt by the sailors to compensate for the effects of the noise. They did so by concentrating on the most important aspects of the combined task, the tracking which they had been told to give the top priority, and the nearer two lights which between them presented two thirds of the signals. By doing so, they were able to achieve as good an average performance in the noise as they could in quiet. When a person first enters a hot room, he becomes more alert or highly aroused. He shows a similar concentration of attention upon what he takes to be the important aspects of a task of this kind. (Bursill, 1958; Poulton and Kerslake, 1965).

There appears to be no attempted compensation when a person

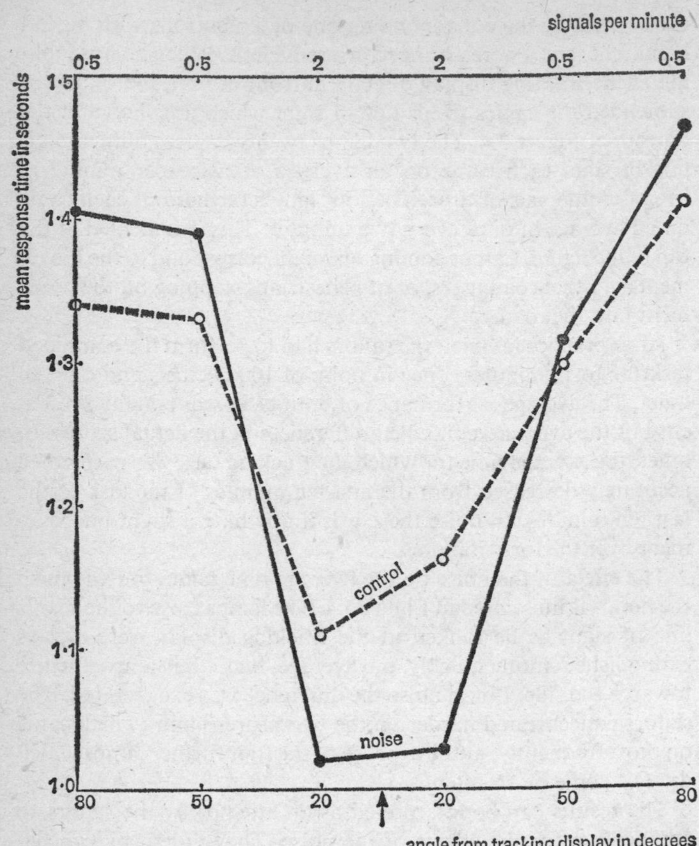

Figure 3.4 The average time taken to respond in noise and in quiet to lamps fixed at different angles to the line of sight. (Results from Hockey, 1970b)

is less aroused than usual, as after a night without sleep. Hockey (1970a) gave twelve young sailors the same combined tracking and lamps task. After practice with normal sleep, they performed the combined task twice, once after a night without sleep and once after normal sleep. At the start, the sailors performed equally well in both conditions. But soon their performance when they had gone without sleep became worse than their performance after normal sleep. After a normal night's sleep, the average time for which the tracking task was performed accurately decreased over the forty minutes of the task. The decrease was almost three times as large after loss of sleep.

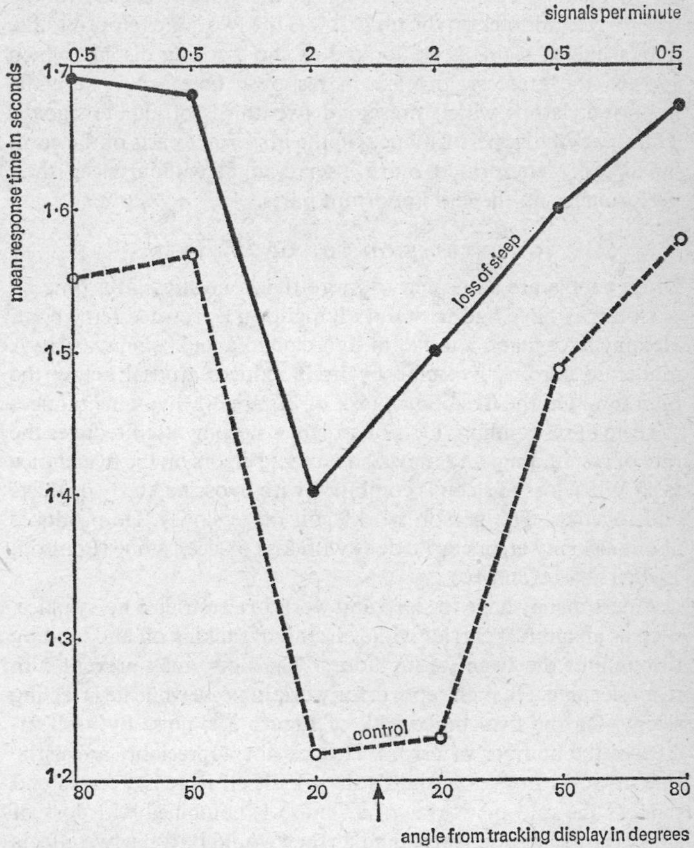

Figure 3.5 The average time taken to respond after a night without sleep, and after normal sleep, to lamps fixed at different angles to the line of sight. (Results from Hockey, 1970a)

Figure 3.5 shows that after a night without sleep the lamps in every position were extinguished less quickly than after normal sleep. The effect came on gradually during the forty minutes on the task. For the first ten minutes there was little difference between the two conditions. For the last ten of the forty minutes the difference was even more marked than that illustrated in Figure 3.5, because the figure shows the times averaged over the whole forty minutes on the task. It was the two lamps closest to the man's line of sight as he looked at the tracking display which showed the greatest increase in response time. They were the important lamps which presented two thirds of all the signals. Thus if anything, performance on the important parts of the combined task deteriorated more after a night without sleep than performance on the less important parts.

ONE STRESS ON TOP OF ANOTHER

Often people are subjected to more than one stress at a time. A person may have had to stand all night on a crowded ferry boat. He may have taken a tablet of hyoscine to avoid being seasick. A moderate dose of hyoscine by itself reduces arousal below the optimum. On the five-choice task of Figure 3.1, hyoscine reduces the rate of responding. Loss of a night's sleep by itself reduces the rate of responding, and may also increase errors on the five-choice task. When loss of sleep is combined with hyoscine, the two effects add together. The person works still more slowly. He produces about as many errors as he does with loss of sleep alone (Poulton, 1970, Tables 9 and 10).

A person may have to sleep and work in a restricted noisy place, such as an aircraft carrier while aircraft are taking off and landing throughout the twenty-four hours. The noise may prevent him from sleeping. He then reports for work in noise while he is feeling sleepy. On the five-choice task of Figure 3.1, noise by itself increases the number of errors. It does not appreciably affect the rate of work. Loss of a night's sleep by itself increases errors and reduces the rate of work. When noise is combined with loss of sleep, errors are not as frequent as they would be if the two effects added together. Also the person may not work as slowly as he does when he has simply lost a night's sleep.

The combined effect can be explained using the arousal model of Figure 3.3 on page 63. Loss of sleep produces inefficiency because it lowers arousal. Noise increases arousal. When noise is combined with loss of sleep, arousal is not as low as it is with loss of sleep by itself. The person who has lost a night's sleep and works in noise, is not as inefficient as a person who has lost a night's sleep and works in a quiet place (Wilkinson, 1963).

There is a more acceptable method of reducing the effect of a lost night's sleep. Telling a person how he is performing increases his arousal. On the five-choice task of Figure 3.1, knowledge of results by itself increases the rate of work and reduces the number of errors. This is the exact opposite of the effect of loss of sleep. If a person is given knowledge of results after loss of a night's sleep, he does not work as slowly, or make as many errors, as he does with loss of sleep without knowledge of results. The two effects tend to cancel each other out. The deterioration in performance produced by a night without sleep is considerably larger than the improvement normally produced by knowledge of results. So giving knowledge of results to a person who has lost a night's sleep does not fully prevent the deterioration. But the improvement produced by knowledge of results is greater when a person has lost a night's sleep than it is when he has slept normally. The combined effect can again be explained using the arousal model of Figure 3.3 (Wilkinson, 1961).

Giving knowledge of results is not always as beneficial as this. If a person is already highly aroused, giving him knowledge of results does not help as much as usual. This is what happens when knowledge of results is given to a person who is working in noise. On the five-choice task of Figure 3.1 noise by itself usually increases the number of errors, without altering the rate of work. In this particular experiment, the increase in errors was not consistent enough to be accepted as reliable. Knowledge of results by itself reduces the number of errors and increases the rate of work. When knowledge of results was given to people working in noise, it had a smaller effect than it did when it was given to the people working in quiet (Wilkinson, 1963).

This effect also can be explained using the arousal model of Figure 3.3. Knowledge of results increases arousal. When a person has worked once or twice with knowledge of results, he is not adequately aroused without it (Brown, 1966a). Without knowledge of results, he might be at the point A_1 in the figure. Giving him knowledge of results might increase his arousal to A_2. His efficiency therefore increases. Subjecting him to noise as well increases his arousal still further, in the direction of A_3. His efficiency is still higher than it was at A_1. But it is not as high as it was at A_2 without the noise.

AVOIDING THE EFFECTS OF STRESS

A person works most efficiently when he is alert, or moderately aroused (Figure 3.3). If he wishes to work efficiently, he should avoid stresses which change his arousal from the optimum. Important or dangerous work should not be carried out under stresses which raise or lower arousal too much.

With the best intentions, a student may find some secluded place in which to study, well away from distractions. Unless he adopts an efficient strategy of study, his arousal will gradually but inevitably fall. Arousal will fall more quickly if the student has run up a sleep debt because he has not been sleeping well. Perhaps he is feeling sleepy because he has not fully recovered from the sleeping tablets which he took the previous evening in order to be certain of a good night's sleep (McKenzie and Elliott, 1965). As his arousal falls, his work becomes less efficient. He may suddenly realize that he has read a number of pages, but cannot recall anything in them. At this stage he may quit study. Or he may persevere, conscientiously but ineffectively.

There are a number of ways by which a student can keep himself alert when he is working alone. He can set himself targets. He can decide to learn the contents of a certain number of pages in a certain time. When time is up, he can note whether he has reached his target or not. This tells him how quickly he is working.

A student should also quiz himself as he goes along. If quizzes are not given in the textbook, he should make up his own. At the end of a section he can quickly note down the main points he has learnt. He can then check them by going through the text again rapidly. Quizzes tell him how efficiently he is working.

This method of study breaks up a prolonged period of work. Study is followed by quizzes and by quick revisions which provide knowledge of results on the effectiveness of the work. Short breaks for coffee or tea between assignments also help to break up a prolonged period of work. Discussing the work with colleagues during breaks may help to maintain interest in it. All these procedures help to keep the student alert.

SUMMARY

A skilled performance involves decisions and precise movements. Figure 3.2 illustrates how the brain works during a skilled performance. The computer of Figure 3.2 is most efficient when arousal is at the optimum level illustrated in Figure 3.3. Stress has a marked effect upon the quality of decisions. Stress has less effect upon highly practised movements which have become partly automatic. When a person is too highly aroused, he may compensate by restricting his attention to the most important parts of the job (Figure 3.4). The effects of a combination of stresses can be predicted fairly well from the arousal model of Figure 3.3. There are ways of preventing the fall in arousal which occurs during quiet study.

FURTHER READING

Christopher Poulton's *Environment and Human Efficiency* (Charles C. Thomas 1970) provides a broad introduction to stress and its effects upon skilled performance. Skilled performance is treated in A. T. Welford's *Fundamentals of Skill* (Methuen, 1968), in P. M. Fitts' and M. I. Posner's *Human Performance* (Prentice-Hall, 1967), and in *Principles of Skill Acquisition*, edited by E. A. Bilodeau and I. M. Bilodeau (Academic Press 1969). C. Poulton's *Tracking Skill and Manual Control* (to be published in 1972) is more specialized. David Legge's book of readings *Skills* (Penguin, 1970) provides a useful introduction to the subject. Perceptual skills are treated in U. Neisser's *Cognitive Psychology* (Appleton-Century-Crofts, 1967).

4
Learning in Practice

John Annett

For several decades the study of learning has been central to the developing science of psychology. Much research has focussed on the acquisition of simple habits by animals or on human learning in fairly unrepresentative laboratory conditions. In this chapter Dr Annett points out that these studies are of limited value when it comes to understanding complex learning situations of the kind faced by education and training specialists. He has for several years worked to extend psychological knowledge of how people acquire the skills and knowledge required in their jobs, and he introduces this field by an examination of some feature of task analysis, programmed instruction, computer-assisted instruction and training simulators.

INTRODUCTION

I make no apologies for the pun in my title. It is generally agreed that there is a gap between the study of learning in the laboratory and the study of learning in the classroom and the training workshop. In a fairly recent standard text on industrial training (Seymour, 1966) the author admits 'To relate the knowledge about the acquisition of skills to these (learning) theories is by no means easy, and many aspects of the acquisition of skill are difficult to reconcile with any of the current learning theories'. Spence (1959) puts the complementary view of an experimentalist: 'The phenomena that the experimental psychologist interested in the problems of learning has taken as the object of his studies, and about which he has to formulate his theories, have little or nothing to do with learning in real life situations, including even the kinds of learning that are supposed to go on in the schoolroom . . . the body of laws and theories that these psychologists have developed had their origin in a very different set of phenomena, namely observations made under laboratory conditions of such simple things as lever-pressing behaviour or the running speed of the white rat, the salivary or leg flexion response of the dog or the blinking response of the human eyelid.'

There are many reasons for this gap between the pure and applied sciences of learning. Chapanis (1967) discusses some of the problems which face the applied researcher attempting to generalize from theoretical and experimental studies, but in the context of industrial training two factors are particularly worth mentioning. In a paper to a conference on programmed instruction in 1963 I put the proposition that there is a basic difference between a theory of learning and a theory of teaching or instruction. The aim of the former is to elucidate the processes underlying learning, ultimately (although this is denied by some) referring to the physiological processes of information storage and retrieval in the brain. A theory of instruction on the other hand is essentially about what a teacher can do to change the learner's behaviour. Clearly at some level of analysis the two will have to match up, to be related one to the other, but in the present state of knowledge and in view of the immediate need to 'engineer' practical learning situations it is both possible and desirable to look at teaching as a process worthy of study in its own right, referring to learning theory only when it helps to settle a matter of practical teaching strategy. The first point I want to make, therefore, is that the sciences of teaching and learning involve different, though ultimately converging strategies.

The second point is this. Laboratory learning studies differ from training research in one important practical way. Whilst the laboratory-based psychologist attempts to explain the acquisition of a lever-pressing response or the reproduction of a list of paired associates the educational or training researcher is interested in how to teach electronics or geometry or a foreign language. In the pursuit of rigour the experimentalist has to *invent* simplified artificial tasks whilst the applied researcher is faced with the problem of how to *analyse* existing tasks before he can plan a systematic attack on the training problem. It is for this reason that the first main section of this chapter describes some recent work on the problems of task analysis.

The term 'educational technology' is currently used to refer to some of the modern developments in applied research or instruction. The word 'technology' is significant in two ways. First it implies that the work is oriented towards producing practical results. It is, like engineering, 'the art of the possible'. Second, the products of engineering technology are, more and more, being applied to education and training in the form of audio-visual aids, teaching machines, computers and simulators. The rest of this chapter is devoted to an all-too-brief outline of recent developments in the use of these technological aids to instruction, particularly in an industrial setting.

TASK ANALYSIS

It is still generally the case that training course syllabuses are based on intuitive analyses of the nature of the desired 'terminal behaviour'. To take a now classic instance, men who are primarily employed in 'troubleshooting' (maintaining and repairing) electronic equipment are typically exposed to a course on electronic theory with rather little emphasis on the techniques of taking the shortest practical route to locate a malfunctioning component. It has been shown (Williams and Whitmore, 1959) that, after training, recall of 'theory' declines progressively whilst actual troubleshooting performance improves with practice on the job. Whatever use electronics theory may have been to the trainee in other spheres it clearly had little to do with successful fault finding. One suspects that much the same might be true in many other cases. How many of us with five years of school French find ourselves incapable of carrying on a simple conversation with a native French speaker?

Given that it is necessary to describe the behaviour we are hoping to teach before beginning to plan a training course, how should one set about this? It might not be unreasonable to expect that psychology should follow the other sciences by developing an agreed system of description and classification of the phenomena to be studied. However, psychology seems to have missed out this stage in its development and there exists no generally agreed set of categories for describing behaviour.

Working in the context of industrial training our research group at Hull has suggested a new way of coping with the analyses of tasks. In industrial tasks, and probably most others, the really important thing is not so much the details of behaviour as what its overall purpose is. An important description of any piece of behaviour is *what it is for*. It will be possible for the same objectives to be achieved in a variety of ways and at the same time some behaviour very similar in superficial characteristics might utterly fail to achieve the overall objective. A television repairman might adopt any one of several possible strategies to find and rectify a fault (though normally there is one best way) or he may go through a drill of checking and replacing parts which is quite unsuccessful.

The first step then is to identify the overall objectives of the task. Next we consider whether these can be broken down into sub-objectives. Figure 4.1 shows the initial stages of an analysis of the task of a process control operator in a chemical factory. The analysis and the corresponding diagram takes the form of a hierarchy. The box at the top states, briefly, the overall objective of the task, namely to purify acid.

Associated with this objective are constraints such as running the plant efficiently and without danger. The whole task is then broken down at the next level into three sub-operations, starting up, running and shutting down the plant. Start-up and shut-down are relatively infrequent and running the plant within tolerance limits constitutes the main day-to-day activity. In certain danger conditions the plant shuts down automatically, an occurrence which can normally be prevented if faults are quickly located and rectified.

At the next level start-up is split into three successive sub-operations, each of which (when described at the next lower level) breaks down into a large number of simple steps mostly involving the activation of various controls in a prescribed order. The start-up is then a very long procedure (taking quite a long time) and shut-down similarly involves long procedures.

The operations involved in running the plant (boxes 8, 9 and 10) are quite different. In 9 and 10 the behaviour required of the operator is seldom repeated in the same form, for his actions will depend on the particular pattern of fault indications shown on the console and he must follow not a sequence but a strategy. The analysis took the form of determining optimal strategies rather than recording actual behaviour which, in these situations, is often sub-optimal. A more detailed description of the task analysis and subsequent training scheme is reported in Annett and Duncan (1971).

This form of analysis is based on the application of a few simple rules. First the description goes from the gross to the particular. Rather than describing the task as a succession of simple acts, like

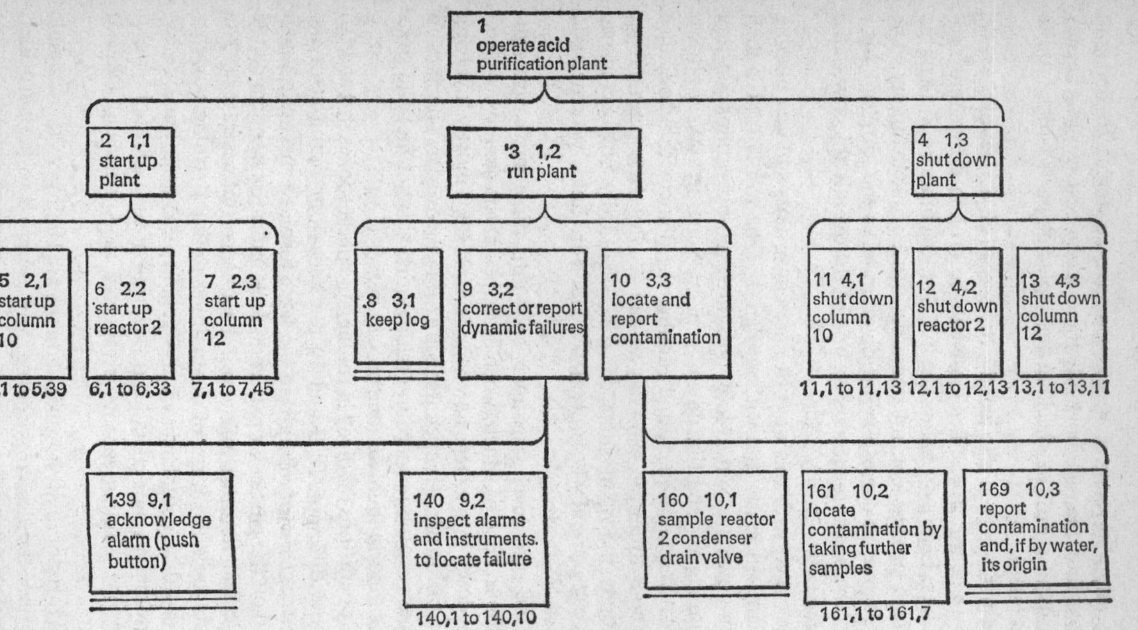

Figure 4.1 Hierarchical description – operating an acid purification plant

telling off beads on a string, one takes an objective, like starting up the plant, and attempts to 'unpack' components, each being defined by a unique set of functional objectives.

The next basic rule concerns how far one needs to 'unpack' each sub-operation. A conventional task analysis adopts one level of description, for instance, describing the physical movements involved. Our method, however, analyses each part of the task only down to the degree of detail required to make a proposal about how to train. For example operation 8, 3.1 refers to keeping the log. This is neither difficult nor critical to the operation and a few verbal instructions and a demonstration is all that is necessary. Other behaviour however requires further unpacking. The rule we propose is that an operation should be redescribed if the product of the probability of failure and the cost of failure is unacceptable to the system. By 'failure' here we mean failure to perform adequately, given some straightforward instruction.

Some 'tricky' elements of a task may have to be 'unpacked' down to a fairly detailed level before the training problem can be identified and a suitable solution proposed. When we get to this level of detail we should find that each operation has three important components, *input*, *action* and *feedback*. A task may be difficult to learn because the input, or signal for action, is not discriminated by the trainee. In this case he must be trained, possibly by some special exercise, to make the appropriate discrimination. 'Action' difficulties can be of two kinds. In the simple case the trainee is merely unaware of the appropriate response but the more difficult case is when he already has an habitual response to this input which happens to be wrong in this situation (like turning a control clockwise instead of counter-clockwise). This kind of difficulty can often best be dealt with by making appropriate changes to the equipment, for relearning is generally a slow and rather uncertain process. Feedback difficulties, like input difficulties, may be a matter of perceptual discrimination, but very often an inability to make a response has nothing to do with any motor deficiency and is simply a failure to appreciate what feedback indicates the correct completion of the response. For example, if a cookery book says 'beat the mixture to a soft dropping consistency' the problem is not beating but knowing just when to stop. Such difficulties are quite common in industry where the operator is dealing with remotely controlled equipment which may delay or mask feedback cues.

TECHNOLOGICAL AIDS TO EDUCATION AND TRAINING

In the first part of this chapter the word 'technology' has been used to emphasize a difference in strategy between pure and applied science. Educational technology implies a direct pragmatic approach to teaching problems as distinct from the investigation of learning processes *per se* which characterizes formal learning research. But technology also has a more conventional meaning to do with the use of equipment and devices. Technology in this sense has in the past fifteen years had an increasingly important effect on both the philosophy and practice of teaching. In this section we will look at programmed instruction and computer-assisted instruction and spend a little time on the problems of training devices and simulators.

Programmed instruction in industry

Programmed instruction first appeared on the British scene in the early 1960s. In 1960, according to Cavanagh and Jones (1970), only about six programmes were commercially available. By 1964 the number had risen to about 200 and by 1967 over 500 programmes were in print whilst many more 'unpublished' programmes were in use. The great majority of these programmes were on technical and scientific subjects, that is subjects of a largely factual nature in which the subject matter admits of presentation in a generally agreed 'logical' order and where in most cases the answers to questions could be classified as 'right' or 'wrong' unambiguously. According to the classification used by Cavanagh and Jones the largest single category was arithmetic on which well over 300 programmes have been at some time or other commercially available in Britain. This is followed by 'engineering' with over 200 titles and 'commercial subjects' with 150. Clearly the sort of material which has been 'programmed' is particularly relevant to industry. Romiszowski (1967) surveyed the use of PI in industry in the previous year, by means of a questionnaire to 2630 organizations. The return was less than 30 per cent and of these 150 firms, or about 20 per cent were using PI and over 130 were planning to use PI during the coming year. Although there is no comparable recent survey there is reason to believe that the growth rate is beginning to slow down and PI is not making quite the impact on industrial training which was predicted in the early 60s.

In the early years the armed services (not included in Romiszowski's survey) led the field in research and development (see Wallis, Duncan and Knight, 1966) just as had been the case earlier in the USA. It would seem that the adoption and use of PI has to do more with the nature of the organization than with the characteristics of the method *per se*. The services, unlike industry, have a tradition of using experimental psychologists in various research establishments concerned with manpower problems and it is really these people, quite few in number, who provided the initial impetus to research and development. In peace time training constitutes the major activity of the services, almost to the extent that a trained body of men could be regarded as the 'product', whereas in industry at large the product is motor cars, plastics, etc. In other words 'management' in the services is more likely to see training efficiency as a high priority goal than their counterparts in civil life. A third factor is size. Romiszowski's survey showed that there was a marked correlation between size of firm and the use of PI. Only 1·7 per cent of the respondents with less than 500 employees used PI whereas 47·5 per cent of the firms employing more than 5,000 did. This sort of relationship between training effort and size of organization is well known throughout the western world and was one of the major factors leading to the introduction of the 1964 Industrial Training Act. It would seem that both attention to training needs and sophistication in training techniques depend on size and this is probably due to the nature of the non-productive support facilities available to larger organizations.

The kinds of problem which arise in the use of PI in industry can perhaps best be illustrated by a project I undertook a few years ago for the gas industry. Although the industry is large by most standards there was at that time only one qualified psychologist on the staff (and he was employed in an administrative role) and so the industry sought outside help in attempting to determine the possible value of PI to its particular problem. Two general sorts of question could be asked – first, were the sorts of skills required by the industry of the kind which could be 'programmed' and second, if so, in what areas and to what extent should there be an investment in PI. Initially at least the industry saw the former question as more important.

The great majority of programmes have been written to teach verbal or 'theory' aspects of tasks and a much smaller contribution has been made to the teaching of manual skills. As part of the project about a dozen short programmes were devised to teach trainee gas fitters how to perform a number of basic manual tasks. These included amongst other things using a water gauge to test gas appliances, reading and adjusting gas meters and soldering joints in metal pipes. In the tasks involving simple procedures a conventional linear format was used. Typically the trainee was at his work bench and supplied with the appropriate tools and equipment. The programme was on cards and each frame described a step in the process and required the trainee to perform some simple act. The programmes were fully illustrated and in particular showed how the work-piece should look at critical stages in the task. In case this visual check on feedback might not be sufficient, at certain critical stages the trainee was required to show a peripatetic instructor his work, inviting comment and correction as necessary. The dozen programmes accounted for only a small part of the whole training scheme, the purpose of which was to train fitters to convert a range of appliances from 'town' gas to North Sea natural gas, a process which required the replacement of certain parts of the appliance.

The basic question as to whether such tasks can be taught by PI was readily answered in the affirmative. For example the programme on joint making was tested on two groups of ten trainees, each with a comparable control group taught in the conventional way. The criterion test consisted of making two test joints. Experimental and control work pieces were coded and labelled and mixed together. They were then scored by an independent judge who allotted marks according to carefully specified criteria. The experimental group averaged 95·8 per cent and the control group 96·3 per cent, the difference being statistically insignificant. Whilst the control groups used a standard instruction period of 165 minutes the majority of the experimental PI trainees completed their task in rather less time. A similar result was obtained with programmes on meter reading and adjustment, the control group scoring 81 per cent and the PI group 86 per cent. In this case, however, the PI group completed their learning on average in just half the time taken by the conventional lesson. These results are quite typical of those obtained in other studies such as those carried out by the services.

This demonstration that PI works in an industrial setting is, however, rather less than half the story. Some very difficult economic and administrative problems have to be solved before the obvious power of PI can be put to work on a large scale. The small number of programmes involved in the experiment required a considerable investment in skilled manpower. They were written by a trained psychologist helped by several subject matter experts working for several months. Even though PI can be shown to be effective it is quite another matter to demonstrate *cost/effectiveness* that is important in training 'productivity'. One crucial factor is, of course, the size of the trainee population. Other things being equal, greater value can be expected for a given investment in programme development if the trainee population is larger. Another organizational factor affecting the use of PI is that the potential saving of trainee time could only be realized if the whole system of lecture/demonstrations and practical work were completely reorganized. Thus it is that the real answer to the application of PI to this industrial case can only be found after a very thorough analysis of the existing training system, a task more appropriate to operational research than to psychology as such. The nature of this problem seems, as yet, to be poorly understood in industry at large and such applications of PI as do exist seem to be rather haphazard, and probably therefore rather unprofitable.

Computer-assisted instruction

Computer-assisted instruction (CAI) is sometimes described as a sophisticated extension of the principles of PI. Whilst there is some justification in this, CAI offers so many different possibilities and introduces so many new problems that it is best to regard it as a separate entity. In PI there has been a general move away from hardware 'teaching machines' towards the programmed text, but CAI reverses this trend. Simple machines turned out to be not central to the teaching function since they were used primarily to turn pages and prevent cheating. The computer by contrast has the ability to perform operations which are non-trivial and to perform them very fast indeed.

A computer-assisted instruction system typically consists of a general purpose digital machine comprising a central processor, backing store of disc or magnetic tape and various input-output devices. Input devices for feeding data into the machine can be paper tape or card readers or magnetic tape readers or electric typewriters. Output can be in the form of paper tape or card punch, or electric typewriter or an analogue display, for example, a cathode-ray tube. Student terminals consist of whatever collection of input/output devices is convenient. Obviously most people cannot read punched tape but they can read typescript and operate a typewriter and through this means can communicate with the machine. Cathode ray tubes (CRT) and other types of electronic visual display have certain advantages (such as being much quieter) and a device called a light pen used with a special CRT enables the learner to 'write' certain types of information directly into the computer. If the CAI system is a large one there may be a separate multiplexing unit (possibly another smaller computer) which will connect up a large number of student terminals to the central processor.

In order to make this collection of hardware teach it has to be provided with its programme of instructions. These instructions consist of material to present to the student and a basic teaching logic, that is, a set of rules which determines how the student will interact with the material. In the extreme case this set of rules will quite simply allow the student to ask for any information contained in the machine, but generally the teacher has in mind some way in which he wishes to control the situation.

One of the principal virtues of CAI is the almost indefinitely wide range of teaching strategies available to the teacher. It is important to realize that CAI as a general concept does not reflect any one theory of learning or approach to teaching. The teacher can, within the physical and data-processing limits of the system embody whatever strategy he likes. One can, for example, set up the computer simply as a drill and practice device which will patiently present an inexhaustible supply of examples, say in arithmetic, and administer and score these exercises. At the same time the teacher can accumulate data on the progress of individuals or groups of students simply for the record or to form a basis for an empirical investigation of the learning situation leading to revision. At a more complex level the teacher could set up diagnostic routines which will explore the student's competence. This sort of approach can be used in what is known as Computer-Managed Instruction (CMI). The student may work through examples 'off-line' and the data can be subsequently fed into the computer for a diagnostic analysis. The computer thus devises a set of instructions concerning remedial or new material to which the student should be sent. A project at the Royal Liberty School at Romford in Essex is pursuing this means of using the computer. But a large computer will normally be able, if suitably programmed, to deal with these tactical teaching decisions on-line and in 'real time', that is, whilst the student is actually working at the terminal.

Without going into details of specific systems we can say something about the functional characteristics of CAI systems. It is generally acknowledged that one important limitation on conventional PI is the inability of machines to 'recognize' student responses when these are freely constructed. The computer offers a great deal more flexibility but there are still limitations. For example a computer can be programmed to recognize not only a correct answer but also a number of common mis-spellings or other trivial mistakes in an otherwise correct answer, provided the programmer can foresee the possibilities and there is room to store them all. The time taken to compare the answer given with all possible answers will be negligible. Additional flexibility is gained by the use of 'key words' recognition. If, for example, the answer to a question is a freely composed sentence the computer may be programmed simply to search through the response for the presence of key words and score the answer on their presence or absence, without regard to word order or the overall wording of the sentence. Yet another alternative is to require the learner to use a specific vocabulary when 'conversing' with the computer. Although CAI greatly extends the range of responses open to a learner there is still a long way to go before computers' pattern recognition capability approaches that of a human teacher.

The second feature in which CAI greatly exceeds conventional PI is in the form of interaction with the individual student. While it is true that some CAI schemes use the computer as little more than a page turner or a means of providing repetitive drill and practice a great deal more is possible. In teaching medical diagnosis, Feurzeig *et al.* (1964) employed a 'Socratic' question and answer method. The rules governing the dialogue allow the trainee diagnostician to request a whole range of information concerning the symptoms of one patient. The computer keeps track of the information requested and may, for example, offer advice about the order of priorities in making tests. The student is instructed to make a diagnosis and the computer, knowing what information he has, can evaluate his conclusions, for example, indicating that the conclusions cannot legitimately be drawn from the data given and so on. The 'conversation' is held in a simple code language but transcripts are none the less very realistic.

Another example of the computer's flexibility is Woods and Hartley's (1970) programmes which will generate problems in arithmetic appropriate to the level of skill of the learner as demonstrated by his actual performance. Because of the size of storage capacity normally available CAI offers the possibility of collecting information about individual learners or groups of learners. This information can then be used in a variety of ways. It could, for instance, be used in the conventional PI manner to modify the material held in store or its sequence, a facility very helpful to programme authors. More than this, given an appropriate set of instructions, student information can be used to modify some aspect of the teaching situation as it occurs. This adaptive facility can be illustrated by a simple programme developed by Dr G. J. Harrison at Hull to control the learning of a list of nonsense syllables. The method of serial anticipation is used, the learner typing his 'answers' into the keyboard of an on-line teleprinter. A very simple adaptive programme simply records correct or incorrect anticipation of each item and at the end of each trial reallocates the total exposure time between items, reducing the time for which correct answers are shown and increasing the time for failed items. Under these adaptive conditions most subjects learn nonsense lists in fewer trials than under non-adaptive conditions.

One notable feature of CAI is the speed with which the digital computer can operate. The speed with which responses can be checked and appropriate action taken is such that with only one pupil to look after a computer would spend a high proportion of its time simply waiting for the student. With appropriate multiplexing a large number of students can be connected to the central processor simultaneously. This is useful since with time sharing the costs of CAI can be reduced to something approaching the cost of conventional teaching.

CAI is in an early experimental stage but it is still appropriate to ask if it may be applied to problems of technical and industrial training. In fact a number of experimental CAI courses are of a technological or industrial nature. For example the Feurzeig's medical diagnosis programme has been adapted by Rigney (1966) to electronic trouble-shooting in the US Navy. Swets and his colleagues (1962) have used computers to teach recognition of sounds. Sound patterns were generated and responses scored by the computer. In one experiment the trainee was able to opt for various kinds of practice, with various kinds and amounts of prompting, or he could opt for tests with or without knowledge of results. Perhaps one of the most obvious applications is in teaching computer technology. IBM have for some years now run courses for their own staff using a multi-access system with the main computer in New York and students 'on-line' from as far apart as Philadelphia and San Francisco. In addition to true CAI where the computer is performing some or all of the functions of a teacher computers can and have been used quite extensively as tools for the learner under his own control. In teaching statistics, for example, the computer can be used simply as a calculating device. Another well established use of the computer is as a simulator and this will be discussed briefly in the next section.

The big question hanging over CAI is of course the possibility of economic justification. At present, computer time is expensive and CAI is the most expensive way to teach. Balanced against this, however, is the rapidly increasing cost of providing human teachers and the trend for computers to become increasingly efficient and less costly. As with PI, usage is an important factor in keeping costs down. Multi-access in which 100 or more students can be taught by a single computer will obviously be more economically viable than small systems in which only one or a few students are taught at any one time. To achieve economic viability it will be necessary to think in terms of fairly large instructional systems based on a very considerable investment in both hardware and software. Such an investment is not likely to occur in the immediate future but pilot work in the last few years has indicated some of the characteristics of these instructional systems of the future.

TRAINING DEVICES AND SIMULATORS

A training device or simulator can be distinguished from a teaching machine or CAI system to the extent that it is not intended as a comprehensive teaching package. It is a means of providing relevant experience but it is not built in such a way as to control the learning process, thus a training device or simulator is a piece of hardware used by the instructor who in fact controls the actual training schedule. Training device is the more general term but we can distinguish between part-task trainers and simulators. Some typical part-task trainers have been described by Seymour (1954) and they have generally been used to permit the trainees to practice some specially difficult or important aspect of the task away from the demands of the real situation. Typically, devices were (a) highly simplified versions of some aspect of the task and (b) provided knowledge of results which were not present in the real task.

The term simulator is generally applied to more elaborate devices which faithfully replicate some real piece of equipment. Best known are the flight simulators for training aircrew, and, of course, astronauts, but any task involving highly complex equipment and involving danger to either the operator or the 'plant' may justify the use of simulators. Even with a very high degree of realism a simulator, say of a commercial airliner, costs a good deal less than the real thing both to build and to operate. Relatively rare conditions due to faults and other emergencies can be produced on a simulator whereas on the real equipment it will often be both difficult and dangerous to induce emergencies simply for training purposes. One further advantage is that a simulator can usually be designed to record the trainee's performance and can therefore be used for both teaching and testing. Arrangements can often be made to feed back test results to the trainee.

Simulators vary enormously in complexity and sophistication. An early example described by English (1942) was a real rifle with a pressure tambour set into the butt which caused a buzzer to sound when the trainee was squeezing just hard enough. At the other extreme there exists a computer-controlled flight simulator system which can mimic the response of a variety of aircraft to movements of the controls. For space-crew training centrifuges have been used to produce high 'g' conditions and zero 'g' can be achieved by flying on aircraft in a parabolic trajectory. In fact engineers have produced some very ingenious solutions to the physical problems of simulation. Our concern, however, is whether what the psychologist knows of learning and transfer can be of any value in the design and use of these devices. It must be understood that the evaluation of training devices and simulators is often only an evaluation in the engineering sense, that is to say whether the device works according to specification, is acceptable to the user and is economic in relation to 'real life' training experience.[1] Flight simulators had been in use for a number of years before any serious attempt was made at evaluation in the sense of measuring the positive or negative transfer from simulator practice to performance on the real task. In fact the engineering point of view (which virtually ignores the psychological variables affecting transfer) is a realistic one because when there is a big discrepancy between costs of simulated and real experience the simulator could be very much less efficient and yet worthwhile. Nonetheless if the transfer value of simulation can be improved by the intervention of the psychologist then so much the better.

Miller (1954) has suggested that the relationship between fidelity of simulation and transfer may not be linear. Another way of approaching this issue is to ask how much more training value does one get by making the simulator more life-like. For example, given a relatively straightforward aircraft simulator how much is gained by having the pilot view a filmed panorama and how much more is gained if the cockpit actually pitches, yaws and rolls as he manipulates the controls. Generally speaking the more sophisticated the simulator the more costly. A particularly controversial issue is whether or not motion cues are necessary in flight simulators. The consumers, that is trainee and instructor pilots, attach high value to fidelity in this respect but experimental studies such as one by Buckhout *et al.* (1963) suggest that these are not always important and may only be relevant to particular sub-skills. For example,

1. Some questions related to this are examined in chapter 5.

fast low-level flight can often provide rather a rough ride. Buckhout's study showed that tracking, that is guiding (simulated) aircraft with simulated buffetting, gave some positive transfer, but other aspects of pilot performance, such as procedures for operating other equipment, were not affected. The essence of the problem of what and how well to simulate depends very critically on what cues the trainee will use in the real tasks and what cues, whilst physically present, are inessential to his performance. Irrelevant or marginally relevant cues, could well be eliminated when, like simulated aircraft motion, they are costly to provide.

The question of the physical stimuli which should or should not be incorporated with a simulator has another aspect, that of the addition of special feedback cues. As was noted earlier a simulator can often be more suited to performance measurement than the real equipment and in some cases it might seem useful to use scoring and recording facilities to provide the trainee with knowledge of results. This sounds an attractive proposition to the psychologist since one of the best accepted generalizations in psychology is that knowledge of results is a powerful aid to learning.

Extensive use was made of additional feedback on gunnery simulators used by the US Air Force during and after the Second World War. A typical simulator consisted of a mockup gun, moveable on a pivot in two dimensions and with a range finder. The gun is pointed at a screen on to which a target is projected. The trainee tracks the target in azimuth, elevation and range and tries to press the trigger when 'on target' in all three. The trainee's controls are linked to the target projector device so that 'hits' could be scored. In one method of doing this a red filter dropped in front of the projector so that a 'hit' target turned immediately to red. On subsequent evaluation trials serious doubt was shed on the value of this technique of providing immediate knowledge of results. A typical finding was that as long as the red filter was available performance improved steadily but removal of the filter cue, as it were transfer to a more real situation, often produced rapid decline in performance to a level not much better than that obtained before training. In fact it was doubted whether the 'filter treatment' had any training value at all. What seems to have been happening in this case was that the red filter provided a cue which the trainee could use to aid his performance to the extent that if he used it, it would be missed when removed. On the whole it would seem better, at least in high speed tasks, not to confuse the display with additional cues but to provide knowledge of results immediately after performance. In this field, however, generalizations are apt to prove misleading and properly conducted evaluation trials are the only safe road. Once again the psychologist can probably be more useful for the experimental techniques he has at his command than by virtue of facts and theories he brings from the laboratory.

SUMMARY AND CONCLUSIONS

It is not possible in one short chapter to give more than a glimpse of the kinds of problems which face the applied psychologist working in training and education.[2] In underlining the differences between pure and applied research on learning it might appear to the student that hours spent in practical classes working with conditioning and rote learning are no more than a waste of time. This is not exactly the impression I would wish to convey, so let us consider briefly the relation between pure and applied psychology in this field. A knowledge of theory and empirical generalizations about learning, including their limitations, is an invaluable tool for the applied psychologist. However, what may be regarded as an incontrovertible fact (in the laboratory) is often in the real-life situation reduced to the status of an hypothesis, or even as Chapanis has put it 'a hunch'.

In the journey from the laboratory to the field the operational definition of critical variables can undergo significant changes. We see this in the extrapolation from reinforcement to knowledge of results. In the laboratory reinforcement normally means providing pellets of food for a hungry rat after a bar press. In a training device it means illuminating the target with red light when the trainee scores a hit. Again some variables like massing or spacing of practice which produce significant effects in the laboratory frequently fail to show up under the weight of other variables in the real-life situation. These points do not constitute a criticism of pure psychology but they are a warning and a challenge to the applied psychologist. I have already dwelt at some length on the

2. Some additional points are covered in the discussion of management training at the end of chapter 12.

difference in strategy between pure and applied research, but although the aims and strategy may be different many aspects of methodology and technique are valid for both kinds of enterprise. Programmed instruction originally arose out of a theory of learning, but CAI and simulation owe relatively little to the theorist. In both cases, however, the applied psychologist is called upon to carry out evaluation studies in which the scientific principles he must use have their direct counterpart in laboratory investigations. The theoretical bases of educational technology are still far too slender for us to be able to dispense with the rigorously conducted field study.

Further, one might ask what contribution applied research can make to theoretical psychology. One way in which such contributions have been made is in the identification of new and interesting behaviour paradigms. The study of vigilance, arising out of the problem of maintaining a watch for long periods, has found an important place in the study of human arousal and attention. In the field of learning, the laboratory psychologist has for many years remained content with a rather limited selection of behaviour paradigms. The analysis of complex tasks reveals some cases where these paradigms seem close enough, for example the learning of long invariant sequences of behaviour, but it also reveals others which have received rather little attention from the learning theorist. An example of this would be the learning of search strategies in fault-finding tasks where the behaviour is not a single chain and each 'element' of behaviour depends on the outcome of previous elements in a systematic way. On the whole we know rather less about how complex skills are learned than we know about simple laboratory skills.

Finally, the applied psychologist, like the engineer, must practise the art of the possible. He cannot isolate himself from the economic and other constraints of the real-life situation. He may feel that a simulator could be built which would provide better transfer of training but he has to reckon with the cost of achieving his ideal. He may feel that programmed instruction is the most efficient form of teaching but he must bear in mind the costs of programming in relation to the level of usage, the impact the use of this new method would have on the existing system and other factors of this kind which will affect the ultimate success of the innovation. When all is said and done being a scientist has a great deal to do with being able to cope with reality.

FURTHER READING

There are many sources on human learning but the beginner may find Part Three of *Introducing Psychology: An Experimental Approach* by D. S. Wright *et al.* (Penguin, 1970) a useful start. R. Borger and A. E. M. Seaborne's *The Psychology of Learning* (Penguin, 1966) provides a readable introduction. Amongst the more substantial texts J. Deese and S. H. Hulse's *The Psychology of Learning* (McGraw-Hill, 1967) is fairly up-to-date and comprehensive.

In the field of industrial training W. D. Seymour's *Industrial Skills* (Pitman, 1966) is a basic text and D. H. Holding's *Principles of Training* (Pergamon Press, 1965) attempts to relate laboratory findings on the acquisition of skill to training. A more basic book on perceptual-motor skill learning is *Principles of Skill Acquisition*, edited by E. A. and I. M. Bilodeau (Academic Press, 1969) but this has a theoretical rather than practical orientation. The Department of Employment has produced a useful series of pamphlets called *Training Information Papers* dealing with new developments in training. No. 6 (1971) by J. Annett, K. D. Duncan *et al.* describes the work on task analysis in more detail.

Several books attempt to relate pure and applied research. Outstanding amongst these is R. Glaser's *Training Research and Education* (Wiley, 1965). *Current Research on Instruction* edited by R. C. Anderson *et al.* (Prentice-Hall, 1969) also contains some useful contributions.

Teaching Machines and Programmed Instruction by Harry Kay, Bernard Dodd and Max Sime (Penguin, 1968) is a readable introduction and Dodd's book *Programmed Instruction for Industrial Training* (Heinemann, 1967) refers to specifically industrial uses. The *Journal of the Association for Programmed Learning and Educational Technology*, published quarterly by Sweet & Maxwell records much of the British research; one issue (volume 5, no. 1, January 1968) is devoted to papers on Computer Assisted Instruction.

Much of the recent work on CAI is only available in the form of mimeoed reports but an early book by J. E. Coulson (1962) introduces the main concepts. The National Council for Educational Technology, 160 Great Portland Street, London has produced several pamphlets reviewing the current state of the art and future projects.

Training devices and simulators are referred to in some of the works already mentioned but are specifically reviewed by W. C. Biel in R. M. Gagné's book *Psychological Principles in System Development* (Holt, Rinehart & Winston, 1962).

5
Psychological Aspects of Man-Machine Systems

Tom Singleton

Psychologists have for a long time been interested in the design of work and work environments. This is partly a matter of social organization and the distribution of responsibilities – topics which are considered in later chapters – but it is also a question of understanding and controlling the ways in which men and machines operate together as 'man-machine systems'. Professor Singleton has made important contributions to this latter field and here he sets into a historical framework three types of ergonomic study – classical, systems and error ergonomics. Throughout the chapter he stresses the need for the applied psychologist to have skills beyond those which are narrowly psychological, and he emphasizes the limitations of experimental laboratory research for increasing our understanding of complex behaviour.

A popular novelist appears on the television screen. With lights flashing on his teeth and spectacles, he delivers a scathing indictment of the age we live in. Machines are becoming more and more complex and dominant and men are becoming more and more limited in their vision and brutalized by continuous contact with these mechanisms. This man arranged the programme on the telephone, he prepared his speech on a typewriter, he got to the television centre in a taxi, his message got across by courtesy of hundreds of machine-orientated men who provided the electric power, the studio, the lighting systems, the cameras, the transmission network, the television sets and the homes they are located in. How well could he function without his spectacles which can only be specified and made by complex machines? What can he do when he gets toothache except get relief from another complex machine operator?

Whether we like it or not we live in a machine age and we are all totally dependent on a technology-based civilization. It is useless to rail against it, it is almost equally useless to make pious statements about the need to ensure that men do not become slaves of machines. In one sense this is inevitable in that if we want a machine to serve us we have to understand it, look after it and control it – which can be regarded as working for it; in another sense it is impossible in that machines can only assist in reaching goals set by their designers, managers and operators. Machines are always extensions of human functions, they are designed by men and operated by men. The way we control them globally is to communicate with the men who control them directly. The problem of control, the problem of design, and the problem of performance are not problems of machines but problems of man-machine systems.

THE MAN-MACHINE SYSTEM

Consider a lathe operator in a Birmingham factory. He adjusts a star wheel with his right hand, releases a clutch with his left hand and activates a motor with his right foot, a metal bar slides into the correct position which the operator can see with his eyes, hear with his ears and feel through the control levers. As a consequence of further control actions, tools move forward in smooth succession to change the outer shape, bore holes, add screw threads and so on. Was the resulting precision component produced by the man or the machine? Clearly a silly question – it was produced by the man-machine system. Consider two tanks approaching each other across a rolling plain in Northern Europe. Eventually one tank commander will locate the opposing tank before he is seen himself. Not because he has better eyesight but because he has a better perceptual technique for continuously scanning the approaching countryside, locating valleys, dips, buildings, roads, sky lines and so on, anticipating continuously where a target might appear. When he sees the target he gives an order to the gunner who performs his particular complex tasks with greater or less skill. If the gun has insufficient range and accuracy then he might still be hit first and then his survival depends on his armour or his avoiding action. Will one defeat the other because it has a more powerful engine or a longer-range gun, or thicker armour or a more accurate gunner or a more alert tank commander? All of these factors are important and any one may be crucial. From the strategist's point of view the relevant measure is the effectiveness of the weapon system. Consider two sports cars at Le Mans approaching the end of a race. One is riding in the slip-stream behind the other but at just the right moment the driver will manipulate the clutch, accelerator, gear levers and steering wheel so that he can slide out and pass the other by a combination of precise timing, engine power, inertia, road holding and favourably low wind resistance. Did the driver or the car win the race? Another silly question, it was the combination that proved superior.

Productivity, efficiency, superiority and other systems criteria depend not on the man alone nor on the machine alone but on both, and also on the effectiveness of their interaction.

If the concept of the man-machine system is so self-evidently valid it is reasonable to inquire why it has taken so long to develop. Why is it that the engineers – the specialists in design and construction – should be trained entirely in matters to do with hardware? Why should they do all the decision making in the creation of these systems? Who thinks about the man half of the system? There are a number of partial answers to these questions.

The human components of a system are beautifully designed, they are flexible, dexterous and adaptable, and for many purposes highly reliable. By contrast the machines, for most of the past two centuries of technological development, have been slow, clumsy, restricted to specific tasks and grossly unreliable. It is proper that the design effort, the care, attention and technological expertise should have concentrated on hardware. Thus hardware technology has developed, directed by the needs of the community and assisted by and assisting the simultaneous development of the physical sciences. The human and biological sciences lag behind partly because there is insufficient incentive in the form of 'need to know' but mainly because of the sheer complexity of human functions. In any case the engineer is human himself, he knows intuitively about human needs and human limitations. Three conditions are required before psychology and other biological sciences can play some part in the design of man-machine systems. Firstly, they must have something relevant to say which is not intuitively obvious. Their technology must not only exist, it must be developed to the point where it can provide more cost-effective answers to problems than those arrived at by experience and intuition. Secondly, the need for the priority of this contribution must emerge, the performance of the man-machine system must be manifestly limited by some human failings as well as hardware failings. Thirdly, it must be possible to do something about it. The hardware technologist must have some reserves which give him the opportunity, not only to design an effective machine, but also to adapt it to the capacities and limitations of the operator.

The progress of science and technology is such that these conditions can now be met but only marginally. The psychologist can sometimes make a contribution which is more than commonsense and depends on some scientifically established principles or facts, but these are uncomfortably rare; such instances of direct applicability are easier to think of from anatomy and physiology than from psychology. Systems often fail because of human limitations, but it can be argued with some justice that the individual can properly be held responsible for many of these failures and that they are not failures of design. The engineering designer does have some spare capacity particularly in electronics but he does have a lot of problems of his own and his primary responsibility remains that of getting the hardware right. Thus the contribution of the psychologist, from the point of view of systems efficiency, is marginal.

However, there is another facet of the situation which strengthens the position of the psychologist. The human operator in a man-machine system is a human being and one responsibility of the designer must be to preserve his health. The term health has been defined by the World Health Organization as not merely absence of disease and damage but total well-being. This is not to suggest that the psychologist can function by simply re-emphasizing the dignity of man. This may need to be done but it is done effectively by the poets and novelists; the job of the psychologist is to support recommendations which, although they may stem from this basic theme are based on scientific evidence relevant to the particular case. The contribution of the psychologist to man-machine systems design rests on the twin foundations of individual well-being and system-efficiency and on the claim that he can make a systematic science-based contribution towards these ends.

Practitioners who specialize in the pursuit of these objectives by the application of biological and psychological knowledge and by the use of techniques for the acquisition of new evidence about human operator performance are often known as 'human factors' specialists or consultants. This particular systems approach to problems of man at work is one of many. For instance, another approach which emphasizes the role of man as a part of an organization is described in detail in Emery (1969).

THE HISTORICAL BACKGROUND

The Second World War is a useful anchor-point in looking at the development of this field. There were a number of earlier streams of relevant work: the time and motion studies of Taylor and Gilbreth respectively, the development of tests by Ebbinghaus, Binet, Spearman and many others, the activities of the Industrial Health Research Board, the development of human experimental psychology of perception, learning and remembering. All these are described in detail in Thomson (1968). There was a hiatus during the slumps of the 1930s when the problem was any job availability rather than the right men in the right jobs. The situation changed dramatically about 1940. From the time and motion study field the work study and training fields emerged (Shaw, 1952; Seymour, 1954), the needs of the armed forces gave a sudden impetus to the use of selection tests (Vernon and Parry, 1949), the work of the Industrial Health Research Board on working hours, rest pauses and environmental conditions became important again (Chambers, 1951). These several developments are summarized in Figure 5.1.

From the man-machine system viewpoint the most relevant war-time activity was the switch of experimental psychologists from theoretical laboratory work to the problems of men at war. The 'Cambridge cockpit' experiments were the focus of this revolution. A group of Cambridge psychologists, Bartlett, Craik, Russell-Davies and Drew, were faced with the problem of studying pilot-fatigue. What we would now call a simulator was built, experienced pilots functioned within it for hours at a time and detailed performance measures were taken by elaborate assemblies of string, pens and rolls of paper (Davis, 1948). Over periods of an hour or more heterogeneous things happened; some dials were attended to equally throughout, on others performance deteriorated markedly, some kinds of errors did not increase, others increased steadily, yet others increased in the early period and then decreased again. Some individuals demonstrated increasing withdrawal and inertia, others showed increased annoyance and violence of activity. To understand the trauma of this experience for the investigators one has to consider the theoretical background with which they were familiar. What they knew about fatigue was based on muscle physiology, on the ergograph, on the conditioning-type experiment and on psychoanalytic theory. The disillusion with classical psychology has been graphically described by Bartlett (1943; 1951b). He took up the position that the useful basic unit of behaviour is the simple skill and that skill psychology would

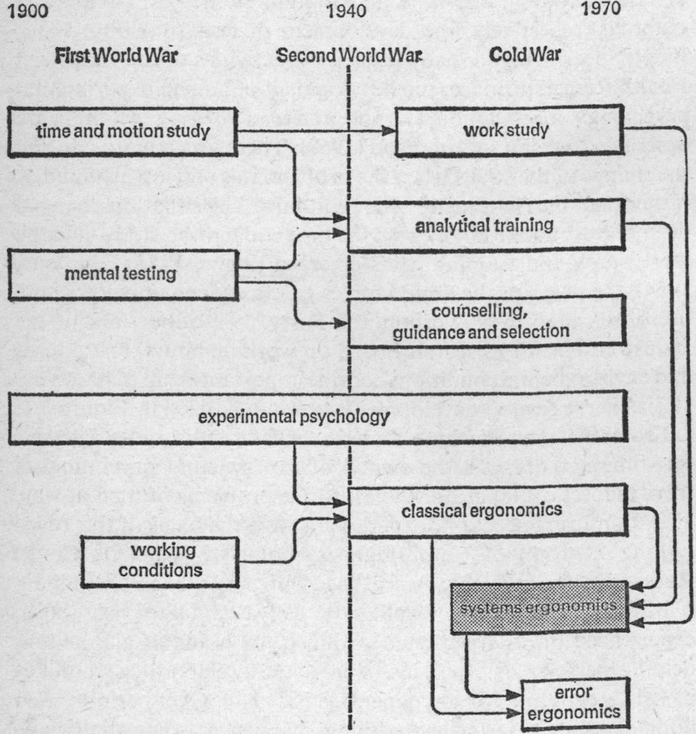

Figure 5.1 Historical background of systems psychology

provide the necessary theoretical background to applied activities. Theoretical progress would be made by understanding the study of real problems using 'unprejudiced observation' and testing the ideas that emerge in controlled laboratory conditions (Bartlett, 1951b). At the same time one of his colleagues, Craik (1947), was beginning to use the analogies of behaviour with servo-mechanisms and other information handling systems.

The partnership of theory and application within skill psychology continued fruitfully for a decade or more after the Second World War but has recently been showing signs of decay. Difficulties on the theoretical side will be discussed later, on the practical side problems began to emerge fairly soon after the war. There was some attempt to transfer the expertise gained on wartime equipment to industry and it was at this time that the term 'ergonomics' was coined. This was conceived as the complement of the more established industrial psychology which dealt with 'fitting the worker to the job' by selection and training methods. Ergonomics was seen as 'fitting the job to the worker' by techniques of work design based on the known limitations of the worker. It was always regarded as including not only psychology but also anatomy and physiology. For instance, the most obvious limitations of the human operator are in size and strength. Work space design based on the specification of limits or ranges such as reach and force available for control operation is clearly a problem for that specialized kind of anatomist called an anthropometrist. The study of presentation of information to take account of human limitations in vision, audition and perception belongs mainly in the province of the psychologist, although the physiologist also has a contribution. There is a similar overlap of contributing disciplines in environmental problems of dangerous and tolerable limits of noise, light and heat. The central role of the physiologist is in the measurement of physical work loads and again the specification of various limits.

All these activities are together classified as classical ergonomics, sometimes called 'knobs and dials' ergonomics. From the human operator side the 'knobs and dials' are respectively the output and input elements of what is called the man-machine interface. Thus, these areas of study are also called 'interface ergonomics'. Probably the main general contribution of this work has been in the vastly improved design of chairs, tables, desks and benches and dials of clocks, voltmeters and other instruments. There have also been many more specific contributions in the design of controls over the whole range from levers to push-buttons, of specialized work spaces and in increased awareness of the problem of optimum environmental conditions. In modifying tasks to suit operators, largely by changing equipment, there were economic problems in justifying the cost of doing so, there were social problems in apparent 'deskilling' of jobs, there were cultural problems of communication between psychologists and engineers and there were organizational problems in operating across traditional boundaries between training, equipment design, health and safety. In fact, very few psychologists succeeded in practising these skills outside the universities and research institutes. Instead of being a problem-orientated practical discipline ergonomics became an academic forum for exchange of ideas between psychologists, physiologists and anatomists.

The practical field was left to the work study practitioners. Even in the military context, once the urgency of war was removed, the psychologists tended to look for more general theoretical problems rather than to cooperate on a day to day basis with the engineers. These varied from pure experimental psychology investigations of laboratory-generated constructs such as the psychological refractory period to the pursuit of a general human operator transfer function with increasing elaboration of non-linearities and noise functions. Another impetus for change was required. It came in the 1950s when the Americans in particular got involved in the Cold War.

In America during the Second World War there were activities similar to those in Britain but conceptually the emphasis was more peripheral in the nervous system sense. That is, there was considerable stress on receptor systems in relation to equipment design. Characteristically, more than half of the book by Chapanis, Garner and Morgan (1949) is devoted to vision and audition. The discussion of movements and controls is largely in terms of selectivity and distinguishability. There is no discussion of learning and training. This particular approach is usually called 'engineering psychology' (Fitts, 1951). There was very little attempt to transfer these activities to American industry (Murrell, 1956) but because of the Cold War there were a number of active creative units attached to the three armed forces. Success and survival in a Cold War where technology is changing rapidly is largely a matter of short development times. The essence of the problem is illustrated by a hypothetical case in Figure 5.2. Suppose that Power A has a development time of four years but Power B takes eight years. Suppose also that the intelligence lag is two years, that is each takes about two years to find out what the other has done. If Power B starts to design a new weapon system in 1950, then Power A will know about it by 1952 and can, if necessary and if possible, design

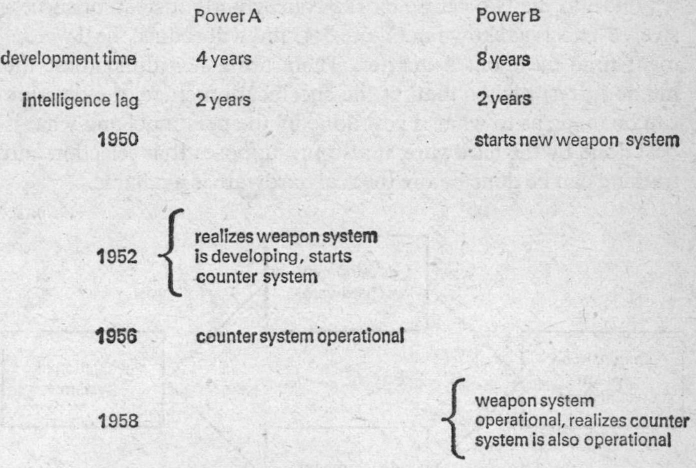

Figure 5.2 The importance of development times in a Cold War

a counter system. Power A will have the counter-system ready in 1956, Power B will have the original system ready in 1958 and will discover at the same time that Power A has a counter system ready. Power B is clearly on the losing end of this game and, with rapidly developing technology, will soon get so far behind that the Cold War is obviously lost. For more extended discussion of this point see Flagle, Huggins and Roy (1960).

It is clearly a good strategy to put a lot of effort into techniques for reducing development times. To anyone not familiar with systems design problems these times of four to eight years may seem very high. One way of illustrating why they are so high is shown in Figure 5.3. If each of these processes takes one to two years then the total time is four to eight years. This block diagram also reveals one obvious way of cutting the development time;

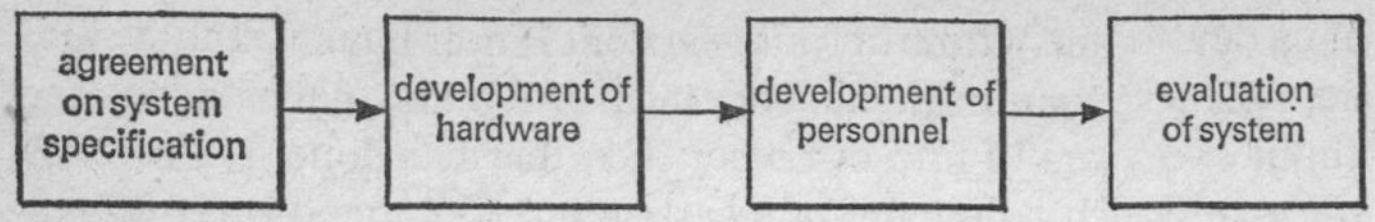

Figure 5.3 Traditional development process

why not do the two centre blocks concurrently instead of successively? This is as shown in Figure 5.4, and will reduce the development time by about a quarter. There are a few difficulties; the method presupposes that, at the specification stage, the decision can be made as to what is best done by the personnel and what is best done by the hardware, it also presupposes that selection and training can be done before the real hardware is available.

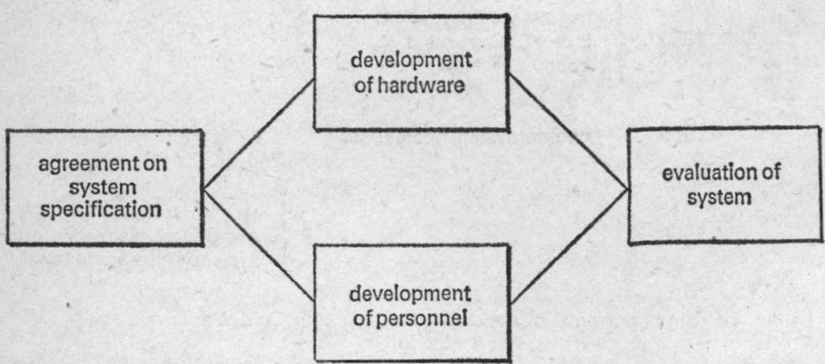

Figure 5.4 Systems development process

SYSTEMS ERGONOMICS

This kind of thinking was the impetus behind the emergence of what is now called 'systems ergonomics'. It has three requirements:

1. Cooperation of psychologists and engineers at the specification stage.
2. Techniques for allocation of function between man and machine.
3. Development of off-line selection and training techniques.

It will be noted that this approach potentially solves many of the practical problems of classical ergonomics. Cooperation between the psychologist and the engineer is improved because the psychologist is no longer primarily engaged in pointing out and attempting to get corrected those mistakes already made by the engineer. Instead they are engaged on the common problems of accurate specification and allocation of function. The cultural problems are reduced because both are now systems thinkers. Many of the cost problems disappear because a good ergonomics design is no more expensive than a bad ergonomics design if it is thought about at the right time. The boundary problems have to be solved because the business of selection and training is now an integral part of the design process.

This systems approach (Singleton, 1967) greatly improved the morale of engineering psychologists because it really did look feasible. However, within a few years it also ran into problems. One difficulty was the inertia of traditional professions: management, engineering and psychology. The senior decision makers simply could not or would not adapt to this new approach (Melton, 1963). Another difficulty was that techniques for systematic allocation of function did not emerge and have not emerged. There have been many debates about why this should be such an intractable problem (Chapanis, 1965; Fitts, 1951; Jordan, 1963; Singleton, 1967; Whitfield, 1967) but it seems to be now agreed that progress cannot be made on these terms. However, all is not lost. The off-line training problem had made extensive progress (Gagné, 1962). The concept of the psychologist as an integral member of the design team remains, and is invaluable. The concepts of a common systems language and of systems-relevant design criteria have improved communication between specialists on the human side and those on the hardware side.

HUMAN ERROR

In the last few years there has been a third stage of development which is not yet well documented in the literature. This is the centrality of the concept of human error in systems psychology. The idea has been around for quite a long time (e.g. Kidd, 1962) but it has only recently become accepted that maybe the best way to think about the role of the psychologists is as a specialist in the reduction of human error (see also ch. 6.) This notion appears to have had a number of separate origins. One is in the continuing world-wide rise of road casualties and the consequent increase in research effort on this particular problem of human error. Another is in the need for reliability in space flight systems and system components. In America this has led to two different approaches: the 'zero defect programmes' which are essentially persuasion-based, and 'error data banks' which attempt to quantify error probabilities and to produce normative and additive data applicable to wide ranges of situations (Swain, 1963; 1969).

These two approaches are based on different basic assumptions about mistakes. The 'zero defect programmes' assume that the problem is one of motivation. Human errors occur because people do not try hard enough, and the way to reduce errors is to get them to try harder. Thus, the people in a production department engaged in, say, making a part of a space capsule, will be subject to exhortation using the various communication media such as posters, films and lectures. The importance of extreme care, the long-term and expensive consequences of errors and the need for extra effort or quality are stressed. As with all propaganda it is difficult to assess how long the effects will endure or, to put it another way, how quickly the worker will adapt to the persuasion so that its effects diminish. It clearly is of some value but the problem which requires great sensitivity and experience is to determine the optimum mode, level and frequency of the exhortation. The error data banks start from the assumption that it is inherent in the nature of all human operations that mistakes are made. The problem is to determine their frequency in given situations, sometimes so that the anticipated frequency can be used to design methods of inspection or replication and sometimes so that failure rates of systems can be predicted. The method is similar to that used in predetermined motion-time systems. Basic units of performance in which errors can occur are identified and the error rate in these units is measured. A new operation under study can then be analysed into these basic units and the error rates for the units are added or otherwise integrated to provide an estimate of the overall rate. The snags here of course are in the assumptions that tasks can be analysed and errors added in these ways. Again the effectiveness depends on the skill and experience of the practitioners.

In Britain, error studies follow the tradition of exploration of particular real situations followed by more controlled study of isolated aspects in the laboratory. Hale (1970) for example, is engaged in comprehensive recording for weeks of routine data entry task from a group of experienced keyboard operators. Just one study of this kind generates hundreds of thousands of readings which can only be analysed by programmes which enable conversational interaction and interrogation of the data file in ways which are noted in chapter 11. This approach is one modern equivalent of Bartlett's 'unprejudiced observation'. Normative data of this kind provide the essential starting point for laboratory studies of speed/accuracy interaction and the separation of corrected errors from uncorrected errors. This latter has implications for equipment design and automatic checking systems as well as for the theory of error detection and correction. On equipment design, for example, the interlock time, that is the minimum allowed time between successive key presses, may require careful optimization since too long a time slows production but too short a time increases the probability of reversal errors. Automatic checking systems often depend on the distinction between constant and random errors; constant errors can be dealt with by compensation, random errors by what Chapanis (1960) calls the 'principle of verification through independent duplication'. Two operators independently punch the same material and their outputs are compared and must agree before acceptance. Single operator error rates of about one or two per hundred are reduced to a combined error rate of two or three per hundred thousand.

Dunn (1970) has been studying accidents to foresters using chain saws by the analysis of the receptor processes required for the task and by the comparison of subjective and objective risks. The hypothesis in the latter case is that if the operator's subjective estimates of risks involved in various jobs do not match the objective risk from past history then the operator is likely to be taking the wrong precautions or ignoring necessary safety procedures. It has emerged that for some tasks the operator's risk estimation is valid, for others it is not. In the former case the problems with sound and vibration information are that the stimuli must be kept above the threshold levels but below the damage levels. In addition when steps are taken to attenuate stimuli, e.g. by ear defenders or flexible handle mountings respectively, then the overall configuration of the stimulus field should not be unduly distorted.

PRACTICAL STUDIES OF COMPLEX SYSTEMS

The control room of a nuclear power station (Whitfield, 1970) epitomizes the task situation of modern industry. The operator observes an essentially automatic process which also has an automatic system to deal with anticipated failures. It is important that complete or even partial system breakdown should never occur. (Not so much because of any danger but because of the cost of starting up again.) The operator provides a second line of defence behind the automatic line and also deals with some apparently simple situations. He is usually necessary because, although the logic of the required response to a given stimulus situation is straightforward (e.g. when two particular alarms occur simultaneously the reactor must be tripped), it cannot be automated since there are a few rare but complicated exceptions to the rule. Thus the human operator is used and he must never make a mistake, that is, fail to react appropriately in a given time. The approach is similar to that used to avoid aircraft crashes on landing and take-off: a combination of otherwise over-qualified operators, high levels of training, elaborate but very clear and rigid rules and instructions, carefully designed presentation of information, unambiguous controls, well-regulated working hours, etc. A research study in this kind of environment requires a range of activities including standard interface design appraisals, task and skill analyses by direct observation and by structured interviews, detailed studies of procedures and elaborate contingency planning. It can only be done by very highly skilled investigators with extensive experience of the particular industry and of all the relevant analytical and experimental techniques.

As another example let us consider an entirely hypothetical military project. This avoids security problems and also gives freedom to provide a somewhat exaggerated picture, idealized in some respects and over-complicated in others. It has been decided that a new weapon system is required consisting of a slow, cheap, low-flying aircraft, highly manoeuvrable and with a high fire power. The first design studies will be carried out by a defence research establishment. Those sufficiently advanced in their thinking will ask for advice from a human factors team. There will be inter-disciplinary group discussions at which the only agreement will be that the project is beyond the state of the art technologically and is impossible in the allowed time and at the specified cost. Having made their token protests everyone will get down to hard bargaining about the share of various cakes. First of all the budget, and then matters such as weight and space. If everyone's first requirements are to be met (in terms of engines and fuels, instrumentation, weapons and ammunition, navigational and other aids, control systems, protection, personnel, etc.), the system would be hopelessly large and overweight. Everybody has to compromise including the human factors people who find that the available workspace is too small for half the available population and cannot possibly accommodate all the controls, and that the proposed external vision conflicts fundamentally in dimensions and compatibility with the required instrumentation displays.

Mock-ups are made and the laborious business of fitting everything in begins. It emerges that there are some fundamental aspects – perhaps population stereotypes or multi-channel activity – on which the research literature is inadequate. Some laboratory experiments are set up and other problems are contracted out to universities or other research units. Everything seems to be going well for a year or two; then there is an avalanche of unexpected problems. The specification is changed because it has been decided that perhaps this aircraft should sometimes be carried underneath another aircraft and so the available workspace height is cut by five centimetres; some of the laboratory experiments become worthless because the engineers find a hardware solution which eliminates the particular problem; on the other hand some new problems appear which the engineers had not predicted (perhaps the vibration or the heating is higher than expected); another instrumentation advance means that new space for information presentation has to be found; the report from the externally contracted work reveals that the research workers started off all right but they quickly uncovered some interesting general theoretical issues and so went off chasing these hares instead of sticking to the problem. Simultaneously there is an edict that the cost must be cut and the time scale shortened. By hard work and inspired guessing all the problems are overcome. Then the manufacturers get involved. They have their own human factors consultants who challenge many of the decisions and recommendations already made; they also add new production constraints. Eventually some prototypes appear and there are serious criticisms from the user evaluations. The strategists raise some very awkward questions about how much reliability and accuracy of performance will deteriorate under battle stress and after a very long operation without sleep or after very long periods of sitting in the cockpit. The workspace designers and the training specialists disagree about the operating routines and check-out procedures.

This description is very general and highly condensed and oversimplified but the intention is just to illustrate that the psychologist working in this environment needs a lot of skills which are not taught overtly in university courses. He must be a gambler as well as a scientist. He must know when to stick and when to twist in all sorts of circumstances, he must know about design compromises, about the need for further experimentation, about the trade-off between required accuracy and available time and resources and so on.

THE CONTRIBUTION OF PSYCHOLOGY TO SYSTEMS STUDIES

The fact that the applied psychologist cannot succeed without many more practical skills is, of course, no excuse for lack of expertise within his profession. Of the three kinds of ergonomics described (classical, systems and error) classical ergonomics in particular depends on a background of knowledge of human behaviour acquired largely through laboratory-based experimental psychology.

Classical ergonomics on design of dials, controls, chairs, ambient environments, etc. depends on either the direct application of general empirical laboratory findings or the comparison in the laboratory of a few likely solutions. For example, if consulted about the design of scales and dials the ergonomist will look up the relevant experiments or summaries of experiments and make his suggestions. These will be of the kind that such and such are 'best' for speed or accuracy. If he is pressed on detail of how much it matters to use exactly the best, what will be the cost benefits, how much will errors rise or speed fall with other than 'best' he will quickly run out of answers because he will run out of experimental data. He will then suggest the reverse procedure whereby, given a few possibilities, he will do a controlled experiment to determine performance on this range. As a competent experimentalist he will generate some information which is reliable but very limited. If pressed again about what happens if the operators try harder or when they get very tired or when the light is poor he will only be able to answer in the most general terms unless he does more experiments which are costly and time consuming. Thus, although this kind of ergonomics can be useful it can also be very frustrating both for the conscientious psychologist and for the engineer waiting for and paying for the tardy and partial answers.

The remedy, of course, is to develop a better theory, a conceptual background in the context of which particular practical problems can be considered and for which answers can be deduced. Unfortunately the history of this approach is not very promising either. When he starts pursuing theory and is released from the responsibility to deal with real people engaged in real tasks the psychologist quickly spirals off into the realms of artificiality. If one looks at recent skill psychology it turns out to be the study, not of people at work and play, but of young men looking at lights and pressing morse keys. If a large enough group of psychologists do enough experiments they generate also enough miniature problems such as minor inconsistencies in results to suggest further experiments designed only to throw light on the original experiments. All this makes for rigorous teaching material and examination questions but the connection with ordinary human behaviour is quickly lost. For example, as apparently consistent human performance limitation is more often a function of the limits imposed by the experimenter than by the characteristics of the subject (Singleton, 1969), too many experimental psychologists have forgotten the principle that the good experiment is based on unprejudiced observation of the real situation.

Systems ergonomics – the second type identified here – is sometimes regarded as not relevant to psychology because, by definition, studies are centred on system performance. However, as Taylor (1963) has pointed out, all experimental psychology measures are, in fact, systems measures. It is not possible to measure human performance unless the human is doing something which means interacting with a machine or with a piece of apparatus in the laboratory. There is no objection to this provided that the experimenter recognizes that he is, in fact, getting measures from a man-machine skill and not from just a human skill. At first sight it would seem that the problem of 'allocation of function' between man and machine could be approached by extensive studies of human performance to provide comparative data on men and machines. This has not proved very fruitful to date. It may be just because it is so expensive and tedious to acquire the relevant data on human performance to feed into the trade-off equations. Alternatively it may be that human operators are intrinsically not comparable with machines (Jordan, 1963).

Another key problem in systems ergonomics is obtaining the task analysis and skills analysis; that is, finding respectively what the operator has to do and how he does it. These techniques are observational and field based (Seymour, 1968) but it is often necessary to resort to laboratory studies to clarify details of the skills involved (Singleton, 1960).

There are a great variety of procedures and methods for these kinds of analysis and, as yet, there are no standard conventions for the presentation of the data arrived at.[1] Often the description is too general to merit anything more precise than a verbal description structured in some reasonably systematic way. For example, the following descriptions of the tasks and skills of a tower crane operator are taken from Singleton (1969).

The task description

1. Function

Decisions – These are dynamic and spatial. The operator must judge distances, speeds and loads, possibly at distances up to 300 feet away and sometimes involving objects to be lifted which are out of view. The operator must decide what forces to apply to a given load to transport it from one location to another, taking into consideration the weight and size of the load, and weather conditions.

Actions – The operator must select control movements using a mental model of control dynamics, allowing for the physical properties of the load and environmental conditions.

Maintenance – Probably the most difficult and dangerous part of the task, since it involves crawling along the jib and other manoeuvres.

2. Information sources

Task relevant – Visual information from the speed and direction of

1. A rather different approach is for instance adopted in chapter 4.

loads and from the banksman. Contours and maximum contrast between the object being lifted and its background are key factors here (figure ground phenomenon). The movement of the trolley on the jib of a tower crane is away from and towards the operator, and it is difficult to perceive speed and distance in this plane. Off-line knowledge such as building procedures is important. So also is a conceptual model of control dynamics (load estimation, inertia, lags). Kinaesthetic feedback may be important on some cranes. There is visual noise due to cab layout, load position, weather and communication with the team on the ground. (The sign language used presents problems of discrimination.)

3. The Environment
Simultaneity – the movement of a load in two or three directions at once. (This may be regarded as a compound skill.)
System emergencies – overload or unbalanced load; slinging failure; collapse of the tower.
Critical errors – the misjudgement of space and movement. The misjudgement of weather conditions.
Psychological conditions – responsibility, isolation, independence, teamwork, and, possibly, prestige. There is an interesting contrast between isolation and teamwork, both of which are inescapable aspects of the task.
Physical conditions – variable illumination, temperature, humidity and general weather conditions. The dangerous nature of the job. The difficulty of access to the cab, and the shortcomings of its internal layout.

Job specification

1. Physical/medical factors
Good visual acuity; no colour blindness
Good hearing
Fitness for climbing into and out of the cab several times a day, and maintaining an erect or nearly erect posture for a long time
No fear of heights – this is essential for undertaking maintenance
General robustness and resistance to temperature change.

2. Personality factors
Capacity to be tough-minded when necessary and not gullible or suggestible
Capacity to make and justify decisions on when it is safe to work and when it is not, in consultation with management
Readiness to work in isolation.

3. Knowledge of . . .
Machine capabilities
Building procedures and safety rules
Maintenance procedures
Concepts of inertia and concepts of centre of gravity of materials
Knowledge of building materials.

4. Skills
Two-handed coordination
Three-dimensional space relations
Ability to drive
Ability to estimate the weights of objects.

Error analysis techniques also depend mainly on field studies rather than laboratory studies. The original work in this area by Fitts and Jones (1947) and Flannagan (1954) was carried out through investigations of practical problems. Laboratory studies have concentrated on discrete tasks such as typing, presumably, because of the difficulty of defining an 'error' in other situations. In continuous tasks or tasks where stimuli and responses are not unambiguously related the term accuracy rather than error is used. The definition of error and accuracy can only be in terms of the goal which the subject is trying to achieve, if they cannot be defined then there is something undesirably vague about the subject's task. To put it in the simplest terms; if the experimenter is not sure whether or when an error is being made how can the subject possibly know?

In summary, the practising engineering psychologist is in a position where the support he gets from academic colleagues is less than adequate. This is true for both concepts and techniques. We do not know enough about human behaviour and, even more, we do not know enough about how to find out about human behaviour. In itself this is not criticism of individuals or groups or professions; it is merely a reflection of the current state of the art. Nevertheless, it must be said that there are more fundamental differences of view between many applied and pure psychologists. The applied psychologist often feels that too many of his academic colleagues are not asking the right questions, are not conducting the right kind of investigations and will never get the right answers. He therefore does his own research following his own principles which have emerged from his practical problems.

THE CONTRIBUTION OF SYSTEMS STUDIES TO PSYCHOLOGY

In looking at research as a potential contribution to real problems the applied psychologist immediately has certain reservations about the work of his academic colleagues at the methodological level. Amongst the many psychologists who have studied learning (see reviews by Borger and Seaborne, 1966; and Annett, 1969) there is a convention born of experimental convenience that it is a process which extends over at most a few days and often over an hour or less. Yet it ought to be obvious that human learning is something which extends over years (Crossman, 1959). Those psychologists not interested in learning as such are prone, for the purpose of their own experiments, to forget that it exists. They sample behaviour at a very early learning stage and treat it as 'behaviour' regardless of learning. It must be admitted that applied psychologists also have been guilty of accepting this fallacy and many comparative experimental studies of machine designs, population stereotypes, etc. are open to this criticism.

In his search for validity and width of extrapolation the applied psychologist questions a number of other laboratory conventions. Is it appropriate that such a large proportion of experiments should be done on students and servicemen? From a recent analysis of two American journals, Schultz (1970) found that more than three-quarters of studies reported over the past five years used students as subjects. Most laboratory experiments have no real purpose from the subject's point of view; this raises serious questions of motivation, the dominant influence of instructions and the confusing effects of different subject attitudes. It is obvious also that man has important circadian rhythms (see ch. 2) but only the students of sleep seem to consider this a variable which should be controlled. Even in the current literature there is a curious hiatus between models of various aspects of skilled peak performance with high information loads (Welford, 1968) and various aspects of the behaviour changes in time, particularly with low information loads (Mackworth, 1969; 1970). It is almost as though the investigators are discussing two totally different information processing systems, but it is all human behaviour. Individual differences are regularly treated as a particular form of experimental error but they are often the key to the problem and some attempt to look at individuals or types of individuals would increase the coherence of our descriptions. In general, just as the machine operator is merely a convenient and sometimes very superficial abstraction for a lot of different human beings working with machines, so also is the laboratory subject a dangerous simplification of a collection of people who inevitably reduce the controlled nature of the situation through their individual skills, aptitudes, prejudices and misconceptions.

From even the earliest work it is clear that the academic boundaries of disciplines were not appropriate. Psychology alone is not enough to deal with any man-machine problem. Take, for example, the design of hand controls. There are psychological problems of identification and selectivity but there are also anatomical problems of size, posture and force application, and there may well be physiological problems of energy expenditure and ambient environmental conditions. There are also control engineering problems involving the interaction of timing characteristics of the mechanism and of the man.

For this kind of reason the Ergonomics Research Society has always been interdisciplinary, involving mainly the four disciplines just mentioned. It is difficult to see how any practitioner can operate effectively without some knowledge of psychology, anatomy, physiology and engineering; it is equally difficult to see how any fundamental research on behaviour can be done without drawing on expertise from all four disciplines. To put it in its most stark form: the living brain is always within a body and behaviour is always a function of both. Similarly behaviour, by definition, is adaptive activity and it will never be comprehended without taking account of the dynamic interaction of the man and the environment including hardware mechanisms.

The theory of manual control (McRuer and Weir, 1969; Young, 1969) is probably the most theoretically advanced part of ergonomics. The research and application is mainly done by engineers and mathematicians but there has always been a necessary leavening of psychologists from Craik to Poulton and Crossman (see Legge, 1970).

The need for an interdisciplinary approach is most obvious in the case of stress studies where a comprehensive attempt is made to describe the current state of an individual in a particular situation (Singleton, Fox and Whitfield, 1970). It seems clear that this cannot be done from one discipline. For any stress situation the psychologist can acquire some relevant evidence by measuring performance changes, the physiologists can acquire other evidence by measuring changes in bodily state, metabolism, EEG's, ECG's and so on, the anatomist can look at changes in muscle tension or in body posture, the biochemist can look at other bodily changes by examining the content of blood, saliva, sweat and urine. Unfortunately, there are no unique correlations between these measures and so, for a given individual in a given situation if any of these measures is not taken there is a gap in the research worker's spectrum of knowledge of his subject's state. The variety of stress situations and combinations of stressors is such that to attempt to analyse systematically all permutations and combinations of kinds and levels of stress in the laboratory is impossible. A more economic and practical approach is to study real situations where a given combination exists. This can become an experimental as well as an observational study by successive elimination of particular stressors.

For both systems ergonomics and error ergonomics the basic techniques for acquisition of evidence are observational rather than experimental. In the case of systems ergonomics there are the twin problems of task analysis and skills analysis already mentioned. For each the complete repertoire of direct observation, charting, critical incident methods, interview, questionnaire and experiment are often needed, but the experiment is subsidiary to the observation. Similarly for error ergonomics the observational analysis, the historical data, the classification of errors, and so on may often need consolidation by experimental work but this latter is not the core of the investigation.

The conclusion from these approaches is that the laboratory experimental method has been overrated. It is one set of techniques for the acquisition of evidence, but only one, and it has limitations both methodologically and in terms of the range of amenable problems. The basic technique is an unprejudiced, informed, systematic look at the real situation from the point of view of the man within it.

SUMMARY

In this chapter we have seen how man-machine systems are an essential part of our modern world and how we must study not only men in isolation but primarily men as part of interactive systems. The historical development of work in this field is described, from its beginnings in time and motion studies, psychological testing and experimental psychology. The Second World War provided an important impetus and brought about a significant change of direction, and since that time several interesting trends have emerged. These all provide evidence for the psychologist's need to work closely with professionals of other backgrounds.

Classical ergonomics is briefly described and the limitations of its 'knobs and dials' approach are illustrated. Systems ergonomics developed subsequently and laid greater stress on interaction between disciplines; a third development is error ergonomics, where the psychologist's major role is seen as the reduction of human error. Several examples of ongoing ergonomics research are discussed and from a more general standpoint the place of psychology in systems studies is examined.

FURTHER READING

References are provided in the text for most of the investigations and specific issues which are described. In addition to these, many of the books and articles cited in other early chapters of this volume are relevant to the work reviewed here. General surveys of the field have been provided by K. S. de Greene (*Systems Psychology*, McGraw-Hill, 1970), L. J. Fogel (*Biotechnology*, Prentice-Hall, 1963) and W. T. Singleton (*Introduction to Ergonomics*, World Health Organization, 1970).

6
Accidents: Some Facts and Theories

Harry Kay

In this chapter Professor Kay considers accidents from several different psychological standpoints. He draws upon research into skilled performance, personality, ageing, equipment design, training and social and organizational psychology to examine the nature and causes of accidents. This treatment is a valuable illustration of how any complex occurrence (in this case an accident) requires conceptualization and investigation by workers of varying backgrounds and interests.

WHAT IS AN ACCIDENT?

We are dealing with a big subject, one that has been called 'the twentieth century disease' (Acres). Safety propaganda may have little popular appeal, and that in itself is a worthy subject of psychological research, but accidents are so common that we all know something about them. Paradoxically we tend to think of accidents as happening to other people, not to ourselves. The whole subject is shot through with such anomalies and we are quickly brought to the conclusion that we shall understand accidents only when we understand human nature.

But we can make a start by clarifying certain issues, one of which is that an accident records the result of an action. Cherns (1962) defines an accident as 'an error with sad consequences'; Arbous and Kerrich (1951) as an 'unplanned event in a chain of planned or controlled events'. We need, then, to distinguish between behaviour and its consequences. We may wish to assess (*a*) the probability of the action leading to the accident and (*b*) the probability that such an action would have resulted in an accident. The two differ from one situation to another, as in the case of a slip on a pavement and on a high tight-rope. There is also a semantic confusion. A drops something on B, injuring B. We speak of B as 'having an accident', meaning he has suffered an accident, but it was the behaviour of A which brought about the accident.

In this chapter we shall restrict our discussion to accidents which cause injury to people and for which human beings are directly responsible. We shall not consider accidents which insurance policies attribute to 'Acts of God' nor shall we examine accidents which damage property or goods but do not cause personal injury. The magnitude of this latter category in financial terms is huge but the statistics would take us into another field. And finally we shall make no attempt to assess the magnitude of human accident statistics in terms of financial compensation; the accident figures tell a sad enough story without any embellishment.

HOW FREQUENT ARE ACCIDENTS?

Within the above limitations how frequent are accidents? Official statistics do not always bring home to us their implications but let us consider those in Table 6.1 which give the recorded accidents for Great Britain in 1968, when the population was approximately

Table 6.1 Accidental Deaths and Injuries in Great Britain 1968 (As given by Royal Society for the Prevention of Accidents)

Source	*Deaths*	*Serious injuries*	*Slight injuries*
Home	7,561	120,000*	1,500,000**
Road	6,810	88,563	253,835
Rail	216	920	11,750
Aircraft	147	unknown	unknown
Water transport	158	unknown	unknown
Factories	625		311,805 (causing more than 3 days disablement)
Farm	136		8,945 (causing more than 3 days disablement)
Coal mines	115	851	139,349 (causing more than 3 days disablement)
Motor vehicles Non-traffic	131	unknown	unknown
All accidents (including falls, drownings etc. other than those listed under the above headings).	18,845	450,000*	3,000,000**

* Estimate
** Unofficial estimate

fifty-four million. We can calculate from the data that, on average, one in every sixteen persons suffers some form of accidental injury each year, though some individuals may have more than one injury. If the figures remain typical of future years as of the past most individuals will have about four accidents in their life, though this is a rough estimate and is limited to reported accidents. The figures for road accidents alone in the 1960s show that approximately one in one hundred and fifty persons in Britain was killed or injured every year. If the pattern does not change, then every child today has almost an even chance of becoming a road casualty during his life. Table 6.2 summarizes the number of deaths by accident on an average day in Great Britain in 1968. Such figures are only a guide but they indicate the main trends.

Table 6.2 Number of Deaths by Accident on an average day in Great Britain 1968

Home	*Travel*	*Work*
21 at home	19 on road	2 in factories
7 in everyday pursuits	1 on railways or air or water	2 in other occupations
Total 28	Total 20	Total 4

WHERE DO SUCH ACCIDENTS OCCUR?

The figures in these tables correct several wrong impressions. More people die or are injured through accidents in the home than anywhere else, including the roads. This, of course, is not to say that the home is the most dangerous place. We have to consider the much larger numbers at any one time in the home than, say, on the roads and the length of time per day spent in the home. Again we have to allow for the range of different age groups in the home with an accent upon the young and old. There are no children working in industry. Even so, the home with its multi-purposes – the workshop of the housewife, the restaurant and social centre of the family, the playroom of the children – is where most accidents happen.

The road accident figures are as startling as we might have feared. Ten times as many die on the roads as in our factories. In the data in Table 6.1, accidents cover all age ranges and of the 6,810 deaths, 2,126 were adult and 636 were child pedestrians.

ACCIDENT DATA

Reliability

The reader will have noted that the data in Table 6.1 are less reliable as the injury becomes less severe. The slight injuries are sometimes estimates or are not known and common experience will suggest that there are many inconsistencies in reporting minor accidents. Some organizations and some individuals are most punctilious, others the reverse. The effect of legislation, as in the recent law in Britain requiring notification of all accidents where the victim is disabled for more than three days, can be to increase the apparent rate of accidents. It is, in reality, an increase in reporting. This can be checked by comparing this rise with the rate for severe or fatal accidents over the same period. It is unlikely that they will go in opposite directions, unless there are other reasons.

Trends

But one of the features of accident statistics is the extent to which they fluctuate with particular influences. Accident data do not appear to reveal fixed patterns inexorably trapping man into some misfortune but rather the reverse. Where the effort has been made to overcome dangerous conditions the pattern of accidents has changed over the years. We seem to have here a sensitive index to the changing conditions man has brought about in his society. For example, as the processes of the industrial revolution came to bear upon Britain in the nineteenth century so the accident rates rose. In 1840 the death rate in England from accidental violence was 0·63 per thousand population. This rate reached a peak in the 1870s of 0·72 per thousand population. In his 'letter' to the Registrar-General William Farr (1865) drew attention to the appalling death on the roads, particularly in London, where 'children, women, old people and even vigorous men are killed weekly by horses and carriages of various kinds' (quoted by Froggatt and Smiley, 1964). A hundred years later the pattern has changed, revealing new influences and the decline of others. Road accidents have risen, now accounting for some 35–37 per cent of the total accidental deaths compared with 8 per cent in 1840, whilst the deaths in factories, mines and workplaces which were so numerous in the nineteenth century have fallen to around 5–6 per cent of the total.

From the point of view of this generation road accidents present the most challenging picture. Throughout the 1960s between 6,800 and 8,000 people died each year from road accidents in Great Britain. We might think that this high accident rate was inevitable until we consider the data for the 1930s when the number of vehicles on the road was only two to three millions but the accident rate was much the same as today. Thus today with a five to six fold increase of vehicles we have much the same total number of accidents.

Utility

Research begins by identifying the questions which need answering and there is no doubt that in the case of accidents we are trying to identify a range of interacting variables. Accidents are not going to be prevented by any one measure – they require action on many fronts.

Accident data provide us with information to guide research efforts and to indicate where action campaigns might be mounted to reduce accidents. In order that useful comparisons can be made between different sources of accident data they need to be expressed as far as possible in a common measure. This involves combining a number of variables such as the accident rate per population at risk per time exposed.

But the key to diagnosis lies in the detailed analysis of accident data. They may have to be broken down into the times of day (daylight or darkness), months of year (weather conditions), different sections of the population in terms of age, experience of the work, and so on. It is from this detailed analysis that we can tease out, say, whether a night shift had few accidents, how far poor visibility increased accidents, or whether a trend for increased accidents with one section of the population could not be accounted for in terms of present knowledge. But we need to guard against accepting a measure which would prejudice the issue. Accidents per distance travelled would be favourable to an airline as compared with a bus company; accidents per time spent in travelling would reverse the bias.

When efforts are made to carry out detailed examinations of accident data we generally find that the records are not sufficiently complete. The type of information required is as follows:

1. *Class of work:*
The industry: size of company: geographical location: the task itself: type of equipment: shift hours worked.

2. *How the accident occurred:*
Time: exact location: prevailing conditions (temperature, noise, lighting): floor surface: how was injury sustained? by what objects?

3. *Type of injury:*
Anatomical location: type of injury (cut, fracture, burn, sprain, etc.): severity.

4. *Personal details of victim:*
Sex: age: height: weight: accident history: length of service.

From examining data collected in many countries it appears that industrial accidents occur primarily in handling material, being struck by falling or moving objects (machinery), by the person falling, or by stepping on or striking against objects. Table 6.3 gives the data for Britain in 1968. The hands and trunk suffer most frequently in industrial accidents whilst sprains and cuts are the commonest type of injury.

Table 6.3 Different Circumstances of Industrial Accidents (1968, Great Britain: Accidents causing more than three days disablement in industry)

Circumstances	*Number of accidents*	*Percentage of total*
Handling goods	84,567	27·1
Persons falling	50,961	16·3
Machinery	49,412	15·8
Striking against objects etc.	29,433	9·4
Transport	26,163	8·4
Struck by falling objects	22,564	7·2
Hand tools	21,314	6·8
Other circumstances	28,016	9·0

WHO HAS ACCIDENTS?

The data so far have shown accident rates may fluctuate at different times or between different classes of work. We may define *accident liability* as the sum of all the factors determining accident rate (see Farmer, 1938). It would follow that an important aim in analysing the statistical data is to identify the variables contributing to that liability. There seem to be three possible areas of investigation:

The individual himself who causes the accident.
The risks inherent in the work itself – the skill of the worker and design of the work.
The working–social environment: accidents and absenteeism: physical factors, e.g. lighting, temperature, noise: stress and fatigue: alcohol: age: safety propaganda and training.

We will consider each area in turn.

THE INDIVIDUAL: ACCIDENT PRONENESS

It seems fitting to begin with the agent himself but it plunges us into the most controversial problem in the field of accidents – are some individuals more accident prone than others? The question seems straightforward. It is asking whether in situations where the accident liability is otherwise equal we may expect one person to have a higher accident rate than another because of individual differences. Such differences may or may not be permanent; some writers have taken accident proneness to represent an inherent permanent state of the individual, whilst others have seen it as fluctuating with changing conditions and experience.

How do we demonstrate accident proneness in statistical data? The problem is deceptively simple and hinges on the distribution of random events. If individuals are accident prone then in a given sample of data they should have a higher accident rate than those who are not. Is it easy to find such distributions? The answer is unequivocal – yes, it is. But, unfortunately, the demonstration that over a particular time sample some individuals have more accidents than others in itself demonstrates very little. We should expect a similar distribution if the events were randomly generated, that is to say, in a restricted sample where all events are equally probable some in fact would occur more frequently than others.

It follows that if some individuals would be expected to have more accidents than others in a random sample, we cannot use the argument that a small proportion of workers are contributing to a majority of the accidents as a demonstration of accident proneness. This, the greater percentage fallacy, has often been put forward as a seemingly plausible argument for the concept of accident proneness. It should be mentioned that in some instances it is palpably absurd. Examples are quoted where 20 per cent of employees have 100 per cent of the accidents. On the face of it this could be an indication of accident proneness but it may mean no more than that there were 20 accidents among 100 employees, sustained in fact by 20 individuals.

We may well ask how it has come about that accident proneness has had such a persistent run over fifty years. There are two reasons, one resting with statistics and one in the attractive plausibility of the suggestion itself.

The statistical analysis was first put forward in a paper by Greenwood and Woods (1919), followed by Greenwood and Yule (1920). The material was most carefully analysed by these authors and is well worthy of attention. Table 6.4 presents some of their best known data. It will be seen that out of the 648 individuals only 201 contributed to the accident total, but even so, 26 have 3 or more accidents. The authors examined their data against chance expectations as given by a Poisson series. This would be assuming that each individual was equally likely to have an accident. (It should be mentioned that some doubts have been expressed as to whether all the subjects employed were at equal risk.) As will be seen from column c the data do not match with this expectation, and in particular too many individuals have three or more accidents. We are near to the birth of an idea.

The authors argued that since their data would not support a hypothesis of equal liability (or of chance expectation) they would consider two other hypotheses. The first was the *biased hypothesis* that all workers started equal but that as a consequence of an accident an individual changed his probability of having further accidents. This bias might increase or decrease the probability in so far as the individual was made more nervous or more careful. In table 6.4 the authors are considering the consequences of the single bias towards increasing the probability, and it certainly fits the data better than chance.

Table 6.4 Comparison of Frequency Distribution of Accidents amongst 648 Women Munition Workers over Five Weeks, and Results from fitting Three Theoretical Distributions (Adapted from Greenwood and Yule, 1920)

Number of accidents per individual (N)	*Number of women with N accidents*	*Expected accident frequency when distribution was:*		
		By chance (Poisson)	*Single-biased hypothesis*	*Unequal liabilities*
a	b	c	d	e
0	448	406	452	442
1	132	189	117	140
2	42	45	56	45
3	21 ⎤	7 ⎤	18 ⎤	14 ⎤
4	3 ⎬ 26	1 ⎬ 8.1	4 ⎬ 23	5 ⎬ 21
5	2 ⎦	0·1 ⎦	1 ⎦	2 ⎦

But their second hypothesis of unequal liabilities started from the assumption that the population was not homogeneous in its propensity to have accidents. The distribution from this hypothesis (column e) is a close fit with the observed data. Later workers, such as Newbold (1926), went on to confirm that the unequal liability theory 'was a great improvement over the Poisson (pure chance)' and when the name 'accident proneness' was put forward by Farmer and Chambers (1926) it was widely accepted. As originally conceived the accident proneness hypothesis states that the initial liability for an accident is not equal between individuals. Thus in those situations where the *non-individual* factors are equal, we should be able to identify accident proneness.

Greenwood and Yule, and later Newbold, were not claiming any dramatic demonstration of accident proneness. On the contrary they emphasized the pitfalls in comparing one distribution with another, and were well aware that other alternative hypotheses might be put forward to explain the distribution.

We must now consider what in fact would be a significant demonstration of accident proneness. The most clear-cut demonstration would be if we could predict which individuals in a group would have the accidents. Such predictions might be based on either of two classes of information; (a) accident repeaters and (b) material from other activities such as tests on personality and motor skills. The strength of this kind of predictive verification will readily be appreciated. It would be equivalent in a game of cards to saying which *particular* cards were likely to fall outside a chance distribution. When this happens we become suspicious of the game.

(*a*) *Accident repeaters*. There have been many attempts to demonstrate accident repeaters. The usual approach has taken a group of workers and examined the correlation between the accidents sustained in one period with those of a second period. Whether we consider correlations between minor accidents in two successive periods, or major accidents, or both, there is no unequivocal evidence to support an accident proneness hypothesis. Newbold (1927) examined eleven groups of male and female workers, ranging in numbers from 19 to 445, and found correlations from − 0·01 to + 0·62 between successive periods. Other workers have found similar variations. With minor accidents Farmer and Chambers (1929) found a mean weighted coefficient of 0·358, and it would be fair to say that the general trend is for correlations to be positive, small and significant. But this could be due in part to the tendency of some workers to report accidents as against others who do not. If this were the case it might be expected that more serious accidents would reveal a trend but they do not. The data of Farmer and Chambers (1939) show correlations for omnibus and trolley bus drivers ranging from 0·058 to 0·328 whilst those of Brown and Ghiselli (1948) are lower. The relationship was not much higher when major and minor accidents were correlated over 14,524 dockyard workers.

It is difficult to make a summary statement about these findings. Some extravagant claims have been made as to how far the data support the case for accident proneness. Several of the correlations are significant though some are not. But none is sufficiently high to be of much value in making individual predictions.

(*b*) *Tests to indicate accident proneness*. It would be most valuable if we could design tests that diagnosed accident proneness outside the accident situation and Farmer, Chambers and Kirk (1933) devoted much effort to this end. They had no success with linguistic type intelligence tests but were able to produce correlations of around 0·20 between accident rates and a battery of 'aestheto-kinetic' tests. Such a correlation is little use for predicting individuals who will have accidents.

Recently systematic attempts have been made to observe driver behaviour and classify drivers according to their habits (Quenault, 1967; 1968a; 1968b). This research did not aim to identify accident-prone drivers as such but it did put forward four categories of driver: safe, injudicious, dissociated active and dissociated passive. Personality tests did not establish a basis for these sub-groups of subjects but by using indices of driver behaviour such as frequency of unusual manoeuvres or near-misses, ratio of usage of rear-view mirror to manoeuvres and ratio of overtaking to being overtaken, definite classes of drivers could be established.

This approach is important. It is a direct measure of behaviour, not the consequences of behaviour, but in a skill such as driving where the probability of an accident becomes high because the frequency of events is so repetitious there is every reason for thinking that this measure of an individual's behaviour will correlate highly with his number of accidents.

A summary of the position on accident proneness

Arbous and Kerrich (1951) in their excellent evaluation summarized the position as follows: 'The evidence so far available does not enable one to make categorical statements in regard to accident-proneness, either one way or the other; . . . This does not mean that accident proneness does not exist, but that so far we have not succeeded in defining it, assessing its dimensions and constituent elements, nor evolved a technique for putting it to practical use.'

In view of all the effort to identify accident proneness we should ask why the evidence is so equivocal. There seem to be three possible kinds of answer:

1. There is no such proneness. It never existed.

The idea that one individual was more prone to have an accident than another seemed so plausible and accorded so well with common experience that it was accepted uncritically by many who did not examine the evidence. But quick and popular acceptance of an idea should make a psychologist cautious and if he fails to find the evidence he must regard it as unproven. This is the case with accident proneness.

On the other hand the concept cannot be summarily rejected. The failure to confirm it may lie with the scientist or it may be that the concept requires modification. Some papers have been a little too eager to write off accident proneness, rather like a black sheep of the family – its history does not reflect too well on our scientific acumen, so let us get rid of it. But there may be more to it than that. (See Mintz and Blum 1949; Froggatt and Smiley, 1964.)

2. Accident proneness has been wrongly conceived.
It is not a permanent, unchanging state of the individual; rather, it is an attribute influenced by both constitutional and environmental factors and varies from one period to another. It will fluctuate with the individual's age, his changing skills and psychological development. This is a plausible hypothesis but it is one which is most difficult to confirm or refute. It suggests that the particular individuals who have accidents in one period may differ in another. It is by no means definite why this happens though some conditions such as fatigue or long attentive duties – vigilance – may be contributory factors. Again different personality types may respond differently to such conditions and indeed to accidents themselves. This whole area is likely to be one of increasing investigation.

3. Accident statistics, by their verv nature, tend to hide individual characteristics, such as proneness.
In trying to make such a case it must be pointed out that accident data are of many kinds and their reliability differ. Data which summate all the accidents in a particular class, such as all heavy vehicle accidents over a national region during a long time span (say a year), aggregate very many incidents, and their reliability is repeatedly demonstrated. But when we turn to the accidents of individuals we are dealing with an altogether different distribution where often at one extreme we have many individuals who have no accidents and at the other a relatively small number who have several – the J curve.

There are many reasons for doubting these data if we try to establish some general case about individual behaviour. For example, the probability of the repetition of an accident by the same individual must vary according to its severity. To state the obvious, an individual cannot repeat a fatal accident. But this is almost the case with severe injuries where there may be absence over many months or inability to continue the same employment. This applies particularly to any comparison time period which an experimenter is likely to use. We are left with minor injuries, which may have different effects on individuals, making some more careful and others more nervous. Accident data on individuals tend to confound these points and since some operate in different directions it is not surprising that the data reveal no clear trends.

But the gravest doubt is related to the small number of accidents contributed by each individual. As we have noted we are not recording behaviour but only the results of behaviour in certain cases. We have no record of an action that might (or should) have caused an accident and therefore we may be making wrong inferences about the individual's liability to have an accident. In other words we have too little information on which to base any expectation that the accident data for one individual will be repeated in another sample of data. For example, suppose we examine the behaviour of motorists at railway crossings controlled by traffic lights and find that one in five thousand vehicles crosses when the lights are at red. But not every crossing at red leads to an accident. Let us say that one in one thousand does. It is difficult to predict individual behaviour from such infrequent accidents. We may instead turn to those classes of events where an 'error' action invariably leads to an accident. Here the fortuitous element is reduced but we find that we are dealing with such a highly selected group (aircraft pilots, steeplejacks etc.) that the findings lose their generality.

It would seem then, that in order to obtain reliable data on individuals we shall have to seek data on the behaviour itself, rather than its consequences. And this has rarely been done.

RISKS INHERENT IN WORK

Drew (1963) estimates that the proportion of accidents due to failure of the human operator remains fairly constant at between 80 to 90 per cent of all accidents and it is to this important section that we shall now turn. Other authors in this volume (Poulton in chapter 3 and Singleton in chapter 5) have already examined the nature of man's skilled performance. Here it is sufficient if we summarize one or two main features of the psychologist's approach to the study of skills, in order that we may then apply them to accidents.

The skill of the worker

A human operator is, essentially, processing information. He communicates in an uncertain world and, by definition, if there were no uncertainty there would be no communication – all would be redundant. In real life, variety (uncertainty) is generally present, and the operator has to process both the signals which arise from the environment and the signals which may arise directly from his own responses. The environmental signals may be outside his control, those from his own actions may be partially under his control, but both present him with information to which he may have to respond.

By the very nature of his complex nervous system man has developed a unique way of controlling his actions in these circumstances and it is essentially a two-stage operation, with each stage having fundamentally different features:

1. *The environmentally controlled mode.* In the first, the environmental or S–R mode, a signal occurs and a response is initiated to it. Performance is intermittent, with measurable time gaps between stimulus and response.

2. *The pre-programmed mode.* In the second, the pre-programmed mode, performance is serially organized with one response triggering the initiation of the next and the whole sequence of action flowing in a smooth and apparently continuous succession.

These two modes are astonishingly contrasted. The first could be conducted by the most rudimentary of mechanisms and indeed would be performed with less latency by a simpler nervous system. In the reaction time situation man is handicapped by the size of his cortex. But the second mode could only be conducted by a highly organized system, capable of learning and thereby predicting a sequence of events. It is the criterion of all skills that they should be conducted as far as possible in the second – the pre-programmed – mode. There is relatively little difference between one individual's ability and another's to operate in the S–R mode but there is every difference at the pre-programmed level.

This bald statement does not attempt to cover the subtle variations in man's perceptual-motor skills where often he is alternating between a pre-programmed sequence of actions and signals which are environmentally controlled. It will be appreciated that it is the nature of some skills to control the environment in so far as the individual determines exactly when and how signals will occur. An example would be a pianist playing solo. In other skills it is very much an exercise in adjusting to the contingencies of the external world whilst maintaining performance (driving a car; playing tennis). But within this broad framework we can say that it is the aim of all skilled operators to perform as far as possible in the pre-programmed mode. The more highly practised the performer, the more likely he is to achieve this.

In terms of achieving a particular goal the more an individual can operate in the pre-programmed mode, the less the information which he will have to process; the more he is forced to operate in the S–R mode, the greater the uncertainty and the more information he will have to process.

Accidents – too much information in too little time

We may now see the immediate application of this to accidents. It is the case that in all accidents the individual has too much information to process in too little time. This point is worth making even though it is a tautology, because it links under one concept many different classes of accidents; for example, an object falling on an individual, a pedestrian slipping on the pavement, the lathe-operator cutting himself, the driver suddenly confronted with an obstruction. But the reason why there is too little time is nearly always because the individual has to switch from his highly organized, efficient pre-programmed mode to his delayed and inefficient S–R mode. In order to adapt to contingencies man has this unique ability to stop a programme and, if necessary, switch to another. But it is at the point of change where he is most vulnerable and where any initiation has the characteristic of the S–R mode. In the case of accidents the operator rarely has time to do more than try to stop the ongoing programmed skill and take the beginnings of avoiding action.

Figure 6.1 is an illustration of how this would appear in a particular accident in the case of road driving. This has been chosen because the time-distance coordinates are easily diagrammed but the same relationship would hold in other kinds of accidents, such as cutting a piece of wood with a knife when the blade slips. The driver is travelling at 45 m.p.h. when at point A he sees that he is approaching a corner. He decides to change gear and at B, C, D he carries out a series of actions using feet and hands to slow the car, change gear and begin to turn the corner. The pre-programmed sequence is quickly performed and he is ready to accelerate as he finishes the manoeuvre, but at X a dog runs in front of his car just as another vehicle is approaching. These represent the external, unplanned events. Several actions might now be possible, such as trying to steer the car past the dog, but the driver has to perceive

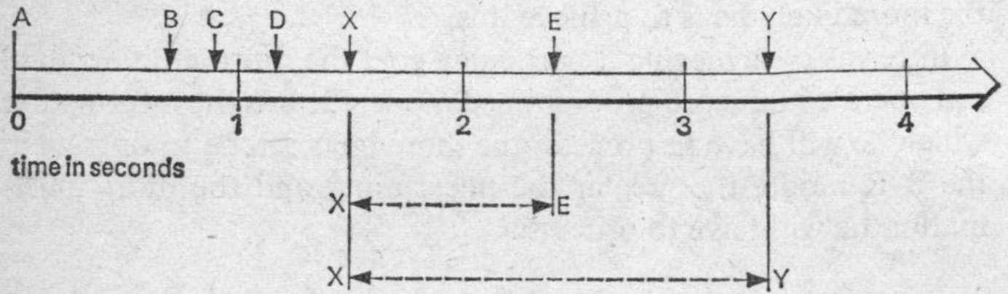

Figure 6.1

the events and decide what action he will take. In the circumstances he brakes at E and stops at Y. It will be observed that the car travels for nearly a second from the time when the dog and the second car are seen, to the time when the driver begins to initiate any action that will bring about any change in the future position of the car. Between points X and E, however active the driver may have been in trying to make a decision about the new external events, nothing happens. From the psychological point of view he cannot yet switch in any new response series because he is trying to interpret the new stimulus. As we witness the end of the planned series of actions and the taking over of the S–R mode there is the inevitable long hiatus as we wait for a response to this unforeseen stimulus.

In any high-speed skill man will be most vulnerable to accidents where specific events cannot be predicted and can force the operator to take up a new action to meet the contingency. Effectively the operator has to discontinue the highly organized series of responses which practice has established and revert to a more primitive level of responding. Man's adaptability created his co-ordinated serial skills which in turn created the situation leading to the accident.

Design of equipment

It is always difficult to assess how far any one accident can be attributed to equipment design, but there are many instances of accidents where an operator, perhaps under stress, made a wrong response because the direction of a control was incompatible with the intended action. Similarly, bad layout of instrument panels can cause dangerous delay to a controller who is urgently needing information.

One of the aims of industrial psychology has been to improve the design of equipment from the standpoint of the operator. It had become and, alas, in too many instances it still is, the accepted practice for an engineer to design equipment paying every attention as to how it would fulfil its function but with little consideration as to how a man would operate it. The absurdities which resulted are now part of ergonomic history – incompatible controls, layout of instruments making them difficult to read at a glance, impossible space for seating – but the priorities are still ignored. Cars are designed too much for sales appearance and too little for their safety.

These points are slowly being met and are considered in greater detail in chapter 5, but a new set of problems has arisen. As machines, particularly with computer control, have become more sophisticated the man-machine interface becomes more critical as the machine imposes conditions which completely change the nature of the work. It is inevitable that we shall come to rely more and more upon machine data, particularly in high speed operations involving quickly changing information, but it has to be accepted that where such systems fail the consequences are likely to be greater. They involve bigger plants, aircraft, shipping and the like.

THE WORKING–SOCIAL ENVIRONMENT

There is increasing recognition that accidents occur in a social context which is often complex and of long standing. We are studying the interaction of variables which range from the individual skill of a worker to others which are embedded in the social industrial situation. In this section we will begin by considering this latter influence.

Accidents and absenteeism

An interesting series of studies has been made by Hill and Trist (1953; 1962) who have suggested that accidents are best considered as a phenomenon in social psychology, where an accident serves as a means of withdrawal from the work situation. They point out that labour turnover has three broadly distinct phases: an *induction crisis* when a large proportion of entrants leave after their initial experience with the firm: a period of *differential transit* when individuals are learning the ways of the firm and a period of *settled connection* of the quasi-permanent employees (Hill and Trist, 1962, p. 6). Length of service is then, an index of the quality of the individual work relationship, and has this characteristic of a high rate of labour turnover in the initial induction crisis phase, declining in a J-shaped distribution thereafter. In a study in the steel industry Hill and Trist analysed the relationship between length of service, different forms of absence and accidents. They considered the absence records of a stable working population over a four-year period and found a definite relationship between those workers who had accidents and those who had most absences for 'no reason' – that is, what the authors described as able-bodied absence for no accepted reason, and designated by them as the 'least sanctioned form of absence'. It was also shown that there was a negative association between accidents and absences requiring prospective sanctioning (seeking and granting of permission before the absence). The authors point out that 73 per cent of absences are of a 'one-day-off' character and argue most persuasively for their hypothesis that 'accidents are social as well as person events, and, in industry, happen by virtue of the fact that the people concerned are members of some kind of work organization. It would seem to follow that the quality of the relationship obtaining between employees and their place of work would in some way come into the question of accidents' (Hill and Trist, 1962, p. 3). Their data support the case of accidents being associated with a motivated form of withdrawal, but it must be mentioned that other workers (Keatinge and Box, 1960; Castle, 1956) have failed to substantiate the argument. As Cherns (1962) points out we are left with the finding that the social context is all important and that to try to study accidents in isolation leads to misunderstanding. We shall return to this in discussing safety measures.

The physical environment

Psychologists have devoted much time to examining how performance varies as external conditions change. Behind such studies is the idea that there is an optimal condition for performing each kind of task. That is to say, when we look at conditions of lighting, heating, ventilation, humidity and noise there is some desirable range within which an operator will function at his best and anything outside that range, whether too little or too much, will adversely affect performance.

There is truth in this view though, as Bartlett (1947; 1948) has pointed out, it is a somewhat naïve statement if we restrict it to the results of performance. A worker may make more effort to maintain a given output in less than optimal conditions. But such an effort may lead to accidents. Each of the above physical conditions represents a study in itself but it is fair to say that all can exert a major influence on performance. Bad lighting may make a simple operation dangerous, though the critical level of lighting will vary between tasks (Tiffin and McCormick, 1966, ch. 8).

Because of the differing temperatures to which a worker may be exposed many long-term experiments have been conducted on this subject and the general effects are known. The main variables are air temperature, humidity, air flow and the operator's mode of attire and activity. Mackworth (1950) showed deterioration in muscular, psychomotor, mental and vigilance tasks, but it was of note that acclimatized men were able to perform optimally at an effective temperature of 79° (85°F: 70 per cent humidity: 100 feet per minute air flow). The general consensus is that conditions for thermal comfort, work efficiency and minimum accident rates are much the same (Surry, 1968).

The effect of noise is extremely complex, particularly in creating emotional disturbances. Noise can damage the auditory mechanisms; prolonged exposure to levels above 120 db will cause permanent damage. Much lower levels may interfere with speech and over and above this loss in communication there may be further interference with working efficiency. Errors have been shown to increase with noise (Broadbent and Little, 1960), whilst non-auditory effects are reported, such as a reduction in touch sensitivity (Broadbent, 1961). Since all urban and social life is reporting ever higher noise levels the importance of this variable is likely to increase rapidly in the future.

Reducing stress and fatigue

An obvious result of more advanced equipment is that it should reduce the stress and fatigue of many operations. Just as we would now accept that it is an inefficient use of manpower to work on a building site without lifting gear and transport, so we are seeing the introduction of automated control systems in steel mills, continuous processing industries and communication networks. These are designed to ease the mental load of work, in the same way as the mechanical digger eased the load of the navvy. Ultimately they will do so but two points need to be stressed. In the interim period during which we learn to use new equipment there is considerable stress whilst new operators are trained for different types of work and the advantages and disadvantages of the new system are gradually assessed. Industry and in particular its electrical engineers face many of these problems today in Western Europe and the stress to maintain a rate of improvement is every bit as great as the stress of the older system. Secondly, goals are unlikely to remain static. As equipment improves performance, new goals will be set. We shall aim to travel further and faster and produce more advanced goods, and the stress of the end state may not be so very different from the present. In other words the days of leisure which are always being predicted may find many workers experiencing much the same stress as they are today.

It is fortunate that the psychologist has paid particular attention to the problems of information processing and the conditions of mental fatigue as these are now the major difficulties with modern equipment. Vigilance studies in particular (Mackworth, 1969) have established how easy it is to fail to see a signal, particularly when the spell of duty is prolonged. We may expect that where conditions put a sustained mental load on an operator every effort will be made to put such a task under computer control, but for some time in the future we must expect that the major machine role will be data handling and the sorting-packaging of information. In other words by assembling more information more quickly and more accurately the computer will make some tasks easier and more efficient. But we should be mistaken if we think that this would apply to all tasks and that the mental load will disappear from the industrial scene. This is not so at present nor likely to be so in the immediate future because there are so many variables in the field of human behaviour which we cannot quantify.

Alcohol

One other factor which influences the state of the operator is that of drugs, particularly alcohol and tobacco. The dramatic effect of alcohol on driver performance has been established in a series of studies, and whereas statistics over many years had brought out how frequently fatal road accidents were associated with high levels of alcohol in the blood, the laboratory data verified how far performance deteriorated with relatively low concentrations (Drew *et al.*, 1959). The consequent legislation in Britain brought about an immediate reduction in accidents during the hours most associated with this type of accident, though for how long this reduction will be maintained is another question.

The significance of these experiments has not been fully assimilated into our thinking about accidents. Perhaps for the first time we have unequivocal evidence of the extent to which performance can be influenced by relatively minor disturbances, in this case small doses of a drug, and how accidents might be reduced by its avoidance. There is a second implication: it shows how narrow is the margin of safety in the skill of driving and how little it has to deteriorate to cause an accident. In high-speed, time-stressed perceptual motor skills of this kind the human operator needs to be at peak efficiency all the time if he is to be safe.

Age

The same point is brought home when road accidents are related to age. The general picture is that two age groups contribute disproportionately to accident totals, the under 25s and the over 65s. It might be argued that the younger group confounds age and experience, and that here lack of skill contributes to accidents.

Certainly this would not apply with the older group (over 65s) who seem to suffer a genuine loss of skill because of factors associated with age. Psychologists have devoted a major effort to examining many of the skills of ageing subjects and there is no doubt that the general trend is for the over 60s to suffer a decline in both speed and accuracy (see Welford, 1958; Bromley, 1966). This deterioration in skill shows up in terms of increased accidents on the roads because there is no age limit to driving. It does not show up as a marked increase in industrial accidents for two reasons:

(a) Most firms have a retiring age limit.

(b) There is a pronounced trend for workers over fifty years to avoid work on time-stressed industrial assembly lines (see ch. 7).

But the high road-accident rate of the younger age group is such a world-wide phenomenon and has been so persistent over half a century that it deserves the most searching investigation. It is likely that several factors contribute to it, including a lack of experience in driving skill and road conditions. But the lack of experience is by no means the main factor as can be shown by holding it constant over different age groups. The young still have most accidents (Surry, 1968). In other words some youthful qualities must contribute to a lessening of driver skill. When we remember that several authorities have agreed that speeding is the greatest single cause of accidents, a possible line of investigation is opened up. To put this another way the Committee of Highway Safety Research of the National Academy of Sciences argued in 1952 that most factors leading to accidents could be corrected by greater caution. This may be what youth lacks, and the efforts to enforce caution by legislation for these age groups should certainly be scrutinized. They may have much to offer towards saving youthful lives.

Safety propaganda

This approach bears directly upon the subject of safety propaganda, which is one of the most complex in the entire field of mass-media communications. There is here a paradox that lies at the very heart of the subject. On the surface we might think that it was the easiest of communications to try to persuade an individual to look after his own interest. All the qualities of greed, self-interest and biological survival might be put forward in support. It might be argued that if advertising can persuade someone to buy something of doubtful efficacy and at a demonstrably inflated price it would be simple enough to sell safety, which enhances the welfare of the individual. It is not. Many safety campaigns misfire; few have any lasting effects, and there is no one method that is certain.

We shall return later to the question why people do not want to be 'saved' as it obviously has far reaching implications for any reduction of accidents, but let us briefly consider why safety propaganda has run into difficulties.

One of the reasons is that it lacks a direct reinforcement. The individual reading a safety poster has probably not suffered the kind of accident to which it relates. He does not therefore apply it to himself and when he does he rarely attributes his safety to its effect. He is more likely to attribute it to his own skill. For this reason propaganda aimed at increasing the skill of the operator, and which suggests the close relationship between skill and safety, tends to be more successful. Where accidents can be associated with lack of training and control there is a direct challenge to the individual either to improve his performance or to assess his skill as being sufficiently high to avoid an accident. It is in this respect that advice is more readily taken from an individual of great prestige or a member of one's own group. The advice of an outsider may be resented and do more harm than good, but the in-member carries his own authority. It is unfortunate that, by definition, he can only influence a smaller number. The same point holds for the relevance of safety posters: the miner does not want advice about the effects of leaving his lorry unattended (see Laner and Sell, 1960).

Reinforcement of a more immediate kind may be achieved by setting targets, scales or charts and keeping an up-dated record of how a particular group is progressing. This has a definite appeal where it is possible to identify a working unit, though there are dangers that it may lead to non-reporting of accidents. It is most valuable in bringing safety into a more central position and keeping it in the minds of workers.

The role of safety officers requires them to be identified with the working group and not be seen as outsiders imposing arbitrary regulations. In the latter case there is always the danger that the new rules will be deliberately flaunted, irrespective of their merits. This adds up to bridging the gap in communications between the 'office' (where safety information may be received) and the shop floor where it is applied. One obvious point is that the communication must be two-way. Every factory has its individual features which require special attention. Equally it is too easy for a safety officer to be out of touch with what is actually happening on the shop-floor. It is often when the work pressure is building up that corners are cut, improvisations adopted and potentially dangerous practices are introduced.

Safety and training

If we accept that accidents are not attributable to any one cause but arise from a number of different features which go to make up the total working environment then it follows that an attitude towards safety and the carrying out of standard safety procedures must be built into normal training. One well-known danger in many firms is that practices are accepted merely because they have always been carried out. In time the workers themselves come to accept the risk which in fact is unnecessary. This may be a matter of clothing (handling metal sheets without gloves; lathe operation of non-ferrous materials without eye protection), the layout of material on the workbench, or the dangerous build-up of work pressures at a particular hour of the day. This is best examined when an analysis is being made of the job for the purpose of training (see ch. 4). Today a reputable training programme would assess the exact objectives of any particular task and then analyse its different activities in terms of both what they contribute to the goal and what they require of the operator. The job is systematically designed around the worker with the necessary tools or instruments being introduced only after careful consideration.

It is at this point where the training programme is being drawn up that the safety elements can be incorporated, not as an afterthought, but as an intrinsic ingredient of the skill itself. The aim is to train the operator so that his concept of the skill includes the safe practices as part and parcel of his work. This can be done. The airline pilot or railway passenger driver has no doubts about his safety priorities. But this seems to be less successful where the actual risk is limited to the operator himself. The training must emphasize that the skill does not lie in reducing the margin of safety but in maintaining it as wide as possible.

SUMMARY

In this chapter we have considered how accidents are a measure of a highly selected part of behaviour, namely those actions 'with sad consequences'. Exactly similar actions which do not lead to accidents generally go unmeasured, but if we are to understand accidents we need to investigate the relationship between them and general behaviour. This is all the more necessary because efforts to establish accident proneness by demonstrating that the distribution of accidents per individual were non-random have not resulted in clear-cut conclusions.

In all accidents there is too much information to process in too little time, and the outstanding feature of many is that an individual has to switch substantially from operating in a pre-programmed mode to an environmentally controlled (S–R) mode. His efficiency drops at the very point where most is demanded of it.

Accidents were considered in their social context and their relationship to absenteeism in the factory. Finally we examined how accidents are influenced by loss of skill caused by fatigue or alcohol or environmental conditions.

FURTHER READING

Arbous and Kerrich's (1951) article on accident proneness is one of the clearest and most readable statements of the problem. McFarland has written on the human factors in transportation safety (McFarland and Moseley, 1954). Surry's (1968) monograph is a useful collection of information with an emphasis upon the human engineering approach. Within standard textbooks M. L. Blum and J. C. Naylor have a sound chapter on accidents in their *Industrial Psychology: Its Theoretical and Social Foundations* (Harper & Row, 1963), as does A. B. Cherns in *Society: Problems and Methods of Study*, edited by A. T. Welford *et al.* (Routledge & Kegan Paul, 1962).

Some of the most illuminating sources are the papers from the Industrial Health Research Board and the Reports from the Road Research Laboratory.

7
Occupational Aspects of Ageing

Stephen Griew

In this chapter Professor Griew introduces the field of 'industrial gerontology'. He examines the extent to which age constitutes a handicap to employment and discusses some possible reasons for the findings which have been reported. Although psychological studies have indicated that over a wide range of jobs there are no marked variations associated with age, some differences do emerge in certain types of work. Professor Griew has himself carried out research into these differences, and he is here able to point to their theoretical significance as well as making some practical recommendations and predictions about future developments.

During the early 1940s a disturbing demographic trend became apparent in most advanced industrialized countries. Due to decreasing mortality and fertility, increasingly large proportions of populations were being found in their upper age groups. Predictions, however cautious the hypotheses upon which they were based, suggested that this trend towards 'population ageing' would be likely to increase over the remaining part of this century and that the first part at least of the twenty-first century would be marked by very high proportions of older people in the populations of advanced societies (United Nations, 1956).

If, as it was usually assumed, ageing is accompanied by a gradual decline in psychological functioning and capacity for work, then countries subject to population ageing would have to plan for a state of affairs in which an increasing proportion of sub-optimally productive members would be dependent upon a decreasing proportion of unimpaired producers. It was this possible economic consequence of population ageing, more than any other, that stimulated the burgeoning of research during the 1950s and 1960s into the psychology of ageing and the occupational performance of older people.

At the same time, the prediction that older proportions of populations would increase led to a massive development of research and social policy-making concerned with the personal problems of older people. The climate was one in which the social desideratum of providing full and satisfying lives for all members of society was readily acceptable, and the special needs of so-called disadvantaged groups were being properly recognized for the first time, and studied with vigour. Older people were seen as potentially one of the most disadvantaged groups of all. And among their most apparent disadvantages, their vulnerability in the labour market was cited as being of particular concern.

Thus, born of economic necessity and enhanced social awareness, the new applied social science of industrial gerontology appeared.[1] It is now a major and expanding field of applied research and practice, with an institute, a journal and many distinguished research programmes to its credit. To quote from the editorial of the first number of the journal *Industrial Gerontology*, it 'is the study of the employment and retirement problems of middle-aged and older workers. . . . Industrial gerontology begins where age *per se* becomes a handicap to employment'. This definition emphasizes the problems of workers, and we shall attack the subject from this standpoint, rather than from that of the problems posed for industry by the ageing of its labour forces. However, there is increasing agreement that age, as a handicap to employment, has implications not only for the individual older worker, but also for his employer and for the economy as a whole. This will become clear in what follows, and the point is now made specifically solely to provide a framework within which the discipline's often apparently conflicting objectives may be reconciled.

AGE AS A HANDICAP TO EMPLOYMENT

Whatever opinions may be expressed by individual workers, employers, or government and private agencies, the acid test of whether age really is a handicap to employment depends on the data which are available about the employment experiences of workers of different ages. If it cannot be demonstrated, for example, that older workers suffer more unemployment than younger workers, that they are excluded from certain sections of the labour market, or that they are being edged out of the labour

1. The term 'industrial gerontology' was coined by Professor K. F. H. Murrell in an article in the 1959 volume of the *Journal of Gerontology*. In that article he both defined the field and identified many of the problems which have since commanded the attention of its practitioners.

force by early, involuntary retirement, then age can hardly be considered as a true handicap to employment.

Age and unemployment

A certain amount of sophistication is needed if one is to point to a problem when one compares the overall unemployment rates of older and younger workers. In fact it has been noted, especially in the United States and Canada, that the rate of unemployment in the age group forty-five-and-over is often below that in the under-forty-five age group. In Britain in July, 1970, unemployment among all males averaged 3·2 per cent, and rates in the age groups forty-five to forty-nine, fifty to fifty-four and fifty-five to fifty-nine were all below this average rate. However, much higher rates in the very young and the very old groups contributed to the overall average rate, and the better than average experiences of older workers could properly be regarded as artefactual upon the very high rates of 7·0 per cent among the over-sixties, and 4·9 per cent among the eighteen to nineteen year olds. In October, 1963, despite lower than average rates in the over-forty-five year old group as a whole, those aged over fifty-five in Canada and the United States showed rates of 6·1 per cent and 3·5 per cent, respectively, compared with rates of 4·9 per cent and 2·6 per cent in the forty-five to fifty-four year old group.

Thus overall rates can obscure reduced participation in the labour force by certain age groups of older workers, and if one looks more positively at actual participation rates (as distinct, that is, from unemployment rates), the picture becomes clearer, as is shown in Figure 7.1. The participation rate of older workers in 1950 was quite markedly lower than younger workers in both industrialized and agricultural nations.

What happens to an older worker who becomes unemployed? In seeking an answer to this question one meets some of the most compelling evidence that exists that age is a handicap to employment. Once unemployed, the older worker tends to remain unemployed for substantially longer than his younger counterpart. Figure 7.2 illustrates this tendency well, and needs no emphasis beyond that which it provides. Another feature of the problem is a greater tendency, noted by a number of authors (e.g. Sobel and Wilcock, 1966), for older than for younger workers to experience

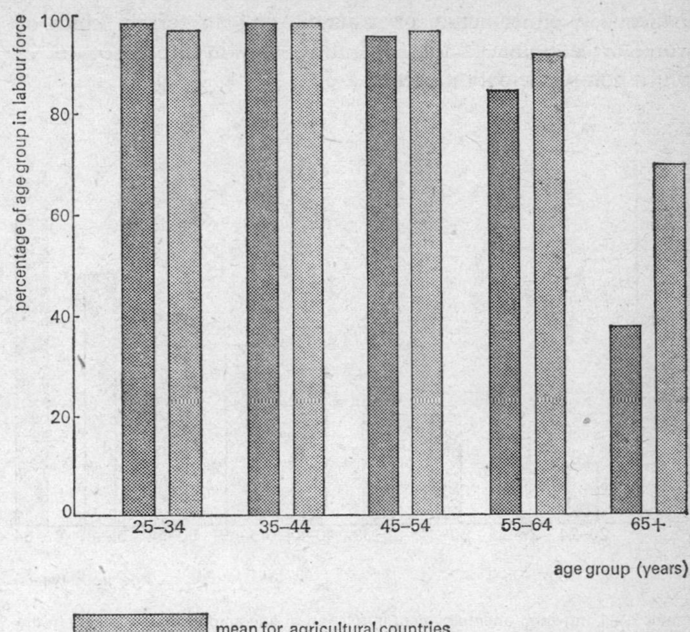

Figure 7.1 Participation of males in labour forces of agricultural and industrialized countries in about 1950. (Based on data reported by United Nations and presented by Riley and Foner, 1968)

a decline in occupational status once they become unemployed. In order to get back into employment they have often to accept jobs lower either in skill or pay than they were accustomed to prior to becoming unemployed.

Age structure of different industries

If the participation of older workers in the labour force is lower than that of younger workers, we may fairly ask whether their lower participation is spread evenly throughout the force, or whether it is restricted to certain sectors only. If it is restricted, then it becomes a possibility that non-participation reflects their inadequacy, either actual or assumed, only in certain kinds of work, or economic factors operating only in those sectors in which non-participation occurs.

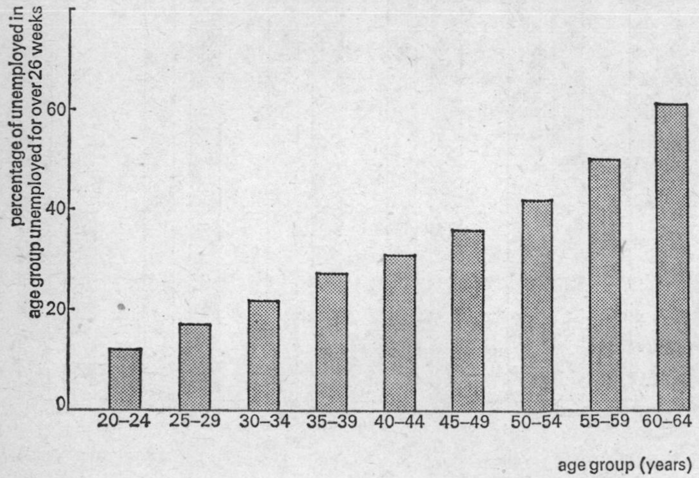

Figure 7.2 Long-term unemployment in relation to age among male workers in the United Kingdom in 1970. (Based on data reported by the Department of Employment)

It will already have been noticed from Figure 7.1 that different rates of participation by older members of the labour force apply in industrialized and agricultural countries. The tendency for a higher proportion of older members of agricultural labour forces to continue participating is found in individual industrialized countries too. Farming may properly be regarded as one of the older trades, one of the less well paid, and, on the whole, one which is declining in most advanced countries; and it is fair to say that it is trades like this that harbour the major concentrations of older workers.

But even within the industrial sector, some industries and trades have higher than an average share of older workers. Murrell (1962) presents data on the age distributions of production workers in three major British industries, and shows the gas, water and electricity industries as having a much higher proportion of older workers (58 per cent over forty) than general engineering (48·5 per cent over forty) or precision engineering (44·2 per cent over forty). These data could be interpreted as reflecting a 'shortage' of older workers in engineering, or, put another way, as demonstrating age as a handicap to employment in engineering.

Even in engineering itself, different jobs show different age structures, and again Murrell shows that the median ages of skilled machinists tend to cluster in the mid to late-thirties, in the fifties in the case of store-keepers, labourers and packers, while the median age of the industry as a whole lies in the early forties.

Older people also appear to be more likely to be employed by small companies than by large ones, and small companies tend, it seems, to be declining the more rapidly (Gordon, 1959). And again, those industries which are growing fastest, such as finance, real estate and insurance, appear to be among those most deficient in older workers (Gilpatrick, 1966).

Compulsory retirement and restrictions on hiring

Another direct manifestation of age as a handicap to employment is to be found in some of the hiring practices and compulsory retirement policies which are reported more and more frequently. The fast-growing industries discussed by Gilpatrick would seem also to be those which impose some of the lowest and most rigid upper age limits for entry. Kreps (1961) reports that, of the firms she studied, only 5 per cent of those employing predominantly skilled labour had compulsory retirement policies; whilst compulsory retirement was a feature of 50 per cent of those which employed the low average of skill seemingly typical of older workers. She also reports that the size of the firm is a major variable in the existence or otherwise of compulsory retirement policies. The probability of there being compulsory retirement will increase, and the proportion of older workers will decrease, as a function of size.

WHY IS AGE A HANDICAP TO EMPLOYMENT?

Unemployment and its duration in older workers, the age-structure of industries and trades, and hiring and compulsory retirement policies, all seem to indicate that age represents a handicap, if not to all forms of employment at least to some. What we must next consider is why older workers should face these handicaps. First, we shall look at some of the economic factors which may operate against them. Next we shall consider whether older workers, on account of their age as such, are poorer productive propositions to employers. Finally, we shall consider certain other factors which appear to be confounded with age and which may be decisive in determining the older worker's chances of success in job-seeking.

Economic factors

It has been suggested that the general change in the demand for labour has been a major factor in determining unemployment among older workers and in promoting their peculiar difficulties in finding jobs when they become unemployed. It has been shown, for instance, that retirement policies in the United States during the period 1930–1960 tended primarily to be related to the state of the economy as a whole (Kreps, 1963), and Sadie (1955) goes as far as to suggest that whenever labour is plentiful, older workers must be regarded as marginal labour, employers rightly giving preference in their hiring practices to younger workers. Kreps goes on to argue that when society produces sufficient goods and services to meet its needs with a decreasing need for labour, it will have either to make a positive decision as to which age-groups are to constitute its labour force, or shorten the working hours of all workers so that all age-groups may continue in employment.

Looked on as marginal labour, the prospects of older workers for continued or extended employment might be regarded as poor, and it has been suggested by Berkowitz and Burkhauser (1969) that the problem will probably only be reduced significantly as society's productivity increases sufficiently to raise incomes to a level at which demand may be expected dramatically to increase. Then, possibly, the need for larger labour forces will return, and with it a need for all marginal labour. Although many would reject the conclusion that the employment prospects of older workers are and must necessarily remain poor until this level of economic growth has been reached, all would agree that they are greatly influenced by structural factors in the labour market.

We have already noted that certain types of industries are declining while other are expanding, and that older workers seem more typically to be employed in those which on the whole are contracting. Given the closure of a company employing a higher than average proportion of older workers, then older workers will become unemployed and will probably remain unemployed for long periods, possibly never to regain a foothold as participant members of the labour force. Furthermore, given the closure of a company in a contracting area, or one in which unemployment is already high, the older unemployed worker will be in greater difficulty still, on account in part of his characteristically low geographical mobility (Saben, 1967).

Perhaps surprisingly, though, older workers do not appear to be the convenient *targets* for redundancy that many assume them to be. Various authors (e.g. Kahn, 1964) report studies that show no greater liability to redundancy on the part of older workers; but all the available evidence confirms the tendency which we have already seen for older workers, once unemployed, to remain unemployed for longer than younger ones.

Many of the purely economic influences on the employment prospects of older workers are summarized by Kreps (1963, 1967) and by Sobel and Wilcock (1966). In summary, it must be concluded that economic factors play a major role in determining re-employment prospects, the operation of upper age limits in hiring, the operation of compulsory retirement schemes, and so on. But greater emphasis seems nowadays to be accorded structural unemployment than gross unemployment; and regional conditions in individual industries would seem to be more important determinants of the older workers' prospects for employment than the state of the economy overall.

Are older workers effective workers?

One possibility cannot be excluded. Older workers *may* be occupational risks in certain jobs. Their most vigorous champion would not seriously try to persuade an employer to recruit a man of fifty into a job as a lightweight boxer or a jet-fighter pilot. Is it not equally possible that one of the reasons why certain less romantic occupations are deficient in older workers may be that accumulated experience has demonstrated that older workers simply do not perform in them satisfactorily?

Such evidence as is available suggests, in fact, that the output of older workers overall is hardly any different from that of younger workers. Data presented by Riley and Foner (1968) show surprisingly little variation with age in output in a number of occupations. Certain other studies, reviewed by Murrell (1962), however, demonstrate slight declines in output as a function of advancing age. And although variations within age groups are usually as great or greater than variations between age groups, making it hard validly to draw any straightforward general conclusions about the relationship between output and age, some occupations do seem particularly to be associated with a pretty clear reduction of output as a function of age of employee.

These occupations tend to involve either work which is under some form of speed stress, work which makes excessive demands on perceptual functioning or work which involves complex decision making against the clock.[2] It is not without interest, therefore, that deficiencies of older workers tend quite frequently to be noted in the more highly skilled engineering trades, in jobs involving piece-work, or where time stress is a distinct feature of the work (see Figure 7.3). It has been argued, further, that the failure to find even more frequent and marked examples of declining output as a function of age in these kinds of jobs may be due to selection factors which conspire to lead to the separation of the worker from his job before his output begins seriously to suffer (e.g. Griew, 1959). Since age structures of employees on such jobs tend to remain fairly constant over time and region (Murrell, Griew and Tucker, 1957; Murrell and Griew, 1958) this would seem to be a reasonable conclusion.

Other things which sometimes worry potential employers are possible increases in accident liability, absenteeism and turnover which may be associated with advancing age. Again, there is ample evidence (e.g. Riley and Foner, 1968) to suggest that in these things older workers, far from being poor risks, are in general very good ones indeed. Figure 7.4 summarizes some

2. Since it is not possible in a chapter of this length to deal with all aspects of the field, no attempt is being made to consider the special problems of the older executive or professional worker. Readers will not be unimpressed, however, with the implications for the manager as he grows older of the reduced capacity for assimilating information and for making decisions which seem generally to go hand in hand with advancing age (Wallach and Kogan, 1961).

data on accident liability and absenteeism as a function of age in various industries, and it will be seen from these that the older worker is either hardly different from, or even superior to the younger worker in his accident liability and absenteeism behaviour. Labour turnover seems universally to decrease as a

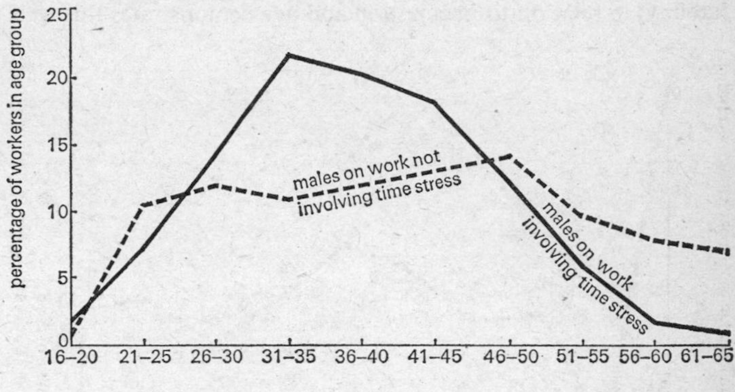

Figure 7.3 Age distributions of workers in occupations with and without time-stress. (Based on data reported by Belbin, 1953)

function of age. Heron and Chown (1960) in Britain report the tendency for markedly fewer older workers to leave firms after training than younger ones, and a remarkable reduction in job-changing characterized the behaviour of older workers in the United States in 1961 (Riley and Foner, 1968). This reduction in job changing may well be a virtue born of necessity, since older people do have the notorious difficulty which we have mentioned more than once in obtaining work once displaced from employment; but a virtue it remains to the employer who wishes to maintain a stable labour force.

It seems, then, that there is no reason to suppose that older workers will necessarily be poorer propositions for employment by virtue simply of their ages. Overall, they may fairly be considered as either equally good, or in some ways better prospects than younger workers. However, as all occupational psychologists know, a worker's actual performance will depend on the complex relationship between the demands of his job and his abilities and aptitudes. Thus, some jobs will inevitably place older workers at a disadvantage *vis-à-vis* younger workers, and it is in jobs of this kind that the satisfactoriness of older workers will be seen as less than optimal. A micro-analysis of a particular feature which overall shows the older worker to be at no disadvantage (accident liability) in relation to occupation and age demonstrates this well

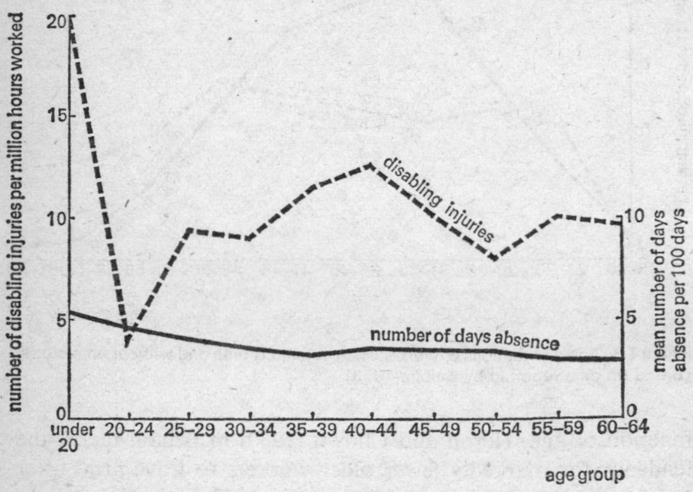

Figure 7.4 Absenteeism (all forms) and disabling accidents as a function of age in workers in various occupations. (Based on data reported by Kossoris, 1948)

(Griew, 1958). Table 7.1 (see p. 163), summarizes the features of jobs which are likely to place older workers at a particular disadvantage.

Other factors

The lower general geographical mobility of older workers has already been mentioned as a factor which is confounded with age to produce additional difficulties in their getting back into the labour force once they have become unemployed. Other factors play their part as well, for instance the unemployed's characteristic low mobility, his low standard of education, his inability to 'sell himself' as a prospective employee, and the disuse or obsolescence of his skills. There is increasing evidence (which accords with one's intuitive assessment of the situation) that older workers in general may be characterized by such characteristics. Another feature of this situation is the variation in education level with age. In 1900 older workers on average had approximately four-fifths of the schooling of younger workers, but in 1950, due presumably to increased opportunity during the intervening years, this fraction had decreased to about two-fifths. Such educational differences between generations necessarily leave the older person at an employment disadvantage, and this disadvantage has increased markedly during the present century.

Berkowitz and Burkhauser (1969), in their elegant analysis of the influence on employment prospects in middle-age of personal investments in education and training made earlier in life, conclude that education markedly increases the middle-aged worker's probability of obtaining work. Employing multiple regression analyses on data from a sample approaching 13,000, they find that in poorly educated groups, probability of employment decreases with age; while in better educated groups this relationship holds to a significantly lesser extent.

Sheppard takes up this kind of point in a forcible argument that age, as such, is a most misleading variable against which to relate any occupational trend. Age at first glance often appears to be the crucial variable, and the simple-mindedness of accepting it as such in interpreting data is responsible in Sheppard's view for 'many half-truths in the mythology of older workers' (Sheppard, 1969a, p. 5). He demonstrates that the confounded variables of skill level and education are crucially important too; and that so long as older workers are at the upper end of one of these socio-economic variables, they will behave much like younger workers.

And these are not the only other variables confounded with age. Socio-psychological variables such as achievement motivation, achievement values and job-interview anxiety, are shown by Sheppard and Belitsky (1966) to be decisively important in determining the frequently unsuccessful job-seeking behaviour of older workers. Sheppard and Belitsky also present data that 'subjective age' is more important than 'chronological age' in determining the outcome of job-seeking behaviour, and argue that positive self concepts and achievement motivation can be developed (McClelland, 1965), and that their development should figure as parts of counselling programmes for older workers.[3]

The factors which we have considered so far relate to the characteristics of older workers. Others which also operate to the older worker's disadvantage relate more to institutions than to job-seekers. For instance, many firms are committed to policies of restricting promotions to people within their companies. This can lead to lines of compensatory promotions down the organization which limit new vacancies to the most junior, and these are often seen by either employers or potential applicants as unsuitable for older workers. Again, it has been reported that some companies, notable apparently in Belgium, pay higher wages to older workers as a general practice, whatever their length of service, and this can frequently militate against the hiring of older workers, particularly in times of financial stringency. Gordon (1959) suggests, in fact, that much apparent 'discrimination' against older workers mainly reflects a concern by employers to protect the interest of their existing employees.

The wider introduction of company pension schemes, and the more general possession of insurance schemes, are frequently quoted as being responsible for some of the difficulties met by older workers in gaining employment, in that the conditions of these schemes frequently exclude the employment of older workers, or increase their costs prohibitively. High pension or insurance costs are frequently quoted by employers as reasons for not employing older workers (Wirtz, 1965), and it has been estimated that as many as 6 per cent of the manufacturing firms which discriminate against older workers do so on the grounds of pensions or insurance costs alone. Whether this discrimination reflects an institutional barrier to employment which simply cannot be overcome is the subject of active debate, and it has been suggested that arrangements can be made to include older workers in pensions and insurance schemes at a very minor extra cost, or at no extra cost at all. Where individual schemes exist which appear to exclude older workers, they may well reflect implicit employ-

3. The construct of achievement motivation is discussed more fully in chapter 12.

ment policies more than inviolable conditions of pension or insurance schemes.

Discrimination against older workers

In addition to those factors which we have already reviewed there is another set which should command our attention, if only briefly, as creating further handicaps to the employment of older workers. These may be grouped together under the heading of 'discriminatory practices'. Employers do frequently discriminate against older workers when hiring labour (Wirtz, 1965), and generalizations about older workers are important factors in the development of recruitment and hiring policies and practices (Gordon, 1959). Before age discrimination can be condemned outright, however, one has seriously to ask whether the generalizations upon which so much appears to be based have any validity when measured against our knowledge of the occupational effectiveness of older workers; and whether discriminatory practices reflect assumptions which cannot under any circumstances be defended in the light of this knowledge. Unfortunately, the whole issue of discrimination generates heat which often takes it outside the arena of applied scientific debate, and questions like these, perfectly proper and reasonable though they are, are frequently left unasked.

It is probably true that many of the generalizations about older workers which result in discriminatory hiring practices are of the kind that Sheppard refers to as half-truths in the mythology of older workers. Some are far less accurate even than half-truths. Some of the practices most damaging to older workers are themselves often intended to protect the older worker from excessive stress or discomfort. Others again which reflect policies applying to younger and older workers alike, tend, largely fortuitously, to operate to the particular disadvantage of older workers, and, when subjected even to superficial evaluation, are seen clearly to operate against the profitability of the company by virtue of being applied with uneconomical inflexibility.

A few examples may help put things into perspective. One of the most widespread generalizations of all, for instance, is that older workers as a group are simply less productive than younger workers. We have already seen that an older person's productivity will depend almost entirely on the job he is doing and on what particular kind of person he is. Here is a generalization which is less than a half-truth. A practice which the writer met personally some years ago involved a firm that always transferred workers to 'light sedentary jobs' when they reached the age of fifty-five. The idea was to protect the elderly from 'heavy work' that involved standing. In fact there is little evidence that heavy work to which a person is accustomed will militate against the older worker, so long as it is not subject to speed stress, and this undoubtedly well-intentioned policy actively displaced older workers from suitable jobs of an unpaced kind into jobs which, in the event, involved a great deal of speed-stress, perceptual activity and decision making; into jobs, in fact, that in general are quite unsuitable for older workers and far more suitable for younger workers. Another practice which is frequently reported is that of insisting that all prospective workers should meet stringent medical standards laid down to meet the demands of the most strenuous jobs. Any medical standards rigidly observed will tend almost automatically to militate against older job-seekers whom the company does not need necessarily to consider for employment in any but the general run of less demanding work.

Whilst it is difficult not to deplore the waste and under-utilization of manpower that results from some of the generalizations and practices which one meets, it is difficult to see much of the so-called discrimination as anything more reprehensible than well-intentioned foolishness, honest misconception and an almost unbelievable degree of ignorance. A lot more time and effort needs to be made available for constructive attacks on this ignorance, foolishness and misconception.

OVERCOMING THE PROBLEMS OF THE OLDER WORKER

Up till now we have been concentrating our attention on diagnosis, trying to determine, if you like, whether the patient is ill and if so why. It is now time to look briefly at treatment. One thing at least will have been made clear by the discussion so far. Industrial gerontology is a mixture of disciplines, and no one of them can be expected alone to contribute solutions to all the problems of older workers. Psychology, though an important contributor of solutions, has little to offer to a discussion of the fundamental economic processes that generate so many of the difficulties which older workers experience due, for instance, to structural changes in the labour market. Whilst it can delineate relationships that account, for instance, for the notable difficulties experienced by older workers in regaining footholds in the labour force after becoming unemployed, it cannot reverse processes of a largely historical nature that result in the tendency for the older worker of this generation to be more poorly educated and less skilled than his younger counterpart. Psychology's contribution to solutions is to be found in the development of measures which mitigate some of the disadvantages which face the older worker. It is able, also, of course, to warn the industrial community of changes in the picture which may be expected when processes which are currently taking place become, in twenty or thirty years time, historical, and some of these changes will be mentioned at the end of this chapter.

The four kinds of solutions which we shall look at are representative of the kinds of solutions to which psychology has already contributed and to the development of which it may be expected to contribute in the future. Although they must necessarily be dealt with extremely cursorily, their treatment should help to exemplify the nature of the psychologist's work in the field of industrial gerontology.

The problems which have been highlighted so far are those due to changes intrinsic to ageing which reduce a worker's probable success in certain kinds of work as he gets older; to his displacement from the labour force by virtue of economic processes that place him at a significant disadvantage when he is in competition with younger workers for the available jobs; and to discrimination against him which has little basis in the facts of ageing. Forgetting for present purposes the essentially economic argument that older workers, in common with other marginal labour, should perhaps be excluded from the labour force, and concentrating only upon the problem of extending their employment prospects, two broad strategies immediately suggest themselves as potentially useful in reducing the effects of ageing as a handicap to employment. They are essentially those that Alec Rodger has recommended for years as 'fitting the man to the job' and 'fitting the job to the man'. These strategies are just as valid for older workers as they are for any other category of worker.

Job re-design for older workers

If by virtue of an incompatibility between a worker's abilities and aptitudes and the demands of his job, he fails optimally to meet the standards required of him, a well-tried strategy is to attempt to modify the job so as to reduce its demands to a level which will allow the worker to cope. This, of course, is to fit the job to the man, or to seek *ergonomic* solutions to the problems at hand.[4] Fitting jobs to older men is as valid an approach to the older worker's problems as any, and it has enjoyed the attention of many industrial gerontologists as a strategy of choice in a wide variety of problem situations that involve the employment of older workers (Griew, 1964). It has many attractions for the applied psychologist. For instance, it reduces the need, when it is successfully applied, to cease utilizing the older worker's established skills and experience, and it obviates the need on the part of the worker to adjust to a novel working environment. Further, it permits the psychologist to apply his knowledge of the psychology of ageing to the solution of problems of ageing in a way that is comparatively rare in applied psychology, which is a field in which solutions are frequently ad hoc, and only marginally related to the knowledge acquired in studying the parent science.

Table 7.1 lists those features of jobs which research in this area suggests are likely to provide difficulty for older workers. Where one of them is met in a working situation in which an older worker is concerned, it should be regarded as a target for modification or re-design. Although it has been shown recently that job re-design as a technique frequently benefits the younger worker as much as the older worker, and although, regrettably, there is still insufficient field validation of it as a technique yet to justify complete confidence in its wide applicability as a problem-solving tactic, it remains an approach of potential power, and one which deserves the field evaluation which so far it has received only rather superficially (e.g. Marbach, 1968). Sheppard (1969b) regards it as one of the more promising approaches to the problems of older workers, and Belbin (1969) notes particularly its potential as a technique when problems of ageing are combined with problems of physical

4. The development of ergonomic concepts and procedures is described in chapter 5.

disability. This is particularly interesting, since job re-design has also been noted as a technique of considerable promise in dealing

Table 7.1 Features of Jobs which are likely to make them Unsuitable or too Demanding for Older Workers (Adapted from Griew, 1964). It is worth noting that this list, as well as being useful as a guide to job re-design for older workers, also serves a function in the vocational counselling of older workers who need guidance into new jobs.

Features of the working environment
Excessive heat or humidity
Atmosphere pollution
Inadequate lighting; glare
Excessive noise
Features of the design and layout of equipment and the work place
Design features causing prolonged stooping, bending, stretching, etc.
Weight of tool or part of body supported by operator without aid
Close visual, or intense auditory activity
Fine discriminatory activity
Complex, ambiguous or 'unnatural' informational displays
Narrow tolerances of accuracy
Hazards likely to cause tripping, stumbling, etc.
Features of the organization of work
Speed of work not under operator's own control (pacing)
Short-term memory requirement
Short bursts of extremely heavy work
Continuous, heavy work
Low distribution of rest pauses
Combinations of features which appear to produce special difficulties
Continuous, heavy work in hot environments
Close visual work or work requiring fine discriminations in badly lighted work places or in presence of glare
Continuous, heavy work of a paced variety
Complex informational displays which have to be read at speeds outside the operator's own control
High levels of accuracy which have to be maintained during paced work
Responding to auditory instructions or signals in excessively noisy conditions

with the employment problems of another significant group of marginal workers, the disabled (Griew, 1969).

Re-training older workers

If an older worker's job resists re-design; if his employer resists the notion of attempting to re-design the job; or if the worker is a victim of structural unemployment, and is forced to seek a new job in middle age; one of his most compelling handicaps is likely to be a lack of skill for any jobs that happen to be available. Until relatively recently it was assumed that the difficulties of training older workers were so overwhelming that re-training them for new jobs in middle age was simply not a feasible solution to any of their problems. An uncritical examination of the literature of the effects of ageing upon learning tended to underline this. However, recent studies of a most distinguished kind by Eunice and Meredith Belbin have undermined this assumption, and it is now clear that older workers may, under a very wide variety of circumstances, benefit from re-training to an extent very similar to younger workers.

Again, this part of industrial gerontology provides the psychologist with an unusual opportunity to apply his psychology. The recent literature on age, learning and training emphasizes the reasons *why* older people often find it is so difficult to learn new material and skills. Frequently it is found, for instance, that it is not learning, as such, which provides the difficulty, but rather certain features of the learning situation, the temporal characteristics of the task, the method of learning employed, or the organization of the material which has to be learned. Armed with such details as this it is possible, as the Belbins have shown so elegantly, to devise methods which permit older people to learn new material and skills as, or very nearly as effectively as, younger workers.

For a full review of developments in this very important area of fitting the older worker to the job, direct reference should be made to readily available accounts of the work of the Belbins (e.g. Belbin, 1965; Belbin and Belbin, 1968).

Counselling the older worker

We have already noted Sheppard's recurring plea that much more attention should be devoted in the future to helping the older worker overcome some of the difficulties which he faces because of his lower levels of achievement motivation, his less robust self-concepts, and so on. Up till now, counselling of older workers has tended to be limited to those traditional forms of occupational guidance which consisted principally of guiding displaced workers, or those facing difficulties, into new jobs, advising them of training opportunities, and directing them towards employers who were known, or thought to have vacancies for and sympathetic attitudes to older workers. Admirable though this approach is as a first step, it does not begin to meet the real needs of older people. Although it is difficult to pinpoint evidence to this effect, it is the common experience of most people who have been involved in occupational counselling of any kind that the highly motivated, confident person will often succeed without external help, while the discouraged and reticent will frequently remain unemployed however much counselling of the traditional kind one gives him.

Up till now very little has been done in an attempt to formalize or systematize this aspect of the counselling of older workers. What happens occurs more by chance than by design, and in the absence of design it is not possible to tease out the elements in a counselling process which make for successful outcomes, let alone submit parts of the process to any kind of hard-headed evaluation. Here is another field in which psychologists have a great deal to offer, and one in which a knowledge of contemporary psychological research may be expected to lend itself to direct application of immediate relevance.

Combating prejudices and misconceptions about older workers

All applied psychologists spend a large proportion of their time collecting, organizing and interpreting data in efforts to identify the problems with which they are being paid to cope. It is not too trite to claim that until these data have been properly digested, the discussion of solutions cannot realistically be started. In industrial gerontology an enormous investment in plain fact finding and relation building has already been made, and psychologists have been in the forefront of this exercise. That they will continue to be cannot be doubted. There are many facts and relationships still to be pinned down, and the psychologist's special training fits him well for this kind of statistical detective work. Apart from helping to identify problems and guiding us towards solutions, these facts and relationships serve another vital function. They represent the ammunition which has to be used in combating the misconceptions, the foolishness and the ignorance which underlie so many of the policies and practices which mitigate so disastrously against the older job-seeker. One would wish to claim, therefore, that one of the psychologist's principal roles in industrial gerontology should continue to be the careful preparation and dissemination of ammunition of this kind.

SOME POSSIBLE FUTURE DEVELOPMENTS

Gerontological practice is very vulnerable to changes in the attitudes and conditions which prevail in society generally. What appears reasonable, even inescapable, to a gerontologist facing problems characteristic of one generation may well strike the gerontologist of the next generation as being irrelevant to the problems of that time. Industrial gerontology is as much influenced by these changes as any other branch of gerontology, and a good deal of its theory is directed to the identification and anticipation of problems which are likely to affect succeeding generations of older workers.

Earlier we spent a little time examining the possibility that economic development itself tends to reduce the need for older workers in the labour force. Although we have not devoted much space to this possibility, industrial gerontology continues seriously to regard it as a possible source of major problems in the future, and as a consequence a good deal of effort is being devoted to the investigation of alternative means of ensuring the incomes of older people (Kreps, 1969), and of providing suitable leisure activities to replace work (Kleemeier, 1961).

Changes in society's priorities may well lead to a situation such that the comparative lack of education of today's older workers may not be reflected in the older workers of the year 2000. Thus many of the employment problems faced by today's older workers may simply reduce in severity during the course of the next thirty years, while today's school-leavers are growing older. This possibility has to be faced, or we may find that thirty years of research to overcome the obstacle of under-education proves in the event to be irrelevant to the needs of the beginning of the next century.

Another question which research in gerontology in general suggests concerns the quite fundamental changes which are taking place in society's very structure. One of the most powerful variables in determining overall adjustment in later maturity is social class (Birren, 1964), and there is growing evidence that social class is influential in determining an older worker's adjustment to his work, his re-employment prospects, his retirement, and so on. To be low on the social class variable would appear broadly to exacerbate the problems of being old. To what extent this variable operates only in so far as it is confounded with many others that are the major sources of variance has still to be determined, but the possibility remains open that today's younger people, developing in a climate that places less value on traditional notions of social class than that which prevailed a generation or two ago, may provide adjustment problems of novel kinds when they become older in thirty or forty years time. Industrial gerontology would be foolish to ignore the fascinating and important issues which are thus raised for the direction and nature of its research programmes during the next two decades.

SUMMARY

The employment prospects of older workers do seem to be poorer than those of younger workers. Once unemployed, they tend to remain so for longer periods than younger workers; they meet certain kinds of discriminatory hiring practices; and they are frequently subject to damaging compulsory retirement policies. These handicaps are not all due to their inferiority as workers. In fact in many kinds of jobs they would seem to be superior to younger workers, but much will depend on the nature of the job. They are subject particularly to structural changes in the labour market, and they are peculiarly vulnerable in that on balance their education, skill level and motivational orientation are not optimally adapted to the process of job-seeking. Re-designing their jobs, and re-training them for new jobs are two promising strategies in dealing with their problems; and a good deal of research needs to be done into techniques for counselling older workers. Discrimination against them can also be combated by painstaking research which undermines prejudices upon which this discrimination is often based.

FURTHER READING

A brief review of changes in performance with advancing age is provided by A. T. Welford in a 1962 article which is reprinted in *Experimental Psychology in Industry* (edited by D. H. Holding, Penguin, 1969), and introductions to the whole field of the psychology of ageing are to be found in *The Psychology of Human Ageing* by D. B. Bromley (Penguin, 1966), and *The Psychology of Ageing* by J. E. Birren (Prentice-Hall, 1964). The massive inventory of research findings in volume 1 of *Ageing and Society* edited by M. W. Riley and A. Foner (Russell Sage Foundation, 1968) is an invaluable source of material of general gerontological interest, and the chapter by H. L. Sheppard in volume 2 of this work edited by M. W. Riley, J. W. Riley and M. E. Johnson (Russell Sage Foundation, 1969) presents a most useful and provocative discussion of the field. Sheppard has also edited the first book to appear under the title of *Industrial Gerontology* (Shenkman, 1970).

8
Theory and Methods of Selection

Pieter Drenth

Scientific psychology has approached from several directions the question of making predictions about future behaviour. An approach which has been particularly fruitful is the one adopted by those concerned to select people for positions in working organizations. Professor Drenth is well-placed to describe this field, being very familiar with both European and North American developments. He discusses selection, placement and classification in terms of three overlapping perspectives – test orientation, criterion orientation and decision orientation. The chapter concentrates on theoretical issues and general conceptualizations, and relatively little emphasis is given to the characteristics of individual tests.

INTRODUCTION

In view of the wide differences between jobs and between people it would be surprising if a group of applicants for a number of vacancies measured up completely and exactly to the psychological demands of the positions. In many cases one has to try to remove person-job discrepancies, and three types of procedure have been applied with this aim. One can try to compensate for individual deficiencies through training (see chapter 4) or one can modify the task so that it becomes adapted to the individual (see chapter 5). The third approach is through selection – attempting to choose the most qualified person for each post. Selection methods may of course be applied in conjunction with the other two approaches, but they do require that one important condition be met, namely that the characteristics or personality traits which are responsible for success or failure in the position can be identified.

Before examining this question more deeply a few points of definition need to be considered. Although the word 'selection' is sometimes used with a very broad reference, it is preferable to distinguish it from two related procedures – 'placement' and 'classification'. One should only speak of selection when it is a question of the organization's accepting or rejecting an individual.[1]

1. One could, like Horst (1962), speak of a 'rejection-model' here

In other situations we may not be concerned to accept or reject but rather to distribute employees over several levels (placement) or over qualitatively different posts that lie on the same level (classification).

However selection is defined it is clear that the process should be part of a general policy in which the management and care of personnel is integrated. In other words, one cannot isolate selection and placement from total personnel policy. It is preceded by advertising and recruitment, and followed by induction, training and education, career planning and general management of personnel.

When this field is viewed historically it is apparent that psychology's original relevance to personnel policy was primarily through the development of selection procedures themselves. Of course selection occurred and still occurs without psychology; references, interviews, impressions of the personnel director, performance during a probationary period and others all serve as bases for decision. But the contribution of psychology to selection has been influential on the one hand through the introduction of new psychological measuring instruments (tests) and on the other hand through an evaluation of the contribution of psychological and non-psychological instruments to the selection process. (These points are extended in chapters 9 and 10.)

As selection psychology developed historically it gradually broadened its outlook. Three aspects can be distinguished which illustrate this gradual expansion: test orientation, criterion orientation and decision orientation. Whilst these are not historical phases which exactly follow each other, they do broadly represent the main changes which have come about. They may be considered separately although they necessarily overlap to some extent.

TEST ORIENTATION

Initially the selection psychologist worked in an isolated way. He stood as it were at the entrance of the company and determined who could enter and who had to remain outside. It is not strange that the psychological test was relied upon to a large extent, since

instead of a 'selection-model', since it is a matter of eliminating as many unsatisfactory applicants as possible.

this instrument differs from other methods of assessment in a number of qualities that make it very suitable for its predictive task. A good test is characterized by the following features:

1. It is sufficiently reliable; that is, its results are not influenced too much by chance factors; it is a relatively consistent and constant, not too 'elastic', measuring staff.

2. It is normative; that is, norms have been determined on the basis of relevant and circumscribed samples.

3. It is sufficiently valid; that is, there is enough empirical evidence for two claims about the test; firstly that it measures the capacity or personality trait which it is supposed to measure, and secondly (and in practice more importantly) that it predicts with reasonable certainty the future performance or behaviour of the tested individual.

In the phase of test orientation, attention was directed primarily and often exclusively to the instrument as such. Numerous forms and specimens were constructed, modified, and adapted to particular circumstances. For a review we may refer to one of the many manuals on the subject (e.g. Anastasi, 1968; Cronbach, 1970; Guilford, 1959; Heiss, 1963; Meili, 1961; Vernon, 1956). The most illustrative for the extent of test production are the periodical Mental Measurement Yearbooks (1938, 1941, 1953, 1965, 1969) issued by Buros, in which thousands of tests are mentioned and discussed.

Figure 8.1 gives an example of the different effects that different 'predictors' (biographical data, ratings, tests) can have. For experimental purposes a sample of 1275 military men were tested before undergoing pilot training. In the figure the numbers of people successfully completing training are shown on the assumption that the highest 500 were selected on the basis of four different predictors or by chance alone. It can be seen that the specially developed pilot test is by far the most successful predictor.

Methodology

In addition, test theory and psychometrics also began to develop. Since the publication on the reliability and validity of tests by Thurstone (1931), many books and articles have appeared; and there now exists (for this development has continued to the present) a sizeable psychometric bibliography.

With respect to methodological viewpoints, the European and American traditions were initially somewhat opposed (with Britain more or less in between). On one side, the approach in which observations, subjective impressions, 'identification' and more or less literary description played an important role was

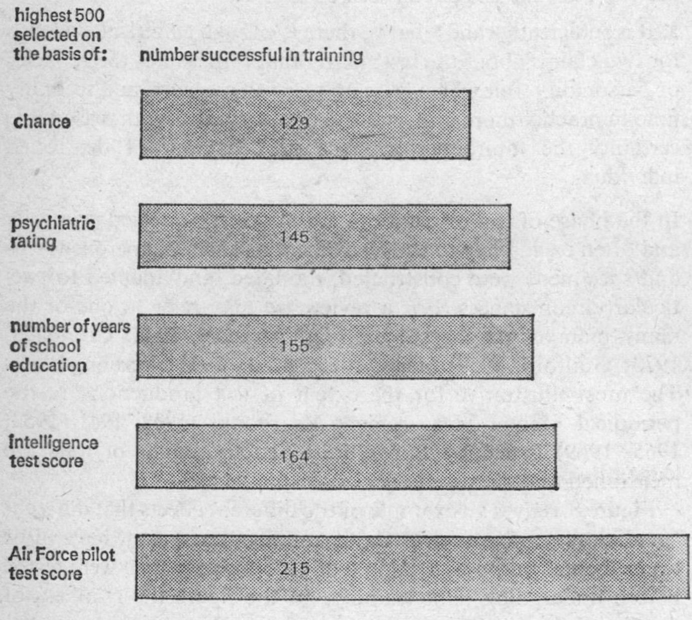

Figure 8.1 Comparison of different predictors against a criterion 'success in advanced pilot training' (Van der Giessen, 1957)

strongly defended in Europe. This viewpoint was supported by personalistic psychology, phenomenology, psycho-analysis and Gestalt psychology. In practice the approach led to the development of a variety of individual observation tests, interview methods, qualitative performance tests, and projective techniques of several kinds. On the other side, in the USA, behaviouristic and positivistic philosophy led to a viewpoint in which objectivity and quantitative treatment of data were especially emphasized. These considerations have, in combination with a strongly pragmatic attitude in American psychology, led to the development of a large range of paper and pencil tests and group tests for all kinds of abilities, aptitudes and even personality characteristics.[2]

Of course such a dichotomy represents an oversimplification, and we can say that more recent selection theory has acknowledged that an empirical, scientifically based foundation is essential for a responsible application of selection principles. But it is also true that the controversy has been stripped of a part of its sharpness and applicability by the distinction between individual and institutional decisions; we will return to this distinction later.

The structure of intelligence

An important side-effect of the emphasis of selection psychology on the test has been a concentration of attention on the nature and structure of intelligence. The extremely pragmatic empirically oriented selection psychologists have recognized that mere attention to the question 'does it work?' (in this case – 'does the test correlate with the criterion?') proves to be fruitless. Not only is there no scientific progress with this narrowly empiricist approach,[3] but also the practitioner reaches a stalemate when he is merely interested in the practical question of predictive validity. Knowledge of what one is measuring, knowledge of the test construct (and therefore an interest in construct validity) is necessary to improve existing predictions, to make sound choice of tryout tests, to be able to make statements about an individual in a new or unique situation, and to be able to pull the sacrosanct criterion from its often undeserved pedestal. This last point is taken up on page 186.

After the spectacular successes of Binet, who concerned himself

2. These developments were illustrated by Thorndike's (1949) book which derived from selection work in the Second World War. It remains a classic in the field.

3. Loevinger (1957) remarks, justifiably so, that to be exclusively interested in the question of whether or not a certain test predicts a certain criterion contributes as little to psychological theory development as the knowledge of the most suitable method to boil an egg advances the science of chemistry.

less with mental processes themselves and more with the end products of intelligent functioning, it took a long time before there was again interest in the nature and structure of intelligence. It was actually Spearman (1927) who continued where Binet's predecessors had left off, and renewed the discussion with his theory of the occurrence of a general and specific factor in every intelligence test. Additionally he attempted to find measures that would correlate with all kinds of intellectual performance, without becoming specifically dependent on, for instance, verbal or numerical achievement. His g-factor (general ability) is accordingly close to the reasoning factor which is measured to a great extent by tests like the Raven Progressive Matrices and Cattell's Culture Fair Test.

In England psychologists such as Burt and Vernon maintained interest in tests for more general factors, while attention in the U S A became strongly directed towards the search for a number of group factors. A leading worker in the latter tradition was L. L. Thurstone (1930) who isolated seven main factors from a series of fifty-six tasks. These factors were called 'primary mental abilities' and were believed to be more or less elementary in the chemical sense of the word. All intellectual performances were considered to be a product of some kind of combination of these primary abilities. These seven factors were: V(Verbal), N(Number), S(Spatial), M(Memory), R(Reasoning), W(Word fluency) and P(Perceptual speed).

Later American psychologists have extended the list of factors. French (1951) produced the French Kit of Reference Tests (mainly on the experiences in the Air Force in the Second World War) with many additional, and of course no longer 'primary', factors. The extreme exponent of factor-intelligence-theory is undoubtedly Guilford (1957) with his structure-of-intellect model, in which he conceives at the moment, at least theoretically, of 120 separate factors!

In this discussion and the related empirical research, the technique of factor analysis played an important role. However, it is now evident that there are so many built-in assumptions that one can never make definite claims about the structure of intelligence on the basis of factor analysis alone. The results in any setting are dependent upon:

1. *The nature of the input variables.* One never finds factor variance that was not first introduced as test variance.

2. *The nature of the samples.* An important aspect here is heterogeneity. Greater heterogeneity promotes intercorrelations and therefore, for example, the chance of finding a common factor.

3. *The number of extracted factors.* The more factors one extracts, the more chance one has of obtaining smaller detail factors (and error factors).

4. *The method of rotation.* It is easy, as the example of Cronbach shows (1970, p. 323) for an investigator, wittingly or unwittingly, to 'rotate away' a g-factor. The choice between orthogonal (statistically independent) and oblique (correlated) factors also clearly affects the outcome of the factor-analysis process.

It is apparent that factor analysis itself is strongly tied to a number of presuppositions, and that the results from its application can never yield a conclusive solution to a theoretical issue.

It is now generally recognized that the discussion about g- and or group- and or specific-factors, besides being a partly semantic question, is also to a large extent a matter of taste. Nowadays more and more emphasis is being put on the so-called hierarchical view (e.g. Burt, 1949; Cronbach, 1970, p. 332; Humphreys, 1962; Vernon, 1950). In this hierarchical thinking one assumes several levels of factors; the higher the level of a factor, the broader its nature and the wider range of performances it is thought to account for. The most widely known, but still hypothetical suggestion for a hierarchical system comes from Vernon (1950). On the top of the hierarchy is the general factor. On the next lower level are located the major group factors (verbal-educational and practical). Then come the minor group factors (verbal, number, spatial etc.) and the lowest level consists of specific factors like vocabulary, grammar, word-fluency etc. If we accept a hierarchical structure of this kind, the question becomes: on which level of the hierarchy do we wish to operate?

The classical model

Another product of this early period of test orientation is the classical model of the construction and evaluation of a test or test battery in the framework of selection. The phases are well known:

1. *Job analysis.* An attempt to understand psychologically which requirements there are for success in the job for which selection is to be made.[4]

2. *Choice of a criterion.* Consisting of an effort to define job performance in an operational form.

3. *Choice of a tryout or series of tests.* This choice is based on knowledge of the particular job. If there are no tests available, one can translate them or construct them anew. At this point the elaborate process of inter-item analysis becomes relevant.

4. *Tryout on an experimental group of subjects.* Ideally a group should only be considered if it is completely representative of the class of individuals for which the test will later be used; this means that one should really test a group of candidates in an application situation.

5. *Validation of the test or battery of tests.* When the experimental group has worked in the company for a sufficient period of time, criterion data should be collected and the association between test results and criterion performance can be established.

6. *Cross validation.* The process described above needs to be repeated with a control group. Tests that appear to be valid with this second group can be considered for use in the final selection battery.

7. *Make-up of the test battery in final forms.* Choosing the tests themselves, determining the weight of the test scores, determining the sequence and so forth.

This account is of course a somewhat idealized one, but the classical model in general presents a number of dangers and difficulties. Five important points may be raised. Firstly, it is often impractical to wait for the long period which in principle is required before the success of members of the experimental group can be measured. In these situations a compromise procedure is sometimes adopted – administering the test battery to employees who currently occupy the position. By these means one has test

4. Some details of this procedure in its application to training are outlined in chapter 4.

data and criterion data available at the outset so that validity can promptly be determined. This information is in terms of 'concurrent' validity as distinct from 'predictive' validity.[5]

The disadvantages of this compromise procedure are twofold. In the first place, only the group that remains after selection, training, and a number of years' work is available. This group is smaller and often more homogeneous than an original group of applicants, and such a difference may have a substantial effect (in this case, negative) on the validity obtained. However, one can eliminate this difficulty by applying one of the several correction formulae for this so-called 'restriction of range' (e.g. Thorndike, 1949). A second disadvantage is more serious. Too often it is impossible just to transfer the results of a concurrent validity study into a predictive validity model. An example from our own experience is relevant here. We found in a particular setting a curvilinear relationship between a measure of motivation and position level of managers (using the latter as an operational criterion for management success). The strongest motivation was found at the middle level, it was somewhat weaker at the top level and weakest at the lowest level. Not much imagination is needed for the interpretation that strength of motivation is caused by position level, rather than motivation (seen as a constant personality trait) being the determinant of the level reached. And the latter was a necessary condition for using the motivation test as predictor of future management success at the entry into the company.

A second danger in the classical model is that the phase of cross validation is often omitted: the investigator proceeds on the basis of correlations found in the first sample. Here is a considerable risk that accidental relationships (the result of chance characteristics of the sample) are taken to be true and generalizable. And this danger becomes greater to the degree that one bases the choice of experimental tests on a 'shotgun' approach. This approach involves trying a large number of tests and other predictors in the hope that at least some of them will turn out to correlate significantly with the criterion. Especially with such a purely empirical procedure, the danger is not inconsiderable that 'chance' correlations will be found.

5. The distinction between several types of validity is discussed fully in the American Psychological Association (1966) publication.

A third problem is that investigators often make unjustified use of the simple product-moment correlation when the data are represented by one or two dichotomies instead of two continuous variables.[6] Underlying assumptions are regularly that the relationships are linear and homoscedastic. This however is not always the case; sometimes the relationships are curvilinear, so that for example low motivation is paired with low achievement, a relatively high motivation with good achievement, a very high motivation again with lower achievement. Deviations from a homoscedastic relationship can also be found, when for instance low intelligence is associated with low school achievement, while the higher the level of intelligence becomes, the less clear is the relationship – the scatter diagram is in this case pear-shaped. Kahneman and Ghiselli (1962) have shown that these kinds of deviations from linearity and homoscedasticity occur with some frequency.

A separate, fourth point is the manner of combination of tests in an optimally predictive test battery. Leaving aside 'intuitive' approaches to combination as unreliable and inadequate, we can note that there are several statistical possibilities.

Firstly a distinction can be made between (a) conjunctive and (b) compensatory relations between test scores. These are illustrated in Figure 8.2, where the simplest, two-predictor situation is exhibited. With a conjunctive relation (represented by (a) in the figure) a candidate who is to be acceptable overall has to pass the minimum requirements on both test X and test Y. Technically this is called the multiple-cutoff procedure. With a compensatory relation ((b) in the figure) a low score on test X (one which would be too low for acceptance in situation (a)) can be compensated for by a high score on test Y (and vice versa). In addition we would employ a combination of both methods, where there is a possibility of compensation but within certain limits. This is illustrated in Figure 8.2 by situation (c). As a more complex example we might take a school examination with five separate subjects. In order to pass the examination overall the requirement may be set that no score lower than 4 (on a 10-point scale) on any of the 5 tests is

6. The correct applications here are respectively biserial correlations and tetrachoric correlations. See for example Nunnally (1967).

permitted, whereas in addition a total score of, say, 30 points is needed.

In this last example the combination of test scores is very simple – mere addition, a linear combination which takes unity as test-weights. There are however many other ways within the limits of a linear relationship by which the weights of separate items can

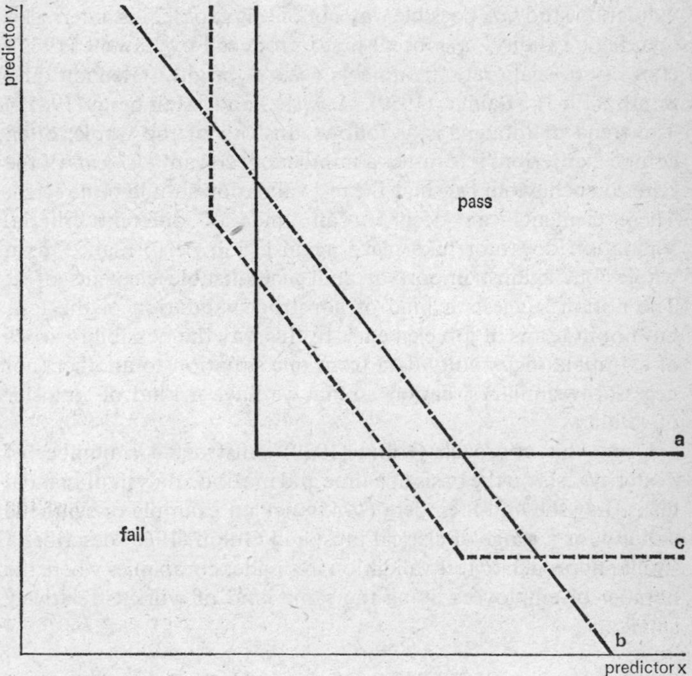

Figure 8.2 Conjunctive (a), compensatory (b), relation of test scores and a combination of both methods (c)

be specified. One possibility is to take the regression coefficient as a starting point, so that tests with greater predictive power relative to the criterion are given greater weights. (Guilford (1956, p. 396) and Albright, Glennon and Smith (1963, pp. 184–9) present graphs and tables to simplify this procedure.) On the other hand several studies have shown that less sophisticated methods of determining weights (using the standard deviations of the tests, or simply adding raw scores) need not yield inferior results (e.g. Lawshe and Schucker, 1959). The choice of weighting models is discussed in more detail by Guion (1956, ch. 6).

A fifth difficulty with the classical approach to selection is that it is often not possible to draw a sample of individuals large enough to meet the requirements of a scientifically acceptable validation study. A possible way out of this problem is in terms of 'synthetic validity', a concept first introduced by Lawshe (1952). (For more elaborate treatments, see Albright, Glennon and Smith (1963), Balma (1959), Lawshe and Steinberg (1955).) The trend of thought is as follows. Instead of the whole, often complex criterion, it is rather a number of relevant *elements* of the criterion behaviour to which the test validation should be directed. These elements can occur in all kinds of different criteria. Validation does not take place against 'job performance' as a whole, but against important and generalizable elements of it. The notion suggests a kind of construct validation of the test, but not in terms of job elements. In this way the possibility arises of extrapolating validity data from one situation to another (not necessarily similar) situation, so that we have a kind of 'transfer of validity'.

Using this approach Griffin (1959) constructed a number of dexterity tests on the basis of a time and motion analysis of manual tasks. Lawshe and Steinberg (1955) give an example of synthetic validity for a range of clerical jobs, and Guion (1965) describes a similar approach to test validation in smaller companies where the number of employees doing the same kind of work is relatively small.

CRITERION ORIENTATION

Such strongly increasing attention to the criterion meant an important widening of the scope of interest. This occurred not only on theoretical grounds, but also for the practical reason that, despite the very considerable energy and ingenuity devoted to the instruments and tests themselves, the resulting correlations with criteria remained of only moderate magnitude.

Conceptual problems

Some confusion exists about the concept of a criterion in relation to ideas about norms, goals and values. There are two main problems: a temporal issue (how long does one have to wait to collect criterion data?), and a question of which level of abstraction is most suitable. As far as the temporal question goes, Thorndike's (1949) distinction between ultimate, intermediate and immediate criteria may be of help[7], but these levels can in practice become somewhat blurred.

With respect to the question of abstraction, three levels can be distinguished. First, the levels of *goals*. At this level it is a matter of formulating the aim of the process in the framework of which a prediction is wanted. We are here concerned with terms such as 'the mental health of society', 'the survival of the company', 'the optimal development of the child' (ultimate goals) or somewhat more concretely with 'social adaptation of clients', 'sufficient capability for work', 'possession of knowledge and skills in a number of areas' (conceptual criteria, see Astin, 1964).

Second, the level of *criterion behaviour*. This refers to behaviour or performance that is considered to be representative of the ultimate goal of conceptual criterion. Parallel to the formulations just cited we find at this level terms like 'therapist's rating of behaviour', 'work performance', and 'school achievements'.

Third, the level of *criterion measure*. This measure or score is nothing more than an operationalization of the criterion behaviour. 'Score on rating scale X', 'number of units per hour', 'score on achievement test Y' are examples of such a measure.

Two important points should be made here. In the first place, the relationship between level one (goal) and level two (criterion behaviour) is not accessible through empirical research. The question of which criterion behaviour is the best translation of a goal which is formulated in abstract and often rather ideological terms (values, ideals, norms) is not a matter for empirical investigation, but one of judged relevance and acceptability. The psychologist will always have to make this judgement in consultation with the persons sponsoring his study. To mention a practical example: the question whether it is preferable to use a criterion

7. See also page 279.

in terms of success during training or one in terms of actual work performance (there can be a great difference between the two; see Ghiselli, 1966) is not an empirical question but a matter of choice.

Secondly, the relationship between levels two (criterion behaviour) and three (criterion measure) is merely one of reliability. Is the score a reliable representation of the criterion behaviour? How far should one make corrections to increase reliability?

A major problem is that the more reliable criterion measures are often the less relevant ones. A score on the final paper and pencil achievement test (at the end of training) is a reliable criterion for the selection of potential pilots, but it is probably not as relevant as an evaluation of their flying skill. A verbal test of cookery knowledge is a reliable criterion but is less relevant than a more direct measure of quality of cooking.

Developments in the criterion

Despite observance of the classical rules for test construction and validation, the results of empirical validation research are still generally poor. In a very thorough study of the validities of very many tests with numerous criteria, Ghiselli (1966) comes to the conclusion that the average correlations for the different criteria lie no higher than the 0·30s or low 0·40s.

It is true that a correlation with a criterion is not the only standard for evaluating the test. Seen from a decision-making viewpoint, one can find situations in which rather low correlations still make a very meaningful contribution to the decision, whereas in other circumstances even a very high correlation has hardly any effect. Nonetheless, it is obvious that in any particular situation the higher correlations are preferable. And seen from this viewpoint, the results, as already indicated, are rather disappointing. The consequences have been that interest in selection research has somewhat diminished, that the psychologist has concentrated on statistically significant rather than practically useful differences, or that he simply returned to selection without research, 'claiming near-miracles of clinical insight' (Dunnette, 1963b).

In the analysis of possible reasons for these low correlations, part of the problem is with the *test itself*. Too often the attempt to construct a test for socially relevant criteria has failed. As an illustration, we might refer to the trouble it took and still takes to construct a satisfactory creativity test or tests of 'social intelligence'. Another part of the difficulty can be located in *design problems*. We have already mentioned the fact that homoscedastic linear relationships are often unjustifiably assumed. Another difficulty is that the groups used for validation research are sometimes much too heterogeneous. Ghiselli's work (1966) shows that the group to be studied can often be classified into subgroups for which either no validation or a much higher validation exists than is indicated by the average correlation for the entire group. With the aid of so-called moderator variables, the predictions can be then refined.

A more general case can also occur, namely, that a good relationship does exist for several homogeneous subgroups, which does not apply for the total heterogeneous group. An illustration of this is presented in Figure 8.3. One can imagine that two groups may differ in their average test score (Y) but not in their average criterion score (X). This may happen in the case of two subgroups of candidate pilots who are tested in a flight-simulator – suppose that one group has had previous flying experience and the other has not. This advantage on the part of one group will naturally show up in the predictor scores (Y, the initial simulator performance) but it might disappear during training and in the final criterion performance (X). This would mean that for the group as a whole the test score will relate rather poorly to the criterion, whereas for the two subgroups separately there may be substantial correlations.

Another set of reasons for low validity coefficients rests in the *criterion*. In the first place measures are often unreliable. All too frequently subjective psychiatric classifications, arbitrary grades or unreliable performance ratings are gratuitously accepted. One cannot expect to obtain acceptable validities with unreliable criteria. Secondly, we should note that insufficient recognition of all kinds of external variables can have a distorting effect on the correlation between test and criterion. Ghiselli's book is surprising not only in the rather low average correlations, but also in the great variety in validities with respect to the same kind of criteria. To cite a few examples: the correlation of intelligence tests with administrative criteria varies from −0·40 to +0·80; space tests correlate with performance of machine operators from −0·55 to +0·65. These results can only be explained by a repeatedly different nuancing of the criterion in question, due to all kinds of organizational or environmental factors. Ronan and Prien (1966) devote an entire section to the extent to which extra-individual conditions affect job performance and therefore the criterion.

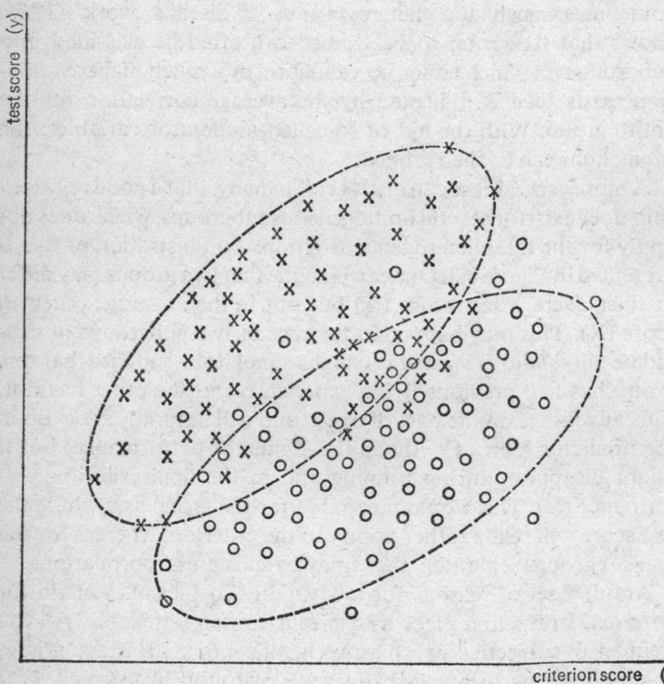

Figure 8.3 Correlations with two subgroups (homogeneous) and total group (heterogeneous)

Thirdly, it should be noted that low correlations are often generated by too simple a model, namely that in terms of a predictor and a single criterion. More often than occurs in practice, it seems necessary to refine the criterion. Three suggestions may be offered:

1. *Multidimensionality.* Although one speaks easily about a 'successful student' or a 'good worker', this does not mean that

one single criterion measure can be found in which the total criterion behaviour is reflected. Toops (1944), in his classic article on the criterion problem, points out that an individual can be good for diverse reasons. A secretary can be good because she types quickly, types neatly, is friendly to clients, maintains a comprehensive filing system, or for other reasons. This idea is discussed in more detail in chapter 10 and has been repeatedly substantiated. For this type of reason Dunnette (1963a) has advised: 'junk *the* criterion'.

2. *Timeboundedness.* A criterion is rarely a timeless, perpetually-valid given. Every criterion choice is bound to the moment of determination, and definitely is not always generalizable. For instance, Fleishman (1954) has demonstrated marked changes in the factor analytic structure of human motor functions during learning. At the early stages of learning a complex coordination skill a large proportion of variance can be accounted for by (a) a cognitive factor (knowledge of rules, procedures, processes) and (b) a more general coordination factor. Towards the end of 100-minute practice time, however, the cognitive factor is replaced by a large specific coordination factor and a smaller motor speed factor. The moment of this process at which the criterion is determined will clearly have repercussions for the question of which tests will correlate highly with it.

Ghiselli and Haire (1960) give a nice example of this in their study of the validity of reaction time, dexterity, distance estimation, mechanical knowledge and the like. They used a profit criterion as an indication of the performance of taxicab drivers during an eighteen-week period. This criterion was estimated four times: during the first three weeks, during the last three weeks, during the total period of eighteen weeks, and in terms of improvement during the eighteen-week period. For our argument the first two criteria are important. Six tests showed a correlation higher than 0·25 with the first criterion, with an average value of 0·36. The average correlation of these same tests with the same criterion determined during the last three-week period was only 0·09. Additionally, three *other* tests showed a correlation with the second criterion which was higher than 0·25. (The average of these three was 0·29.)

3. *Static or dynamic character.* Not only is it important to note at which moment a criterion is measured, but it is sometimes also possible and helpful to make use of what we can call a dynamic criterion. In that case the criterion does not consist of a 'single take' (e.g. performance level after a certain period), but of the *improvement* in performance during a certain period. In the article mentioned above, Ghiselli and Haire point out the usefulness of this idea. Bass (1962) gives an experimental example with an actual work criterion, and Manning and DuBois (1958) apply the principle to the prediction of improvement of school achievement.

Indirect criterion research

This section on criterion orientation may be concluded with a few words about a useful side-effect of this kind of critical analysis of the criterion. This side-effect has also arisen from the increasing attention to construct validity instead of the predictive validity of a test. We said previously that the choice of the criterion is ultimately the responsibility of the sponsor; but this does not mean that the psychologist must gratuitously accept and try to predict any criterion which is suggested to him.

To what kind of objectionable situation the politics of 'hands off the sacrosanct criterion' can lead is shown in the well known example of Travers (1951), in which a questionnaire designed to measure leadership qualities was validated against a rating criterion. In analysis of the data it appeared that, for example, weights for alternatives such as 'from a large city', and 'from a merchant's family' were negative, while weights for 'from the country' and 'from industrial occupations', were positive. In an attempt to explain these facts, it emerged that these item weights clearly reflected the anti-semitic feelings of the judges in the company concerned. Taking over this criterion uncritically only perpetuates and sanctions such a prejudice.

Continuing along this line of thought, Lovell (1967) has pointed out that the very unsubtle item 'I am a negro . . . yes/no' would be a valid and therefore useable predictor of industrial promotion, school performance and criminality in some parts of the USA. If, however, this item were used, an investigator would be contributing to the maintenance of deplorable situations and forces. In other words the psychologist, in his sometimes desperate endeavour to construct good predictors and to find high validities, runs the risk of neglecting an often more important and far-reaching assignment, namely that of analysing the nature and consequences of the criterion, and confronting the sponsor with the repercussions of his choice. Hofstee (1969) has used the fitting terms 'indirect criterion research' and 'inverted diagnostics'. Indeed, a correlation says as much about the criterion (seen from the predictor) as it does about the predictor (seen from the criterion).

DECISION ORIENTATION

The accent in much thinking and writing about selection has been placed on the decision aspects of working with and advising through tests, particularly since the first appearance of Cronbach and Gleser's *Psychological Tests and Personnel Decisions* (1957). Interest in these features had naturally been present before; after all, the use of a regression formula for the prediction of satisfactory performance already involves working with probabilities and chances of success. But the advantage of a systematic and explicit decision orientation is that the various assumptions and elements in the decision process are exactly identified, and that the place and contribution of the test becomes clearer. One is compelled to make a clear distinction between several decision strategies in which the test plays a different role and fulfils different demands on different occasions.

In decisions of all kinds, two elements can be identified: first, the chances of certain outcomes, and second, the values of these outcomes. In order to reach a decision, it is in principle necessary for the decision maker to be able to attribute a value to the different possible outcomes and to try to compare the evaluated outcomes on some sort of quantitative scale.[9] Of course this is not always an easy task. It is very difficult to compare on a scale a slow but accurate worker with a fast but less accurate one, or an efficient but not well-liked department-head with a somewhat less productive but very pleasant leader. Nevertheless, a decision approach brings out the need for an explicit evaluation and quantitative comparison of these outcomes. The chances of each outcome next have to be determined, perhaps by conducting predictive test

9. A more detailed discussion of these ideas is presented in chapter 11.

research to allow calculation of the probabilities of a particular person reaching different levels of criterion performance. It is naturally very important to distinguish between the evaluations placed on different outcomes and on the probability of these outcomes; a decision will be based on some form of combination of the separate pieces of information.

When we try to *classify* the decisions in which tests may play a part, a first important distinction to be made is that between individual and institutional decisions. With the first kind of decision, the focus is on the individual who makes the decision or for whom the decision is made. Each decision is made once, and the payoff from the decision may vary between individuals even when they have the same chance of a certain outcome, since the perceived value of an outcome can vary between them. Examples of such individual decisions are occupational, career and school choice (see ch. 9) as well as individual career planning within a company.

Within an institutional framework on the other hand a whole series of repeated decisions may occur. The value of the outcomes is determined here by the institution (the school, company or society) and is constantly the same for each particular decision. The utility of the whole decision-making strategy is determined by the average payoff of all decisions separately, so that it becomes a matter of maximizing this total yield or minimizing the loss. Examples of these institutional decisions are admissions to a school, selection for a company, examination for military service.

It we assimilate beside this the distinction between the dichotomy of yes/no decisions on the one hand and the choice on the other hand between different alternatives that themselves can further vary with respect to level or nature, we come to a taxonomy of decisions as represented in Figure 8.4. The most important kinds of decisions are indicated here but naturally this does not rule out other important distinctions between test decisions. The distinctions between 'interrelated' and 'not interrelated' decisions (with a restricted or required quota) and between single stage versus sequential decisions, among others, come to mind.

The importance of this decision approach is threefold: firstly, it generates a more exact determination of the contribution of the test to the decision-making process; secondly, it increases the possibility of making a more adequate choice of the right test type for a certain decision; and thirdly, it produces a more correct determination of the requirements for the test, recognizing that these depend on a variety of factors that have to be assimilated into the decision-making process. Quite different kinds of tests will be needed in a simple selection situation as compared to a procedure in which a number of people have to be distributed

		institutional decisions	individual decisions
univariate information	dichotomy yes–no	selection	choice yes–no
	classes	placement	choice of level
multivariate information		classification	qualitative choice

Figure 8.4 A taxonomy of decisions

optimally over several qualitatively different jobs. There are also differences between a question such as whether or not someone should take further college training and an 'open' question such as 'what kind of profession shall I choose?'. The approach also places emphasis on the fact that the test is only 'responsible' for the determination of probability of success; since a lot more has to be taken into consideration in order to reach real decisions about people, the role and contribution of the test becomes more realistic and modest. Making decisions is more than using tests!

As an example of this line of thought, let us return to the selection situation in which a test predicts a criterion performance with validity as summarized in Figure 8.5. The vertical axis embraces the critical criterion score: above this value one is judged satisfactory, below it one is deemed unsatisfactory. The horizontal axis extends around the critical test score above which one is accepted and below which one is rejected. The meaning of selection lies in the fact that the ratio of satisfactory to unsatisfactory

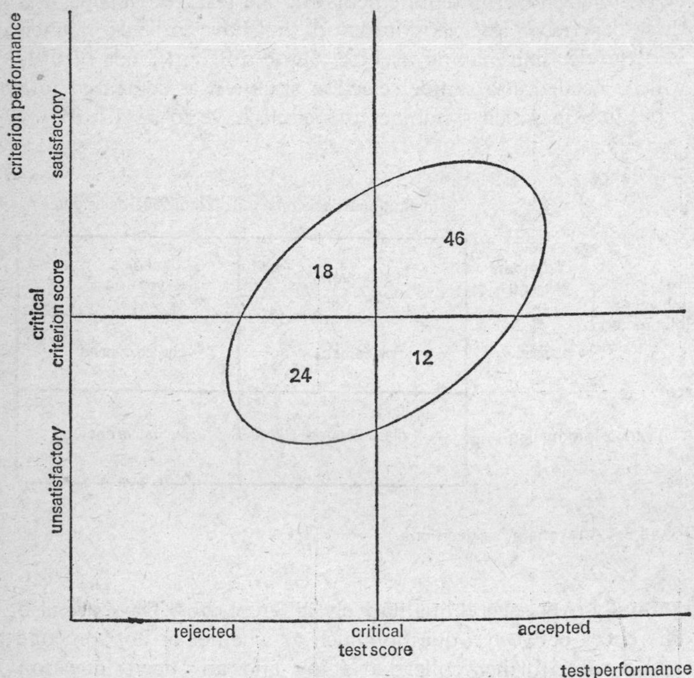

Figure 8.5 A hypothetical selection strategy for a group of 100 applicants

people (the so-called success ratio) is more favourable ($\frac{46}{58} = 79\%$) for the group on the right of the critical test score than it is for the group as a whole ($\frac{64}{100} = 64\%$).

But, as Figure 8.6 brings out, there are many factors besides validity alone which determine the value of this success ratio. This figure represents variations in four features by contrasting two possible situations in each case. The first illustration (diagram (a)) is the customary example about changes in validity: the narrower scatter-plot yields a higher correlation. A second feature affecting the success ratio is the average level of ability of the group of applicants (diagram (b)); this may be viewed in terms of differences in the antecedent probability of success. Diagram (c)

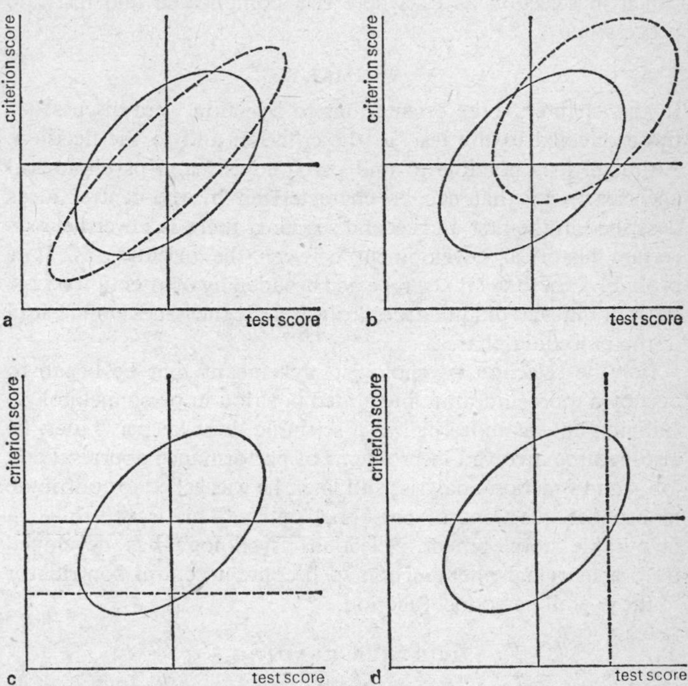

Figure 8.6 Interrelationships between validity, antecedent probability, selection ratio and success ratio

shows how changes in the definition of what is satisfactory criterion performance affect the ratio, and diagram (d) makes a similar point about variations in the number of candidates to be accepted (the so-called selection ratio).

Which decision must be taken depends on the evaluation of the various elements relevant to this decision-making process. Cronbach and Gleser (1965) and Rulon *et al.* (1967), among others, have developed several formulae for determining the optimal strategy for selection, and for placement and classification decisions as well. For a complete treatment, we refer to these books. The point to be made here is that this line of thought has provided a scientific and rigorous basis for decision making which in selection as elsewhere is a complicated and intricate process.

SUMMARY

In this chapter, three orientations to selection were discussed – those directed to the test, to the criterion and to the decision. Although it is possible to find psychologists and psychological agencies today that can be characterized by the central ideas described in the first and second sections, there is nevertheless a certain historical development between the orientations. It is probably best to say that a repeated broadening of attention occurred, but that this did not necessarily exclude the issues emphasized in the preceding phases.

For the selection psychologist, this meant that he began to occupy a more and more integrated position in personnel policy. Initially, he was more or less a scientific door-keeper. Later, he also became involved in problems of performance appraisal and job – and function-analysis; still later, he was asked to contribute to broader questions of personnel policy. This is, we think, a favourable development. Selection psychology has developed from a marginal phenomenon to become a central contributor to the overall personnel function.

FURTHER READING

Of the several general introductions to selection theory these four are representative: L. J. Cronbach, *Essentials of Psychological Testing* (Harper & Row, third edition, 1966); M. D. Dunnette, *Personnel Selection and Placement* (Belmont, 1966); R. M. Guion, *Personnel Testing* (McGraw-Hill, 1965); C. H. Lawshe and M. J. Balma, *Principles of Personnel Testing* (McGraw-Hill, second edition, 1966). Other references are cited in the main part of the chapter.

In the more specific field of test theory H. Gulliksen's *Theory of Mental Tests* (Wiley, 1950) has long been authoritative, and the second edition by R. L. Thorndike of E. F. Lindquist's *Educational Measurement* (American Council on Education, 1951; second edition, 1971) is also valuable. Other useful texts are P. Horst's *Psychological Measurement and Prediction* (Wadsworth, 1966) and J. C. Nunnally's *Psychometric Theory* (McGraw-Hill, 1967). More advanced treatments of test theory are provided by F. M. Lord and M. R. Novick, *Statistical Theories of Mental Test Scores* (Addison-Wesley, 1968) and W. W. Rozeboom, *Foundations of the Theory of Prediction* (Dorsey Press, 1966).

All these are American sources. Work in Britain is illustrated by the contribution of P. E. Vernon (*The Measurement of Abilities*, University of London Press, 1956; and *Personality Assessment*, Methuen, 1963). German texts include that by G. A. Lienert (*Testaufbau und Testanalyse*, Julius Belt, 1961). Volumes by R. Magnusson (*Testteori*, University of Uppsala Press, 1966) and M. Reuchlin (*Methodes d'Analyse Factorielle à l'Usage des Psychologues*, Presses Universitaires de France, 1969) are from Sweden and France respectively. Developments in the Netherlands are exemplified by A. D. de Groot's *Methodologie* (Mouton, 1961) and P. J. D. Drenth's *De Psychologische Test* (Van Logehum Slaterus, 1968). The latter is reprinted in German by Barth Verlag (1968).

9
Occupational Choice Theory and Occupational Guidance Practice

Ruth Lancashire

In this chapter we turn to research, theory and practice concerned with the ways in which people take up and progress through their careers. Theoretical writers are described as either 'differentialists' or 'developmentalists' and representative work of both kinds is described. Mrs Lancashire has been closely involved in guidance work for some time, and in reviewing the field she draws attention to the wide disparity between theory and practice: the questions which interest the theoretician are often quite divorced from those which matter to the practitioner.

My parents never thought much of me; I was a diffused child. One day, they saw me floating matchboxes in a puddle. 'Oho!', said my father, 'so it's water he likes, is it?' I didn't like to say it was matchboxes. Next week they bought me a sailor-suit and told all the neighbours. When I saw that suddenly everyone recognized me, I didn't want to argue and become a stranger again. So I joined the Navy. On the other hand, my brother, who worshipped naval things, was somehow seen to be a chartered accountant.

Nigel Dennis: *Cards of Identity*

Many occupational psychologists are interested in how people choose their jobs. This interest has sometimes arisen out of their own difficulties in choosing, since psychologists are often torn between the arts and sciences, attracted both to intuition and to scientific method. However, there are less personal reasons for trying to understand occupational choices in that their outcomes are important contributors both to work satisfaction and to effectiveness. Whether an occupational psychologist is concerned with problems of mental health and individual adjustment at work or whether he is interested in the maximal use of natural resources, if he hopes to influence occupational behaviour he must first try to understand it.

Psychologists are not the only ones who are interested in how people choose their jobs or the organizations they work for; economists, sociologists and other behavioural scientists also have ideas which contribute to an understanding of this aspect of work behaviour. Psychologists, by focussing their attention on psychological processes, have tended to neglect the considerable limitations provided by economic and social factors. Sociologists such as Miller and Form (1964) tend to feel that by the time race, nationality, class, family and area of residence have played their part, not only has the range for occupational choice been severely restricted but so also have work expectancies. In a similar vein, Macrae, making out a case for vocational guidance in the early nineteen-thirties, felt it necessary to apologize for doing so at a time when people were less concerned with the problem of choosing suitable work than with that of finding any work at all (Macrae, 1932; 1934). Certainly if we were to consider only economic and social factors we would have to admit that for the majority of people in the world occupational choice is almost non-existent. It does occur, but mainly within industrialized societies, and research into choice can only be considered valid so long as its social context is clearly defined and the results not given a wider significance.

Where psychologists have concerned themselves with choice behaviour in relation to work they have tended to view choice not as a peripheral decision but as one involving the whole personality, and they have therefore considered it valid to use the findings of general psychology in their studies. However, the flow is not seen as merely one-way, from general psychological theory to specific theories of occupational behaviour. Several writers see the study of occupational choice, in its turn, as a means of understanding personality, and some even imply that decisions about choice of work can actually form or modify personality. For example Roe (1964) felt that occupational behaviour can be as indicative of basic personality dynamics as any other part of the behavioural repertoire and that its study can consequently contribute to general theory.

People who have attempted to develop theories or at least formulate hypotheses about occupational choice can be grouped broadly into two classes. There are those who have concentrated their research interests on individual differences, who have been interested to discover to what extent and in what way people in one field of work differ from those in others. There are other workers who have been more concerned with how any one individual develops ideas about work in general and the stages he goes through in developing and modifying his ideas. The first of these groups may be referred to as differentialists and the second as developmentalists. As with all classifications this one tends to be an overstatement, and differences between the various writers are differences in emphasis rather than in conceptualization. For example, Holland (1966) who has concentrated on developing classificatory systems for workers and for jobs based on differential need satisfaction has nevertheless been interested in how such differences have arisen.

Three main research designs have been used in these studies. The first is a within-groups design whereby test scores and material from inventories, interviews and so on, have been used to compare people within different occupations, to compare those who leave with those who stay in any one occupation and to compare the successful and less successful. The second is a follow-up design in which peoples' occupational choice behaviour is recorded at different periods and attempts are then made to discern patterns over time and to account for them. The third is a between-groups approach whereby different age groups are examined at one point in time in order to by-pass the lengthy procedure of the 'follow-up'.

THE DIFFERENTIALISTS

This group assumes that people have different abilities and personalities, that jobs have different requirements and that occupational choice is a kind of matching process. The differentialists aim to develop a theory or series of hypotheses that will allow jobs and people to be described in the same set of terms, and the satisfaction and likely stability of an occupational choice is judged by the congruence of the two sets of terms for any individual. Such theories usually imply that patterns of ability, interest, strategies, disposition and so on, are developed early on in life, and that although modifications occur these are slight.

The origins of the approach can be seen in the writings of Parsons (1909). For Parsons the choice of an occupation consisted of three phases:

1. A clear understanding of oneself, one's aptitudes, abilities, interests, ambitions, resources, limitations and their courses.

2. A knowledge of the requirements and conditions of success, advantages and disadvantages, compensations, opportunities, and prospects in different lines of work.

3. True reasoning on the relation of these two groups of facts.

The early differential researchers at first saw ability and special aptitudes as the main psychological determiners of occupational choice. Later were added interests and values and more recently personality dynamics. All, however, have used essentially the same 'matching' concept.

Tyler (1964) has admirably summarized the work of those who have concentrated on individual differences in intelligence, special aptitudes and interests. For example it is generally held that people tend to gravitate towards a type and level of work appropriate to their level of intellectual potential. However, studies show that intelligence, as conventionally assessed, appears to be only indirectly related to choice of career via the medium of education. Harrell and Harrell (1945) showed in their study of the test scores of some nineteen thousand Second World War enlisted men on the Army General Classification Test that, although there were significant differences between the average scores of men in different occupations, there was a considerable overlap in range. Similarly, if a person's interests are like those of people in any occupational group who have found their work satisfying, then he will be inclined to choose this occupational area and remain within it. Generally it has been found possible to differentiate between occupations by the scores on interest inventories and to demonstrate that there is a tendency for people to choose and stay in areas where their main occupational interests are found to lie. Strong (1955) found an 86 per cent agreement between interest scores of college men and the occupations they were engaged in some twenty years later.

However, it has been left mainly to those using some aspect of personality as the differentiating criterion to develop all embracing theories of occupational choice. Some of these have drawn directly, or indirectly, from psychoanalytic literature and are, in consequence, open to many of the criticisms applied to 'psychoanalytic' writers, especially lack of clarity in definition.

Some of the major work exploring the realm of occupational

choice from the 'personality' angle has been done by Anne Roe. Her studies of alcoholics and the relationship between art and alcohol led her to see a link between personality characteristics and occupation. She explored the relationship by using information derived from biographical interviews and projective tests to differentiate between various kinds of scientist and between degrees of success in the different branches. For example she found that physical scientists tended to be withdrawn and anxious with rigid and compulsive reactions, whereas psychologists were generally uninterested in intellectual controls.

Such studies enabled her to develop two assumptions – that personality differences exist between occupational groups and that such differences are, to a considerable extent, rooted in childhood. Her interest in Maslow's need reduction model (see ch. 13), and the role of need arousal and satisfaction in personality development, led her to stress particularly the contribution of child-rearing practices to later adult behaviour and attitudes in general and to occupational choice in particular.

Roe (1957) assumed two basic feelings of parents to children – warmth and coldness – and from these she constructed six possible parent–child relationships – overprotective, overdemanding, rejecting, neglecting, casual and loving. She predicted that these different relationships would predispose people to select different occupational fields as adults. She had already developed a classificatory system for jobs, modified by Moser, Dubin and Schelsky (1956), based upon a 'people' – 'non-people' continuum of interest. This produces eight categories – outdoor, technology, science, business organization, business contact, service, arts and entertainment, and general culture. The continuum in fact becomes a circle with the more backroom cultural careers linking up to outdoor careers, neither having much people contact.

In attempting to link early childhood atmospheres with the degree of 'people-orientation' in occupational choice, Roe met considerable difficulties, for example, both parents do not necessarily have the same attitudes to their children and children may accept or reject parental attitudes. Although neither her earlier studies nor her later work with Siegelman (Roe and Siegelman, 1964) have produced the consistent results she hoped for, in reviewing her own and similar studies (1964) she feels that the thesis that different personalities choose different kinds of work has been generally upheld and stands best for broad groups of work and for higher levels of occupation.

Roe's work has been criticized on a number of counts particularly as to its naïvety in attempting to account for occupational choice by the use of one bi-polar factor. Her use of the interview has been challenged in that she has assumed by this that people are able to make their motives explicit. Additionally her attempt to construct a theory has been criticized on two further counts. First, that although she has claimed to have derived her ideas from Maslow she provides no clear systematic deductions from his theories which can be tested by her evidence. Secondly, by using the Rorschach Ink Blot Test she has displayed her analytic bias which, it is claimed, has prevented her from collecting independent data to establish her hypotheses. She seems rather to have fallen between two stools in her attempt to theorize.

A more comprehensive exploration of occupational choice has been provided by Holland (1966). He sees people as developing hierarchies of preferred strategies for dealing with developmental tasks from the interaction of their particular genetic and constitutional make-up and the cultural and interpersonal forces with which they are brought in contact. Choice, for Holland, is the result of a person searching for work situations which provide outlets for his particular hierarchy.

Through studying jobs Holland has classified working environments into six broad groups and has assigned a personal orientation for each. Any job does not fall exclusively into any one of these groups, nor do individuals take up only one of the accompanying orientations. Individuals are seen to differ according to the arrangement of the hierarchy of their preferred orientations. The six orientations are motor, intellectual, supportive, conforming, persuasive and aesthetic. Each orientation is made up of a variety of factors such as attitudes, aptitudes, habitual responses and so on. For example, people with an intellectual orientation have a need to understand the world, they prefer to 'think through' rather than 'act out' problems, they tend to possess unconventional attitudes and values and generally try to avoid interpersonal problems. This list of orientations can be matched to Roe's classes and to the various scales of the Kuder Preference Record.

Holland views the actual occupational choice an individual makes as depending not only upon his hierarchy of orientations but upon intelligence, aptitudes, self-evalutaion and job knowledge as well. The ease of making the choice will be related to the clarity of the hierarchy. If, for example, a person has a number of orientations with approximately equal pulls, then he could possibly vacillate or delay choosing. As with Roe, Holland sees choice as a matching process, in this case between personal hierarchies and the demands and satisfactions of a job.

To test out his ideas Holland has chosen both longitudinal and cross-sectional methods and has carried out studies aiming to predict initial occupational choice and to predict change in occupational direction. Although Holland has been criticized for claiming theoretical status for what is really only a series of hypotheses based on descriptive stereotypes, nevertheless, his ideas and studies have stimulated research workers in the field of occupational choice and many practitioners have found his classificatory system the most subtle and useful of those available.

THE DEVELOPMENTALISTS

Developmental theorists attempt to redress what they feel to be the static quality of the classifying and matching model. They tend to see occupational choice not as something occurring at one point in time but as an evolving sequence of vocational decisions. The approach is essentially longitudinal, interest starting with the first childish phantasies about work and finishing with the reflections on retirement. These theorists usually attempt to divide working life into age stages and try to develop norms of vocational behaviour for each stage. There is the general implication that a greater maturity is achieved as each stage is successfully accomplished.

The major sources for such theorizing are understandably the writings of educationalists and child psychologists concerned with general development. For example, Buehler (1933) is frequently quoted, and her life stages of growth, exploration, establishment, maintenance and decline, have been used as a starting point by many writers interested in the developmental approach. Havighurst is a more recent source. He considered the process of socialization as a long sequence of graduated characteristic developmental tasks, success at any one task being dependent upon how previous tasks had been tackled (Havighurst *et al.*, 1962).

Ginzberg and his associates (1951) were the first to attempt a comprehensive developmental theory of occupational choice – an attempt prompted by their surprise at finding that people were quite prepared to give vocational guidance without any adequate theory of how occupational choices are made. Their theory has three basic elements to it:

1. Occupational choice is a process.
2. As a process it is largely irreversible.
3. Compromise is an essential part of choice.

They dispense with the concept of choice as a rational decision, made at a certain point in time and leading to the acquisition of a 'perfect niche'. Instead they postulate that occupational choice is part of a lengthy and arduous process of growing up, with occupational maturity accompanying general maturity when the phantasies of childhood give way to the hard facts of 'reality'. The phantasy period, which they suggest lasts until about eleven, is one in which the child believes he can become whatever he wants. This belief becomes tempered, they find, first by interests, then by capacity, and, towards the later teens, by an increasingly clear value system. Then comes a realistic period in which a compromise has to be sought between these factors and the opportunities and limitations of the environment. They divide the realistic period into three stages – exploration, crystallization of ideas, and finally the emergence of a career specification.

The authors' main aim is to present a developmental theory establishing norms of behaviour for chronological age. However, they acknowledge individual differences by suggesting that these occur in the timing of the sequences, and in patterns of ability and interest. Chown (1958) found that although a similar general pattern of developing occupational attitudes could be found for young people in this country, it failed to reproduce in detail Ginzberg's stages.

Super, who has worked longest approaching occupational choice as a problem of development, has drawn from Ginzberg, but has extended and loosened his concepts of stages. For example, Super sees reality testing as starting as soon as the self begins to be differentiated from others; similarly he sees phantasy operating at all stages of vocational thinking, although he accepts a general movement in the direction of increasing realism.

In proposing developmental stages, Super and Overstreet (1960) attempt to chart the development of an individual's 'self-image'. This they see to be the solid core of a person, built from the interaction of inherited and constitutional make-up and the opportunities to play various roles, and capable, in its turn, of directing behaviour. Super has three broad phases to describe the growth of the self-concept: formation – this is up to the early teens, when development is through identification with key figures, and during which, choice, dominated by needs and phantasies, gives way to choice from interests and capacities with the increasing social participation and reality testing of an individual; this is followed by a period of translation when the 'self-concept' begins to be translated into occupational terms and tentative choices are modified against this developing self-consciousness; finally after a trial work period comes the period of implementation when effort is made to establish and maintain oneself in a particular career.

Super sees vocational development, then, as developing a 'self-concept' as a worker; he sees vocational adjustment as the process of seeking work where the requirements are consistent with one's views of oneself; and he sees job satisfaction as related to the degree of this consistency. His interest is to understand and perhaps, therefore, to be able to predict, career patterns and sequences of jobs, and this concerns him more than predicting occupational choice in its more conventional sense, that is, as choice at one point of time. He has yet to define clearly, or point to ways of assessing, the 'self-concept', but is attempting to develop a series of dimensions for this (Super *et al.*, 1963).

Super has generally preferred to take a longitudinal approach and has used a follow-up study of nearly three hundred boys, started in 1951, not only to explore his ideas about the 'self' in vocational development but to attempt to discern sets of predictors associated with this. He has in fact been criticized for not linking more closely his findings from his longitudinal studies of career patterns and his theoretical formulations which have generally been found to be too general and too loose (Carkhuff, 1967).

Tiedeman has accepted from Ginzberg the idea of occupational choice as a process, and from Super, the central position of the self (Tiedeman and O'Hara, 1963). He views occupational identity as part of a wider identity and occupational development as that part of general personality development arising from the confrontation of 'the problem of work in living'. Like Super he interprets a career as a sequence of jobs and has been exploring a variety of theoretical models for understanding career patterns, and a number of statistical techniques for their differential prediction.

In formulating stages of development Tiedeman has drawn heavily upon Erikson's (1950) concept of psychosocial crises which accompany each stage. A period of anticipation occurs in which many alternatives are considered and these are open to phantasy, are often transitory, and are generally fairly diverse in character. Then ideas begin to be crystallized and are modified by further exploration. Actual choices emerge with the increasing consistency of pattern of occupational attitudes.

Tiedeman has concentrated, to a greater extent than Super, upon the actual process of choice. He has become more interested in the way in which people go about making a choice than in the actual content of the choice, and sees 'style of choosing' as a possibly better basis for prediction and counselling. This way of thinking about choice is echoed in the way some advisers use psychological tests in vocational guidance where more, or as much, interest is shown in the way a person approaches the tests, in his strategies for dealing with problems, than in the actual test score.

A number of authors have also focussed their research interests on the actual process of decision making in vocational development. They have drawn upon diverse aspects of general psychology. Hilton (1962) has applied Festinger's theory of cognitive dissonance, Miller (1968) attempted to use learning theory, and Ziller (1959), Kalder and Zytowski (1969) and Gelatt (1962) have preferred more classical decision theory models. The last have each attempted to develop a 'risk' model seeing occupational choice as similar to a gambling decision and aim, thereby, to introduce a greater rationality into the process. A typical kind of experiment contributing to this type of theorizing is one where subjects were asked to rate careers in order of preference. They were then asked to re-rate the same occupations after information (falsified) was given about their chance of succeeding in any one of those chosen. Not surprisingly 50 per cent of those who had rated a career high lowered their rating when told that they stood little chance of succeeding in it; whereas of those who rated an occupation low 91 per cent raised their rating on being told that they had a good chance of success.

THE RELEVANCE OF THEORY TO PRACTICE

Generally theorists concerned with occupational choice and practitioners in the field of occupational guidance have had limited communication. The practitioners have largely avoided attempts at developing all-embracing theories but have rather considered the contribution of separate variables when they have had the time to take up research issues at all. Theorists, intent upon pursuing their curiosity, have often neglected to direct their findings to affect practice seriously.

Certainly in Great Britain there is a considerable gap between theory and practice. A careers officer carrying the size of case load that makes it difficult for him to see all his school leavers once, and then only for a relatively short time, can only feel frustrated when reading Super. A careers teacher, allowed Friday afternoons for 'career work' and allotted a small cupboard in a corridor for career information, is likely to experience nothing but irritation when urged to explore a young person's methods and strategies for making decisions. The fact that there is inadequate support and consequently inadequate facilities for careers advisers to carry out their jobs effectively whether in schools, in further education, in the Youth Employment Service, or in work, is no argument for sheltering them from the ideas emerging from research workers which challenge the systems in which they function. Trainees should emerge from their courses with 'fire in their bellies', as one tutor put it, to spur them to attempt to close the gap between present facilities and those based more closely on the knowledge that is being built up about the development of vocational attitudes and about choice behaviour.

The concepts of 'choosing a career' and of 'fitting a square peg into a square hole' are no longer valid if they imply some kind of rational assessment at one point in time that can be expected to last a life-time. The work of Ginzberg, Super and others stressing the time element in the development and implementation of occupational ideas shows choice rather to be a gradual process, starting long before school-leaving age and continuing through working life up to the adjustments necessary on retirement. Occupational guidance is coming to be seen as an ongoing conversation between guider and guided, where both expect, accept and learn to deal with, changes in abilities and circumstances against a changing political, economic, technological and sociological background.

The ideas about vocational guidance in schools developed by Daws and his co-workers at the Vocational Guidance Research Unit in the Psychology Department at Leeds (Daws, 1968) and, more recently, for an all-age vocational guidance service by the Department of Employment, illustrate attempts to translate the developmental aspect of occupational choice into practice.

The emotional and subjective elements to career choice, highlighted in the work of Roe and Holland, are also beginning to have their impact on practice. Although the view of vocational guidance accepted in this country restates its test orientation and its concern with the rational assessment of potential, nevertheless it is probably true that the majority of vocational advisers have neither had the time, nor, until recently, the training to develop a more subtle approach. However, against the background of the kind of research touched on in this chapter, it is no longer possible to view the client as a passive audience receiving information about himself and beneficial advice. Motivation and personality are now known to affect how a person views his abilities and to influence how effectively he can use them. The work of Super, Tiedeman and their colleagues suggests that how an individual perceives his own situation is more likely to determine how he acts than how others perceive it. If someone is to be helped to a practical decision or series of decisions, then the picture of how he sees himself (which needs patient eliciting), how others see him (which contributes partially to how he sees himself), and how he is seen by a trained adviser using reliable and valid techniques, will all have to be skilfully combined into a 'realistic' picture which the client can accept, make his own, and act upon. This cannot be achieved by an interview starting with the adviser interpreting a client's scores on a battery of tests and pointing out the work he feels would consequently be suitable or unsuitable to the client, which is still the practice in some agencies. Against the theoretical background sketched in this chapter an adviser would rather initially seek to elicit how far the client had got with his own thinking about himself in relation to work, the part his working life was likely to take in his broader 'life plans', and his attitudes to general career areas and to specific careers.

This is not to suggest, however, that psychological tests should be neglected, but rather that there should be a fuller understanding of their strengths and weaknesses and of the ways that they can contribute to vocational guidance. The differentialists, attempting to provide some scientific basis to the old adages of 'birds of a feather flocking together' and 'like seeking like', have been able to demonstrate that although considerable differences exist between people working within the same broad career area, and even between people holding similar jobs, nevertheless successful and satisfied workers can be roughly differentiated by intelligence, special aptitudes, interests and personality and that these aspects can be assessed. Test norms can be established to differentiate groups in a rough and ready way but it is always necessary to have fairly wide tolerances as far as score ranges are concerned.

Work on differences between occupational groups and similarities within them can also provide occupational advisers with useful material for the 'information giving' aspects of their work. Grouping or mapping out jobs can help people with different patterns of ability seeking different kinds of work satisfaction to widen their aspirations, for often if one member of a family of jobs is a likely choice, so could others be within the same family.

These are just a few ways in which practitioners can draw on the many theorists working in the field of occupational choice. However, it is not always easy to abstract practical implications from research work in this area and there is need for much closer communication between theory and practice to provide frameworks within which the work of occupational advisers can become more meaningful, and to provide more direct tests of the validity and usefulness of theories of occupational choice.

SUMMARY

The last twenty years have seen a multiplication of attempts at developing comprehensive or partial theories to account for occupational choice. Some theorists have focussed their ideas upon differential choice between occupations, attempting to tease out the kinds of characteristics that lead people to develop careers in one kind of work rather than another. Others have been more interested to discover how people develop ideas about work and to discern the stages through which vocational thinking passes.

Although various of the 'theories' and hypotheses have not stood up particularly well to testing, nevertheless they have helped to change the climate of thinking which has affected both research programmes and practical occupational guidance. There is still a considerable gap between theory and practice and a real need for 'interpreters' to bring the two together.

FURTHER READING

Papers by the main research workers in the field are presented in these four collections: *Counseling and Guidance*, edited by J. F. Adams (Macmillan Co., 1965), *Man in a World at Work*, edited by H. Borow (Houghton Mifflin, 1964), *The Theory and Practice of Vocational Guidance*, edited by B. Hopson and J. Hayes (Pergamon, 1968), and *Vocational Guidance and Careers Development*, edited by H. J. Peters and J. C. Hanson (Macmillan Co., 1966). Other useful texts are J. O. Crites's *Vocational Psychology* (McGraw-Hill, 1969) and S. H. Osipow's *Theories of Career Development* (Appleton-Century-Crofts, 1968).

10
Judgements about People at Work

Peter Warr

This chapter is in many ways complementary to the previous two. These were concerned with selection and vocational guidance, both of which involve judgements about how someone matches up to a job. It is the judgement process itself which is examined now. In this chapter two main forms of organizational judgement are considered – staff appraisal schemes and selection interviews. Research into each of these is set in the framework provided by a general conceptualization of the process of 'person perception'.

At work and throughout our home and social life we necessarily receive and transform huge amounts of information about other people. It is research into this process – commonly referred to as 'person perception' – which provides the subject-matter of the present chapter. We shall first look broadly at some recent work in the field and then turn to examine two relatively formalized illustrations of person perception in organizational settings. Attention will be focused on staff appraisal schemes and on selection interviews; in both of these cases organizations have developed procedures for eliciting and processing information which is used as a basis for decisions about their members.

THE PROCESS OF PERSON PERCEPTION

If we are to examine the judgements which people make about each other we have to develop some ways of measuring what these judgements are like. There are several approaches to this but most researchers are agreed that it is helpful to think of a personal judgement in terms of a series of dimensions. We might judge that a stimulus person should be placed towards the 'tense' end of a scale from 'relaxed' to 'tense', that he is more industrious than lazy or that he is about average in creativity. There are naturally many different scales which might be applied, and it is apparent that in studying the process of person perception we have to learn about those which are used in a particular context. In doing this we might be said to be acquiring information about the Attributive Component of a judgement – that part of a judgement to do with the characteristics, values, intentions and so on which are attributed to a stimulus person.

It is important to note however that the dimensions on which we place someone when we are attributing characteristics to him are not always the same ones: they vary between situations and between perceivers. When forming an impression of applicants for a salesman's job, for instance, a perceiver might be applying scales to do with verbal fluency and persuasiveness; but when he is himself in the role of salesman he will view potential purchasers in rather different terms. Furthermore the dimensions of attribution which make up an impression will vary from judge to judge. There is little doubt that different childhood and adult experiences result in differences between individuals in the personal dimensions they apply (e.g. Bannister, 1966; Warr, 1970).

The Attributive Component is thus the main feature of any judgement, but two other aspects are also important – the Expectancy and the Affective Components. The first of these is necessarily implied by the attributive nature of perception: when we attribute, say, intelligence to someone we are in effect predicting that he will behave in certain specifiable ways. Personal judgements may in this sense be seen to go beyond mere descriptions of a person to include expectancies about his likely behaviour and reactions (c.f. Kelly, 1955). The Attributive Component and the Expectancy Component of judgement are thus logically interdependent.

The Affective Component is slightly different, being more to do with the reactions of a perceiver than with the assumed characteristics of a stimulus. When judging a person we do not only attribute characteristics to him and make predictions about him; we also respond to him in terms of liking, attraction, respect, sympathy, interest, and so on. There is no doubt that these affective responses colour our judgement in many ways so that we adjust and discount information to form an impression which fits our feelings and attitudes and which is itself a consistent one; illustrations of this process are presented at several points in the chapter.

Other features of the person perception process are incorporated in Figure 10.1.[1] This is set out as a flow diagram such that arrowed

1. Note that in several important respects this diagram parallels the model presented by Poulton in chapter 3.

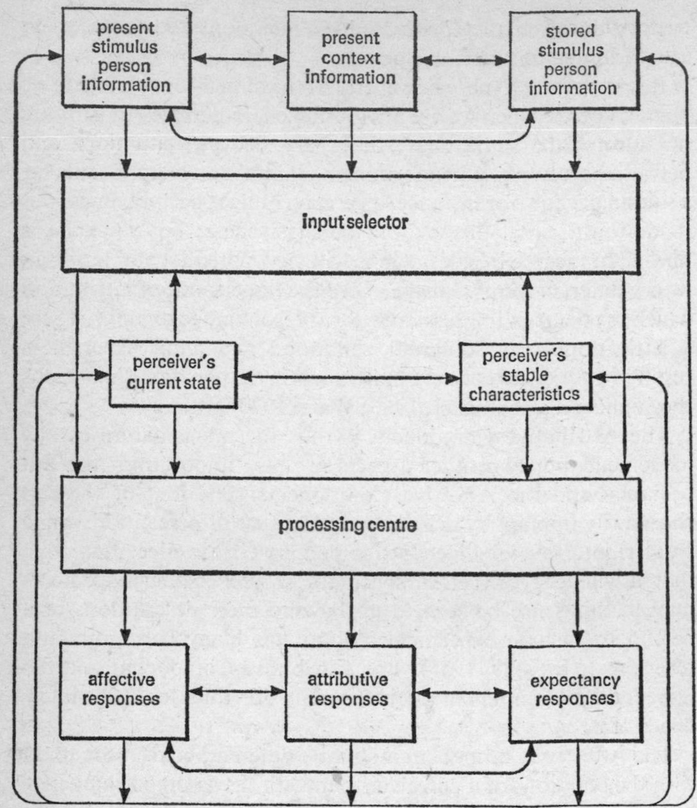

Figure 10.1 A schematic representation of person perception. (For a more complete account see Warr and Knapper, 1968)

lines indicate the flow of information and influence. The three judgement components at the bottom of the diagram are seen to feed back into a component at the top called 'Stored Stimulus Person Information'. This draws attention to the fact that our impressions of people are cumulative, since earlier judgements affect later ones. Our perceptions are also necessarily derived from information about what a person says or does and about the circumstances at the time of judgement; these two features are indicated by the other components at the top of the diagram.

Below them is a component referred to as the 'Input Selector'. This component is necessary since we cannot possibly process all the information available at one time; we have to select some of it and filter out the rest. As Broadbent has pointed out in chapter 1, such a process occurs in judgements of our physical environment as well as of social objects. It is likely that we have to *learn* to select only certain aspects of other people in the same way that acquiring a psycho-motor skill (car driving for instance) involves learning to discard less relevant stimulus information.

Moving down the schematic representation of the process in Figure 10.1 we come to two important and interdependent features of the judge himself. The 'Perceiver's Current State' refers to his perceptual set, his intentions and needs at the time; and his 'Stable Characteristics' are personality factors, attitudes, age and other less transitory characteristics. Both sets of variables are shown in the diagram to influence the Input Selector and also the Processing Centre.

It is the latter which may be said to be at the heart of the judgement activity. The material which is selected from the environment and from memory is somehow processed to yield the judgements which we form and which themselves feed back into later judgements. One way of viewing the Processing Centre is in terms of a complex series of 'decision rules'. We might assume that through experience we develop a range of probabilistic rules about people. These rules are generalized expectancies which form the basis of inferences. They might be of the form: 'If a person has characteristic X, then infer with probability p that he has Y' or 'If a person does A, then infer with probability q that he will do B'. In this way we might suppose that incoming material about someone is slotted into relevant decision rules to yield a judgement.

Such a processing activity is clearly a complex one, and it is only imperfectly understood; we still have to learn more about the rules which are available and the way they are used in a particular context (c.f. Warr and Coffman, 1969). One pressing question concerns the way several separate inferences about attributes become combined into an overall judgement. We might infer that a job applicant is likely to be industrious, rather undependable, quite creative, a pleasant social companion, fairly strong-willed, slightly below average in health and fairly knowledgeable about the job. How do these several probabilistic inferences coalesce to yield an overall selection decision? It is clear that in practice we need to consider other applicants, the main features of the job, salary required and so on before a decision can be reached. But can we say anything in general terms about the way perceivers combine the many inferences which they inevitably make?

The considerable research literature on this question is mainly oriented around empirical tests of variations on a general linear theme (e.g. N. H. Anderson, 1965; Manis, Gleason and Dawes, 1966; Rosenberg, 1968; Warr and Smith, 1970). The general linear model of combination may be reformulated in terms of a more specific averaging model, so that we might predict for instance that an overall decision is simply the average of the separate inferences. Or we may examine the decision in terms of a more complex procedure which involves allotting different weights to the separate items. When this is done it is generally found that some form of weighted averaging model provides a fairly good description of judges' decision-making behaviour.

This account of the perceptual process is of course rather a sketchy one. A more detailed description has been presented by Warr and Knapper (1968), at which point many research investigations into person perception generally were reviewed. The present chapter will mainly be restricted to aspects of person perception within organizations, and an attempt will be made to link reported research with the general framework presented above.

APPRAISAL SCHEMES

Most large organizations have developed procedures for recording and collecting information about the way their personnel are evaluated. These procedures are usually brought into operation once a year, they are mainly restricted to managerial and 'white-collar' jobs and are usually referred to as 'management appraisal' or 'staff reporting' schemes. In outline the schemes operate by requiring managers to record in a prescribed manner the impressions they have formed of each of their subordinates; in terms of Figure 10.1 appraisers have to select and process some material from the component labelled Stored Stimulus Person Information.

The judgements which are made and the action which follows them depend upon the aims of a particular company's scheme. The general intention is to ensure that an organization makes the best and fairest use of its employees, but this overall objective may be subdivided, as follows:

1. *The assessment of future potential.* Here we are mainly concerned with the Expectancy Component of the judgements which are made. Questions of prediction are likely to be asked on the appraisal form so that 'talent spotting' judgements for promotion and transfer may be made.

2. *Manpower planning.* A related objective is to collect data which allow projections of retirements, likely labour turnover and possible imbalances in manpower. These aims are at an organizational level, whereas those in 1 are more concerned with the appraisal of individual members.

3. *Improving current effectiveness.* The appraisal schemes in many organizations are intended to contribute to the success with which people carry out their present jobs (rather than being entirely oriented to promotion and other changes). They may incorporate procedures for establishing work objectives for each person, for identifying training needs or for checking on selection outcomes.

4. *Salary administration.* In some organizations another objective of the annual reporting scheme is to provide the basis for decisions about salary increments which may be granted to each individual.

5. *Providing information to employees.* One commonly-expressed aim of an appraisal scheme is to provide 'feed-back' to employees about their judged successes and weaker points. This objective is often thought to be attainable through an annual 'appraisal interview', and research into such interviews is considered later in the chapter.

Appraisal systems differ between organizations in their aims, but all of them have as a central function the recording of personal judgements. In some cases these judgements are intended to be entirely about the way a person carries out his job, but in the majority of cases superiors are asked to record their impressions of personality characteristics. We have seen that for this to be possible we have to determine the dimensions of judgement which are to be applied in the particular context. In most cases an organization specifies dimensions which are to be used for all employees, but it is also quite common for unrestricted 'pen portraits' to be requested.[2]

The dimensions which are used are regularly chosen in a fairly *ad hoc* way, and the problems arising from this will be considered shortly. In many organizations five-point attributive ratings are requested in terms of features like: knowledge-of-work, conscientiousness, responsibility, energy, relations with colleagues, penetration, organizing ability, speed and accuracy, mental alertness, oral expression, expression-on-paper and creative ability. The judgements so recorded are of considerable psychological interest within the framework of Figure 10.1 as they derive from situations where measurement procedures are fairly controlled (as in the laboratory) but where the judges' task is of personal significance and practical importance (conditions which rarely obtain in the laboratory). Let us examine some findings from research into the use of such scales.

The use of rating scales for appraisal

Five main lines of research into the use of rating scales in appraisal schemes may be distinguished; these concern the range of response, the reliability of judgements, differences between judges, relationships between scales, and the prediction of overall gradings.

1. *The range of response.* One of the aims of an appraisal scheme which was noted above was the assessment of future potential. The hope here is that judgements of different people which are

2. The generally-applied scales have the virtue of allowing easy comparisons between individuals; the free descriptions are less desirable in this respect but they have the advantage of permitting the application of special scales in individual cases. A choice between the approaches hinges on the purposes to which the material is to be put (Warr and Haycock, 1970; Warr, Schroder and Blackman, 1969).

recorded on appraisal forms will be sufficiently dispersed for discrimination between members of the organization to be possible. Several investigators have examined the degree to which responses are in fact spread out over the scales provided and have noted that the majority of judgements are usually very close to the middle of the scale, tending slightly to the favourable end (e.g. K. H. Rowe, 1964). In one study of the application of 15 scales to almost 150 employees I noted that more than 60 per cent of judgements were at the mid-point and that the extremes of the five-point scales were never used.

Such findings have sometimes been taken to suggest that the use of rating scales for appraisal is inadvisable, but methodological work makes it clear that such a conclusion would be unnecessarily gloomy. Increased dispersion may be achieved by suitable instructions and training, and by a stricter attention to the selection of relevant scales. These points are taken up below (p. 217).

2. *The reliability of judgements.* The degree to which judgements of people are stable over time has been extensively studied. There is no doubt that test-retest reliability coefficients are in general of a satisfactory magnitude (Warr and Knapper, 1968, ch. 2) and that this general conclusion may be extended to company appraisal schemes (Stockford and Bissell, 1949). However it is particularly important to note that scales differ between themselves in their reliability; those whose meaning is clear and unambiguous are regularly found to generate more reliable judgements than scales whose terms are open to varying interpretations.

3. *Differences between judges.* Individual differences in judgement were summarized in Figure 10.1 as deriving from a person's stable characteristics and from his more transitory state. Stable differences in personality are unquestionably sources of differences in response patterns. People are consistent in their liability to make or to avoid extreme judgements (Warr and Coffman, 1970) and in their tendency to be lenient or severe (Stockford and Bissell, 1949); the correlates of these differences are in need of further investigation.

The 'current state' influences in appraisal schemes are less likely to include emotions and perceptual set than is the case in other instances of person perception; they are likely to be more apparent in a judge's attempts to attain consistency in completing an appraisal form. He will probably rehearse his ratings several times to ensure that they fit together into a coherent pattern; this process has long been recognized as central to perception and remembering (see Bartlett's (1932) discussion of 'effort after meaning') but because of the deliberateness with which appraisal judgements are made it will here be especially evident.

4. *Relationships between scales.* It is well established that dimensions of judgement tend to cluster together: studies which have examined the intercorrelations between responses on different scales invariably reveal overlap and redundancy. The average intercorrelation between appraisal form scales which have been chosen on an intuitive, non-statistical basis seems to be around 0·35, although individual pairs of scales may of course be more or less closely associated. In view of the strong pressures to consistency in judgement and of the semantic links within some groups of scales, this overlap is theoretically quite acceptable, but it should be noted that on a practical level it can cause concern. Several of the dimensions used for recording judgements are likely to be fairly redundant, so that in practice the organization is obtaining more-or-less the same information in different guises. A possible way to overcome this is examined below (p. 217).

5. *The prediction of overall gradings.* A related question concerns the overall impression which an appraiser has of the subordinate he is judging. Almost every appraisal form requests an overall judgement about suitability and the extent to which this global evaluation is predictable from the separate scale values is a matter of considerable research interest. Laboratory studies of the combination of material were briefly reviewed on page 212, where it was concluded that a fairly straightforward averaging rule often accounts quite well for the data.

This appears to be the case for appraisal-form judgements too: correlations between the median of separate scale-judgements and overall gradings are usually found to be around +0·80. As another illustration of perceptual consistency this is theoretically quite reasonable, but we may once again question whether it is acceptable on a practical level. With such redundancy in an appraisal form it is very probable that some organizations could usefully reduce the rating process to a single overall judgement, at least in the case of some employee groups.

Applying research to remedy appraisal-form deficiencies

The previous section has drawn attention to several difficulties with the conventional rating-scale approach to appraisal. We have seen that judgements are likely to be close to the mid-points of the scales provided, that reliability of judgements hinges upon the use of relatively unambiguous items, that judges are likely to rehearse their responses to such an extent that the normal pressures towards consistency become exaggerated, and that this consistency extends to the association between scale scores and overall gradings. Is it possible to develop sets of scales which might avoid these difficulties?

One approach which is being adopted in some organizations is to treat the construction of an appraisal form more as a research question than as a matter for individual or committee suggestions.[3] Applying techniques originally developed by clinical psychologists (e.g. Bannister and Fransella, 1966) we can elicit from members of management dimensions of judgement which are directly relevant to the employees in question. These elicited dimensions can be applied on an experimental basis under instructions which encourage the use of a broad range of scale points. Checks for reliability can be incorporated, and the data obtained can then be submitted to principal component analyses. These statistical analyses can serve as a basis for selecting smaller sets of judgement dimensions which are relatively uncorrelated with each other and with the overall gradings.

Such a procedure will in a sense make more objective the subjective material which is recorded on an appraisal form. The development of scales of this kind should regularly be accompanied by careful training for the staff who will use the form; it is known that by these means reliability of judgement can be further enhanced (e.g. Stockford and Bissell, 1949).

3. It will be recalled that this discussion refers only to the use of rating scales in appraisal; decisions about other features of an appraisal scheme are considered in the next section.

Other features of an appraisal scheme

The previous section has concentrated on research into the impressions which are recorded on appraisal forms, but it was earlier pointed out that appraisal schemes have several other aims. One particularly important possibility is the use of appraisal forms as a means of informing an employee how successfully his superiors think he is carrying out his job. This possibility has generated quite a lot of research.

In some organizations it is customary for an appraisal form to be seen and countersigned by the person to whom it refers. (This is usually referred to as an 'open' reporting system.) In other cases the report form may not be made available in this way, but a manager may be required annually to conduct an 'appraisal interview' with each subordinate broadly along the lines of his report. The objective in both cases is to provide knowledge-of-results (as perceived by superiors) and to encourage an individual to perform his job more adequately.

Research has suggested that these objectives are not easily attainable by the techniques in question. Social interactions are usually conducted in a way which minimizes personal criticism and boosts the parties' self-esteem (e.g. Goffman, 1956), but the appraisal interview is established with the explicit purpose of breaking both of these norms. It is not surprising therefore that such encounters are likely to be uncomfortable and unwillingly joined (McGregor, 1957; K. H. Rowe, 1964).

One programme of research examined ninety-two appraisal interviews in a large company. In each case a research worker was present at the interview itself and questionnaires were completed before and after the appraisal period (Kay, Meyer and French, 1965; Meyer, Kay and French, 1964). It was clear that although the interviewers tried hard to provide criticism which was constructive the situation generated frequent threats to the subordinates' self-esteem. This was almost inevitable since it emerged that the bosses' impressions of their subordinates were consistently less favourable than those individuals' own self-perceptions. People being appraised reacted in a consistently defensive way, denying their bosses' suggestions or introducing alternative interpretations. The investigation included a follow-up study in which attempts were made to relate bosses' suggestions for improvement to actual work changes later. It emerged from this that there was a *negative* association between the number of threats or criticisms in the appraisal interview and the subsequent goal achievement of the subordinates. On the other hand the use of praise was uncorrelated with later changes.[4]

In general bosses think that appraisal interviews are more useful than subordinates consider them to be (Stewart, 1965) but it is not surprising that there are individual differences in attitudes towards the procedure. French, Kay and Meyer (1966) have suggested that personality differences in dependence-independence may be central here, but their results did not reach statistical significance. More clearly established is the fact that individuals who are fairly satisfied with the day-to-day supervisory performance of their boss are more likely to be satisfied with the way he handles the appraisal interview (Burke and Wilcox, 1969). And subordinates who perceive that they have some influence over the outcomes of an interview are more appreciative than those who have less opportunity for participation (French, Kay and Meyer, 1966).

Additional problems arise in those cases where completed appraisal forms are examined by subordinates. Stockford and Bissell (1949) have shown that open ratings are very significantly more favourable than those which are not seen by a subordinate, and we may view this in terms of conflicting communication goals. The completed appraisal form is a means of communicating a superior's impression of his subordinate, but it is evident that communications generally have to be tailored to fit the situation and the recipient. In so far as a 'true' representation of an impression can be attained, this usually has to be modified before it is communicated to others. We might suspect that a closed report is more an approximation to 'truth' than is an open one.

This is not to deny the importance of providing feedback and discussing a person's work performance with him. These goals can however be more readily attained if the feedback is more

4. There are difficulties of interpretation here, since the variation between individuals in their level of competence is likely to be a confounding factor. This will mediate the level of a superior's criticism and also a subordinate's achievement.

closely linked to behaviour – throughout the year as the situation arises rather than at annual intervals. The emphasis in many organizations is currently moving away from appraisal interviews as such towards work-planning and review sessions. Here the aim is to encourage subordinate participation in forward-looking goal-setting rather than merely to provide an opportunity for a superior to let a subordinate know where he stands. In this respect annual interviews are probably more valuable as a means of improving current effectiveness (objective 3, p. 213) than they are as a means of providing feed-back (objective 5, p. 213). For recording and communicating managers' impressions and expectancies about their staff (objectives 1, 2 and 4), some variety of appraisal form is quite essential.

THE SELECTION INTERVIEW

The second research area to be covered here is the selection interview. Psychologists have long been interested in this form of decision making and research trends have broadly paralleled those in the field of person perception more generally. On the one hand there has been concern for knowledge about the *accuracy* of the judgements which interviewers form, and on the other hand the *process* of interviewing has been examined to learn about important variables and their interactions. These approaches may be treated separately.

Interviewers' accuracy

Studies of the accuracy with which interviewers can predict later performance have generally been carried out within the framework of the approach to selection which in chapter 8 was characterized as 'test orientation'. Here the classical emphasis is on the correlation between a predictor and a criterion, and such a correlation is taken as an indication of the test's validity. In the selection interview field most reports and commentaries have stressed how small are the validity coefficients obtained: the modal figure is probably somewhere between 0·20 and 0·30. Yet this value should be set against the average validity coefficient of the supposedly more 'objective' psychological tests in occupational prediction. This also turns out to be between 0·20 and 0·30 (Ghiselli, 1966, p. 125). So it might be assumed in so far as we can make a general statement that the selection interview is not significantly less valid than the test.

But can we make a general statement? The evidence from research into interviewing is notable for its confusion and inadequate empirical foundations; and reviews by Mayfield (1964) and Ulrich and Trumbo (1965) make it clear that cheerful overall conclusions about validity are in reality no more justified than are gloomy ones. The data on which summary interpretations have to be based are drawn from a remarkably heterogeneous range of situations. In some research settings the interviews lasted an hour or so, but in many others ten minutes was usual. Some validity studies have even been reported of interviews lasting under three minutes. In some reported cases the interview was quite unstructured whereas in other settings it was structured to the extent of being in effect an orally-administered questionnaire (possibly containing a mere eight items). Some studies relied on single interviewers but others employed a panel of people; in some situations the interviewers were experienced and trained, yet others made do with untrained assistants. Some interviewers had no prior information about the candidates, whereas others were previously allowed to study biographical material, written references and other forms of background evidence.

In addition to these variations in actual procedures we should also note the wide differences between criteria studied. Job success has of course been the most common follow-up measure, but results from studies predicting training performance or more particular features of behaviour (e.g. Crissy, 1952) have sometimes been combined in discussion with data about this main criterion. As chapter 8 made clear, the adequacy of a criterion measure is often as problematic as the accuracy of a predictor. A further problem of interpretation arises from the fact that investigations have been carried out at several organizational levels and in very different functions. This is of course very desirable, but it has resulted in an unhealthy willingness to treat as comparable the prediction of success on the part of such varied people as students, manual workers, army officers, drivers, salesmen, secretaries, psychiatric patients and engineers.

It would seem essential that psychologists in their search for generalizations do not extend their net as widely as this. A general statement about the predictive validity of a one-hour semi-structured interview carried out by trained professional interviewers who are predicting managerial success in production jobs would be worthy of attention. But a general statement about 'the validity of the interview' based on evidence of the kind presently available is one which verges on the meaningless.

The approach which in chapter 8 was labelled 'decision orientation' is likely to be more fruitful here than is a mere concentration on validity coefficients. The value of an interview arises partly from other sources – to inform a candidate about the job, to answer his queries, to learn about his idiosyncratic, non-standard features, or even to persuade him to continue with a firm application for the post. And the interview is most usefully seen as only one of several selection components. It may be employed to yield inferences about particular attributes (social skill, perhaps) whereas other devices (a relevant aptitude test or a written reference, for instance) might be preferable in forecasts about other characteristics or behaviours.[5] Furthermore, interviews may be required to play quite different roles on different occasions – perhaps initial screening in one case and the final selection stage in another.

Such an approach implies that research into accuracy has to shift its attention away from validity coefficients *per se* to examine different forms of value in different decision-making situations. This move is well illustrated by the work of Mayfield, Carlson and their colleagues who have developed procedures for incorporating several types of interview into a general framework which also includes objective measures and work records (Life Insurance Agency Management Association, 1968).

The interviewing process

These same investigators have also contributed significantly to the second line of research which was noted earlier – the process of interviewing itself. Work in this field may be reviewed under three overlapping headings – the interviewer, the interviewee and their interactive relationship.

5. An illustration of how this can work successfully in practice is given by Grant and Bray (1969).

The interviewer. Research into the way an interviewer processes information about a candidate constitutes a special case of research into person perception more generally. As such it might be viewed within the framework discussed at the beginning of the chapter and summarized in Figure 10.1 (p. 210). It was noted at that point that a central research question concerns the nature of the attributive dimensions which a judge employs in a particular setting. We need here to concentrate on techniques for eliciting the dimensions of judgement, and although much work of this kind has been reported none of it appears to have been conducted in a selection interview setting. More usual here are studies which specify for the interviewer a set of rating scales and which involve factor analyses of his reactions. Interview work of this kind needs to be supplemented by research designed to allow interviewers more freedom in generating their own judgement dimensions.

Turning from the Attributive Component of judgement to the Expectancy Component, we come upon another research topic which is in need of development. The Expectancy Component is here represented by the predictions about a candidate which are made as part of an interviewer's judgement. There appear to be no published studies of interviewing which specifically examine this feature, but its obvious practical and theoretical significance make it clear that research progress is to be expected. A third feature of judgement which was isolated at the beginning of the chapter is the Affective Component. This is partly represented in the interview situation by the accept/reject decision which is taken, and several investigations have been carried out into the way this decision is predictable from particular attributive judgements.

As was mentioned earlier such a combination process is often adequately accounted for in terms of a weighted averaging model. However the adequacy of any model naturally depends on which attributive judgements are used as a basis of the test: if these are not salient to the interviewer it is unrealistic to seek strong predictions of overall acceptability from individual attributions. Hakel, Dobmeyer and Dunnette (1970) have shown that information seems to be combined in a manner which has been described as linear (p. 212), but that significant configural effects also occur. These imply that a particular cue may be weighted differently on different occasions, depending on the other cues which are available. Studies in other areas (e.g. Goldberg, 1970; Slovic, 1969) yield similar interpretations though the degree of importance of the configural process is not yet clearly specified.

An ancillary question concerns the relative contribution made by the candidate's appearance and his other characteristics. Carlson (1967a, 1969) has indicated that appearance has much less influence on a selection decision than has descriptive information about an applicant, but this importance ratio presumably hinges to some extent on the judgement which is being made. Non-verbal cues are for instance likely to be particularly important in inferences about an interviewee's nervousness or his social behaviour.[6]

As Figure 10.1 illustrates, judgements made during a perceptual encounter feed back into a memory store and are available to influence subsequent judgements. There have been several investigations into the way this operates during selection interviews, and it is clear that implicit decisions are usually made early in the encounter. Springbett (1958) noted that the outcome of the great majority of interviews was settled within two or three minutes, and it appears that the usual sequence of events is for the interviewer to form an initial impression (based partly on the completed application form) and to look for confirmation of this impression. Thereafter he is normally set to select mainly consonant information about the candidate, or he may 'switch off' altogether and merely complete a ritual which is formally supposed to continue for some time.

There is however an interesting difference between interviewers' sets for positive and negative information about a candidate. It seems that the most persistent set is to select negative information (that which implies rejection). This is plausible in the light of the interviewer's regular need to reject most of the applicants and to select only a small proportion of the original sample.[7] It is apparent

6. Research into this question soon meets methodological problems of equating the 'amount' of verbal and non-verbal information which is made available to a judge. To compare a large quantity of descriptive material with a limited visual input can bias the results considerably. It may be that a general answer to the question of relative importance is logically impossible.

7. A related point is connected with the knowledge-of-results which an interviewer obtains. In practice he rarely learns about the outcomes of his work since follow-up checks are infrequently made. But in general he is more

that an early implicit decision to reject an applicant is more resistant to change in the light of subsequent information than is an implicit decision to accept him (Bolster and Springbett, 1961; Springbett, 1958). Carlson and Mayfield (1967) have shown that negative decisions are more reliable (between interviewers and over time) as well as being more readily made.

This aspect of Stored Stimulus Person Information and perceptual set has also been studied in terms of 'primacy' and 'recency'. Many laboratory experiments on person perception in general have tried to ascertain whether primacy effects ('first impressions count most') are more important than recency effects, or whether neither influence is predominant. Much of this work is of a very artificial kind, and attempts to extend conclusions about primacy to real-life settings are unwise (c.f. Warr and Knapper, 1968, ch. 6). As we have seen the interviewer's set to negative material is likely to overwhelm any serial-order effects of the kind found in the laboratory, where judges are likely to be passive recipients rather than active perceivers. In practice this means that primacy effects occur in interviews when the implicit decision is a negative one, but that a recency effect is more possible when unfavourable information is preceded by favourable material (Carlson, 1971).

The context in which a judgement is made is another feature incorporated in Figure 10.1. As far as interviewer judgements are concerned, it is obvious that such contextual features as the general standard of applicants and the number of places to be filled will affect a decision (Carlson, 1967b). More interestingly it emerges that an interviewer who has as his frame of reference a group of several applicants is likely to be more reliable and more cautious than one who has to decide about a single candidate (Carlson, 1968). Another contextual variable is the sequence in which applicants are interviewed. P. M. Rowe (1967) reported data suggesting that an interviewer would be subject to contrast effects, in that (for instance) an average candidate coming after several extremely good ones would be judged as below-average. Later work (e.g. Carlson, 1970; Hakel, Ohnesorge and Dunnette,

likely to be castigated for a bad recommendation than he is to be praised for a good one; his bias is therefore likely to be to reject rather than to accept too many applicants.

1970) has, however, shown that contrast effects are trivial even in experimental conditions established to encourage them.

This disparity between outcomes raises again the irrelevance of much laboratory research. Rowe's experiment required introductory psychology students to rate 103 sets of six adjectives in terms of likeableness as a friend. Both Carlson and Hakel and his colleagues were able to investigate managers who were professionally responsible for selection interviews but both studies were restricted to written descriptions of hypothetical job candidates. The difficulties of 'live' research in this area are obvious and the latter studies might be acceptable as compromise solutions; but conclusions about selection interviews which derive entirely from the scale ratings of undergraduate students in the laboratory are in general quite unwarranted.

Turning to individual differences in perceptual activities we may note that the Stable Characteristics of an interviewer (his age, background, personality, and so on) are represented in Figure 10.1 as potentially influencing both the Input Selector and the Processing Centre. Detailed research findings from interview studies are not yet available but several promising lines of research have been opened up. It is clear for instance that selection officers are likely to differ in their notions of the ideal candidate (e.g. Hakel, Hollmann and Dunnette, 1970). Interviewers who operate by closely structuring their encounters are likely to show more between-judge consistency than those preferring unstructured interviews (Carlson, Schwab and Heneman, 1970). (This does of course not necessarily imply that they are more accurate.) Interviewer consistencies also extend to their willingness to make 'accept' decisions: the percentage of candidates accepted by each of a sample of personnel selection officers on three different occasions has been reported to remain fairly constant (P. M. Rowe, 1963). The correlates of these individual consistencies have yet to be explored; so far we at least know that amount or type of interviewing experience do not appear to be influential factors (Carlson, 1967b).

It is also apparent that different items of information are selected on different occasions and by different interviewers (e.g. Mayfield, 1964), and that different weightings are employed in processing the material that is selected (e.g. Hakel, Dobmeyer and

Dunnette, 1970). Yet we are still uncertain about the way these differences are associated with other variables, and progress here must be awaited.

The interviewee. The studies described in the previous section were selected to illustrate within the framework of Figure 10.1 the perceptual processes of the person who is conducting a selection interview. An alternative research approach is to concentrate upon the candidate who is being interviewed, and to inquire into his perceptual experiences.

Only a limited amount of work of this type is available. One relevant study is by Alderfer and McCord (1970), who examined how candidates evaluated different interviewer styles. It is perhaps not surprising that supportive, interested behaviour on the part of an interviewer was appreciated, but as the authors point out this can be important in those employment situations where applicants are scarce so that acceptable candidates have to be encouraged to pursue their initial enquiries

The interactive relationship. Finally we may turn to studies of the social interactions which take place during a selection interview. Much work carried out by social psychologists into small group processes (e.g. Cartwright and Zander, 1970; Gordon and Gergen, 1968; Mann, 1969) is of course relevant here. One important feature which distinguishes the interview from many other forms of social interaction is however the asymmetrical role relationship which exists: the interviewee is in general dependent upon the interviewer's behaviour so that he mainly has to follow the guidelines which the latter lays down.

Some research into social interaction has concentrated on the non-verbal signals which serve to communicate feelings and to synchronise behaviour. Features such as physical proximity, body orientation, facial expressions, gestures, pauses and eye movements are potent sources of information about a person. Work in this field has been summarized by Argyle (1967; 1969), Duncan (1969) and Sommer (1967), and one illustration will have to suffice here.

This is the pattern of *visual* interaction which takes place during an interview. Two people engaged in conversation look at each other on average between 30 and 60 per cent of the time; for the rest of an encounter they look somewhere to the side. These movements of a person's eyes are partly used to control the pattern of verbal interaction, so that a person starting to talk looks at the other but then looks away as he continues speaking. From time to time during his utterance he looks back briefly, but as he comes to the end he looks at the other person more steadily to indicate that he may now take over. Individual and situational differences in looking behaviour have been studied; it is of some interest to students of the interview that a steady gaze is often felt to communicate both interest in the other person and an attempt to assert superiority.

Research of this kind is obviously important to increase our understanding of the selection interview process, and further developments will be valuable. Other studies have measured the proportions of an interview during which the interviewer and the candidate are speaking. It emerges that on the whole interviewers are likely to talk more than are candidates, and that this difference is especially marked in cases where the interviewer decides to accept an applicant (C. W. Anderson, 1960). It seems probable that this arises partly out of the implicit decisions which tend to be made early in the encounter (see p. 224). More detailed studies have applied content analysis techniques to the interaction. Sydiaha (1961) reports that an interviewer is more likely to exhibit positive social-emotional behaviour (measured in terms of Bales's (1950) category system) in cases where the candidate is accepted than when he is rejected.[8]

Another promising line of investigation has examined how the topic under discussion (a candidate's previous employment, or his education for instance) influences such variables as length and reaction time of utterance. Questions with obvious face validity are likely to elicit more prompt and longer replies than are other enquiries (Matarazzo *et al.*, 1970).

To conclude this discussion of the selection interview, it is appropriate to note that the two themes which have been developed

8. As Ulrich and Trumbo (1965) point out, these results carry the paradoxical implication that an observer can better predict the outcome of an interview by studying the interviewer than he can by recording what the candidate does!

are not as independent of each other as this presentation might suggest. Research into interviewer accuracy and into the interviewing process have so far mainly been carried out by people of different inclinations and professional backgrounds. As both types of work progress we may anticipate a fruitful integration both of findings and of practical recommendations.

SUMMARY

Two forms of organizational judgements about people have been examined in the context of a general framework of person perception. This perceptual process is seen to involve the selection of information from the environment and from memory and its transformation into judgements which embody attributive, expectancy and affective components. Transitory and more stable differences between perceivers influence the process, which is seen as a continuous, closed-loop activity.

Appraisal schemes were viewed in terms of several organizational objectives. Research into the judgements made by appraisers has concentrated on variability, reliability, inter-judge differences and relationships between scales and overall gradings. Another main research area is the appraisal interview itself, and research has suggested ways of increasing the effectiveness of this encounter.

Studies of the selection interview can be classified in terms of the accuracy of the interviewer and of the process of interviewing itself. Research into accuracy presents a very confused picture, but studies of the process in terms of the interviewer, the interviewee and their interactions have advanced considerably in recent years.

FURTHER READING

In addition to references cited in the chapter, there are several useful books about appraisal. *Staff Reporting and Staff Development* by E. Anstey (Allen & Unwin, 1969) is a general introduction with an emphasis on British civil service techniques. Two American texts are *The Appraisal Interview* by N. R. F. Maier (Wiley, 1958) and R. Fear's *The Evaluation Interview* (McGraw-Hill, 1958).

Practical hints on interviewing are provided by E. Sidney and M. Brown in *The Skills of Interviewing* (Tavistock, 1961) and by G. Shouksmith in *Assessment Through Interviewing* (Pergamon,

1968). A rather disjointed account of some early research appears in E. C. Webster's *Decision Making in the Employment Interview* (McGill University Press, 1964), and a general review of interviewing studies (mainly in fields other than selection) is presented by C. F. Kannell and R. L. Kahn in chapter 15 of G. Lindzey and E. Aronson (eds.) *Handbook of Social Psychology*, volume 2 (Addison-Wesley, 1968).

11
Decision Making Since the Computer

Max Sime and Michael White

Many chapters of this book deal with decision making in one guise or another; indeed some psychologists would even maintain that 'decision making' and 'psychology' were broadly synonymous. Nevertheless a relatively circumscribed subject-matter has emerged over the past twenty years which has an undisputed right to the title. The authors outline this topic in terms of two main activities – information search and information integration. They contrast models which are more normative with those that are more descriptive; and throughout the chapter they examine the role of the computer, both as a research tool and as an aid to the decision-making process.

The study of decision making has a long and distinguished pedigree, originating in the eighteenth century with Daniel Bernoulli's deliberations about gambling and business choices. Significant contributions have been made by mathematicians, economists, statisticians and political theorists, and in the last twenty years or so the topic has taken its place as an important part of psychology (Arrow, 1963; Edwards, 1954; Edwards and Tversky, 1967). Yet it is a very large topic, similar in breadth to 'thinking', 'behaviour', 'information processing' and 'judgement', so that to say of someone that he is investigating decision making does not really delimit his activities at all closely.

In this chapter we shall first examine in very general terms what is common to the many studies of decision making, but we cannot go on to detail all the varied approaches which have been attempted. Instead we shall place our emphasis in one area where exciting developments are particularly likely to occur – the role of computers in decision making. It is only twenty-five years ago that the first practical computer was built. Since then there has been a tremendous rate of development, not only in numerical calculation, but also in using computers for non-numerical symbol manipulation, for controlling the activities of machines, for simulating complex processes and for implementing models of real or hypothetical environments. Because of these developments computers offer significant advantages to a psychologist studying decision making. On the one hand he can use them to analyse complex psychological processes and so to increase his theoretical understanding; and on the other hand their practical application in organizations may be expected to yield changes in the characteristics of day-to-day decisions. The theoretical and the practical possibilities will both be explored in this chapter.

THE MAIN FEATURES OF DECISION MAKING

We describe behaviour as involving a decision only when the situation has certain characteristics. In the first place there must be some element of choice: a number of alternative actions must be open to the decision maker and he must have to select from these. Secondly, the alternative actions must have some consequences, so that each option confronting the decision maker must map on to a set of outcomes. Finally, the outcomes must (if the decision is to be of any significance) be mapped on to the utility domain of the decision maker; each potentially achievable state must be worth something to him.

This characterization of a decision situation is close enough to the truth for most people to give qualified assent to it if pressed, but it is at a very general level. To introduce content into the description we have to make some specific assumptions which may be more questionable. We might for instance assume that the decision maker assigns probabilities to each of the outcomes he has in mind, or that he evaluates all the outcomes on a single scale of utility so that they can more easily be compared. We might further assume that the outcome which has the greatest expected pay-off (probability multiplied by utility perhaps) is the one which will be chosen.

As we shall describe below many distinguished studies have been carried out on the basis of these very assumptions. Yet they seem to imply a rather limited view of a complex psychological process. If the decision maker in fact has such a perfect model in his head (one where all the possible outcomes are known and have clear probabilities and values attached to them) then he has no decision to make – merely an action to perform. By applying a standard processing routine he has already attained the state to which his decision making efforts are directed, and there is very little for the psychologist to study.

Yet we know that real-life decisions are often extremely difficult to reach, and we might expect that people cannot usually apply a straightforward 'probability-times-utility' routine. The reasons why this routine is often inapplicable are important ones: they point to a set of assumptions which characterize a somewhat different approach to decision making. These other assumptions emphasize the importance of actual and perceived uncertainty. A decision is called for only when some uncertainty exists, so that we might argue that making a decision is a matter of reducing uncertainty. When the uncertainty has been removed, a decision is no longer needed – it has already been made. The decision does not occur at the end of this process, in a sense it *is* the process.

The uncertainty with which a decision maker has to deal is of two kinds – objective uncertainty existing in the environment and subjective uncertainty arising from the fact that he is incompletely informed. In any complex situation some relationships between components will be unspecifiable. This applies even if relationships between pairs of variables are deterministic (having probabilities of zero or unity), since even so the consequences of large numbers of components in combination become very difficult to trace. Where some consequences of actions are themselves probabilistic, the assessment of probabilities in interaction becomes even more difficult. In many complex situations, then, even the best-informed judge will find prediction difficult.

But judges are in practice often far from well-informed, and this leads on to the second form of uncertainty – that which exists within the man's model of his environment. A decision maker may not be aware of all the alternative actions open to him, he may not have considered all the outcomes of those alternatives which he has recognized, or he may not be able to assign precise probability values where these are required. Before he can reach a decision he has to acquire or assume a great deal of information. In this sense decision making is a process of *information search* as much as of *information integration*.

This distinction provides the main theme of this section. We have rather overdrawn the divergence between approaches, but broadly we can view decision making in terms of two sets of assumptions.

One set concentrates upon the way a person *integrates information*: probabilities and values are assigned and combined in specified ways. This way of viewing decision making is a narrow one, and we prefer the second perspective, in terms of how someone *searches for information* and procedures which may help him resolve his uncertainty.

NORMATIVE MODELS OF DECISION MAKING

Let us now move on to examine some of the research into decision making which has been reported by psychologists. Many laboratory studies have been given force and direction by specific models which have been applied to the process of decision making. These models may loosely be classed as either 'normative' or 'descriptive'.

In many fields of investigation, subjects' behaviour is examined against a model of what in some sense the behaviour 'ought' to be like. It is assumed that people's activities are at least sufficiently similar to the account provided by the model for a comparison between behaviour and the model to be worthwhile. When a conceptualization is used in this way as a standard for comparison we might refer to it as 'a normative model'. Other accounts of a process are more clearly 'descriptive' – their aim is a precise specification of what a person does rather than suggestions about what he should do. We will return to descriptive models shortly, but in this section three illustrations of the normative approach are presented.

Bayes's theorem. Consider an apparently simple experiment. There are two bags of poker chips. The chips are known to be of only two colours, and there are different proportions of the two colours in the two bags. These proportions are also known to the subject in advance. One of the two bags is picked at random. The subject is then allowed to look at the counters, one at a time, and on this evidence to judge the probability of it being one particular bag out of the two. A particular problem of this kind is presented in Figure 11.1, and you may like to have a quick try at getting the answer yourself.

The problem was in fact initially described by Edwards, Lindman and Phillips (1965). They suggest that the experiment, for all its apparent simplicity, represents the essence of a sequential decision process which is quite prominent in the real world. A scientist, a businessman, or a detective will rarely make a decision of any importance on the basis of a single item of evidence. Instead, he will accumulate information until he becomes sufficiently confident to choose between the various alternatives which he is considering.

What is particularly interesting about this kind of situation is that the 'best' decision can be precisely calculated by means of

Can you estimate probabilities?

Given these observations:

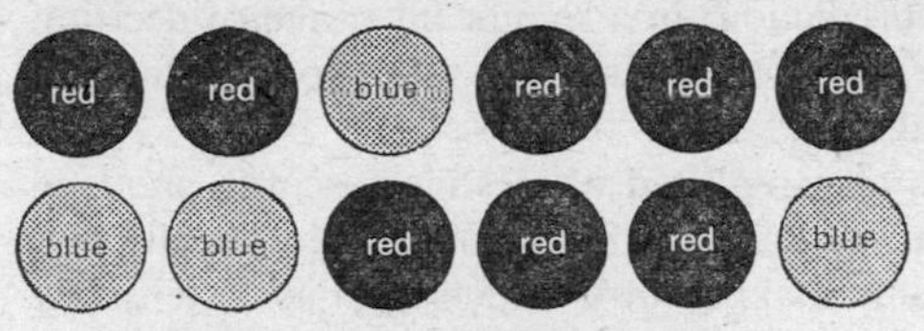

What is the probability that the 12 counters were drawn from Bag A rather than Bag B?

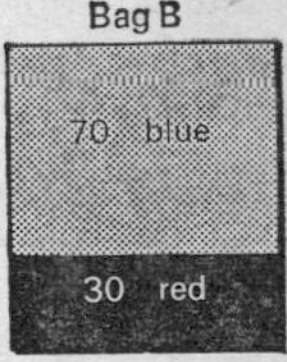

Figure 11.1 Can you estimate probabilities? Given these observations: red red blue red red red blue blue red red red blue. What is the probability that the 12 counters were drawn from Bag A rather than Bag B? See text for answer. (From Edwards, Lindman and Phillips, 1965)

Bayes's Theorem, so that a subject's estimate can be compared with this normative solution. (Those who wish to find out how Bayes's Theorem can be applied to such problems might examine the paper by Edwards, Lindman and Phillips, 1965.) By the theorem, the probability of the sample coming from bag A is about 0·97. But most people are much more cautious in their estimates than this, typically deciding that the probability is somewhere around 0·75.

Edwards and his colleagues report a variety of experiments comparing subjects' behaviour against the normative Bayes's Theorem (see also Edwards and Tversky, 1967; Phillips and Edwards, 1966), and conclude that people do adjust their estimates as new evidence becomes available but that they do so far more cautiously than the evidence justifies. This tendency is known as 'conservatism'. In the present context we are concerned not so much with the precise details of conservatism as with the general point that its existence is usually indicated in terms of a deviation from the normative prediction: in a significant range of decision situations people are more conservative than they 'ought' to be in a statistically optimal sense.

Audley (1967) has also reported interesting research showing ways in which people's decisions differ from the theoretically best solution. One decision making task which he has extensively explored is the 'expanded judgement'. Typically, two different classes of stimuli are presented, one stimulus at a time, and the subject judges which class is the more numerous after each presentation. As time goes on, he accumulates more evidence and should be able to modify his estimate. One version of his experiment required subjects to make a guess before any evidence had been presented to them. Audley found that a longer accumulation of evidence was required to change that guess to a new conclusion than was needed to arrive at the same conclusion when the guess had not previously been made. Similarly, 'runs' of evidence (where several successive items of information are all the same) are given undue weight and their effect is hard to neutralize. (See also Audley, 1970.)

The experiments were not limited to artificial tasks. One used evidence from an actual court case, but this evidence was presented experimentally in two different sequences. The sequences had a large influence on whether the mock verdict was 'guilty' or 'not guilty'. Again, the employment decisions made by personnel officers were studied under controlled conditions. It was found that the provisional employment decisions reached after studying an application form, and taking first sight of the candidate, were excellent predictors of the final employment decisions made after carrying out the complete interview; the later evidence either added little of value or was largely discounted. It is interesting that this conclusion was also reached in the studies described in chapter 10, although the research workers cited there have quite a different methodological and statistical orientation.

Dynamic programming. Another set of normative models derives from dynamic programming techniques. These provide a means of mapping a *sequence* of activities so that a choice made at one point affects the choices which are then available. They are primarily used to yield an optimal solution to problems of sequential choice.

Figure 11.2 represents a problem which is amenable to this kind of approach. Elithorn, Jagoe and Lee (1966) allowed subjects thirty seconds to find a solution, and the solutions were compared with the results of several relatively simple mathematical algorithms. The interest of these workers was primarily in the field of perceptual skills, but Amnon Rapoport (1969) pointed out that choosing a sequence of points in the maze can be considered as a multistage decision task which is analogous to many important business decisions. He argued that although an optimal solution to problems of this kind can in principle be found by the application of dynamic programming models, an individual is in practice unlikely to use such a computationally complex procedure, especially if he is working against time. Instead, suggests Rapoport, he will have some 'suboptimal strategy', in which for instance he may consider only a section of the problem at a time. In Rapoport's experiment one-ninth of subjects achieved optimal performance, while a further one-third produced solutions which were exactly predicted by one or another of a small set of sub-optimal models derived from mathematical programming.

Some earlier experiments by Amnon Rapoport (1966; 1967) indicate that the dynamic programming model and its various sub-optimal variations give a better fit to decision-making behaviour as the tasks become more realistically difficult. The 1966 paper reported a task where the subjects tried to minimize costs in a simplified business game, with computer-calculated feedback given after each decision point. A modified dynamic programming

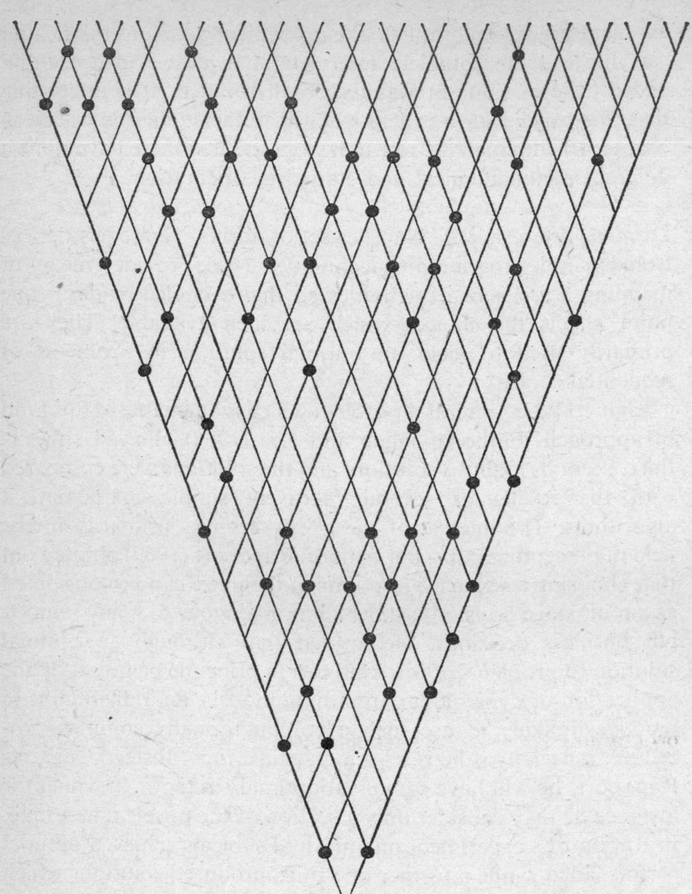

Figure 11.2 The Elithorn visual maze (from Elithorn, Jagoe and Lee, 1966). The problem – finding the route from bottom to top right which passes through most dots, without doubling back – has a similar structure to many business decision problems

model, which took account of feedback and looked ahead only over a limited number of trials, gave a close fit to the actual quantitative decisions made by one group of individuals, although another group, which appeared to use feedback in a different way, was not accounted for. The 1967 study is based on a more complicated and explicit business game. The subjects performed close to the theoretical optimum, and the deviations from this could be explained as an intelligent interpretation of the experimental situation. For instance, they guessed that there would be limited series of plays and so, cunningly, ran down their stock levels progressively to cut down their stockholding costs.

The theory of games. Another normative mathematical model is provided by the theory of games, which deals with decision making where the choices of different individuals affect one another. A discussion of the theory of games is outside the scope of this chapter (see the suggestions for further reading at the end), but the introduction to the subject by Anatol Rapoport (1966) has an emphasis which is specially relevant to the present section. He argues that the most fruitful situations for psychological experiment are those where the observed behaviour departs from the 'rational' choices prescribed by games theory. It is these differences which are likely to give clues and insights into the nature of decisions.

The fruitfulness of this approach is illustrated in a study by Messick (1967). The experiment revolved around a two-person zero-sum game: that is, for every amount won by one person's play, the same amount would be lost by the other person. In this case one of the players was not in fact a person, but a computer programmed to play a particular strategy. This strategy is an adaptive one (it varies according to what the opponent has done), and it can be defeated by a cyclical counter-strategy, which exploits the regularities in the computer's play. Of course, a more cunningly programmed computer (or a real human player) might then switch to a different strategy and turn the tables. Game theory affords a different approach: it prescribes what is known as the 'minimax' strategy as the best possible defence against one's opponent, irrespective of what strategy this opponent may employ.

Human players did defeat the computer soundly in this game. But they did so without using either the minimax or cyclical counter-strategy. Messick attributes their excellent performance to their tendency to play two much simpler component strategies:

Strategy 1: If you win a play 'stay' (repeat the choice).

Strategy 2: If you lose, assume your opponent will 'stay' and play the best available move on that assumption.

Although these strategies are based only on the previous single play and therefore involve little load on the subject's memory, they capitalize on the computer's adaptive strategy almost as well as the theoretically optimal counter-strategy would. Intuitively, it seems more likely that people use strategies like these for sifting information than that some analogue of a mathematical model is involved.

Computers and normative models

Although there is no logically necessary association between the study of normative models and the employment of computers, the two are likely to go together. At one level the computer is invaluable in the construction of complex mathematical models and in the speedy calculation of predictions. Experimental work in this field has advanced considerably as psychologists have become more familiar with computers and have had more ready access to them.

Another way in which computers have contributed to work with normative decision making models is in providing 'experimental environments'. In the dynamic programming work for instance, the computer is used to generate a problem environment which changes continuously and realistically. Not only can a subject obtain rapid feedback about his actions, but in addition the computer can ensure that the environment changes adaptively – reacting meaningfully (and in line with a consistent strategy) to whatever the subject does.

Work with normative models of decision making has undoubtedly increased our understanding of the process. But there is a tendency for investigators to concentrate so hard on subjects' deviations from their chosen model that they do not examine other possibilities. Discussions by researchers in this area are likely to include remarks of the kind 'if only subjects were completely rational, they . . .' or 'if people were Bayesian, they . . .'. The impression is given that man is unfortunately limited by his poor memory or by his inability to process information quickly enough; if only these defects could be remedied all would be well – he would be rational, or Bayesian, or have other 'optimal' qualities. Yet other authors see no special advantage in setting up some model of rationality, and then measuring man's behaviour against it. They prefer a more open investigatory approach at this stage, trying to describe what people do rather than to test its rationality. Let us turn to this work now.

DESCRIPTIVE MODELS OF DECISION MAKING

Bruner, Goodnow and Austin (1956) have provided a most stimulating account of the procedures which people employ in developing abstractions or concepts. Typically these investigators presented subjects with concept-learning problems where each of several stimuli varied on several attributes. The subject had to find which attributes were the relevant ones and which values of the attributes defined the concept. Figure 11.3 illustrates the task.

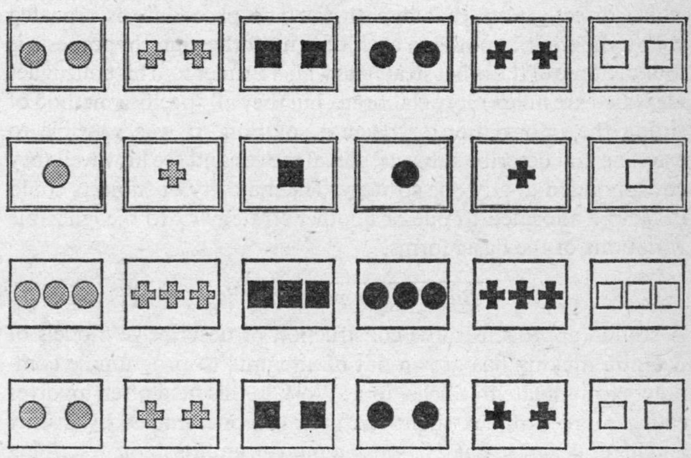

Figure 11.3 Finding the concept. The problem is to identify a concept (a combination of attributes) given only that particular instances are either positive or negative. The instances shown here are part of a set of 81 devised by Bruner, Goodnow and Austin (1956)

In one form of this experiment the subject had the complete array of information available to him from the outset and he was free to search among this array in any order he chose. In another variation the subject was fed stimuli one at a time and he could state his hypothesis about the concept at any stage. In each case the researchers recorded the trial-by-trial pattern of responding. They were more concerned to analyse the nature of intermediate steps than they were to provide summary statistics of performance such as the number of trials or time to solution.

From their analyses of what subjects did before they reached their final decision Bruner and his colleagues were able to develop some understanding of what strategies were being adopted. They defined strategies operationally in terms of 'regularities in decision making', and were careful that the particular strategies they examined were not derived on an *a priori* basis but by observation of subjects' actual responses.

One particularly simple strategy which they identified is 'successive scanning'. The subject in this case hypothesizes or guesses what the concept is, then picks out an item from the array which directly tests that hypothesis. The procedure is repeated with a different hypothesis each time until the right hypothesis is found. Some of the other strategies which Bruner and his colleagues identified are much more elaborate, but they all specify a method of sifting the information to reach a solution. It was possible to examine and describe subjects' actual moves and see how well they corresponded to any one strategy. The majority of subjects could in fact be allocated to one or another strategy or to recognizable variations of the basic forms.

Building computer models

A related approach to the construction of descriptive models of decision making has grown out of attempts to programme computers to simulate this behaviour. Work in this field often involves rather more complex situations than the one studied by Bruner and his colleagues, but it has in common an emphasis on describing what people do as they work through the varied stages of their decision making activities. Several programmes were written in the latter part of the 1950s which seemed to simulate human thinking. One of these proved theorems in symbolic logic, another solved problems in geometry, another played a good game of checkers, and so on. What is of particular interest here is not the capability of such programmes but the methods of analysing decision making which grew out of them. These methods have been presented elsewhere – in a famous paper by Newell, Shaw and Simon (1958), in a short book by Simon (1960), and in a more detailed discussion by Newell, Shaw and Simon (1962). We will not describe the results they obtained in their pioneering work but instead summarize the methods used. In the next section, we will move on to some applications of the methods which are probably less widely known.

Data collection. The first step in the Newell, Shaw and Simon method is to obtain 'verbal protocols' from people while they are engaged in solving a problem or making a decision. The protocol is a detailed record, usually captured by means of a tape recorder, of what the individual says he is doing while he is actually doing it. This carries a stage further the approach of Bruner, Goodnow and Austin in getting an external record of the search and hypothesis-testing processes in decision making.

Identifying information processes. The protocols, and any other evidence which is available, are studied to identify typical 'information processes'. An information process is any operation or sequence of operations which the individual uses in searching or manipulating the problem with which he is faced. As far as possible they are directly equated with the steps in the person's thinking-out-loud. For instance, information processes used in the Logic Theorist programme of Newell, Shaw and Simon (1958) include the normal logical devices of substitution and detachment, and these processes in turn make use of a sub-process of similarity comparisons. In fact Simon (1960, pages 22–24) stresses that no new or sophisticated processes have to be discovered to create a theory of complex decision making. What is required is a way of linking together processes which are already well known or are easy to find.

Flow charting and programming. The linking together is usually achieved by means of a computer programme. Such a programme is a set of completely specific instructions which can be executed by a computer. An abbreviated version of the programme is usually drawn as a flow-chart; this merely labels the information processes and shows their interrelationships. Each information process can be thought of as a sub-programme with its own defined sequence of instructions. Rules must also be defined which will govern the sequence in which the sub-programmes will be used when faced with particular types of problems, or at different stages of the decision process. This overall structure which links up the sub-programmes and controls their utilization and, sometimes, their modification is referred to as the 'executive programme'.

Testing and validation. The total programme embodies the final description of the decision processes, and this description can be submitted to a variety of tests of its adequacy. The programme can be run on a computer to see whether it 'works' in the sense that it produces an appropriate solution or decision. If so this demonstrates that the description is at least sufficient to account for some problem-solving or decision making behaviour. The validity of the description will depend on what range of problems or decisions it will handle, and the extent to which it also produced plausible intermediate steps on the way to its conclusion. Evidence of this kind is presented by Newell, Shaw and Simon (1958).

The executive. These studies illustrate how in a computer system a programme operating at a higher level than the rest can utilize other programmes to achieve an objective. It might identify the type of problem to be dealt with and then transfer control of the relevant operations to a subordinate programme. It might also arrange for the modification of sub-programmes and retain overall control of some form of learning process within these sub-programmes. Some psychologists see a fruitful analogy here with the organization of human cognitive processes. The idea of a hierarchical structure headed by an executive is a rich and intriguing one, and it has recurred in several guises throughout the development of psychology. Neisser (1967, p. 293) quotes Bartlett's observations that our ability to use experience selectively implies 'that an organism has somehow to acquire the ability to turn round upon its own "schemata" and to construct them afresh' (Bartlett, 1932, p. 206).

In advocating the fruitfulness of such concepts for psychology

Neisser suggests that many theorists have reacted against them for fear that they lead to infinite regress. If a high level controls a lower level what controls the high level and what in turn controls that? He points out that in a computing system there is a *highest* level. The analogy to be sustained soon faces the question of how the highest level rules themselves become organized. In the case of a computer system they were written by a programmer. In the case of a man either he was born with them or he learned them. The high level control in any learning artifact so far realized remains invariant through learning, but it is not clear that principle dictates this. What does seem clear is that work on the design of intelligent artifacts, including attempts to simulate human thought processes, will clarify our concepts of hierarchical control structures, and separate the boundaries of practice from those of principle.

Describing real-life decisions

The type of analysis described in the previous section is often referred to as an information-processing analysis. The investigator analyses what a person seems to be doing as he processes information to reach a decision; when the several stages and sub-goals are clear, the investigator creates a computer programme which basically is intended to replicate his description of subjects' behaviour. He then checks the output from his programme against observed behaviour to gain some indication of its adequacy.

This analytic technique has been applied in many areas of experimental, laboratory psychology, including problems in memory, language and concept learning. But one of its attractive features is that it is not limited to simplified, laboratory tasks. If anything, it seems to work better with apparently rough and informal decision processes than it does with highly exact and formal ones. Each of the three examples given in this section concerns the bread-and-butter decisions made by skilled professional people in their jobs.

Investment decisions of a trust officer. One of the most surprising, yet successful, applications of an information-processing analysis is Clarkson's study of the investment decisions of trust officers. This has been published in book form (Clarkson, 1962) and also in Cyert and March (1963a) as a chapter-length summary. The trust officer is a bank official specializing in the administration of trust funds. His decisions, leading to the purchasing of stocks, often involve large sums of money. In order to invest this money well, he must consider the financial needs of the client and a great variety of information about the economic situation. His task would normally be described as requiring a high level of skill and judgement.

The initial description which Clarkson proposed for analysing these investment decisions is of the same form as that of Newell, Shaw and Simon (1958). There is a *memory* containing the various types of information which need to be considered, there are *search procedures* and selection rules, which can be applied to the contents of the memory, and there are *decision rules* which determine the operation of the model and the final selection of the investments. In this case considerable effort goes into defining the decision rules, since these are akin to 'rules of thumb' developed by a trust officer rather than to general rules of logic.

The decision rules and search procedure were first investigated in detail through intensive analysis of verbal protocols. Clarkson then developed a computer programme to replicate the trust officer's behaviour. This programme is a lengthy one, and it is only possible here to pick out a few of its main features. One notable point is the use of simple binary rules to build up complex decisions. Another point which the programme illustrates is that complex information can be searched very economically if one has a small set of categories into which the information must finally be sorted. An example of this is shown in Figure 11.4. A wide range of information is available in memory concerning the beneficiary of the trust. However in the programme the *purpose* of the information is simply to determine which of four alternative investment policies should be pursued on behalf of the beneficiary, and these distinctions can be made on relatively simple considerations.

The trust investment programme is a delightful demonstration of how complex judgement can be analysed in terms of simple processes. The complexity resides in the organization of these simple processes into long and adaptable sequences of behaviour. But how well does the model work? It was tested by providing it with the same information as possessed by the trust officer,

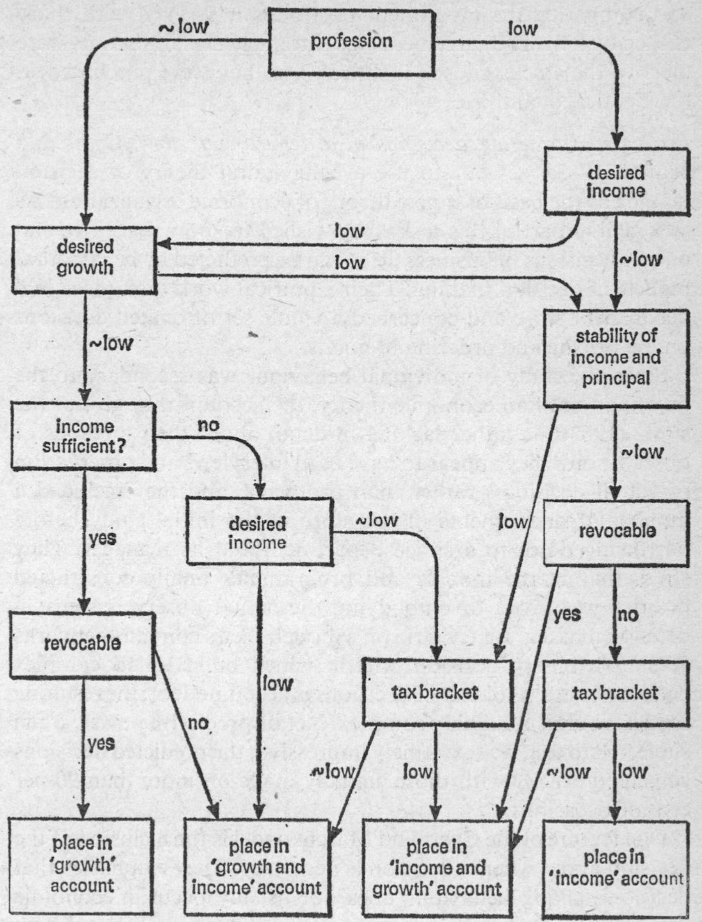

Figure 11.4 Clarkson's flow-chart analysis of how Trust Officers select and use information about the beneficiary of a trust to determine the investment policy. (From Cyert and March, 1963a)

and comparing the investment portfolios it selected with those chosen by him. The agreement was extremely close. Not only were most of the stocks chosen identical, but they were purchased in the identical quantities.

Pricing and ordering decisions in a department store. Cyert and March (1963a) set out to use a behavioural theory of decision making as the basis of a new theory of economic organization. As an essential part of this task, they wished to show that price and output decisions in business firms can be predicted by behavioural models of decision making. Their empirical work took place in a department store and concerned a whole set of related decisions on the pricing and ordering of goods.

Since the study of individual behaviour was secondary to the presentation of an economic theory, the account they give of the study (1963b) is rather lacking in detail about their methods of observation. They appear to have used interviews and observation of actual decisions, rather than protocols, and they included a number of departments of the store in the initial study before narrowing down to a single department and its manager. They stress that in the models and programmes finally constructed priority was given to embodying the actual observed steps in decision making. Like Clarkson's model, theirs contains networks of simple binary decision criteria which build up to complex decisions. As a whole set of decisions is accounted for, the resulting model is correspondingly complex. Yet its predictive power, when subjected to test, was extremely impressive; the predicted decisions coincided exactly with those actually made on more than 90 per cent of occasions.

One feature of the Cyert and March model is the inclusion of the decision about when a decision is necessary. They emphasize that decision-making behaviour does not usually occur in economic organizations unless it is triggered by some external stimulus or perceived problem. An example of such a stimulus is that an item in a department store is not selling. This triggers search activity until a sufficient explanation is identified. But so long as the merchandise is selling at an acceptable rate, no search activity will be commenced, and no new decisions will be taken concerning the item. This aspect of decision making can be seen to be extremely important when one considers a decision maker, such as a manager, who has many potential problems and must decide which ones to deal with at a given time. The flow of problems has been graphically described in studies by Marples (1967) in which individuals kept written notes of their activities. But the psychology of problem selection is still largely an unexplored territory, although two early theoretical discussions by Simon (1955, 1956) have suggested that it is a very general aspect of adaptive decision-making behaviour.

Employment decisions by a selection psychologist. A study by Smith (1968) shows how the information-processing analysis can be applied to employment decisions made by a psychologist using a battery of psychological tests. The methods used by Smith are the by now familiar ones: verbal protocols, construction of a flow chart and programme, building up the final judgements from sequences of simpler distinctions, then testing the decisions of the computer programme on specific cases, here against the judgements of a psychologist. Since the final decision could be one of four categories – accept, reject, accept at risk, or check for more information – there is a 25 per cent chance of the computer model being in agreement with the psychologist even if their decisions are unrelated. In fact the computer programme made the same decision as the psychologist in twenty-two out of twenty-four cases, and another psychologist awarded a 'mark' of 94 per cent for the correctness of the programme's evaluations.

Information search and integration

In the opening section of this chapter we drew attention to two separate perspectives on decision making. One of these we labelled the 'information integration' approach and the other 'information search'. We may now see how this dichotomy relates to our other conceptual distinction – between normative and descriptive models.

In fact there is at present quite a close fit here, although this is more an empirical than a logically necessary matter. The normative models which have been developed (in the light of Bayes's Theorem for instance) have tended to deal more with information integration than with search behaviour. This is understandable since probability theory has been developed by mathematicians and statisticians for many years and as a clearly-formulated set of combinatorial principles it gives rise to precise models against which to examine human performance.

On the other hand there are fewer logical models available for application to information search, and psychologists emphasizing this aspect of decision making have necessarily had to start more from scratch. In consequence they have tended to work with descriptive models of the kind we have outlined. It is important to note however that there is no logical objection to the generation of normative models of information search or descriptive models of information integration. An example of a normative model applied to information search is provided by Sayeki (1969), and further developments would be most valuable.

THE COMPUTER IN ORGANIZATIONAL DECISIONS

For psychologists the introduction of computer methods into organizations presents an added dimension of complexity and excitement to the study of decision making. Although computers are at present still mainly employed in industry and commerce as very rapid numerical calculators (dealing with wages, stock control and other complex but routine processes), they will gradually exert increasing influence in the less routine field of managerial decision making.

Much of the literature on this topic is of a very rarified normative kind. As Stagner (1969) notes, 'it sets forth, with impressive mathematical treatment, the decision processes in which corporation executives should engage if a number of quite unrealistic assumptions can be met. The articles have been characterized, perhaps unkindly, as our modern version of "how many angels can dance on the head of a pin?"' (p. 1). Stagner himself shows the way in which important psychological processes of group cohesiveness, competitiveness and managerial style are major determinants of what actually is decided (Stagner, 1969); these processes have no place in orthodox economic theories of the firm.

We cannot here examine all the features of decision making as it occurs in social and organizational settings. Important treatments have been provided by Clarkson (1968), Collins and Guetzkow (1964), Cyert and March (1963a), Dion, Baron and Miller (1971), Kogan and Wallach (1967), Simon (1960) and others. Our focus will be on the role of computers in this activity. First we will note some studies examining the effects of computers on organizational decision making up to the present; in our final section we shall turn to the future, and speculate a little about how computers will become increasingly used in their capacity as decision aids.

Brady (1967) collected information, primarily by interview methods, on the effects of computer methods on the decision making of top-level managers. His broad conclusion is that computers have had only a slight effect so far, but he observed some isolated cases where the effect was large, and noted several changes in decision-making processes:

Situations were more extensively analysed.

A wider range of alternative solutions was considered.

The consequences of decision alternatives were worked out more fully.

A study by Stewart (1971) used a longitudinal method of investigation, data being collected by repeated interviews and by observation while the computer method was being introduced. The main consequences for decision making, observed in a large company developing the use of mathematical models for long-term planning and policy analysis, included the following:

The scope of planning was increased, e.g. by considering a longer time-period.

There was a wider search for alternatives.

Methods of evaluating risk in decisions were modified.

Assumptions about the decision situation were quantified and revised.

Decision rules, and the goals which underlay them, were questioned and in some cases altered.

There was increased integration of decision activities across organizational groups.

A conceptual scheme, relating these and other possible types of change to underlying problems in the activities of organizations, has been proposed by Stewart and White (1971). They emphasize that there is not any invariant effect from the use of computer methods. The actual effects depend upon the way managers apply the methods to the problems, and indeed upon the characteristics of those problems themselves. For instance, the type of effects which may take place when computers are applied to a problem of detailed control in an organization are different from those which may be observed when a problem of long-term planning is being tackled. From a psychological viewpoint, it is not hard to put forward hypotheses why there should be such differences. For example, the computer's contribution to a problem of detailed control may be largely through providing a large and reliable 'memory' for large amounts of information; while for long-term planning, it may provide the computational power to deal with long sequences of interacting variables. One possibility mentioned by Stewart and White is that computer systems can fail due to a mismatch between the computer method and the problem to which it is being applied. In one of the cases presented by Stewart (1971), such a mismatch seems to have occurred. The problem appeared to be one of developing a consistent plan or strategy for a production plant, but the method applied was one of detailed control. Management attention became narrowly focussed on detailed control problems, with the result that strategic decision making actually deteriorated.

Computers as decision aids

We now look in a little more detail at the ways in which computers can be expected to affect the decision-making process in the future, and how the psychologist can be expected to contribute. Broadly speaking, computer methods may enable decision makers to adopt different strategies for information search and information integration. These changes interest the psychologist in two different ways. First, from a *theoretical* viewpoint, he can gain understanding of decision-making processes by observing how they change when the computer is introduced as a catalyst. Second, from an *applied research* viewpoint, he can actually assist in the changes by using psychological knowledge as a contribution to the design of total man-computer systems.

One function, which computers have already carried out on a

large scale, and which is likely to continue in the future, is the collection, sorting and aggregation of large masses of routine information (stock control, invoicing and so on). This may have the effect of relieving managers and staff of tedious, time-consuming chores. However, there is not much evidence to suggest that this affects decision-making processes (Stewart, 1971).

Other methods, more directly concerned with decision making, are now becoming established. Chief among these are the mathematical modelling methods. We have already mentioned dynamic programming, which is one of a family of methods which finds optimum solutions to problems of certain types. Another class of methods are the simulation models (Gershefsky, 1969), which do not calculate a single optimum solution: instead, the model can be used to test out the consequences of *specified* decisions. Although different in principle, these kinds of models seem to be used in the same way by decision makers: to provide rapid and safe experience of manipulating the environment, in much the same way that training simulators (for aircraft pilots, say) are used (see ch. 4). A manager can try out his ideas and hunches to see '*if* I do this, *then* that will happen'. The use of models can be said to make his environment more 'transparent' – it is as if he can see through it and into it in a way which was not possible before. The detailed psychological mechanisms behind this metaphor remain to be investigated. They may include enhancement of feedback, or increased opportunity for 'learning heuristics by hindsight', as discussed by Newell, Shaw and Simon (1962).

Another set of computer techniques for increasing what we have called environmental transparency might be embodied in a 'management information system'. These systems naturally vary between organizations in their sophistication, but their essential feature is the provision of periodic statements of the state of some part of the environment. For instance, at the end of each week managers of production departments might receive information from the computer about the week's production activities and about likely trends in the immediate and more distant future. There are many problems attached to the operation of management information systems which require psychological study. In essence these involve questions of how material can best be perceived and assimilated. Many contemporary management information systems are very efficient in producing large quantities of print-out, but are less effective when it comes to ensuring that each manager integrates the material which is significant to him. Sometimes the sheer quantity of output results in compressed formats not readily assimilable by the human eye. More often, despite the efforts of systems analysis, attempts to discover the exact information required and the time constraints imposed by particular decision problems have been less than completely successful.

More studies are required of the way in which managers actually use information in making their decisions. In fact, a study by Greiner, Leitch and Barnes (1970) throws doubt on whether the emphasis by systems designers on quantitative information systems is an appropriate one. Their investigation concerned managerial judgements about the performance of operating units – a typical situation for which a management information system may be used. However it was found that managers generally preferred qualitative to quantitative criteria, and moreover those groups of managers depending more on qualitative criteria were more consistent and concordant in their judgements. This study appears to open up a large field for investigation.

One possibility about which there is much speculation at present is the increased use of 'on-line' facilities by managers. Much computer work is carried out 'off-line' on a batch system. Jobs are put in the computer's 'queue' and dealt with without intervention from the manager awaiting the information. In contrast, 'on-line' use of a computer can incorporate some element of 'conversation' between the person and the machine: a manager might ask a question and obtain an immediate response or he might change the state of the system to bring it up-to-date and then ask a question which is immediately answered. The computer can itself ask the operator for more details or it can prompt a particular action. 'On-line' systems in principle allow more flexibility and adaptability.[1]

1. The on-line use of computers has similar advantages for the psychologist in his laboratory experimentation. Material may be presented and adapted in the light of a subject's reactions, so that (for instance) correct responses to a stimulus in a learning task result in that stimulus being presented less frequently than other, unlearned items.

Looking into the future, we can imagine senior managers sitting at their desks operating a small console in conversation with a distant computer as they reach complex decisions. This on-line facility would bring together the two forms of decision activity which were outlined at the beginning of the chapter. At that point we distinguished between information search and information integration, the former being concerned with the acquisition of information to reduce uncertainty, and the latter with the calculation of combined probabilities and utilities. In organizational settings these two types of activity are much less separate than our earlier discussion might have implied. On-line decision making allows the manager in principle to seek out new information, to be reminded of possibilities and to be given simulation facilities to explore likely outcomes. He can also use the computer to combine probabilities and to apply differential value weightings to outcomes which are of interest to him. So in this type of system, the computer's role is both in search and in integration.

But much of this is still 'in principle' only. We need to learn more about how man and computer can comfortably interact. How can a non-specialist learn to 'talk' to the computer, how can the computer convey essential points to the manager? Partly this is a question of hardware design, and ergonomists are already making a contribution to rapid development at this point, which is within their own traditional area of specialization. For instance, keyboards and printers are giving way to instantaneous visual displays which change at a touch. But there is also much else to be done in the broader field of man-machine systems design, which is reviewed in chapter 5, and which might be called 'cognitive ergonomics'. A great deal has to be learned about the acceptable characteristics of man-machine languages, from the point of view of intelligibility and ease of learning, and the cognitive ergonomist will be working on the design of such languages just as the more traditional ergonomist will be working on the design of hardware.

Another use of the computer as a decision aid – perhaps the most ambitious – is to give it a complete section of the decision process as its own province. If we know that a computer handles certain processes more efficiently than a man, we have the opportunity of using it for these processes and employing the man on other aspects of the task. It is clear that computers can easily apply fixed, complex rules whereas the man often does better in a less deterministic capacity. The computer can speedily execute a mass of complicated operations to solve an economic problem, but the man is more ready to observe that the real problem is not an economic one at all.

This approach to the use of computers in decision making is connected with the name of Ward Edwards. In a recent study (Miller, Kaplan and Edwards, 1967; 1969) the approach has been developed to design a complete decision making system, coping with a realistic and complex situation. In this system the human contribution is a series of specific value judgements concerning probabilities and utilities. The computer's contribution is to apply elaborate mathematical procedures to the judgemental data, and to factual data made available within the system, and to produce the best set of decisions.

The authors point out that the design of the system is based on two broad conclusions from previous psychological investigation: that men are extraordinarily good at judging individual magnitudes, frequencies and so on, but rather inefficient at combining their judgements in complex ways to reach decisions. They prove their point by experiments in which the decisions from their man-machine system are compared with decisions made by experienced men on the basis of the same information. The system using human judgement together with computer calculation is much superior.

SUMMARY

This chapter outlines two broad approaches currently adopted in the psychological study of decision making: the 'normative' approach and the 'descriptive' approach. The studies cited show how the use of computers has extended the scope of both.

The normative approach, where man is measured against some theoretical standard, can now be used in realistically complex situations. The consequences of adopting theoretically optimum decision procedures can readily be calculated by computer. Furthermore, computers allow the researcher to build task environments which, although complex, are precisely controlled. These task environments can be programmed to adjust their status according to the person's actions so that complex sequential decision processes and interactive situations can be studied.

Both approaches are valuable but descriptive studies are particularly enhanced by the use of computer models. The attempt to observe and state directly the decision procedures which are actually used in a given situation requires a method of evaluating the resulting description. A model embedded in a computer programme is ideal for this purpose. On the one hand it represents a precise formal description and on the other it can be tested for accuracy by comparing its output with that of the decision maker it simulates. This approach has had notable success when applied to complex 'real life' decision tasks.

The chapter views decision making not simply in terms of the integration of information to arrive at a choice of action but also in terms of the process of searching for relevant material and procedures. We therefore conclude with speculation about the emergence of increasingly sophisticated management information systems and the role of psychologists in this development.

FURTHER READING

A good starting point for someone who wants a broad not-too-technical introduction to the field is the BBC's 1967 publication *Decision Making*. The collection of readings edited by Ward Edwards and Amos Tversky (*Decision Making*, Penguin, 1967) is a valuable set of papers concentrating on the classical treatment in terms of information integration and choice. It includes two review papers by Ward Edwards which provide many signposts to further exploration.

Several of the controversies and innovations of decision theory have centred round the Theory of Games. *Two-Person Game Theory – The Essential Ideas* by Anatol Rapoport (University of Michigan Press, 1966) is a stimulating if unorthodox introduction to the subject, R. D. Luce and H. Raiffa's *Games and Decisions* (Wiley, 1957) is a long but lucid exposition, specially slanted towards social science applications.

For those who wish to follow through the experimental work on thought processes, there is an introductory text by L. E. Bourne, *Human Conceptual Behaviour* (Allyn & Bacon, 1966) and an interesting collection of papers edited by B. Kleinmuntz,

Concepts and the Structure of Memory (Wiley, 1967). A fascinating but difficult development of the information processing theory is E. Hunt's *Concept Learning: An Information Processing Problem* (Wiley, 1962).

A treatment which concentrates on individual differences is H. M. Schroder, M. J. Driver and S. Streufert's *Human Information Processing* (Holt, Rinehart & Winston, 1967). And an industrial application of the information processing analysis is H. Tonge's *A Heuristic Programme for Assembly Line Balancing* (Prentice-Hall, 1961) – a monograph which provides many insights into the methods of heuristic programming.

12
Managers: Their Effectiveness and Training

Stephen Fineman and Peter Warr

Social behaviour both within and outside organizations is in large measure a question of interpersonal influence, and this topic has been studied by psychologists under several guises – in investigations into conformity, attitude change, mass media and propaganda, brain-washing, social facilitation and leadership. An emphasis on the last of these characterizes the present chapter, where research into managers is set against a broad framework of attempted answers to the basic psychological question 'Why does this person behave like this?' The authors are actively working on research into managerial personality and behaviour.

There are those people at work who are clearly labelled as 'managers'; yet many others – teachers, hospital matrons, army sergeants, company directors, trade union officials, bishops, university professors, committee chairmen – are also holders of managerial jobs. As managers they retain some sort of technical or administrative responsibility for the work of others. They are said to 'lead' subordinates in their work and are usually granted a degree of formal authority over them. In addition to these distinguishing features they also tend to be primarily concerned with ideas, facts and decisions which are passed on for others to turn into action.

Managers in industrial and non-industrial organizations play a vital part in today's society and the way that they perform their functions has a marked influence on local and national prosperity and on the well-being of a large number of employees. Consequently managers have increasingly become objects of study. What do they do? What are their backgrounds? What do they need to know? How can they learn more? How effective are they? What do their subordinates think of them? What do they think of themselves? It is not surprising that psychologists have played a large part in these studies. The manager is no extraordinary creature; he is merely a person in a particular role and persons-in-roles are the subject-matter of psychology.

THE PSYCHOLOGIST'S VIEWPOINT

The psychologist in any field is faced with a formidable amount of behaviour to explain. He attempts firstly to classify or describe his subject matter, so he has to find particular labels for the *behaviour* he observes. After this process he might consider some personal *attributes* to account for the behaviour he has described. Here he is likely to invoke features of someone's personality, his attitudes, values and interests, his motivation and skill, his knowledge and experience. As tests of the explanatory value of these attributes the psychologist will concern himself with the prediction of certain types of behaviour from measured attributes, and will also note how his predictions may depend upon the *context* of the behaviour. This demands a description of features of the physical and social environment, such as the task in hand, the degree of stress, or the influence of other people.

However, psychologists are not only interested in describing and linking behaviour and attributes; they are also concerned with their *effects*. In any area of study the nature of these effects has first to be specified in some detail, after which we can move on to see how cause–effect links are modified in different contexts.

We can bring together these several notions to generate a framework into which research results of many kinds can be set. We have seen that in broad terms the psychologist's task is to unravel the interrelationships between attributes (A), behaviour (B), context (C), and effects (E). Within this A, B, C, E setting he also has to insert D – the descriptions which he chooses to apply to the four main components.

We can summarily represent many (though not all) research possibilities in the diagram of Figure 12.1. This is laid out to indicate that we are basically concerned with the associations between B and E, and A and E, and A and B, and with how each of these associations is likely to be influenced by C. We have in addition to select the most fruitful descriptions (D) to work with when we are studying each of the components A, B, C, and E.

The discussion of research into managers which follows is organized around this framework. We shall consider each of the four components to identify those aspects which at the present time seem to be the ones which are most significant and productive-of-research. The arrowed links in Figure 12.1 will then be examined in a description of research findings to date. Finally we shall consider attempts which have been made (primarily through training) to bring about effects which appear in any organizational setting to be particularly desirable ones.

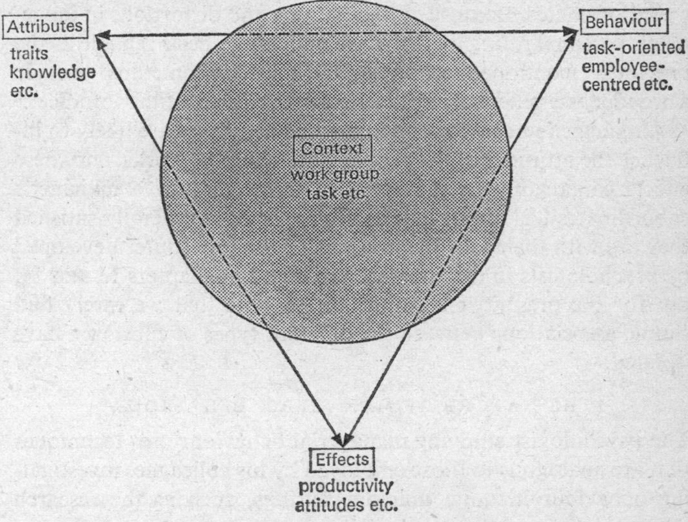

Figure 12.1 A research framework for studying the interrelationships between attributes, behaviour, context and effects

THE NATURE OF THE EFFECTS

In many studies of managers attention has been focussed upon the consequences of their behaviour or of their personal attributes. It is now common to isolate two main 'effects' for study – the success of the manager in productive terms and the attitudes he generates in his subordinates and colleagues. These features may be viewed as the major criteria in studies of management selection and training procedures.[1]

In some circumstances a manager's productive success may be measured reliably in an objective quantitative fashion. We might,

1. Additional conceptual and methodological issues in criterion research are reviewed in chapter 8.

for example, be able to examine indices of his section's effectiveness which are based upon standard times established by work study engineers, or in other cases there may be measures of production costs, sales, scrap levels and so on. Alternatively a manager may be rated for effectiveness by superior managers, by colleagues or by subordinates. Because of fluctuations and distortions in judgement, personal rating methods are unlikely to be as reliable as the previously mentioned techniques, but they can sometimes provide a broader assessment of effectiveness than can quantitative indices.[2]

A manager's behaviour and personal attributes are likely to influence the attitudes of the people with whom he works, and these effects can readily be measured in terms of how a manager's subordinates feel about him as a boss or how generally satisfied they are with their job. Illustrations of the procedures developed by psychologists in this area are presented in chapters 13 and 14, but for the present it is important to note that we rarely find simple associations between the different types of effects we have isolated.

THE NATURE OF MANAGERS' BEHAVIOUR

The psychologist studying managerial behaviour uses techniques that are analogous to those employed by his colleagues investigating behaviour in quite different settings, such as the research laboratory, the psychiatric hospital or the nursery school. Several basic approaches are possible. The investigator may *directly observe* and record ongoing behaviour, he might collect *retrospective* data about the behaviour, or he can adopt a *self-recording* procedure whereby the people in whom he is interested record what they are doing as they are working. Let us look at each of these in turn.

Managers can be observed at work and records can be made of what they do, with whom, where and when (e.g. Copeman, Luijk and Hanika, 1963). A continuous recording procedure of this kind is likely to be very time consuming and it often yields an unwieldy amount of data. More acceptable techniques have been developed which allow sample observations to be taken at random intervals. This approach was used by Thurley and Hamblin (1963) in their examination of the work behaviour of different

2. Research into appraisal techniques is examined in chapter 10.

groups of British supervisors. If the presence of the observer does not unduly influence those people being observed, direct observation can provide a reasonably comprehensive picture of the day-to-day activities of a manager.

Retrospective data (the second type noted on page 262) may be obtained directly from managers through interview or questionnaire techniques. In either case the manager is asked to state what he *thinks* he does in his job. Often this method yields descriptions of behaviour which tend to differ from what managers in fact do when directly observed: there are more interruptions and 'wasted' periods than managers themselves assert, and much more time is devoted to personnel problems than they believe to be the case (e.g. Burns, 1957). Other retrospective descriptions may be obtained from a manager's subordinates, his peers or his own boss. It is important to note however that data about a manager collected from different sources do not always yield the same picture (e.g. Fleishman, 1953a; Webber, 1970).

Self-recording of managerial behaviour usually takes the form of the manager noting in a diary what he does. This record might cover a continuous period, or it may relate to a sample of occasions. Burns (1957) studied seventy-six British top managers who kept a diary for between three and five weeks. He found that the managers spent from 42 per cent to 80 per cent of their time in discussions and only a very limited time formulating plans by themselves. Stewart (1970) analysed diary records kept by 160 managers over a four-week period. Each subject noted down 'incidents' at work in terms of 'where?', 'who with?', 'what type of interaction?' (committee, telephone etc.) and 'what topic?'. Cluster analysis of the data suggested five main groups of managers: specialist advisers, who spend most of their time writing reports; emissaries, who spend a lot of time away from the company; trouble-shooters who continuously have to cope with crises; discussers, who are repeatedly involved in scheduled or unscheduled conversations; and committee-men, who do most of their work at formal meetings.

The differences between the classifications we have mentioned illustrate the major problem faced by an investigator using any of the three basic approaches to behaviour measurement – how can he best impose some ordered system of description on to his material?

It may sometimes be enough to describe managers' behaviour in terms of percentage-of-time-spent-talking, but often we will want to apply dimensions which are more abstract or which have a greater degree of psychological substance.

In selecting descriptive dimensions we will usually have to start with relatively *a priori* concepts which seem to be intuitively plausible. For instance in the late 1930s, Lewin, Lippitt and White made a significant contribution to contemporary thinking by working with the notions of authoritarian, democratic and *laissez-faire* leader behaviour (Lewin, Lippitt and White, 1939). Later writers, such as Tannenbaum and Schmidt (1958), found it helpful to talk of a single continuum of leadership behaviour varying from 'boss-centred' to 'subordinate-centred' and the notions of 'participative' leadership (Argyris, 1957; McGregor, 1960) and 'benevolence' (McMurray, 1958) have also proved fruitful. These descriptions of managerial behaviour are plausible ones, but they do not pretend to cover the whole spectrum of possible activities. More comprehensive descriptions of behaviour are required so that analyses can be developed which extract the underlying major factors or components.

This strategy was the one adopted by the Personnel Research Board at Ohio State University in the 1950s. Their investigators collected a 'pool' of over 1800 statements representing types of manager behaviour. The statements were derived from interviews, observation, questionnaires and organizational manuals (Stogdill and Shartle, 1948). Experts sorted the items and arrived at nine assumed major dimensions of leader behaviour. Items representing these supposed dimensions were embodied in a 150-item questionnaire (the Leader Behaviour Description Questionnaire), which was administered to several large samples for retrospective descriptions. The results indicated that the items in each assumed dimension did not intercorrelate notably more highly than did those in separate assumed dimensions; furthermore the dimensions as they stood were far from independent (Fleishman, 1953a).

At this point statistical procedures of factor analysis entered the research, and several studies generated two major factors, 'Consideration' and 'Initiating Structure', together with the minor components of 'Production Emphasis' and 'Social Sensitivity'.

The major factors are defined by Fleishman (1969) as follows:

Consideration. Reflects the extent to which an individual is likely to have job relationships with his subordinates characterized by mutual trust, respect for their ideas, consideration of their feelings, and a certain warmth between himself and them. A high score is indicative of a climate of good rapport and two-way communication. A low score indicates the individual is likely to be more impersonal in his relations with group members.

Initiating Structure. Reflects the extent to which an individual is likely to define and structure his own role and those of his subordinates towards goal attainment. A high score on this dimension characterizes individuals who play a very active role in directing group activities through planning, communicating information, scheduling, criticizing trying out new ideas, and so forth. A low score characterizes individuals who are likely to be relatively inactive in giving direction in these ways.

Subsequent investigators (e.g. Halpin and Winer, 1957; Stanton, 1960) have confirmed the independence of the Consideration and Initiating Structure dimensions, and Harris and Fleishman (1955) have presented reasonably good stability coefficients.

It is important to note that these two major components of manager behaviour are thought of as being statistically independent, so that a particular manager may display behaviour which is at any point along each of the dimensions. Since the two components have on several occasions been extracted from more complete descriptions of what managers do, we may have some confidence that they are valid and significant aspects of their behaviour. This form of leadership-behaviour description has been adopted directly by other investigators such as Blake and Mouton (1964) who have labelled the dimensions 'concern for people' and 'concern for production'.

Likert (1961) has worked with empirically derived dimensions of 'employee centredness' and 'job centredness', which are defined similarly to Consideration and Initiating Structure but which are not said to be statistically independent. Similar approaches have been developed in Bales and Slater's (1955) direct observation research that isolated 'social-emotional' and 'task-oriented' leadership behaviour, and in Fiedler's (1967) and Reddin's (1970) accounts of 'relationship-oriented' and 'task-oriented' leadership behaviour.

In summary of this section we can note that there are three main techniques for measuring managerial behaviour: direct observation, retrospective description by self or others, and self-recording procedures. In each case we have to determine the descriptive dimensions which are to be applied to the data. These may be selected on an *a priori* basis or they may derive from systematic analysis of more comprehensive empirical studies. In the latter case there is considerable agreement that two dimensions appear to be most salient; these reflect an orientation towards people and an orientation towards the task.

THE LINKS BETWEEN BEHAVIOUR AND EFFECTS

Let us now look at research studies which have related the measures of managers' behaviour that we have described to measures of the effects of that behaviour.

Beyond statements of 'good' and 'not so good' ways of spending time at work (e.g. Drucker, 1966) we have no quantitative evidence of the precise effects of different forms of day-to-day managerial activity as measured by direct observation or by diaries and other records. Research into these recording techniques has not yet extended beyond the actual mapping and classifying of behaviour patterns, and we must await developments in the field.

Most work on the effects of managers' behaviour has used retrospective descriptions and there is considerable evidence (e.g. Halpin, 1957, Halpin and Winer, 1957; Likert, 1961, pp. 16–18) that subordinate satisfaction (one of the criteria noted earlier) is related to democratically oriented supervision. There are also several studies (e.g. Argyle, Gardner and Cioffi, 1958; Weitz and Nuckols, 1955) that indicate that satisfaction with democratic supervision is associated with less absenteeism and lower labour turnover. However, we must be cautious in inferrring from these findings that a straightforward linear relationship exists, such that every increment in democratic leader behaviour is accompanied by an increase in subordinate satisfaction. The research results are at least partly due to the fact that *very* authoritarian supervision is almost by definition unacceptable to subordinates. Furthermore, the preference for democratic, consultative leadership is very much an in-general one; Sadler's (1968) survey of more than 1500 employees shows that, although this was the modal preference, more authoritarian styles were not infrequently appreciated. Preference for autocratic, non-participative leadership became more frequent as attention switched from higher grades of employee to lower ones.[3]

Looking at how manager behaviour affects a section's productive success we find several investigations which have contrasted the behaviour of managers whose sections are high-producing with those that are low-producing. These studies have shown that the typical high-producing manager is perceived as more employee-centred than is his low-producing counterpart. (See Likert, 1961 and 1967 for a review of these investigations.) On the other hand, the picture here is not quite as clear as with the employee-attitude data, and the methodological difficulties facing a researcher are often considerable. Sales (1966) points out that results can sometimes be attributable to differences in work group absenteeism or labour turnover, and Anderson's summary of forty-nine experimental studies sounds a cautionary note for those who feel intuitively that a democratic approach to management *must* be 'the best':

> The evidence available fails to demonstrate that either authoritarian or democratic leadership is consistently associated with higher productivity. In most situations, however, democratic leadership is associated with higher morale. But even this conclusion must be regarded cautiously, because the authoritarian leader has been unreasonably harsh and austere in a number of investigations reporting superior morale in democratic groups (Anderson, 1959).

Research that has utilized Consideration and Initiating Structure dimensions of managerial behaviour has the advantage of a background of empirical derivation. Thus we are reasonably confident that the dimensions are stable and replicable, and it may be that these behavioural descriptions will be consistently associated with measured effects. There is certainly a belief (e.g. Blake and Mouton, 1964) that the ideal manager is one who is both very concerned for people and has a high concern for production. What is the evidence?

3. This point is amplified by the studies described in chapter 15 which show that employees differ widely in their desire to participate in managerial decisions.

Reviews which are similar in outcome have been provided by Anderson (1966), Korman (1966) and Lowin, Hrapchak and Kavanagh (1969). It emerges that despite optimism by research workers in the 1950s there are no generally observed associations between a manager's Consideration or Initiating Structure and the effects of his behaviour interms of the criteria discussed. Lowin, Hrapchak and Kavanagh (1969, p. 240) conclude that:

> there appears to be much evidence that Consideration and Initiating Structure can each correlate positively and negatively (depending on other variables), and only weakly if at all with effectiveness and morale indices.

However, it might be that instead of a straightforward association there is a *non-linear* relationship between behaviour and effects. Fleishman and Harris (1962) looked for an optimum balance between Consideration and Initiating Structure. This is illustrated in Figure 12.2 where their employee-grievance results are summarized; a similar pattern emerged for labour turnover. The study also revealed that there were critical levels at which increased Initiating Structure and decreased Consideration began to relate to grievance or labour turnover. Similar findings have been reported by Skinner (1969) in a study of textile-firm foremen, but it is still an open question whether non-linear relationships will be observable when productivity effects are studied more directly.

Most studies of the effects of manager behaviour leave uncertain the direction of causation: does the behaviour cause the effects, is the reverse the case, or is there a more complex (perhaps circular) causative pattern? Suppose we do find a significant positive correlation between considerate behaviour and employee productivity; it may be that the managerial behaviour is causing the productivity levels, but it is also conceivable that managers will show more consideration when their subordinates are working well. Alternatively both of these influences could be at work. Studies by Jackson (1953) and Lowin and Craig (1968) do provide strong evidence that managers can affect how subordinates behave and feel, but the manager is also definitely influenced by his subordinates. Furthermore, it is possible that other factors, such as employment levels or the market for a section's product, are sometimes the

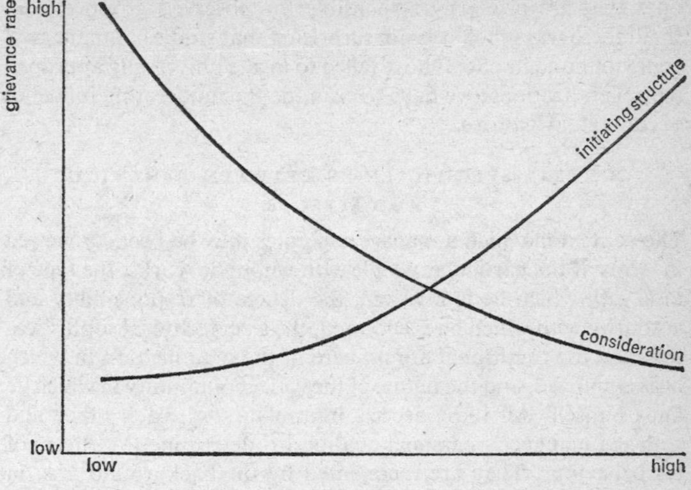

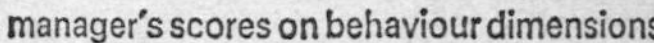

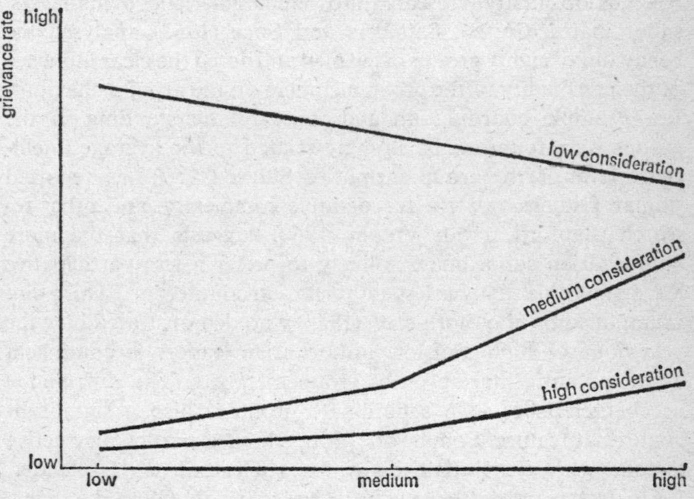

Figure 12.2 Schematic representation of some results of Fleishman and Harris's (1962) study of effects of manager behaviour

ones that are primarily responsible for observed group effects. In all these ways then it is not surprising that studies of managers' behaviour and its effects have failed to locate universally appropriate generalizations; we have to examine the moderating influence of contextual features.

CONTEXT-SPECIFIC LINKS BETWEEN BEHAVIOUR AND EFFECTS

The context in which a manager operates may be broadly viewed in terms of the particular people with whom he works, the type of task with which he is involved, the degree of responsibility and authority with which he is endowed, the size, technical sophistication and the traditional atmosphere of the organization in which he is employed, and the nature of the wider community in which he finds himself. All these aspects interrelate with each other and with the manager's personal qualities to determine the effects of his behaviour. They are represented by the background area in Figure 12.1.

Let us look firstly at research into the characteristics of managers' subordinates. Cattell, Saunders and Stice (1953) analysed the behaviour of eighty groups of ten men and noted the clear influence of the personality of the group members on the group behaviour. For example coordination and mutual understanding in the groups were found to be strongly related to the average intelligence level of the group members. Stager (1967) has reported similar findings relative to cognitive complexity, and other research (Sanford, 1950; Vroom, 1960) suggests that the more authoritarian subordinate is likely to prefer a less participative leadership style than his less authoritarian counterpart. This point is amplified by Haythorn *et al.* (1956) who demonstrated how the behaviour of high and low authoritarian leaders is contingent upon the authoritarianism of group members. The *distribution* of characteristics in a subordinate group is also a significant contextual feature. Some work groups have a particularly active member who often initiates his own acts of leading (e.g. Hollander, 1961). In this respect he may be a 'key man' on whom the supervisor's effectiveness depends.

Studies of leadership under different task requirements (e.g Carter, 1953; Shaw and Blum, 1966) show that the actual task with which a manager is involved can significantly determine his influence over his subordinates. Thus, in a highly unstructured task, a manager's influence is diluted because he has no clear set of work procedures to follow, whereas his influence in a more structured situation is more certain because of the self-directive nature of the task.

The degree of authority or power possessed by a manager is another aspect of the context which sets a limit to how far he can bring about desired effects. The considerable amount of psychological research on power is well documented by Collins and Raven (1969). One may conclude that how and when a manager utilizes different aspects of power at his disposal, and whether such power is seen by his colleagues as appropriate or legitimate, are factors likely to be highly instrumental in his effectiveness as a leader.

There are some interesting findings related to contextual factors such as work-unit size and geographical location. Vroom and Mann (1960) have shown that the acceptability of authoritarian supervisory behaviour is greater in large units than in small ones. Studies by Blood and Hulin (1967), Katzell, Barrett and Parker (1961) and Turner and Lawrence (1965) point to the fact that workers in large conurbations are more willing to adopt a subordiate non-participative role than are employees in smaller rural townships. This point is raised again in chapter 17.

Also in chapter 17 is a review of the ways in which organizations may be categorized in terms of degree of specialization, lines of command, centralization and so on. It is apparent that these aspects of organizational structure will have a strong potential influence on the effectiveness of a particular management style. The way in which this potential influence manifests itself is however not yet clear, and this is another area in which research developments are awaited.

MANAGERIAL ATTRIBUTES

Rather than taking managers' behaviour as our starting point we might instead concentrate upon their attributes – stable personality dispositions, attitude and value systems, motivational tendencies, knowledge and skills. Are there any attributes which predict who will emerge as a leader? Are there any 'leadership qualities'? Reviews by Gibb (1969) and Mann (1959) of psychologists' work on leadership make it clear that in an informal group situation (where rules are not formally assigned) people who take the lead are likely to differ somewhat from other group members. In general they are likely to be rather more intelligent, self-confident, adjusted, dominant and extraverted than non-leaders, but recent writers on this subject are unanimous that the distinguishing attributes can vary from situation to situation.

There is also some evidence (Gibb, 1969) that we may expect to observe similar distinguishing features in formal groups and organizations: the filtering-out process of promotion will make it likely that *in general* the people designated as managers will be more intelligent and will have had more formal education. Additionally, it would seem probable that managers will be more knowledgeable than their subordinates in certain job-related respects but less knowledgeable in others.

THE LINKS BETWEEN ATTRIBUTES AND EFFECTS

There is a fair amount of evidence that certain attributes are linked to the 'effects' criteria we have described. Traits such as originality, aggressiveness, intelligence and clarity of self-expression have been shown to be more indicative of promotion-potential than are tact and cooperativeness traits (Bruce, 1953; Fleishman and Peters, 1962; Roadman, 1964). Furthermore, 'inner-directed' characteristics such as imaginativeness, forcefulness and self-confidence are judged by successful managers to be more important than 'outer-directed' qualities like agreeableness, caution and social adaptability (Porter and Lawler, 1968, ch. 5). Another managerial attribute is the amount of job knowledge he possesses; it would seem reasonable to assume that managers with limited knowledge of their job will engender negative attitudes in their subordinates, especially if this deficiency is linked with behaviour seen as unacceptable in other ways.[4]

Perhaps the largest single body of research that has explored the direct relationship between a managerial attribute and mana-

4. Job knowledge is an attribute which is regularly lacking in newly-appointed managers (Warr and Bird, 1967). It is however more open to change than are many attributes; this point is taken up again at the end of the chapter.

gerial performance is in the work which has followed the initial suggestions of McClelland *et al.* (1953) about achievement motivation (*n* Ach). Let us look at this work in some detail.

The achievement motive is presented as a relatively stable personality construct, which is of particular importance for managerial success (McClelland, 1961; McClelland and Winter, 1969). The high *n* Ach manager tends to set moderate goals for himself, to work harder when the chances of success are neither too small nor too great and to show a preference for personal responsibility and control over his own work. Additionally, he likes reasonably quick and concrete feedback about the results of his actions, and he tends to be active in learning about the environments in which he has to operate. Some versions of achievement-motivation theory incorporate a motive to avoid failure, so helping to explain the behaviour of the low achievement person who acts more to avoid the discomfort of failure than to seek the satisfactions that may come from success (Atkinson and Feather, 1966).

In evaluating these approaches we need firstly to examine the measuring techniques used. McClelland bases his conclusions on the projective Thematic Apperception Test (TAT) (Murray, 1943) whereby subjects tell stories about the perceived content of a series of pictures. The fantasy so derived is content-analysed by expert judges according to a complex scoring system. It would appear that the high sensitivity of the TAT to the conditions of testing (see Murstein, 1963) and its low test-retest reliability renders the measure psychometrically weak and unsuitable for individual prediction purposes in specific situations. However, at a more general level the TAT has been successful in predicting particular effects: for example, studies by Andrews (1967), Grant, Katovsky and Bray (1967) and McClelland (1961, pp. 267–8) indicate that managers with high *n* Ach get more promotions and pay rises, are judged as more effective and are also associated with more successful firms than are low *n* Ach managers.

The TAT measure of achievement motivation is administratively inconvenient and lacks face validity for general use in organizational settings. These reasons together with the psychometric criticisms noted above have encouraged many investigators to develop alternative measures. Some of these are projective tests (e.g. French, 1958; Hurley, 1955), and others are tests of the self-report type (e.g. Edwards, 1954; Gough, 1960). Unfortunately, however, several studies have shown that these various indicators of achievement motivation do not intercorrelate very highly, if at all (e.g. Klinger, 1966; Weinstein, 1969). There could be several reasons for this. It may be that we are investigating a multi-dimensional phenomenon so that different tests are tapping separate independent achievement areas, which are not always unified into a single general component. On the other hand one may argue, as does McClelland, that whatever the TAT *n* Ach score is measuring, 'the same thing is not likely to be measured by any simple set of choice-type items' (McClelland, 1958, p. 38).

The absence of high correlations between supposed measures of achievement motivation could also be due to response factors within the tests themselves. Self-report questionnaires may be administratively convenient but they are very open to social desirability influences and are likely to be boring from the point of view of the respondent. Much published research has relied on college students who are notably willing to complete questionnaires with the minimum of concentration and involvement, and the results from investigations with large batteries of tests completed at one sitting should always be treated with some reserve.

Nevertheless the work of McClelland and his followers provides a reasonable basis for hypothesizing a general achievement motivation construct that could subsume more specific factors that are situationally relevant. The achievement syndrome is clearly a plausible one, and we might expect high *n* Ach managers in general to be more effective than low *n* Ach managers – an expectation that has some empirical support.

CONTEXT-SPECIFIC LINKS BETWEEN ATTRIBUTES AND EFFECTS

Although we may find links between certain personality traits and measured effects, these links are rarely strong ones (see ch. 8, p. 182). It seems likely that the most meaningful associations will result from considering the importance of traits relative to specific situations. Thus we can view a manager's effectiveness as a function not only of one or a few personality traits, but of how his traits relate to a particular task in a particular group in a specific organization. For example, studies have shown that, although leaders are in general more intelligent than non-leaders, they will be ineffective if they are *very much more* intelligent than their group (Gibb, 1969, p. 218). 'Over-intelligent' leaders may be seen by the group as 'not one of us' and too remote from their problems to act effectively.

Some researchers in the field of achievement motivation have attempted to specify situational constraints. We find that Atkinson and Feather (1966) have explored differences between tasks of different perceived difficulty and attractiveness, and McClelland and Winter (1969, pp. 15–19) have pointed out that measured high *n* Ach need not necessarily guarantee success unless the opportunity to succeed is available.

The overall picture for context-specific links between attributes and effects suggests that those situational aspects that were earlier described as modifying behaviour-effect relationships are also at work on the attribute-effect associations.

THE LINKS BETWEEN ATTRIBUTES AND BEHAVIOUR

The third link in Figure 12.1 on page 261 is that between attributes and behaviour, and is essentially a representation of the predictive validity of our measures. When we study leader attributes can we locate associated patterns of behaviour? Our discussion of distinguishing managerial attributes implied that we can. We summarized Mann's (1959) evidence for a relationship between directly-observed leadership behaviour and measures of intelligence, adjustment and extraversion in various groups. On a more practical level, it is likely that managers who know their job well behave differently at work from those whose knowledge (an attribute) is very limited, and that variations between managers in radicalism-conservation will influence the way they run their organizations.

Nevertheless our ability to predict a person's behaviour from his measured attributes is generally increased when contextual features are included in research paradigms. Gibb summarizes the relevant research on traits as follows:

> In every instance, the relation of the trait to the leadership role is more meaningful if consideration is given to the detailed nature of the role.

> A person does not become a leader by virtue of his possession of any one particular pattern of personality traits, but the pattern of personal characteristics of the leader must bear relationship to the present characteristics, activities, and goals of the group of which he is a leader. (Gibb, 1969, p. 226).

Such an approach implies that the relationship between managerial attributes and behaviour should be examined separately in differing work contexts. Taking as illustrations the manager behaviour measures of Initiating Structure and Consideration outlined earlier we might ask how these are predictable from *n* Ach scores in different kinds of job or at different levels in the organization. Or we might ask about different types of *n* Ach ('professional' and 'social' perhaps). But having asked we must move on, for studies of this kind have yet to be made.

TOWARDS A POSSIBLE SYNTHESIS

We have discussed different ways of measuring managerial behaviour and attributes, and how these measures can relate to each other and to different effects. We have also emphasized the importance of various contextual features that can modify our predictions; but we have not so far attempted a broad theoretical synthesis which makes specific predictions about particular situations.

One recent approach to a comprehensive unifying framework is found in Reddin's (1970) '3-D Theory'. This adds to the dimensions of Consideration and Initiating Structure (here renamed 'Relationships Orientation' and 'Task Orientation') a third dimension – 'Effectiveness'. This latter is said to depend upon the context, which is itself viewed in terms of five elements – technology, subordinates, co-workers, superior and the organization. The theory is carefully worked out and is sophisticated in presentation, but has not yet been the subject of published empirical validation.

A rather similar approach, which has developed out of empirical tests conducted over a fifteen-year period, is that of Fiedler (1967). His basic postulate is that a leader can be characterized by a specific personality attribute that reflects a consistency of goals or needs over different situations. Two main goal orientations are suggested, one reflecting a need to be successful in task performance, and the other relating to good interpersonal relationships. Fiedler's 'contingency model' states rather directly that the effects of these attributes are contingent upon three aspects of the situation; these are the relationship between a leader and his followers, the leader's position power within the organization, and the structure of the group's task.

He provides methods for measuring each of these situational variables as well as his own indirect measure of leadership attributes. This index is derived from scale judgements made about one's 'least preferred co-worker' (LPC) – the person with whom one can work least well. Someone who describes his LPC very negatively on the rating scales is said to be a more task-oriented leader than is a person who has a high LPC score; this latter type of leader is thought likely to behave in a more relationship-oriented way.

Of the three contextual variables – leader – member relations, task structure and leader's position-power – Fiedler regards the first as most important. For descriptive purposes each of the three is treated as dichotomous, so that leader-member relations are classified as 'good' or 'moderately poor', tasks are rated as 'structured' or 'unstructured' and the leader's position-power is either 'strong' or 'weak'. The three dichotomous variables yield eight classes of context, and Fiedler groups these in the way shown in Figure 12.3 to represent the extent to which a situation is favourable to a leader.

The figure summarizes sixty-three median correlations derived from a wide range of different groups, and clearly demonstrates how the effects of leader behaviour are contingent upon the situation. The task-oriented leader (as assumed from a low LPC score) is most effective in favourable or unfavourable conditions whereas a relationship-oriented leader (inferred from a high LPC score) is likely to be most effective under conditions of moderate favourability or unfavourability.

The contingency model is a well-developed illustration of how the components of Figure 12.1 – attributes, behaviour, context and effects – can be brought together in practice. The model is undoubtedly a valuable conceptualization and there is now sufficient evidence to support it at least in outline. It is not without criticism however, especially with respect to the LPC measure which seems

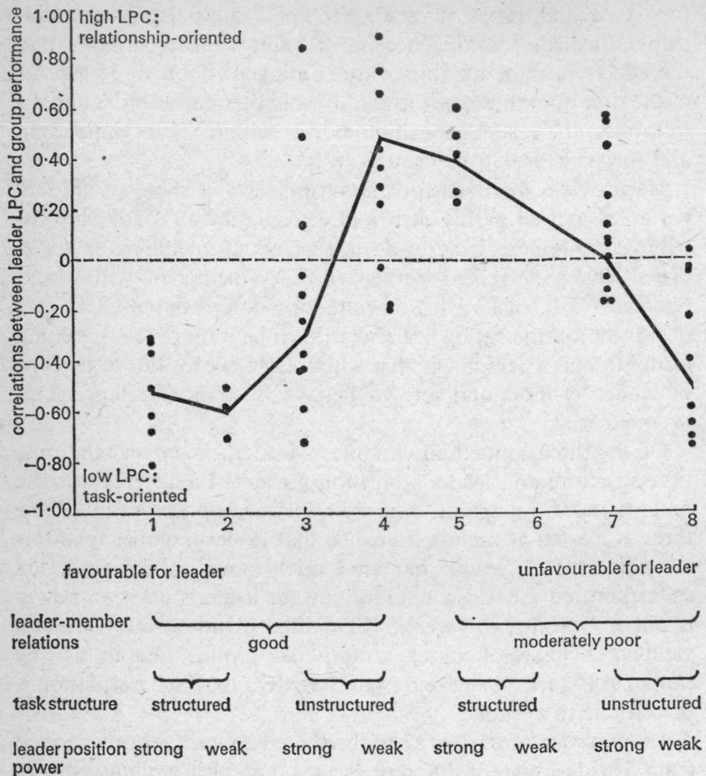

Figure 12.3 Fiedler's (1967) representation of the relationship between leaders LPC scores and group effectiveness for different classes of context

to be somewhat arbitrary and dependent upon particular rating scales (Yukl, 1970), and also to be difficult to interpret (Bass, Fiedler and Krueger, 1964; Fishbein, Landy and Hatch, 1969). We cannot be sure that the LPC score is indicative of a consistently-applied task-oriented or relationship-oriented behaviour. Studies by Graham (1968) and Sample and Wilson (1965) show that in fact high- and low-LPC leaders engage in similar amounts of task- and relationship-oriented behaviour overall, but that the two types of leaders are distinguished by their sequencing of task and relationship behaviour. The low-LPC leader tends to be far more directive from the start, but is likely to be considerate after having organized the task, and the high-LPC leader tends to operate in the reverse sequence.

Although there have been well over fifty studies contributing to the development of Fiedler's model, relatively few of these have involved industrial, real-life samples. Wider cross-validation in this area is now desirable. Despite these several deficiencies the theory has marked heuristic value, and as such merits considerable scientific respect. It should provide a springboard for the development of more sophisticated measures of manager behaviour, attributes and effects, and of those contextual variables which it is now certain must be incorporated into attempts accurately to predict the performance of a manager.

CHANGING MANAGERIAL ATTRIBUTES AND BEHAVIOUR

In this final section we shall examine what can be done within an organization to optimize managerial attributes and behaviour. This is in practice largely a matter of selection and training, and we might expect that personnel policies for these activities would embody at least implicit assumptions about attribute-effect and behaviour-effect links. As we have seen, there is still much doubt about the nature of these.

Some principles of selection are discussed in chapter 8, and training is examined in chapter 4. In the present chapter we shall only look briefly at some features of managerial training in so far as they bear upon the overall research framework we have described.

Can training change managerial attributes and behaviour at work? This question has often been examined through studies which attempt to evaluate particular training programmes. One way of evaluating training in items of its outcomes has been described by Warr, Bird and Rackham (1970) in the following manner:[5]

1. Immediate outcomes of training. Changes in knowledge, behaviour or attitude which are present immediately after training.

5. See also page 181 in chapter 8.

2. *Intermediate outcomes of training*. Changes in knowledge, behaviour or attitude which are present in the work situation some time after training.

3. *Ultimate outcomes of training*. Changes in organizational effectiveness rather than in trainee knowledge, behaviour or attitude.

Let us look at some of the published research findings in terms of these levels of evaluation.

Fleishman (1953b) was concerned with the *intermediate* outcomes of human relations training provided for foremen. Using questionnaire measures of Consideration and Initiating Structure he found that, although there were desirable changes in foremen behaviour immediately after training, they soon settled back into their earlier ways. Their behaviour, in fact, seemed to be determined more by the 'leadership climate' in which they worked than by the training they had received; foremen whose superiors valued considerate behaviour tended to adopt this as their norm, whereas in other climates considerate behaviour was exhibited to a much smaller extent – irrespective of whether training had been received. Similar results have been reported for other human relations training courses by Harris and Fleishman (1955) and for more specifically task-oriented training by Bird (1969); the intermediate outcomes of manager training are very limited unless the leadership climate is favourable.

The *ultimate* outcomes of training to change managerial behaviour have been looked at by Blake and Mouton (1964), who have claimed that managers trained to behave with a high concern for production and an equivalently high concern for people (see p. 265) are likely to have a significant influence on their organization's profitability. Unfortunately, the 'before and after' data used in their study, without a control group, leave the results open to alternative interpretations. It is possible that situational factors, such as variations in market conditions or organizational improvements, could account for the observed changes.

It would appear from the evidence available that it is not easy to change managerial behaviour at work through training. Successful training programmes have to be tailored to individual work situations so that managers *as a group* come to adopt new ways of managing. Certainly training programmes for individuals which leave aside the context are unlikely to yield profitable intermediate outcomes (cf. Warr, Bird and Rackham, 1970).

Is it possible to alter managers' *attributes* through training? To materially change the personality of mature individuals is no easy task. One extreme manifestation of this view is held by Fiedler (1967) who recommends that we should concentrate on changing a man's work environment rather than altering his personality. In this way the manager can be placed in a situation that will optimize his effectiveness. There is some evidence (e.g. Campbell and Dunnette, 1968; Mangham and Cooper, 1969) that T-group training in 'social sensitivity' may sometimes be reflected in work behaviour, but whether the inferred personality changes have occurred solely because of the training content and whether they are long lasting ones are still open questions.

McClelland and Winter (1969) provide some evidence that intensive training with highly selected managerial groups can lead to increases in achievement motivation and consequent changes in work behaviour. However, there is virtually no evidence that managers can be trained to be more intelligent, self-confident, adjusted and so on: this in an area where very little research has been performed. On the other hand, we are confident that other forms of attributes such as specific knowledge, skills and awareness of sound decision-making procedures are quite open to training (e.g. Glaser, 1965; Kepner and Tregoe, 1965; Warr, Bird and Rackham, 1970). A well-planned programme of training can be very influential in changing attributes of these types. But whether a manager will be able to *apply* his new knowledge and skills effectively is less certain.

SUMMARY

This chapter has been addressed to an instance of the basic psychological question 'Why does this person behave like this?' Our focus has been a person in a managerial role and we have suggested that research framework involving attributes, behaviour, context and effects may be helpful here (see Figure 12.1). The discussion presented within this framework has highlighted the fact that a considerable body of knowledge has been acquired about behaviour-effect links, but that attribute-behaviour and attribute-effect relationships are far less fully explored. In all cases however, we are painfully ignorant of the precise nature and influence of the contextual factors. It appears that psychological research at the present time has as great a need to explore contexts as it has to explore people; when we can describe and classify contexts in ways which are conceptually and empirically satisfying, then we shall be better able to understand our proper object of study – people behaving within these contexts.

FURTHER READING

Good reviews of psychological research into leadership can be found in C. A. Gibb's 'Leadership' in *The Handbook of Social Psychology* edited by G. Lindzey and E. Aronson (Addison-Wesley, 1969), and in C. A. Gibb's *Leadership* (Penguin, 1969). More specialized writing on managerial behaviour are F. E. Fiedler's *A Theory of Leadership Effectiveness* (McGraw-Hill, 1967), R. Likert's *New Patterns of Management*, (McGraw-Hill, 1961) and D. C. McClelland and D. G. Winter's *Motivating Economic Achievement* (Free Press, 1969).

13
People's Motives at Work

Frank Blackler and
Roger Williams

Psychologists' laboratory-based research into motivation has often concentrated upon physiological processes or upon the behaviour of animals. This research is notably irrelevant to real-life working conditions where long-term social and personal considerations interact in complex ways. Some attempts have been made to develop theories applicable to motivational patterns at work, and these are examined in the present chapter. The authors review the incentive value of money, of good social relationships and of the intrinsic interest of work itself. They note some individual difference parameters, and illustrate theories of the motivational process in terms of goal setting, equity and expectancy. Throughout the chapter they emphasize the limitations of each approach as well as its advantages.

Why some people resent their jobs while others are enthusiastic about them, why some people look for additional work while others seem to avoid as much as they can, are questions which concern everyone interested in people's behaviour at work. It would be convenient if simple answers existed to these and related questions, but it is our belief that they do not. Paradoxically though this should be no cause for despair – understanding will only follow when the delicacy and complexity of the problem is appreciated.

A number of separate questions each falling under the heading 'the psychology of motivation to work' should first be distinguished. In everyday conversation it is usual to explain people's behaviour by reference to their purposes. When a person's motives are understood, behaviour which previously may have been strange becomes commonplace. In the study of motivation, the first question asked is therefore 'What purposes and motives do people have at work?' Do people work, for example, because they like what they do, because of the friends they make or simply to acquire money?

A simple list of motives and intentions, while of great interest, is only the first step towards understanding motivation, since experience tells us that the motives of one man are not necessarily the motives of another. Individual differences need to be recorded, for a second question is 'what conditions tend to promote the development of some motives and intentions rather than others?' Experience also tells us that while two people may each want the same thing one may try harder to get it. When faced with difficulties one person may persist while another may give up. How do we account for such differences in the strength of people's motivation? Psychologists have studied the conditions under which behaviour is sustained and dissipated, and have attempted to explain the processes involved.

With this overview in mind we consider in this chapter some theories about the nature of men's motives, examine research which has documented individual differences, and briefly discuss explanations of how it is that some people experience stronger motivation to work than others do.

THE WORK OF TAYLOR AND THE MONEY MOTIVE

When considering what motives people may have at work, the question of the importance of money invariably arises. It is often stated, probably correctly, that money is an important factor for most people, but from this limited insight it seems only too easy to conclude that money is *the* important thing. People are basically self-centred the argument goes, their actions at work are invariably designed simply to maximize personal material gain.

A modern view of such a doctrine was formulated by F. W. Taylor. Working in the Bethlehem Steel Company, Taylor observed that labourers were loading pig-iron on to railway carriages at an average of twelve-and-a-half tons per man-day. After studying the operations involved he concluded that men given sufficient incentive should each be able to handle nearly four times that amount. To prove his point one individual, noted for his respect of money, was selected for demonstration. For an increased wage this man laboured and rested according to the most precise instructions from Taylor; nothing he did was left to chance. As predicted the man's output rose to forty-seven-and-a-half tons daily.[1]

1. Taylor is associated with the development of what became known as 'scientific management'. A general account of this is presented by Tillett, Kempner and Wills (1970).

Taylor was concerned to secure maximum output for minimum cost, a problem faced by managers everywhere. His solution was to regard men as individual machine-like units. In his view the causes of inefficiency in men, just like in machines, were unnecessary movements, fatigue and poor physical environment. So to combat low output men should be carefully selected, they should be instructed as to their every movement, and their working environment should be carefully controlled. Especially, their desire for money should be maximally exploited to ensure high rates of working.

By some criteria Taylor was dramatically successful. The number of wagon loaders at the Bethlehem works was reduced from five hundred to one hundred and forty, and as the wages of these men were only increased by 60 per cent considerable financial savings for the company resulted. But he became a hated man as far as the workers were concerned. Perhaps this is an understandable result, for while the social theory implicit in his work is bad enough (for example, that men are essentially instruments to be manipulated by their employers) the psychological assumptions are frightening. It would seem that he thought men were basically lazy, irrational and untrustworthy and that it was important that their energies should be channelled by exploiting their inherent greed. We should add that in our experience it is not that managers believe they *themselves* are like this, but rather that they believe their *subordinates* are! So finally it would seem from Taylor's assumptions that we need to distinguish an élite of self-controlled individuals whose role it is to manipulate their fickle colleagues by astute use of the power of money!

In fact a large number of studies of what people themselves believe are most important to them in their jobs indicate that money is not the overriding factor Taylor believed it to be. For example Stagner (1950) reports a study of 7,000 employees in one organization. Only 7 per cent stated that their rate of pay was the most important thing to them in their jobs. A steady job and work they enjoyed were said to be the most important by as many as 36 per cent and 15 per cent respectively. And in an interesting study of employee benefit programmes, all of approximately equal cost to the employer, Nealey (1964) showed that more workers from his American sample preferred full hospital insurance or the introduction of unionization to a proposed 6 per cent pay rise.

But it remains true that our social and economic system in the West places high premium on the incentive value of money. Interestingly enough though, a body of evidence is building up to suggest that companies are likely to award financial increments to their employees *whether or not* they become more effective in their jobs. We can reasonably assume that people's skills on the job will increasingly develop as time goes by. Similarly it seems reasonable to suggest that a person's effectiveness in his job at any given time will be predicted to some extent by his performance in the recent past. Given all this, if salary increments are awarded according to developments in effectiveness then correlations between people's level of pay and their increments over a number of years should be fairly predictable. As performance presumably improves and as salary increments should reflect this, the associations will not be perfect. On the other hand, as performance levels over adjacent periods in time should be somewhat related, pay increments should bear *some* relation to previous pay. But Haire (1967), in a study of the increments awarded in three companies, noted that in two of them the moderate correlations between salary levels and expected increments, where more effective performance determined them, were not observed. These two firms seemed to award increments on a very haphazard basis; correlations between salary levels and increments followed a random pattern. And this may well be the case in a great many organizations. Despite the fact that managers only too often express undying faith in the incentive value of money, they may raise people's salaries when they present themselves punctually for work, when they are smart and cleanshaven, when they have firm handshakes – rather than when they do what we suppose they are paid for, namely a good job of work.

Often, then, despite their expressed beliefs managers do not reward effective performance with salary increments. But even when they do, the money motive may not prove to be as powerful as people expect. The evidence for this comes as much from research which deals with the success of incentive systems as it comes from documentation of failure. Viteles (1953) and Marriott (1957) in reviews of incentive schemes for non-salaried personnel conclude that they do tend to increase performance effectiveness.

But, as Opsahl and Dunnette (1966) have pointed out, the introduction of incentive plans is more often than not accompanied by other changes. Increased output may be a response to any of a number of factors, like changes in company policies, or changes in work methods. Consistent with this suggestion Whyte (1955) observed that, when incentive schemes do work, paradoxically this may *not* be because people want more money. He suggested that the attempt to meet newly-set production goals becomes a kind of game, or that it may be that people mainly want to please their supervisor, or perhaps that working fast is rather less tedious than working slowly.

And on the negative side we know that incentive plans may not reach what potential is estimated for them because people often voluntarily restrict their output to an implicitly or explicitly agreed norm. This cannot be accounted for by the money motive and Hickson (1961) in a British study identified a number of possible causes. He claims that output may be restricted because people are uncertain that initial productivity bargaining procedures will be continued, they may fear that increased output by the majority may facilitate job reductions in the company, or fear that existing social relations on the job may be disrupted by changes countenanced by them. In other cases people may simply reserve the right to work hard only when they feel like it, and indeed they may find that restricting output is of itself rewarding to them since it asserts their independence from management.

We know then that financial reward for employees is by no means necessarily their overriding concern at work. We know that management practices may not even be designed to exploit what incentive value financial reward does have for people. And we know that incentive schemes are often regarded with suspicion by workers, and when they are effective this may be for other reasons than the money motive. So we can be categorical in our conclusions. People often do not work hard solely or primarily for money; and attempts by management to manipulate employees' behaviour by exploiting acquisitive inclinations are often unjustified and sometimes dangerous.

THE HAWTHORNE STUDIES, AND THE IMPORTANCE OF SOCIAL RELATIONS AT WORK

Impetus to quite a different (though equally restrictive) view as Taylor's of the ends to which behaviour at work is directed, came from a series of experiments at the Hawthorne Works of the General Electric Company in Chicago (Roethlisberger and Dickson, 1939). Here, to begin with, the effects of various degrees of illumination on the efficiency of workers assembling and checking electrical components was studied. Surprisingly, it was observed that not only did the output of workers given better lighting improve, but so also did that of a control group given no such advantages. A follow-up study demonstrated that even when lighting was reduced to the equivalent of *moonlight* two girls selected for study maintained high levels of production.

Clearly variables beyond that of lighting had confounded the results of the experiments. In an attempt to identify their nature piece rate working was introduced for a group of workers, various schedules of rest pauses were tried, and shortened hours were introduced. Nearly all these strategies were accompanied by increased productivity. But consistent with the earlier work it was found that the complete *removal* of all improvements was itself accompanied by further increases!

These experiments have not been without critics (for example Argyle, 1953; Carey, 1967), yet as Cubbon (1969) points out their importance is that they spell the death-knell to the man = machine = isolated unit ideas discussed earlier. Seemingly, many of the workers studied felt privileged in that they were singled out for study, all were given more freedom in dividing up their work, good relations between group members had developed. These factors all emerged as significant aspects of work motivation.

Subsequently, at the Hawthorne works an extensive employee interview programme was instituted. The results seemed to confirm the special importance of social relations at work and these were investigated further in a study of a small group of workers over a six-month period. The primary finding was the existence of several cliques among the men, each of which had recognized standards for behaviour. Workers who produced either more or less than was considered acceptable by other clique members were subjected to various sorts of pressures to conform.

As a result of these studies a conception of motivation to work which was quite different from Taylor's came to appear plausible. It could be argued (see Mayo, 1945) that men obtain their sense of identity by their association with others, that meaning at work is sought through social relations, that men are more responsible to the social pressures of their peer groups than the controls of management. Some studies producing evidence consistent with these views can be found in the literature, for example Trist and Bamforth (1951) in a study of the effects of technical innovation in coal mines, and Whyte (1948) in a study of the behaviour of restaurant staff.

Yet we know that a number of behaviours can be observed which cannot be explained by formulations concentrating exclusively on the importance of social relations. Notable here is the behaviour of 'rate busters', people who insist on working exceptionally hard despite ostracism from their work-mates. And in his review of the literature Vroom (1964) points to differences in motive patterns to be found in different workers. Sales and personnel people, for example, seem to find social contact important while production managers like to work more with mechanical things. Mayo's formulation is, like Taylor's, a half truth which overlooks many important observations. On a purely intuitive level indeed Mayo's view is too simple; we are reminded of the ball-bearing inspector who liked her work 'because they're all different'. It should come as no surprise to learn that all of us to some extent seek some meaning in the work itself. And the next two theories we examine touch on this very point.

MASLOW'S THEORY, AND ACTIVITIES VALUED IN THEIR OWN RIGHT

A somewhat more sophisticated account of people's motives has been suggested by Maslow (1943) and presented to the business world by McGregor (1960). For our present purposes the interest in this theory centres firstly around the various goals towards which he proposes that men's behaviour is directed. These he lists as follows:

1. Physiological needs (such as food, water and drink) which are basic to the survival of the organism.
2. Safety needs, that is the need for a threat-free environment.
3. Social needs, including the need to be accepted by others, for affectionate relations with others, to be part of a group.
4. Esteem needs, such as self respect.
5. Self-actualization needs, that is the importance of self-fulfilment, the need to do things that fulfil a person's potential.

This list draws attention to a variety of needs that people may experience. Further, Maslow emphasizes that people often want to do things simply because they are felt to be worth doing for their own sakes. Normally we do not question why people for example play games, listen to music, or read novels. We accept that these are valuable activities in their own right. The term 'need to self-actualize' draws attention to the fact that people do certain activities for no reason beyond this; perhaps they work in large part for the same reason.

Maslow is also provocative in that he suggests there is an order of priority in the matters important to people. Thus, it is suggested that physiological needs will dominate behaviour until they are largely satisfied, then safety needs will come into play; when these are satisfied social needs will operate, and so on up the hierarchy. From his clinical experience Maslow believes that mental health depends on the satisfaction of each of the five need areas he describes, and that only the person who satisfies his more basic needs and who attends to the higher-order ones will reach his potential. If this is so, the implications for management practice are clear: employees need not only money and acceptable colleagues but also work which is of itself considered interesting or valuable.

The general approach to understanding behaviour that Maslow proposes is an attractive one. As Hall and Lindzey (1957) point out, probably no psychologist would take issue with a theory of behaviour which emphasizes that a number of variables influence behaviour so that we should try to understand particular events in the context of a wider system. Yet it remains true that only little research has been conducted into the detail of Maslow's philosophy, and his point of view is as much an article of faith as it is an empirically verified theory. In a series of surveys Porter (1961; 1962; 1963) has tried to assess the relative importance of Maslow's need areas to different types of people by examining differences between management levels and types. While Porter is able to interpret his findings in terms of Maslow's model the point needs to be made that interpretation is quite different from testing. And this is the crunch as far as Maslow is concerned; it has proved easy to interpret situations by his model but rather more elusive to actually test it out.

There are a number of difficulties in Maslow's theory. Firstly people might be expected to move up and down this hierarchy quite frequently – before and after meals let us say! The difficulty here is that when lower-level needs are not satisfied people (according to Maslow) will not *primarily* be concerned with higher needs, and the extent to which their attempts to satisfy these higher needs are thwarted will represent deprivations of such needs. However, when people's more basic needs are satisfied and they begin to attend to the higher order needs more earnestly, any blocks to attainment of these goals now will constitute a real threat to happiness. Unfortunately Maslow is not of much help in attempts to predict how frequently deprivations become real threats, or real threats reduce to mere deprivations, so it is difficult to make his theory operational and to make detailed predictions of behaviour.

The order in which he presents motives may be misleading. The priority he proposes may well reflect the priorities experienced by people living in certain sectors of American society, but it may not be relevant to other people. To use Maslow's jargon, perhaps some people 'self-actualize' through their social relations; in more common parlance this means that perhaps some people find that satisfactory social relations are not dependent for their value on anything else, are worthy goals to be aimed at in their own right.

And yet the theory continues to find favour with psychologists. In part this may be because they appreciate Maslow's general postulation that behaviour is initiated to rectify imbalance in physiological or psychological functioning. (For a detailed reformulation of this see Wolf, 1970.) We conclude that his model is misleading, taking the point up again in connection with Herzberg's theory. However we believe that Maslow is important because he directs attention to the point that many motives may direct behaviour, and that people may engage in activities simply because they believe they are valuable and not because of other extrinsic motives.

HERZBERG'S THEORY AND GENERAL COMMENTS ON THEORIES OF MOTIVES

A theory which has provoked great interest on the part of managers and psychologists alike is Herzberg's Two Factor Theory. Like Maslow's, it draws attention to the point that people like doing things they find valuable; unlike it, it has generated a wealth of research.

The theory is based on the finding (Herzberg, Mausner and Snyderman, 1959) that when people described times when they felt very *satisfied* at work, they seemed to be describing different activities from those when involved describing more *dissatisfying* times. The finding is perplexing; normally it would be assumed that the presence or absence of a certain factor (say for example responsibility) would give rise to satisfaction or dissatisfaction accordingly. But the fact remains that Herzberg and his colleagues discovered that content analysis of people's stories suggested that:

1. Good times at work were the product of factors like achievement, advancement, recognition, responsibility and the work itself.
2. Bad times at work were the product of factors like poor company policy, interpersonal relations, salary, security and poor working conditions.

In short, the work which people did and the rewards which were contingent on their performance seemed to be associated with satisfying times and not with dissatisfying times; the reverse being true of the context and conditions under which the job was done.

Herzberg interprets these findings to suggest that man is directed by two basic and quite different needs, the need to avoid pain and the need to self-actualize:

> To summarize, the human animal has two categories of needs. One stems from his animal disposition. It is centred on the avoidance of loss

of life, hunger, pain, sexual deprivation and other primary drives, in addition to the infinite varieties of learned fears that become attached to these basic drives. The other segment of man's nature . . . is man's compelling urge to realize his own potentiality by continuous psychological growth. Perhaps there are primitive glimmerings of [this] characteristic in sub human species. Recent experiments on the curiosity and manipulative drives of animals suggest such possibilities. (Herzberg, 1966).

If Herzberg is right, then managers should not expect their subordinates to put more effort into their work as a result of improved working conditions as such an improvement would simply serve their need to avoid pain. Positive results would be the result of programmes designed to give workers increased responsibility, better recognition, and the like; these would serve their need to self-actualize.

Because of Herzberg's relatively simple prescription, it is hardly surprising that he has had considerable impact. However it would seem to be the general consensus in psychological literature, that his theory does not withstand critical scrutiny. As House and Wigdor (1968) in their review of relevant literature point out, the results of Herzberg's study are inconsistent with previous evidence. Vroom (1964) examines a number of studies dealing with the relation of performance and satisfaction and shows that – contrary to predictions from Herzberg's model – dissatisfied workers (who presumably would not be activated by their need to self-actualize) are often likely to work as well as are satisfied workers (who presumably are activated by this need). And King (1970) in an excellent discussion of evidence relating to predictions from the Two Factor Theory describes a number of studies which suggest that workers do in fact feel bad about factors like achievement, responsibility etc. (just as they feel good about them): similarly that they feel good about factors like company policy, salary etc. (just as they feel bad about them).

The problem (as for example Quinn and Kahn (1967) and Hinton (1968) identify it) is that studies which support Herzberg's position have invariably used his technique of inquiry, while studies which do not support it have examined the question in different ways. Vroom (1964) has probably explained this discrepancy by his suggestion that when describing times they found most satisfying, people tend to put themselves in the best light; but when they are describing bad times, defensive processes operate so that people put more emphasis on the failure of others. In short, the story-telling technique may be producing biased data. Wall, Stephenson and Skidmore (1971) have noted that people who were asked Herzberg's questions when they were under pressure to portray themselves in the best light (in a selection interview) produced data more confirmatory of the Two Factor Theory than did people under no such pressures.

And yet the importance of the Two Factor Theory should not be overlooked. Herzberg has dramatically challenged our traditional thinking about the nature of attitudes. Moreover his writings are instructive by their very mistakes. A point consistently overlooked in the literature is that Herzberg's interpretation of two basic 'needs' is an absurdity. The word 'need' has two meanings. Firstly, psychologists (for example Hull) use the word as a technical term; it refers to states that can be measured *independently from behaviour* initiated to change them (like the weight-loss of a rat deprived of food). On the other hand it has use as a literary device in everyday language simply to emphasize that certain things are *important* to people, and does not say *why* this is so. So one may say 'he needed the money', and 'need' here is used to point out that money was a powerful motive for the individual concerned; it does *not* refer to any state that is identified independently from behaviour.

'Need' used in the literary device sense is essentially a normative term. It draws attention to the fact that people do enjoy doing certain things, but it does not (like technical term use of the word) offer explanations of the processes at work here. Yet because Herzberg discovered that certain items appeared important to a group of accountants and engineers, he talks (see the quotation on pp. 292–3) as if certain predispositions can be inferred for all men. This cannot reasonably be done; all he might say is that certain things seem important to the people he studied.

Conclusions from the study of the Two Factor Theory are salutory. In the first place psychologists should clarify their terms and stick to only one use of a given word; Maslow who may use the word 'need' in the literary device sense has been interpreted in a different way (for example by Campbell *et al.* 1970). While this is unfortunate, the second point we might learn is that perhaps we should abandon the search for overall theories about the nature of men's motives and intentions, and more fruitfully examine the conditions under which given ones appear. We know relatively little about what people do find important, and we should not draw a blind over our ignorance by becoming advocates of simple generalizations and easy prescriptions.

THE IMPORTANCE OF INDIVIDUAL DIFFERENCES

A considerable number of studies have documented the fact that different kinds of people have different motives and intentions. McClelland (1961) for example, who has extensively studied the importance of achievement, reports large differences in its perceived importance to people from different cultures. Again studies with interest inventories (Wald and Doty, 1954) show that managers prefer to exercise persuasive powers more than do non-managers, and Morse and Weiss (1955) note that managers more than other groups lay emphasis on achievement or accomplishment. Indeed part of the process of giving vocational guidance to people is founded on the assumption that people's particular interests should be met by the jobs they do.

One point to remember is that while work may be an important feature in people's lives this may be so because of various reasons. A team of industrial sociologists led by Goldthorpe have documented one of the possible roles that work may fulfil for people. These workers (Goldthorpe *et al.* 1968) studied a sample of two hundred and twenty-nine manual workers, all married and all between the ages of twenty-one and forty-six. Members of this sample lived in the Luton area, and at the time of the study were earning not less than £17 a week – a high level of earnings at that time. Overall, Goldthorpe and his colleagues concluded that these particular workers had an 'instrumental' approach to their work. By this they mean that the workers did not appear to expect or to receive satisfaction from the interest of their jobs or from their association with their fellow workers. Rather their work was quite simply a means to an end outside their working situation; they saw advancement mainly in terms of a rising standard of living and material possessions.

Of especial interest to us in this section are the reasons suggested for the sample having this particular orientation to work. Firstly, because of their ages the financial responsibilities that the workers were facing were probably more acute than they were likely to have been before or were likely to be again. Secondly, as no fewer than 70 per cent of them came from an area outside that in which they currently lived, there was a high degree of geographical mobility amongst the sample. And thirdly, a proportion of the sample appeared to have been socially mobile in a downward direction. All these factors may explain why work had its particular instrumental meaning to Goldthorpe's workers.

Age is noted in chapter 7 as a most important variable to be identified in our understanding of individual differences in motivation. The middle-aged or older worker may experience more difficulty than his younger colleagues in adjusting to rapid technological change (see ch. 7). Again, as people grow older fewer ways may be open to them to cope with any disturbing circumstances. As people marry, buy houses, raise families, become trained and experienced at their jobs so it become increasingly difficult for them to extricate themselves from difficult situations. So job security – to cite but one factor – may assume an increasing level of importance to the older worker. On the other hand a high level of earnings might be more important to the person in an early stage of his career than it is to the older man. For him the newly acquired financial burden of a new house or young family is likely to be fairly acute. Paradoxically, in this connection, in our society it is people about the age of fifty who tend to be most highly paid, and this is so despite the fact that the strength of the money motive is likely to be less at that age.

It would be logical to expect that people's approach to work will be influenced by their personalities. A study reported by Vroom (1960) confirms this. He asked supervisors to rate the amount of influence they had in decision making and to indicate their attitudes to their jobs. At the same time Vroom obtained scores from each of them on a scale measuring authoritarianism. He found that for those who obtained a high score on this scale there appeared to be no relation between influence and job attitudes. But for those supervisors low on authoritarianism there was a marked positive relationship between the degree of influence they felt they had and their attitudes to their job. This topic is considered further in chapter 15.

Another factor which may prove useful in understanding the nature of an individual's motives has been identified by Korman (1970). So far we have implicitly assumed that men are self-enhancing and rational in the sense that they will try to attain whatever they think most desirable. At first sight Korman appears to have thrown a spanner into the works here. He has reported studies which suggest that only people who have high self esteem (i.e. see themselves as competent self-sufficient individuals) try to attain what they think desirable. Those with low self esteem seem to say to themselves 'I do not like what I am, and am not going to let me have what I want.'

While this is possibly an oversimplification, Korman believes it summarizes a large body of research using different samples and studying people in a wide variety of situations – vocational choice being an important one. Indeed it is supported by the finding that even where the person with low self esteem is provided with fulfilment of his desires he is not satisfied. Such people seem to ignore their own feelings – as they have little faith in their powers of decision they have learned to distrust themselves. More research is needed on the decision processes of people with low self esteem; certainly they are not conducted on a hedonistic basis. And more research is needed also to find how easy it is to change people's self esteem. However the implications of Korman's work are considerable, and research in this field will certainly help to better understand individual differences in people's motives.

TOWARDS AN UNDERSTANDING OF THE MOTIVATIONAL PROCESS

In this section we briefly consider three theories designed to explain how motives work, theories not concerned so much with specific motives as with the motivational process itself. We discuss goal setting, equity theory and expectancy theory; each of these has direct relevance to the world of work.

Goal setting

Locke and his co-workers (see Locke, 1970) have been concerned with the effect of setting oneself goals to aim at and the strength of motivation to attain these goals. A most important part of their work has been concerned with the level of *difficulty* of the goals people set. Stedery and Kay (1966), have examined this variable in connection with supervisors' performance in a manufacturing industry. It was found that those perceiving the difficult goal they had been set as 'challenging' had a 28 per cent decrease in defective items – while those who saw the goals set as 'impossible' had an *increase* of 35 per cent in fault units. And Berlew and Hall (1966) suggested that if newly-hired college graduates did not perceive their first job as challenging and in tune with their abilities they either left or did not put much effort into their work.

These findings are consistent with Locke's conclusion from laboratory studies that the degree to which performance is affected by motivational factors (as distinct from say level of skill or trustworthy equipment) is a result of the goals people set themselves. Clear, hard goals which are accepted by people help them to organize their effort and strive towards attainment. So far however we know little about why it is that certain people accept difficult objectives, and some of the comments we make in the next chapter have a bearing on this. Certainly the problem should not be dismissed lightly, for as Atkinson and Feather (1966) point out people for whom success is important tend to prefer tasks which are of intermediate difficulty. The role of this type of personal goal setting in the behaviour of managers is examined further in chapter 12.

Equity theory

Another area of research which is currently of importance is in the field of balance or dissonance theories of motivation. One branch of this, equity theory, has been especially applied to problems of motivation at work and to pay in particular (see Pritchard, 1969). Possibly too it might be extended to include the findings of Locke and his associates, and aspects of the exchange relationship between boss and subordinate.

The basis of the theory is that a person is said to compare the ratio of his inputs to his job to what he gets out of it. If the two ratios are not equal then he will attempt to reduce the discrepancy in some way (see also ch. 16). Early work in this field was conducted by Adams and his associates (Adams, 1962; 1963; 1964).

It was found that subjects working on various tasks in experimental situations tended to increase their performance when they felt overpaid. If they were overpaid on a piece rate basis they attended to the quality of their output (increased quantity would only upset the situation more), while subjects overpaid on an hourly rate of pay tended to increase the quantityof work that they finished. It should be emphasized that the important variable here is people's own perception of fairness or unfairness. Certainly, it would seem plausible to suggest that when people perceive they are not paid enough, they may reduce their output.

While the implications of equity theory seem exciting and while it is without doubt an important contribution to our understanding of how motives work, it is by no means easily applied to industrial situations. It is difficult to define the specific variables involved which people see as their inputs and outcomes. Age, skill, education, experience, effort, loyalty, for example, might all be thought to be inputs, while outcomes might be pay, status, satisfaction with the work itself, fringe benefits or a trustworthy boss. How any discrepancy between inputs and outcomes is resolved in real-life situations is not easy to predict; there are always many possible methods. And an interesting point is that the 'fair reward' principle on which equity theory is based may not actually explain very much. While we may consider a reward to be perfectly fair even so we may not be satisfied by it; fairness is possibly only one of the elements we take into account when assessing the value of a goal to ourselves. Similarly, we observe people who 'take advantage of' favours bestowed on them, who do not repay goodwill with goodwill.

Expectancy theory

Finally, we briefly examine a type of explanation of how motives work which directly deals with people's perceptions of a situation. Vroom (1964) suggests that an individual's motivation to carry out a particular act is a function of two variables: firstly, his expectancy that certain outcomes will result from his behaviour (e.g. more effort means more money), and secondly, the strength of his preference for the outcomes (e.g. how much money he wants).[2] Vroom suggests that this strength of a person's preference

2. Similar conceptions are described in chapters 8 and 11.

is dependent on the extent to which he believes it will help him to obtain other outcomes, and on how attractive these are (e.g. more money means we can buy a new car, and we want one very badly).

This kind of formulation has been elaborated by other writers. For example, Graen (1967) categorizes goals into those set externally (by boss or work colleagues) and those a person sets for himself. And Campbell *et al.* (1970) suggest there are two types of expectancy to consider: firstly, the chances of people actually producing more if they try to, and secondly, the chances of them receiving any reward should they be successful. As Lawler (1970) points out, the expectancy that my effort will be converted into performance can be said to depend on how realistic are my perceptions of the relationship between my effort and performance level, on my perception of my current situation and on my past experience in similar situations.

It can easily be seen that it would be no mean measuring task for the psychologist to establish the nature and extent of all these variables. And indeed expectancy theory becomes all the more complicated when it is realized that the expectancy that certain outcomes are contingent on certain behaviours is also said to be dependent on a complex of factors. What really matters it seems is the *net* attractiveness of the events that are felt to result from this performance. If the psychologist wanted to investigate a particular situation therefore he would have to discover all the events a person thought might result from certain behaviours, how attractive each of these is felt to be and how likely the person thinks it is that they will follow from his behaviours. Assume there is a young executive thinking of changing his job. His motivation to get the new job might depend (among other things) on the necessity for him to move house and its attendant outcomes (e.g. the chances of getting a reasonable house in an attractive area, the chances of making new friends, and his wife finding a new job, of the children finding new schools, and the results of increasing the distance between his relatives). Other important factors might be the outcome of money and status (new promotion prospects for example, the chances of salary rises, the state of the organization he is thinking of joining and its position in the market, the possible fringe benefits of the new job), and a further area of concern might be the job itself (what it will be like, whether the new boss will be satisfactory, the hours to be worked, the responsibility to be taken, and so on).

The reader can doubtless think of many other possible outcomes which the young executive might consider. Expectancy theorists would have us believe that people go through the process of sorting outcomes such as these – giving each a valence and probability index, then rationally and logically adding the product up at the end and acting accordingly. This theory and others like it (see chapter 11) are clearly of limited practical value; it would be impossible for an observer to make firm predictions, as he could not obtain the necessary data.

And in truth it does not seem likely that people behave rationally and logically to the extent required by expectancy theorists. Everyday experience suggests that people do not weigh the pros and cons of each and every action to such an extent. Furthermore research has suggested that important decisions (when we might think people ought to sit down and logically assess the possibilities) are often fraught with stress. And we know that under stress people do not consider the wider perspective but tend to focus on minutiae, becoming less rather than more capable of rational decisions (see ch. 3).

Yet on the positive side such accounts of the motivational process sometimes give us a real insight. Emphasis on the chances of increased performance and on the chances of receiving a promised reward is all to the good. It is often forgotten that in work organizations not only are people's goals likely to be far from clear, not only is their power to effect their attainment often radically limited, but rewards frequently do not reflect a person's level of performance to any great degree.

CONCLUSIONS

We began this chapter by emphasizing that understanding the psychology of motivation is not any easy task. And this is the note we must end on. Certainly it is possible to learn a lot from the empirical work reported and the theories that have been suggested – yet a lot remains quite clearly unknown.

Taylor's views on the importance of money have been shown to be false, the theories developed from the Hawthorne studies were seen to be unsatisfactory, and neither Maslow's nor Herzberg's accounts of motives and motivation are by any means all that people would like to believe they are. Similarly attempts to explain the process (rather than the content) of motivation are by no means completely successful. And yet we know that incentive schemes fail for perfectly understandable reasons and that they work for rather more unexpected ones. We know that employers do not make realistic use of what incentive value money may have and that they should consider alternative schedules of rewarding workers. We know that people may often work hard simply because they find their jobs interesting. We are beginning to understand something about individual differences in people's motives at work. And while our formulations of the process of motivation still remain unsatisfactory, we are beginning to break away from the need/drive reduction models. These and other lessons can be gleaned from our review.

One point is worth emphasizing. Applied psychologists – like all scientists who attempt to put into practice research findings – naturally emphasize what they know already; scientists working in pure research fields emphasize more what they do not know. Since applied psychologists are trying to help managers and workers who have to face real and immediate problems, there is often a temptation for them to overlook gaps in their knowledge. This is unfortunate. In the field of human behaviour, we are faced with tremendous and exciting problems, and we should not attempt to gloss over them. Applied psychologists who are working in the field of human motivation should recognize that they are only students of the field and not its masters.

SUMMARY

In this chapter three questions basic to the study of work motivation are identified. First, it is asked what motives do people have to work at all? Second, why do different people have different motives? Third, how can different strengths in people's level of motivation be accounted for?

The work of Taylor, the Hawthorne experiments, Maslow's theory and Herzberg's theory are all considered in the first part of the chapter. Each is noted to contribute to our understanding, yet it is suggested that none does full justice to the topic. Taylor's work is instructive because of the undoubted importance of the money motive, the Hawthorne experiments draw our attention to the significance of social factors in the work situation, and Maslow and Herzberg both emphasize that people may work hard because they like the task they have to do. But each of these formulations overlooks certain factors and none of them can accommodate the wide variety of human experience at work.

In the discussion of individual differences Goldthorpe's work is reviewed and the importance of differing background circumstances is emphasized. Personality and age factors are examined, and in the discussion of different levels of motivational strength the nature of goal setting, equity theory and expectancy theory are all considered. It seems that people who see their work objectives to be challenging try harder to meet them than do other people. Equity theory emphasizes that people expect a fair return for the amount of effort they invest in their jobs. Expectancy theory deals directly with people's perceptions of their work situations and tries to identify the various factors which they take into account in their decision making.

Finally, a number of conclusions from the review are suggested. While we are beginning to appreciate the variety of factors which help determine people's motivation to work we should avoid the temptation to gloss over gaps in our knowledge and propose easy solutions to the very exciting questions we are asking.

FURTHER READING

A general review of some of the topics covered here is to be found in J. A. C. Brown's *The Social Psychology of Industry* (Penguin, 1954). This has been reprinted several times and is very readable, but it is of course now rather out-of-date. A more recent and more specialized presentation is in V. H. Vroom's *Work and Motivation* (Wiley, 1964). Two books which provide an interesting contrast are *The Motivation to Work* by F. Herzberg, B. Mausner and B. Snyderman, Wiley (second edition, 1959) and *The Affluent Worker* by J. H. Goldthorpe and co-authors (Cambridge University Press, 1968). A more philosophical approach is adopted in R. S. Peters's *The Concept of Motivation* (Routledge & Kegan Paul, 1958); and D. McGregor's *The Human Side of Enterprise* (McGraw-Hill, 1960) is a good illustration of a text written primarily for managers.

14
Motives and Behaviour at Work

Roger Williams and Frank Blackler

This chapter complements the previous one and allows the authors to develop further some of the points introduced earlier. They now examine more closely the links between attitudes and behaviour and show how these relationships are far from simple. We might be able to predict someone's behaviour from a knowledge of his attitudes, but only if we take account of several moderating factors. Another theme of the chapter is the importance which people attach to being able to anticipate and control events in their environment; research studies of stress, job design, organizational change and effective leadership are viewed within the single perspective of their effects on the clarity with which employees can predict and interpret events around them.

ATTITUDE SURVEYS: INADEQUATE WAYS OF STUDYING MOTIVATION AND BEHAVIOUR

Most people probably believe that the satisfied worker is the hard worker, and that the dissatisfied worker is the one who avoids as much as he can. Indeed it is often assumed that when people have favourable or unfavourable attitudes towards something they will behave accordingly. So the person who is racially prejudiced is not expected to bestow favours on the ethnic group he dislikes, nor might one expect the dissatisfied worker to contribute much to his organization.

Psychologists have often defined attitudes with just such thoughts in mind. Thus Allport many years ago suggested that an attitude was 'a state of preparation or readiness for response' (Allport, 1935). Attitudes are, according to this view, learned predispositions to react in certain ways. Should this be the case then we have a convenient way of predicting behaviour at work: all we need to is to measure people's level of job satisfaction and infer from this how they will work. If we believed that this was true then this chapter would be simply made up of instruction in designing attitude measures and of a review of research concerned with attitude formation and change. However, we must emphasize that all the evidence suggests that there is no such simple relationship between attitudes and behaviour. As long ago as 1934 LaPiere published a study which suggested that expressed opinions and intentions bore very little relationship to actual behaviour (LaPiere, 1934). Again, Brayfield and Crockett (1955) concluded that there was no consistent relationship between attitudes and opinions about work and job performance. Nine years later Vroom (1964) in reviewing twenty studies noted the extreme variability between the relationship of performance and satisfaction. Some satisfied workers work well, but others do not.

Little is known about the causes of such different reactions. Part of the trouble is that investigators have often only measured overall satisfaction at work instead of also studying people's attitudes to more specific factors such as their working conditions, their boss or their pay (c.f. Warr and Routledge, 1969). This emerged in the previous chapter where we noted that an interest in the work itself (one component of overall job satisfaction) seems to be associated with a tendency to work harder, whereas the evidence for such an association in the case of satisfaction with pay is rather more equivocal.

Another possible reason for the failure of global attitude measures to predict behaviour at work might arise from the very great range of levels of skill which is often involved. Wide differences in skill could in effect swamp a satisfaction–performance relationship, because highly skilled but dissatisfied workers might easily perform better than do less skilled but satisfied people. To examine this possibility we need to be able to hold constant skill levels and then examine the relationships between satisfaction and performance; this is not too easy.

Other factors which might influence whether or not attitudes to work are predictive of performance arise from the immediate pressures of the environment. One of these is the social influence exerted by the reference group of which a man considers himself part. Such groups very much influence the way we perceive our environment, a point nicely illustrated by Lieberman's (1956) investigation of factory workers subsequently made foremen or shop stewards. It was found that compared to control groups those workers who were promoted to foremen developed more positive attitudes towards management and more negative attitudes towards the union. On the other hand those who became shop stewards became more pro-union while their attitudes towards management remained the same. Other illustrations of this effect are presented in chapter 16.

But aside from the point that social pressures influence our attitudes there is still the question as to the extent to which such pressures influence actual behaviour. Much relevant work has been done in the applied situation to see how group standards influence the performance of individuals in the group. Laboratory experimentation by Schachter (1951) suggested that groups where co-workers were strongly attracted to one another exerted greater influence over the behaviour of their members than those where members had little mutual attraction. A major field study in this area was carried out by Seashore (1954). His sample was composed of 228 work groups in a large heavy machinery manufacturing company in the United States. Seashore considered that a group was cohesive if the members of that group perceived themselves to be a unit, preferred to remain in the group rather than leave, and thought their group was better than other groups in terms of the way the men got along together. It was found that members of highly cohesive groups were more likely to produce at the same level than were members of groups low in cohesiveness. It was also found that highly cohesive groups were more frequently either very high- or very low-producing groups; in addition cohesive groups tended to have lower rates of absenteeism and labour turnover and higher job satisfaction than less cohesive groups.

From this then, it is possible to imagine a situation where a worker, very satisfied with his job, belongs to a group with whose members he thoroughly enjoys working, and yet his productivity is low in common with his work-mates. In order to predict behaviour therefore it is not enough to know how much a person likes his work as a whole or the extent to which he is subject to social pressures; we also need to know what kind of behaviour any such social factors will sanction.

In some cases, of course, the behaviour sanctioned by the group will lead to high productivity. Van Zelst (1952) conducted a study which serves to make this point. He studied two groups of carpenters and bricklayers on a large building site who had been working together for about five months. The employing organization allowed him to reorganize the workers in teams of two – based on their own preferences. In fact he was able to arrange things in such a way that twenty-two pairs worked with their first choice partner and twenty-eight with their second choice, leaving only eight isolates. The results in behavioural terms were a decrease in both labour and material costs, and in labour turnover. It seems clear that in this instance the social pressures sanctioned an increase in effort towards the employer's best interests.

Another variable which may mediate the relationship between group cohesiveness and productivity is the nature of the task the group has to perform. Lodahl and Porter (1961) have demonstrated this effect. In a study of over five hundred workers in an airline maintenance base they noted that the men were organized in a number of work groups each led by a 'lead man' who had little or no formal power of reward or punishment. In this situation it was found that a positive relation existed between group productivity and group cohesiveness and the popularity of the 'lead man', but more detailed examination showed that this relationship was strongest in groups where successful completion of the tasks on the job involved the groups in a high degree of cooperation. In other words, the power of the group to influence performance was greatest when the interdependence of task activities was greatest.

In this discussion of the immediate pressures of the environment we have inevitably moved further away from the idea that a man's attitude alone will dictate his behaviour. One might want to argue however that if only we could hold constant all the various pressures on people from their environment then a person's attitude to his work would be seen to dictate his behaviour. But this is hardly a practicable course, and again it assumes that attitudes are best understood as learned predispositions to react in certain ways. If this were a reasonable definition of an attitude then it could be understood in stimulus-response terms: an attitude then would be understood as an implicit response (in a person's mind) to certain stimuli (say his job) which in turn itself would become a stimulus to behaviour. Applying this model, a rat placed on an electric grid learns it is a painful situation, develops an attitude, which in turn prompts him to take evasive action.

Yet this very application of such an understanding of attitudes points to the stupidity of saying that attitudes are learned predispositions to react. It is ridiculous to say that rats learn *attitudes* towards electric grids or for that matter towards anything. What we do say is that rats experience *aversions* to objects like these. It is inappropriate to talk as if animals are capable of *evaluating*, and it is this process of evaluation that is implied by the term attitude. Man makes judgements of right and wrong, good and bad, just and unjust, and all the rest. Attitudes are the result of his capacity to evaluate. Objects, actions, situations, are viewed through value systems and judgements are made accordingly. Attitudes defined in such a way should be understood independently from behaviour and do not imply any straightforward relationship to it.

But if it is true that attitudes have been studied in too gross a way, and that our definitions of them have been naïve, it is also true to say that we know little about how to measure them. Attitudes generally and job satisfaction in particular, are hypothetical variables *inferred* from a number of statements or actions a person makes with respect to something. So certain responses would be grounds for saying a person has a favourable attitude towards his work while others would be grounds for postulating unfavourable attitudes. The difficulty, as we see it, is in deciding on what grounds we will accept responses as indicative of favourable or unfavourable attitudes to work.

The customary solution to this difficulty has been to assume that favourable attitudes are the product of exactly the same factors as unfavourable ones. So, if a worker has responsibility he will be satisfied; if he has none he will be dissatisfied. It is assumed that attitudes can be conceptualized as if they fall along a continuum with favourable attitudes at one end, unfavourable at the other, and a neutral point in the middle. Thurstone-type scales explicitly use that model. Likert-type scales too, when people are asked to express varying amounts of agreement or disagreement with certain statements are scored in such a way that the linearity of attitudes is assumed (Jahoda and Warren, 1966).

While linear models such as this appear to make light work of problems of quantification, it may be that positive and negative evaluations are not opposites. Possibly, Likert and Thurstone scales only create artefacts. We believe that despite all its shortcomings, the real value of Herzberg's work (discussed in chapter 13) has been to point to the possibility that while a worker may be satisfied when given, say, responsibility, he may not be actively dissatisfied when he has not been given it. He may be dissatisfied, let us say, by bad company policy, but possibly not actively satisfied by good. We do not know for sure that, because the presence of certain factors is valued, their absence will be greeted by abhorrence, nor that because some factor is associated with distaste its absence will necessarily be greeted by enthusiasm. Oppenheim (1966) nicely makes this point when he says we do not know whether attitudes are 'more like concentric circles or overlapping ellipses or three dimensional cloud formations'.

Our argument is then that the 'commonsense' method of studying the effects of motivation on behaviour by using the concept of attitudes may be misleading. This is not to say that the concept is unworthy of study in its own right, for the occupational psychologist is as interested in people's job satisfaction as he is in their job performance. In fact the influences of pay (discussed in the previous chapter) of a person's boss (see chapter 12) of intrinsic factors like the nature of a person's work (see Chapter 13) and of a person's co-workers on his attitudes to work certainly merit close study. The point is, however, that we do not believe that any simple insight into overt behaviour is likely to result from such a study alone. Attitudes cannot be expected to have a straightforward relation to behaviour. They are difficult to define and we do not completely know how to measure them. So it is necessary also to look elsewhere if we hope to understand why people behave as they do.

AN ALTERNATIVE: THE SITUATIONAL APPROACH

The approach we prefer is also a 'commonsense' approach, in that it is one all of us use in our everyday attempts to understand behaviour. Customarily we observe a person's behaviour in one situation, form a hypothesis about him, and test this out in other situations. To refine this a little, we suggest that people's behaviour in situations in which they are known to be highly involved should be studied. And we should observe them on occasions when they change their customary modes of behaviour. Through such study important variables might be identified, and it should be possible to formulate tentative laws about behaviour. This is essentially a scientific approach to understanding behaviour – the laws would be supported by evidence from various sources and not just from studies of one type (c.f. Mischel, 1968).

In the remainder of this chapter we examine such situations. First we look at situations which people experience as stressful, and secondly, those in which they have been observed to change their behaviour. Our study of stress raises a theme which is observed to run through many of the remaining topics examined.

Stressful situations at work

Several of the basic causes of stress at work have been enumerated in chapters 3 and 6. An approach which gives rather more emphasis to social psychological factors has been developed by workers at the University of Michigan (Kahn and Quinn, 1969), who draw attention to three common causes of stress at work. They identify these as role ambiguity, role conflict and role overload. A 'role' here is defined as a set of behaviours expected of anyone occupying a particular job. Role ambiguity refers to situations where information available to a job holder about what is expected of him is inadequate. Role conflict is where two or more individuals expect different, incompatible behaviours of the same individual. And role overload exists where a worker experiences a conflict of priorities because some expectations which people have of him he can meet and others he cannot.

Managers might well notice the deplorable frequency with which such situations are encountered in industry. In a national survey of the American labour force reported in 1964, Kahn and his team found that 35 per cent of workers were disturbed by lack of clarity about the scope of their responsibilities, while about 30 per cent were disturbed either because of uncertainty of what their co-workers expect of them or because of uncertainty about their supervisor's evaluation of them or because of both. Forty-eight per cent of the sample reported that from time to time they felt caught in the middle of two sets of people who wanted different things, and 45 per cent were disturbed by 'feeling they have to bear a work load such that they cannot finish during an ordinary working day'.

We have no reason to believe that such findings would not be duplicated in any study outside America, and managers should not underestimate the consequences of such stress. One finding has been that role overload can be associated with cardiac diseases. Miles (1954) studied forty-six coronary patients and forty-nine controls; half of the former compared with only one-eighth of the latter reported they 'had worked long hours with few vacations under considerable stress and strain'. And in a similar study Russek (1965) reports that prolonged emotional strain associated with job responsibilities preceded attack for 99 per cent of the coronary patients he studied, whereas accounts of similar strain were reported in only 20 per cent of normal control subjects.

But this is to digress a little. We are basically concerned here to document the nature of stressful situations. In the case of role ambiguity, an employee perceives that he lacks basic information concerning what he ought to do or how he ought to do it. In the case of role conflict, stress occurs when individuals cannot decide between two conflicting ideas as to how they ought to behave. In the case of role overload, it is impossible for a worker to complete all the tasks others expect of him given the constraints present in his situation. In short, all these instances appear stressful because they tend to result in an individual *being unable to achieve important goals through no fault of his own.* In the ambiguous situation he cannot find the stepping stones that lead to the achievement of acceptable goals, in the conflict situation the stepping stones are in opposed directions, and in the overload situation he is unable to cover them all.

A number of strategies have been observed to help people cope with role stress. One way is to give them warning of what is likely to happen when they have no experience of important forthcoming events. So Janis and his colleagues (Janis, 1958) record the effectiveness of informing patients awaiting major surgery of likely outcomes. And another related phenomenon is reported by McGrath (1970) who concluded that practically every study of task performance under stress shows that practice or experience was effective in reducing performance deterioration. Both these strategies seem effective because they help people to improve their predictions of what will happen under the onset of stress.

Working with others when under pressure also seems to help, especially if these are people the individual under stress has previously met. Possibly, others will give guidelines as to acceptable course of action, or possibly someone in the group may adopt a directive role. Either outcome enables a person experiencing stress to predict more easily how he should behave. Related work has been reported by Kogan and Wallach (1964) and McKenzie (1970) who have highlighted the phenomenon of 'risky shift'. When people make decisions in groups they generally advocate more risky alternatives than when they make solitary judgements; it may be that 'collective responsibility', when no one person can entirely be held responsible, encourages more extreme decisions.

Circumstances in which people change their behaviour

Next we turn to discuss conditions under which people have been observed to change their behaviour in some way. We discuss programmes of job enrichment or enlargement, studies of the conditions under which innovations are willingly accepted, rearch into job change, and take a brief look at research into effective leadership. Although it has not been possible for us to discuss all pertinent variables that have been shown to promote behaviour change in this review we feel confident that common threads can be identified through all these varied topics.

Job enrichment and enlargement programmes. Current interest in job enrichment and enlargement is discussed in chapter 15. At this point we merely wish to note that most of the published studies in this field have been concerned to analyse results in terms of changes in performance, that is whether quality or quantity of output varies as a result. Too few studies have been primarily concerned to explain why changes actually take place.

Because of this it is difficult to identify with any precision the exact nature of the variables that brought about the changed behaviour in these programmes. People's jobs have been redesigned certainly, but there is often doubt as to whether or not any changes (regarding, for example, increased responsiblity or more varied tasks) were accepted *voluntarily* or not. Studies after the event suggest they may often seem to have been, but it is possible that workers are reacting just as much to the interest shown in their progress by outsiders as they are to the job changes themselves or even that they are just keen to accept the *status quo*. Again many studies (for example Morse and Reimer, 1956), did not actually specify in their published reports the exact nature of any job changes involved. Others fail to consider the part played by changes in levels of pay consequent on job redesign. Neither should it be overlooked that many job enrichment programmes have been introduced in progressive firms with good employee relations; perhaps the schemes would not have had altogether satisfactory outcomes in less enlightened firms.

In the light of these difficulties we must be careful not to draw general conclusions from the published work. We *do* know that the simple attempt to make people's jobs wider or richer in content is in itself no panacea for management. Wildebois (1968) describes a failed job redesign programme. In this case young single girls had little interest when changes introduced involved them in more output – perhaps such changes interfered with more important things to them like their social life. And Ramondt (1968) reviewed work in six organizations showing how the antagonism of lower management minimized the success of redesign programmes.

Where job redesign programmes have been accompanied by more positive outcomes however, it seems to be the quality rather than the quantity of output which is most affected. Lawler (1969) reviewed many relevant studies in a useful attempt to explain this result. His hypothesis was that this effect was due to job changes resulting in 'intrinsic rewards', for example feelings of accomplishment, of growth, of self esteem. But ideas like 'feelings of accomplishment, of growth, of self esteem' are by no means easy to define or make operational in any study. And in fact the *specific* variables which Lawler examined were increased knowledge of results, increased use of valued abilities and increased opportunity for job control. As Lawler is able to conclude it may be that workers do react favourably to these, yet this is but small reason to favour his hypothesis. A simpler explanation of their effects might be extrapolated from the approaches of the University of California and the London Tavistock Institute. Both these research centres (see Davis, 1966; Emery, 1966) separately advocate the importance of people possessing clear goals, of control over variables affecting performance, and of clear feedback about performance. Job enrichment programmes may serve to meet these criteria; we would suggest that any move to explain their effects by using concepts such as 'intrinsic rewards' may be unnecessary.

Of interest to this discussion are three studies of job change concerned with voluntary acceptance by workers. Strauss (1955) observed the introduction of an assembly line pattern of work in a plant where this had not previously been in operation. The eight girls involved demanded greater control than had been provided over the pace of the belt at which they worked. As they were paid on a piece-rate basis, in effect they subsequently obtained greater control over their earnings. Babchuk and Goode (1951) studied the reaction of eighteen salesmen to the introduction of a new payment-on-commission system. It was noted that they voluntarily set themselves quotas and pooled their earnings; in this way (like Strauss's girls) they controlled their level of pay. Emery and Thorsrud (1969) observed a forced job enrichment programme which was unsuccessful in its early stages. They report that subsequently a number of people volunteered to take part in a similar experiment differing from the first only in that participants had greater control over their ability to produce high quality work.

The acceptance of innovation. In this section we very briefly look at some work concerned with voluntary acceptance of innovations to develop the theme touched on in the last. 'Diffusion research' is our starting point; as its name suggests, this considers the process of social contagion by which new ideas, practices or products are spread through society (Rogers, 1960). Studies carried out under this title vary widely from the acceptance of new methods in agriculture to the acceptance of drugs by doctors. From a broad range of studies however we can conclude that an innovation's chances of being adopted depend on the extent to which people can predict the effects of its use. So the complexity of an innovation is important, as are the chances of communication about it. Again, the chances of adoption seem to be dependent on the degree of risk involved here: if it can be tried out on a limited basis, or if it is seen to have very clear advantages, it is likely to be more acceptable.

The concept of the two-step flow of communication is also relevant to behaviour change. Here the hypothesis is that information flows from impersonal sources like the mass media initially to the 'opinion leaders' and that these people in turn influence others who are less affected by the impersonal sources. The hypothesis originally stemmed from an analysis of the ways in which people came to a decision concerning how to vote in an election (Lazarsfeld, Berelson and Gaudet, 1948). Related work has been reported by Katz (1957) who reviewed four studies undertaken at Columbia. One of these was his own team's research into the diffusion of a new drug among doctors, and it was apparent that the two-step hypothesis was broadly supported.

Another area where the concept of opinion leadership is currently proving of use is highlighted by the recent research at the Massachusetts Institute of Technology (Marquis, 1971). The work suggests that the idea of opinion leaders helps explain the process underlying successful scientific and technical innovation emanating from industrial laboratories. It was observed that certain individuals in the laboratories have far greater contact with the scientific world through attending meetings and conferences and by reading technical journals. Just as with Katz's doctors, it was these people who were consistently consulted for advice by their colleagues in the same organization, and it was their advice which was related to the subsequent development of profitable innovations.

Our earlier discussion on stress served to make the point that personal influence is important in situations which are uncertain. In these situations any change leading to an improvement in prediction is desired, and clearly one of the most obvious methods of achieving such an improvement would be to find someone whose opinion you can trust and to learn from him. This would be a question of gaining and using 'social support' to maintain psychological stability and the predictability of your environment.

Changing a job. Changing jobs is a topic which is discussed in chapter 9, and we wish to make only a limited comment here. Shuh's (1967) review failed to find any clear causal connection between the variables often studied and job change, and it seems in fact that two major classes of variables have largely been overlooked. On the one hand the very importance of jobs to people has rarely been assessed, and on the other hand researchers often do not take into account the attractiveness of possible alternative work. If we can learn from research done to date it is that detailed analysis of how an individual feels about factors like his present pay, boss or opportunities for self development needs to be supplemented by inquiries with a wider perspective.

Linked with the importance of people's expectations, is the idea that people may leave jobs if these do not meet their notions about what they as people are like. Ross and Zander (1957) noted that leavers differed from stayers in the amounts of autonomy and recognition they received. It might be inferred that if people do not have enough control over variables affecting the attainment of performance standards by which they judge themselves they will perceive any judgement that is made as unfair. Wickert (1951) studied six hundred telephone operators and service representatives; job leavers felt they had less chance to make decisions on the job and felt they were unable to make important contributions to the success of the company they worked for.

For some time we have been interested in one particular type of labour turnover – the tendency for graduates recruited directly from university to leave their first employer within two years of joining. The phenomenon is so widespread that it is not possible to place it simply on any one organization's selection and training methods. The reasons are probably deeper and are likely to hinge upon the perceived ambiguity of the new situation.[1] The graduate is used to the educational system, whose clear goals and informative feedback give him a basis upon which he can form judgements of himself and upon which others can base their judgements. In the world of business no such basis for judgements apparently exists. To the new graduate this may mean that no one understands him, knows how to treat him or even cares how to treat him. The system on which industry is based is therefore somewhat foreign to the graduate, and in the absence of clear feedback he finds himself in a strange, ambiguous, apparently alien environment.

Effective leadership. The nature and effects of different managerial styles and qualities are examined in chapter 12, where many rele-

1. This notion may be generally applied to the concept of an 'induction crisis' which is considered on p. 138.

vant studies are reviewed. Much of this work can be interpreted in terms of the main theme of this section. It may be that a particularly important characteristic of effective leadership is the extent to which it reduces ambiguity and enhances predictability in one's working environment (c.f. Kelvin, 1970).

Sadler's (1968, 1970) study of preferences for particular styles of leadership showed that managers with distinct and identifiable styles were more effective in promoting confidence and satisfaction whatever style they adopted. As the discussion in chapters 12 and 15 indicates, employees do not always want democratic, participative leadership (although many of them do!), and we might see this in terms of their wish to avoid too much ambiguity and uncertainty. Fiedler's contingency model (see ch. 12) suggests that the leadership style which is most effective varies from situation to situation. An interpretation of his classification of situations as more or less favourable for leaders (see Figure 12.3, p. 278) would be that the favourable situation is one where leaders are easily able to predict the outcomes of their actions. When the group's tasks are clear there is little likelihood that people will question their decisions; if they have power behind their arms then demands made are unlikely to be resisted. In such a situation the effective leader does not promote ambiguity where none exists, while in a situation where these conditions do not exist (and it is obviously rather more difficult to lead) the effective leader is the one who resolves high levels of ambiguity. And when it is neither extremely easy nor extremely difficult to lead, the leader will be effective when he encourages his group to involve themselves in problem-solving activities.

INTERPRETATION AND IMPLICATIONS

In this short chapter, our review of situations where people are known to be highly involved and of occasions when they have changed their customary modes of behaviour inevitably has been selective. We have been able to include only a small number of studies. Yet we believe a number of common threads can be identified, that may indicate a general framework applicable to other work.

Note that our discussion of stress served to make the point that role ambiguity, conflict and overload are all unpleasant because people who experience them do not know what they should do nor how they can do it. Stress might be reduced when a person's situation is made less ambiguous and more predictable. Research in job redesign is not easy to interpret, yet it seems that clear performance standards are important, as is control over variables affecting their attainment. Diffusion research indicates that people only change when they can weigh up how much they will be affected by innovation. And the finding that the normal flow of opinion is from the mass media to opinion leaders and from them to others can be explained by the suggestion that opinion leaders are used by others as examples to help them make predictions. In considering why people change jobs we observed that people seek control over variables which are important to them. In our discussion of the role of the boss, we noted that the inconsistent leader (whose behaviour is difficult to anticipate) was seen to be a source of stress. And we can conclude from Fiedler's work in the field of leader effectiveness, that leaders are effective when they help their followers to predict and control their environment.

Two concepts seem to be of recurring value in explaining the phenomena considered here. Firstly, it seems important to people that they are able to *predict* events, and secondly we note that people seek to exercise *control* over certain variables. The identification of the importance of the processes of prediction and control no doubt goes a long way to explain what we *mean* by the very idea of motivated, purposeful behaviour. Yet more than to simply clarify what we understand by such ideas, we can now interpret people's behaviour at work within this framework. By emphasizing the centrality of the processes of prediction and control, managers and psychologists alike will better be able to understand the behaviours of those they are concerned with.

To a greater or lesser degree, what matters to us all is that our lives should be fairly predictable. Great upheavals in how we are to spend our time are disturbing, as is uncertainty about what is expected of us; and when expected outcomes are not contingent on our behaviours we are distressed. In our society some major factors relevant to our capacity to predict are our ability to maintain our income, to preserve and develop our status with others, the state of our health, the type of person we associate with. When any of these is disrupted, uncertainty is involved. And note that work is central to all of them – a man's job often dictates his income, his status, to some extent his friends and even perhaps his health. We all seek control over relevant features such as these.

But although this argument seems to be one biased towards stability, it is apparent that in many circumstances change can be welcomed. The introduction of new ideas and techniques at work must go on all the time, but many of the current rush of programmes to redesign jobs and to change the work environment overlook the point which the missionaries to Africa in the nineteenth century forgot. If we force people to change to a new way of life which upsets rather than replaces traditional values then we must expect trouble. By all means let us give individuals the fullest opportunity to develop themselves. But we overlook at our peril the fact that some people prefer to develop themselves away from their jobs in their spare-time activities; and the fact that self development is very much the second priority if opportunity to test oneself further means that one's ability to control a comparatively predictable environment is endangered. Job-enrichment programmes often give people new chances to try out their abilities at holding down increased responsibility, but often they carry the implied threat that should they fail, life may be made more difficult. In such a case where employees feel they cannot predict likely outcomes it is hardly surprising that they are against the programme.

The days of blanket reward systems giving the same to everyone, of automatic promotion up career ladders, of allocations of rewards and punishments with little explanation as to the whys and wherefores, are probably over. They should cease because, we suggest, people like to know where they are going, they like to have some control over the circumstances which affect the stability of important factors such as their earnings and status, and they like their rewards to be fair and contingent on their performance. Treating people in this way means that we have to find out what matters to each individual, what each individual will perceive as fair and as rewarding or punishing. It means treating people as individuals, and if there is anything that can be said with any certainty after reviewing the literature it is that what matters to every person is to be treated as an individual by those who matter to him. And that goes for those who work with him as well as those who live with and love him.

SUMMARY

In this chapter research from a number of different areas is reviewed in an attempt to break away from simple overall theories of behaviour at work and to acknowledge the rich variety of human experience in the work situation.

The relationships between attitudes to work and performance at work are first discussed. It is easy to assume that it is the satisfied worker and not his dissatisfied colleague who works harder, but research does not in general confirm this pattern. Reasons why this may be so are discussed and it is argued that rather than study overall attitudes the effects of particular variables in the work situation should be examined. In this connection the influence of a person's co-workers is particularly stressed.

We then move on to review research into situations where people are known to be highly involved and into circumstances where customary modes of behaviour are changed. Causes of stress at work and behaviour which copes with stress are discussed. Job-enrichment programmes, the processes of acceptance of innovation, of changing jobs and of effective leadership are each briefly considered in the light of people's need for stability and predictability. Our general conclusions are that people like to be able to predict the development of personally important events and that they like to have some control of relevant variables.

FURTHER READING

This chapter is in many ways an extension of the previous one, and the additional sources cited there are also relevant to the material now discussed. Other books of readings which cover the field of motives and work behaviour are *Studies in Personnel and Industrial Psychology*, edited by E. A. Fleishman (Dorsey Press, revised edition, 1967) and *Management and Motivation*, edited by V. H. Vroom and E. L. Deci (Penguin, 1970).

Detailed examinations of the nature of attitudes and attitude change are provided in volumes 2 and 3 of the *Handbook of Social Psychology* edited by G. Lindzey and E. Aronson (Addison-Wesley, 1968 and 1969), and in M. Fishbein's *Readings in Attitude*

Theory and Measurement (Wiley, 1967). A general treatment of social psychology which emphasizes people's need to predict events around them can be found in P. Kelvin's *The Bases of Social Behaviour* (Holt, Rinehart & Winston, 1970).

15
Some Aspects of Employee Participation

George Hespe and Alan Little

One of the most pressing issues in contemporary industrial relations is the degree of employee participation in a working organization which is most appropriate. This topic has been discussed by people of many different backgrounds, and in this chapter the emphasis is on psychological considerations; studies by psychologists are set within the framework of a broad examination of different forms of participative practice. Participation is seen in terms of the sharing of power, information and profits; and some research into each of these is described. The authors have themselves carried out studies in this field, and a summary account of part of their work is presented here.

Clearly emerging from the discussion in the last two chapters is a viewpoint of man as the possessor of various needs whose higher echelons are equivalent to a requirement for greater involvement with the world about him. One obvious way in which this may be achieved is through greater involvement, or participation, in his employing organization. However, whilst management and workers may see the desirability of more involvement by employees in the activities of the enterprise, there is but little agreement on the manner or extent of this participation. At one extreme advocates of workers' control would view workers' involvement in areas of decision making, previously dealt with exclusively by management, as simply an intermediate stage in the inevitable progress to a situation of workers replacing management. Other employees might be more satisfied with the *status quo*. The views of those managers who hold any favours for the notion of greater employee involvement may range from the employee having a little more say in his own working conditions to the opinion that employees should be shareholders in the enterprise with adequate representation at board level.

THE PROBLEM OF DEFINITION

The researchers' prerequisite of establishing parameters for participation has itself presented a considerable problem since there is no universally accepted definition of what exactly we mean by the term.[1] Essentially, however, we are concerned with a concept of sharing in three functions of the enterprise's activities, namely:

1. *Power* – to what extent and by what means should employees be enabled to influence the decision-making structure of the enterprise?

2. *Information* – what information relevant to the functioning of the enterprise should be passed to employees and what methods of communication should be used?

3. *Profits* – should employees' earnings be more closely geared to the financial success (or failure) of the enterprise?

There are basically two methods of approaching research work in this area. One is a fairly broad descriptive approach in terms of the structure and functioning of various kinds of participative procedures. The other entails studies, ranging from simple laboratory settings up to complex organizational environments, which investigate the effects of differences in personal and situational participation characteristics on employee effectiveness and satisfaction.

Research on participation following the first approach includes extensive international surveys such as those of the International Institute for Labour Studies. Also, more intensive studies of one form of workers' participation in management in a small number of selected organizations have been reported in the literature – for example, the work of Emery and Thorsrud (1969) on the representation of workers on the boards of companies in Norway. Various useful conceptual frameworks have been proposed. Walker's (1967) is based on two complementary components; the first, 'participation potential', takes into account the cultural setting, size, location and technology of the enterprise while the second, 'propensity to participate', is dependent on the willingness and ability of employees involved to participate. The interaction of these two components, suggests Walker, gives rise to a wide range of possible organizational climates, in which participation schemes may flourish or wither.

1. For a detailed discussion of the problem of definition of workers' participation in management see Walker (1970).

Walker's scheme, however, while useful conceptually deals with participation at an abstract level. We need to analyse what we mean by participation in greater detail.

A CONCEPTUAL MODEL OF PARTICIPATION IN ORGANIZATIONS

Globerson (1970) has put forward another useful model which breaks down the participation concept in terms of five 'spheres' or dimensions, each graduated into different levels on the basis of degrees of specificity or generality. Globerson's model provides us with a useful way of structuring what is a very wide and heterogeneous area of discussion, and his broad scheme is a good starting point for further debate (see Table 15.1).

Some forms of participation do, by their very nature, offer more scope than others when examined on the basis of an involvement criterion, although it must be borne in mind that the actual level of participation is not strictly defined by the particular organizational form present – a company may show a great deal of informal participation without the existence of any formal schemes. This aspect will be considered in the following broad and non-exclusive discussion of the main types of participation programme. The ordering of the various schemes is not rigid – works councils, for instance, could fit in at many levels, depending on the amount of practical power they yield.

This discussion tends to exclude informal participation, which occurs to some extent in every organization, and may in practice be more important than the formally prescribed arrangements. Participation through trade unions is also omitted from consideration; as discussed in chapter 16 this tends to be more concerned with bargaining, often in an atmosphere of confrontation with management rather than of participation in it. (There are of course cases of management and trade unions functioning effectively together in the democratic management of a company.)

Profit sharing

This need not involve the mass of individuals, or indeed their representatives, in detailed discussions with management, although employees participate in the organization to the extent of sharing in the success of their enterprise. However, profit sharing

Table 15.1

	Spheres	*Levels*				
		1	*2*	*3*	*4*	*5*
A	Institutionalization	Voluntary	Plant agreement	Industry agreement	National agreement	Government law
B	Decision making	General information to personnel	Joint consultation	Passive participation in management	Active participation in management	Self management
C	Subject matter	Wages, salaries and fringe benefits	Safety and hygiene	Welfare	Plant operations	All
D	Personal participation	Individual	Selective groups	Functional units	Full plant representation	Entire personnel
E	Material gain	Basic wages and salaries	Incentives	Bonuses and prizes	Profit sharing	Profit and loss sharing

might be an effective adjunct to another scheme which did give employees more opportunity to participate in organizational decisions since it would tend to involve them more in ensuring that the right decisions were made – in the interest of their own financial well-being. Profit-making schemes are typically institutionalized at the level of plant, or sometimes industry, agreement.

Suggestion schemes

Suggestion schemes, which usually offer financial incentives or prizes for ideas which increase workplace efficiency are a fairly low-level rudimentary type of participation programme and are typically concerned with suggestions for the improvement of specific working methods, materials handling, safety, hygiene, and so on. Although every member of an organization is part of the scheme, active participation is necessarily an occasional thing and is typically found to consist of voluntary efforts by a few individuals, the vast majority of employees remaining somewhat apathetic to such schemes. This is not to say that the schemes are not useful – in British industry, where they are very common, many valuable ideas have been thrown up by them. By themselves, however, they do not seem significantly to increase overall participation in an organization.

Job enrichment

Job enrichment is a fairly low-level system in terms of the actual level of decisions in which it involves workers. The introduction of such a scheme may, however, have far-reaching effects higher up the organizational structure, since it does give to employees responsibilities and decision-making powers previously held by their superiors. Job enrichment involves the *active* participation of shop-floor employees, typically in decisions concerning their own work areas and functions. Its theoretical background has been discussed in chapters 13 and 14. Briefly, it is based on the notion that the increasing specialization and simplification of work in modern industry leads to monotony, boredom and general dissatisfaction and, hence, to undesirable work behaviour in terms of absenteeism, lateness and frequent job changes. Job enrichment and its antecedents, job enlargement (in which an employee may be allowed to perform a sequence of tasks rather than a single repetitive one) and job rotation (in which employees circulate among different functions), attempt to reverse the specialization trend by giving employees more varied tasks which, it is claimed, will interest them more in their work and also make them more productive.

More important from the point of view of our discussion, however, is the fact that job enrichment differs from its predecessors in that employees are asked to take over some of the responsibilities previously held by superiors or by colleagues at a slightly higher level in the organization (Paul and Robertson, 1970). An assembler might be asked to assume responsibility not only for producing the requisite quantity of an item but also for controlling the product's quality and himself rejecting items which fail to reach the required standard. A machine operator may be allowed to do his own setting and maintenance as well as operating his machine, or a clerk may be given authority to make decisions on what commodities he needs to requisition from the stores without recourse to a superior for approval. Job enrichment involves adding another dimension to a person's day-to-day work – a planning and controlling (and hence a decision-making) dimension. In the sense that more initiative, involvement and responsibility are required of an individual, his job has been 'enriched'. Protagonists of the approach suggest that as a result he will respond with greater dedication and satisfaction which should lead to welcome dividends in terms of increased efficiency and reduced absenteeism and labour turnover. Job enrichment may co-exist with many different kinds of payment system, although basic wages and salaries are probably the most common: such schemes are typically decided by plant agreement.

Production committees

Many production committees and joint consultative committees owe their inception to special circumstances such as the war or its aftermath. For example, 'joint production committees' were set up in Britain, Canada and the USA during the Second World War, while French 'comités' (discussed on p. 329) came into being, in a country which had been generally slow to adopt participative procedures, as a result of the priority to increase production after that war.

This type of system is fairly common in British industry, and is typically organized at plant level. Production committees are usually purely advisory bodies and have no decision-making authority on issues that are traditionally management's responsibility. Committees typically consist of staff representatives together with groups of people elected from a department. They discuss none of the issues which are normally negotiated by trade unions, but consider only 'neutral' issues, such as plant operations, safety and hygiene. Any member of a department workforce can be elected on to a production committee but representatives do not have a great deal of actual decision-making power. The committees, however, provide a useful forum for the airing of problems and sharing of information. They may co-exist with any type of payment system.

Scanlon type systems

Probably the most highly-developed approaches and examples of the participative management of an enterprise on a company-wide scale are the several examples of the so-called 'Scanlon Plan' (Lesieur, 1958). The Scanlon Plan involves factory-wide incentive systems for sharing the economic results of productivity and is typically institutionalized at the plant agreement level. It complements the existing management hierarchy in the organization with a network of joint labour-management committees which deal with employee suggestions, attempt to solve production problems and develop new plans for improvement. They can deal with most topics apart from remuneration. These committee networks involve representatives of rank-and-file workers so that most of the workforce remains passive in terms of actual decision making, although the committee representatives are involved in key policy decisions. The successful plan, however, claims to involve employees to a greater extent in goals for productivity, costs, prices and profits, since each individual has an economic stake in the success of his company. Whilst this type of scheme is most prevalent in the USA, an increasing number of British companies use similar types of systems.

Works councils

All the systems discussed so far vary greatly in the amount of actual participation in company management they confer on employees, according to the particular setting in which they are installed, the degree of commitment to their success and so on. More than any other system, however, works councils can mean very different things in different countries – they may be institutionalized at many levels from plant agreement to government law, for example. This section will be sub-divided into some of the better-known national forms of participation by works council.

1. *French Comités d'Entreprise*. Since 1946, it has been compulsory to set up a committee in every undertaking employing fifty or more workers. Normally, the head of a company acts as chairman and his committee consists of a number of elected workers according to the total workforce employed. Elections are usually held by ballot every two years, candidates being put forward by trade unions as representatives for the employees of an undertaking. Negotiations as to conditions of employment are excluded from committee meetings,which are normally held monthly, as are grievance procedures which are a matter for management and unions. The committees, like British production committees, are purely consultative bodies, except in so far as welfare activities are concerned. However, although the head of the undertaking always has the last word on organizational problems, management has to justify its proposals and take the views of the committee into full account. Clearly, the majority of workers remain passive in this system of participation, although their elected representatives have some impact at a fairly high level in organizational decisions, albeit only in an advisory capacity.

2. *Legally enforced German Works Councils*. Legally enforced works councils have a very long history in German industry, dating back as far as 1848. These councils are the legally prescribed representative body of the employees, elected by secret ballot every three years. To some extent they perform the functions of a trade union at plant-level, negotiating with management for shop-agreements while the trade unions are more concerned with

industry-wide wage levels and working conditions. Works councils consist only of employee representatives and are thus independent from management – an important feature which distinguishes them from production committees in British industry or the French type of works council. Corporation rights provide for the works councils to influence management's decisions although management's decision-making power is unaffected. Although the majority of employees take no active part, their representatives on the councils do have influence in high-level decisions. Furthermore, they can appeal to 'labour courts' in the event that management does not take into account their objections to a planned course of action. As far as the economic situation of their undertaking is concerned, works councils receive periodic reports, special economic committees being set up in larger companies.

3. *Co-determination.* In the coal and steel industries of Germany, formal participation has been extended to other levels under the 'co-determination' system. This system operates at two levels:

(a) Works councils (as described earlier).
(b) A supervisory board – consisting of between a third and a half employee representatives, elected by the works council and trade union, together with management representatives and a neutral member. Its function is to review all business matters and control decisions made by the management board, on to which it elects a full-time member – the labour director, who is usually a trade unionist and concerns himself mainly with personnel issues. The supervisory board can be authorized by shareholders to exercise veto powers over certain management decisions but it does not normally interfere in the day-to-day management of the enterprise. The internal representatives on supervisory boards are elected by works councils but are not otherwise controlled by the councils and do not formally consult with each other. The works council solves problems with the management board (including the labour director) and only then do the problems come before the supervisory board.

4. *Yugoslav Workers' Councils.* In Yugoslavian company organization, the workers' council is the highest authority and this takes part in all decisions up to the highest levels. Membership varies ac-

cording to the size of the undertaking and members are elected annually for a maximum period of three years by workers and staff. The council (together with a local 'people's committee') appoints the director who, with a management board, manages the firm under the direction and guidance of the council which typically holds its meetings monthly, these being open to all employees. As is pointed out below, this is how the system operates in theory and the balance of power may not be like this in practical terms. Council approves plans for production and marketing, makes decisions on wages and the use of profits and is also responsible for the hiring and promotion of employees.

Studies by Kolaja (1961, 1965, reported in Emery and Thorsrud, 1969) show, however, that as far as board meetings are concerned, management personnel carry much more influence in companies than is indicated by the formal organizational structure and title of self-management. In fact, while workforce representatives and others may frequently voice opinions, the director seems to take the bulk of decisions. Thus it appears that the system offers a great deal of representational participation but that not all the decision-making power is used. Of course, the management committee must report back to the highest body – the workers' council – but Kolaja shows that the director has a dominant role even at this level. It is particularly true that financial and technological management problems are handled by management with formal approval of non-management people who usually do not have the necessary expertise to participate actively in some areas and limit themselves in general to personnel affairs. Kolaja concludes that because the bulk of important organizational problems are, in fact, handled by management, the workers' council legislation has not given workers more autonomy.

Employee directors

The employee director system has become established to some extent in several European countries, usually at an industry agreement level, and is perhaps the form of participation which involves the least number of individual workers in an organization and is most remote from the workforce as a whole. This is particularly so in larger organizations where many employees may never have heard of the idea despite it being extant in their own company.

The system consists of a number of representatives, usually with considerable shop-floor experience, who are nominated to sit on the management board and advise on policy. Clearly, most employees remain passive in this form of participation and the degree to which they are represented in management's decision making is predicated on how representative of them their particular employee director is. Obviously, the worker director system can co-exist with any type of payment policy.

Kibbutzim

The kibbutz movement represents a rather specialized and localized type of participatory system, found largely in Israel. It is much deeper than a mere industrial system and involves the communization of production and consumption and de-emphasizes the family as the intermediate social unit between individual and community. A kibbutz acts as a body in production, marketing and purchasing and the philosophy of kibbutz life requires subordination of individual to collective will. Kibbutzim function through elected leaders and committees with all members of a kibbutz community free to attend and contribute to meetings. This feature together with the economic interdependence of individuals means that all members can play their part in running the organization if they so wish. Kibbutz life necessarily involves sharing of profits and losses among the whole community.

Co-ownership

This involves complete control and ownership by the employees of a firm, the distributable profits of the enterprise being shared out amongst all employees in direct relation to their earnings. All employees (except perhaps those who have only recently joined) have voting power and control the company through votes at an annual general meeting like shareholders do in a conventional company. They may also exercise indirect control through a works committee elected on the basis of one-man-one-vote which deals with welfare matters and acts as an advisory body to the board of directors of which its chairman is a member. Typically schemes of this kind involve fairly small companies.

EMPIRICAL STUDIES OF PARTICIPATION

So far participation has been discussed in terms of a broad descriptive approach and the different forms in which the basic philosophy has been expressed in industry have been described. We now turn to a second research approach, complementary to the first, which involves the more systematic manipulation of variables in experimental and organizational settings, rather than observation and assessment of existing participation programmes.

The psychologist frequently applies his expertise to industrial research based on a three stage process. Somewhat paradoxically the first stage is the development of hypotheses founded on experimental work in the psychologist's laboratory. The findings from this type of experimentation may then be tested and refined by means of 'micro' experiments, normally using small groups or one small department in an enterprise. The experimenter's third task may imply the reformulation and refinement of hypotheses developed through stages one and two in a 'macro' fashion, that is by considering the whole of the enterprise as the experimental group. (Here is another example of the interdependence between laboratory and field studies discussed in some detail by Broadbent in chapter 1.)

One of the pitfalls which the psychologist at work must avoid is that of assuming that an observed result in, for example, stage two (the 'micro' stage) should be replicated in stage three (the 'macro' stage). The latter stage may have very different environmental conditions in terms of group size, payment systems, managerial policies (formal and informal) and many other social factors. These variables are of critical importance in research at the macro stage and need to be fully considered in attempts to generalize the results from other stages of research.

Let us now consider three examples of this transition of experimental work from the laboratory situation through the micro stage to the macro type experiment. Early in the chapter we considered participation in terms of the sharing of power, profits and information, and we shall look at an example of each of these at the three stages of research.

Sharing of power

1. *Laboratory work*. Lewin, Lippitt and White (1939) investigated the variation in behaviour and attitudes of children in a specially organized club when subjected to different types of leadership, namely, authoritarian, democratic and *laissez-faire*. They found that the children led by authoritarian leaders (who determined policy, dictated activities and were arbitrary and personal in evaluation of activities) developed little of their own motivation with respect to the club's activities. Although the children worked productively when the leader was present, the lack of personal motivation towards group goals clearly evidenced itself in

(a) Change of behaviour when the leader left the club.
(b) Absence of motivation when the leader arrived late.
(c) Lack of carefulness in the work.
(d) Lack of initiative in offering spontaneous suggestions in regard to club projects.
(e) Lack of pride in the products of the group's efforts.

The democratic type of leadership, involving group decisions on activities, was preferred by the group members and appeared to lead to better interpersonal relations, higher morale and greater productivity. This leadership behaviour was in many senses 'participative' in that power was not held exclusively by the leader.

2. *Micro-level work*. A classic illustration of experimentation at this second level is represented by the work of Coch and French (1948) who conducted an experiment in a pyjama manufacturing company. The fundamental independent variable was the degree to which workers were permitted to participate in planning a needed production change. Some workers were allowed total participation whereas others were allowed only indirect participation (through representatives) or no participation. The results showed that participation in any degree yielded significantly higher production than did no participation at all.

3. *Macro-level work*. The influence of the previous type of research is clearly seen in some of the macro-level studies involving the extension of the power enjoyed by employees, for example the work of Marrow, Bowers and Seashore (1967) when implementing

an extensive change programme in the Weldon Manufacturing Company. This company had been taken over in 1962 by the Harwood Manufacturing Company, previously their leading rivals. Subsequent to the takeover it became apparent that Harwood's philosophy of involving employees in the company's decision-making structure was not reflected in the traditional authority system at Weldon. It was considered that a change to the Harwood participative approach might lead to improvements in factors such as productivity and reduced labour turnover where Harwood was considerably more successful. The results of the change programme were quite marked. Within two years the return on invested capital changed from a 15 per cent loss to a 17 per cent gain. Labour turnover and absenteeism rates were reduced by 50 per cent whilst productivity increased by more than 30 per cent. Changes in attitude measurements were also seen to reflect a move in the direction congruent with the aims of the change programme.

In view of the impressive results obtained from these three types of studies of the sharing of power one could readily be excused for considering increased influence by employees in decision making as a panacea for many industrial shortcomings. This is a viewpoint which we believe to be quite erroneous since there are many situations, for example in military settings in time of combat, when autocratic decision making is likely to be more effective than that of a group. As Vroom (1969) points out, the relative effectiveness of a decision-making style depends on the importance attached to quality, acceptance and time variables; different styles will be preferable in different settings. Such a conclusion was also reached in chapter 12, where power sharing was considered from a slightly different standpoint.

Sharing of profits

Our discussion so far has been restricted to research work in that part of the sharing concept concerned with power. Let us now review some of the investigations connected with the sharing of profits.

1. *Laboratory work.* A considerable amount of research on financial returns from working has concerned itself with theories

of equity and inequity. Essentially inequity is seen to exist when inputs (for example skill, experience and amount of effort expended) are perceived to be discrepant from outcomes in terms such as pay, status and intrinsic job satisfaction.[2]

Adams and Rosenbaum (1962) tested the hypothesis that laboratory subjects when led to believe they were overpaid would reduce their sense of inequity by increased work effort. Subjects were paid three and a half dollars an hour to carry out interviews. Half of the subjects were told that they were adequately qualified and paid equitably whilst the remainder were told that they were not qualified and therefore overpaid. As predicted the latter group carried out significantly more interviews than the control group. The theory would predict that subjects overpaid on an hourly basis would increase their work output, whereas for those overpaid on a piecework basis increased work would merely increase the feeling of inequity since it would exaggerate their overpayment. Adams and Jacobsen (1964) tested the hypothesis that overpaid subjects on piecework would reduce inequity by reducing the quantity of their output. The results of this experiment, in which subjects were presented with a proof-reading test, showed that the overpaid experimental group read significantly fewer pages than did the two equitably paid groups, thus substantiating the hypothesis.

2. *Micro-level work*. Earlier in this chapter we sounded a note of caution to the effect that differences in situational variables may mean that we may not generalize from one type of study to another. In consideration of equitable payments and laboratory *vis-à-vis* micro studies we see a clear example of this. Whyte (1955) carried out a series of case studies on economic incentives and found that the establishment of individual states of equity, as might be expected from the laboratory studies above, was confounded by the emergence of a dominant factor of restriction of output to a level which was acceptable to the group as a whole, that is a norm. As noted in chapter 13 workers are subjected to pressure from co-workers to hold their production around a cer-

2. A more complete account of this concept is presented in chapters 13 and 16.

tain level. Those who conform to these standards are accepted by their colleagues whilst those who greatly exceed or fall short of this level are rejected and become unpopular. This factor – so significant at the micro level – is not usually apparent in laboratory studies.

3. *Macro-level work.* One of the best examples of experimentation with profit sharing at macro level is in the application of the Scanlon type of plan. This was discussed earlier in the chapter (see p. 328).

Sharing of information

One of the problems to be solved in the quest for better industrial relations is concerned with the 'whether, what, when and how' to share information with employees. Again we may see the link between the laboratory, micro and macro studies which attempt to throw light on the problem.

1. *Laboratory work.* Leavitt (1951) conducted an experiment which demonstrates the effect of the communication structure and amount of information available within a group on the members' satisfaction and performance. By an arrangement of communication networks between group members he restricted in varying degrees the number of available channels of communication. For example, in a 'circle' arrangement members may only contact those on either side whereas in the 'wheel' network the central member may contact any of the other constituent members although their contact is restricted to a link between themselves and the central member. The task was to find which symbol on the cards handed to group members was common to them all. The results of this experiment clearly showed that the communication network employed had a significant effect on members' behaviour and satisfaction. In terms of the fastest correct solution the wheel was found to be most efficient whereas the circle tended to afford greater satisfaction. Other relationships indicated that the degree of centrality of a member greatly influenced his satisfaction level.

2. *Micro-level work.* Bales (1950) investigated the successfulness of a conference as a means of communicating ideas and its effect on behaviour. Observers recorded the remarks of in-

dividuals in small groups whilst discussing various business problems. Experimental groups took part in four sessions of forty minutes each and their method of operation in terms of patterns of communication was observed. Analysis of the data indicated that the difficult problem of group communication is not just with the leader but rather among the entire group membership. After manipulation of the size of committees Bales considered that in order to obtain optimum participation by members, the group should be limited, in most circumstances to a maximum of seven members.

3. *Macro-level work*. Of late there is increasing interest amongst managements and employees in improving communication procedures within their enterprises as a whole. In Britain formal methods for transmission of information towards higher echelons of management frequently centre around appropriate suggestion schemes, sectional and departmental committees, works councils and occasionally employee directors. These have been described above. The passing of much information from management to employees is often based on notice board announcements of committee minutes together with articles contained in company publications such as house magazines and newsletters. Several British organizations are currently introducing the Briefing Group system to improve the downward transmission of information. This system places the responsibility on senior management of giving relevant information on the company's affairs, in both an oral and written manner, to departmental management and then ensuring that this information is transmitted in face-to-face fashion to employees in groups of approximately fifteen to twenty members.

It is of importance to realize that an enterprise's communications system functions on two levels, that is the formal level, as exemplified in the above paragraph, and also at the informal level. An example of the latter would be in the sharing of information between a manager and his subordinate in a non-crisis type of face-to-face meeting on the shop-floor. There is a growing awareness amongst management that time must be made available to meet employees in this informal manner and that handsome dividends in the acquisition of useful production ideas and a higher level of mutual trust fully justify the time so expended.

EMPLOYEE ATTITUDES TO PARTICIPATION

The remainder of this chapter will be concerned with the attitudes of shop-floor employees to various forms of industrial participation and the organizational and individual factors influencing such attitudes. People's propensity to participate is clearly a variable with crucial influence on the success of any scheme, and it is a factor which has been badly neglected as a topic for research. The idea that participation in some (possibly unspecified) form is morally necessary to recognize workers as full human beings with certain undeniable rights has been widely propounded, but we must first discover if workers in fact wish to exercise such rights. It seems quite possible that in some case the traditions, expectations and ideology of a workforce would actually constitute limitations on the applicability of a participative approach. Thus, analysis of orientations to work which are found to prevail is more useful than quite general assumptions about the needs which all workers are deemed to possess.

One of the few studies which has concerned itself with employees' attitudes to increased participation was that of Holter (1962) in seventeen companies in the Oslo area. Holter's data arose out of a larger study of age and sex differences in behaviour and attitudes in the work situation, and three questions out of eighty-six particularly concerned themselves with attitudes to participation. Holter found a widespread desire on the part of employees for more information about the management and plans of their firms. She also found 'a general, uncommitted but quite extensive belief that there ought to be more "industrial democracy" in the enterprise'. From the point of view of personal participation the desire was for increased participation in decisions regarding an individual's own work and conditions, with comparatively few individuals wishing to participate in company matters as a whole. Banks's study (1963) measuring propensity to participate in the existing organizational framework in terms of interest in becoming a trade union or works council representative seems to support this finding. Very few men were interested in becoming an active participant in decisions at a higher level than those concerning their own jobs. In these decisions they wished to be represented, but not representative. Similar findings are reported by Flanders, Pomeranz and Woodward (1968) and Blum (1968).

This greater interest in 'local' as opposed to 'general' participation seems to be quite usual. We must however incorporate into any account of employee attitudes those contextual variables which are likely to mediate a particular set of findings. Amongst the important mediating factors are the size and location of the organization, its technology and structure, the degree of unionization and the present extent of participative procedures. Turner and Lawrence (1965) amongst others have shown that the geographical location of a plant (and hence the backgrounds of a large majority of the workers) plays an important role in shaping the attitudes of workers and influencing their behaviour. Size, technology and other organizational features are, of course, additional variables which may affect the results of any investigation. The type of occupation involved (department store sales girls, coal miners or skilled machinists for instance) and the age level, previous employment history and mobility are all of consequence here. So are variations in personality traits such as dependence, achievement motivation, and so on.

We are at present examining employee attitudes to participation in an attempt to specify the significant inter-organizational and inter-individual factors. So far we have interviewed nearly five hundred employees in eight different enterprises. This is not the place for a detailed presentation of our findings, but some salient points may be mentioned. These will be set in the framework of the three types of sharing noted earlier – sharing of the profits, the information and the power of the enterprise.

Profits

There was higher overall interest expressed in participating in some sort of profit sharing scheme than we anticipated. Over 50 per cent of employees showed enthusiasm for the notion, but there was a marked difference between those who worked on a one-man-one-machine basis (frequently paid by piecework) and those who worked on any other arrangement. Of the former only approximately 25 per cent of employees showed interest in profit sharing within their enterprises whereas over 70 per cent of the latter group did so.

Information

We found that the spread of information by the written word (for example through company newspapers and notice board announcements) has two major limitations. Firstly, employees all too frequently do not read them (or only read selected portions such as the sports page). Secondly, many employees do not consider that this is the correct method of giving them the information they want on company affairs. Neither do employees desire the transmitter of this information to be a works council or trade union representative. The majority places the onus of presenting information, on mutually agreed areas of the company's business, quite squarely on the shoulders of management.

Power

Throughout the chapter we have cited several different forms of power-sharing. One way of classifying these is in terms of how closely or otherwise the sharing arrangements influence an individual's day-to-day activities. Some forms of participation are really quite 'distant' in that the individual employee at his regular work place may feel relatively unaffected by their existence. Examples here are employee directors and some forms of works councils in large organizations. At the other extreme is 'local' participation, in which an employee may have considerablc influence over decisions about his own work arrangements. Job enrichment and certain styles of participatory behaviour by junior managers are illustrations of attempts to increase local participation.

It is quite likely that attitudes to local and to distant participation operate rather differently and that they are influenced by different background factors. Our present research is examining this question. For the present, however, data are available about the extent to which employees feel they should be enabled to influence management's decisions in ten different operational situations. These are laid out in Table 15.2 which summarizes the average opinions from the first three companies studied. The range of situations presented here is a fairly broad one, although it does not of course, cover the whole spectrum of possible decision-making situations.

Table 15.2 The average Response of Employees from three Industrial Organizations to a range of Decision-Making Situations.

Subjects were asked for their views on the way management should deal with the following situations.
For each situation a cross was placed under heading *a, b, c, d* or *e*.

	a This is a management matter	*b* We should be asked our views but it is up to management	*c* There should be negotiations, but if no agreement management should go ahead	*d* There should be negotiations, no action until agreement	*e* This is a matter on which management should accept what we say
To allocate profits between investments, dividends, reserves etc.					
To introduce new working methods					
To introduce work study methods					
To discharge workers no longer needed					
To change the method of payment					
To introduce a pension scheme or modify existing scheme					
To change starting and stopping times					
To alter works rules so as to change disciplinary proceedings					
To set up new procedures to deal with absenteeism					
To dismiss an individual or group of individuals for disciplinary reasons					

Those employees displaying apathy towards increased decision-making participation may be expected to register their scores towards the left-hand side of the continuum, whilst a general desire for 'workers' control' would be reflected in a move to the right extreme of the continuum. It is quite apparent that, in these three enterprises, there is only very limited support for any notion of workers' control based on employee dominance of the company's decision-making structure.

As far as differences between individual members of an organization are concerned, three points may be noted. First, one finding which is common to all the organizations studied, is that the more an employee influences the decision-making structure (and here quite clearly skilled workers are prominent) or alternatively perceives that he influences the decision-making structure of the company, then the more he wishes to participate in the company's affairs. Thus, an increase in the number of skilled personnel on the shop floor, together with any increase in participation on the part of employees, is likely to result in a general movement of employees' mean scores to the right-hand side of the decision-making continuum in Table 15.2. The second point to be mentioned in connection with individual differences and one which is related to the finding that the more an employee participates in his enterprise then the greater will be his desire for further participation, is the part played by age as a determinant of the desired involvement level. It seemed likely to us that the demand for increased participation within a company might come more from the younger age groups who typically seek more change. However, the results of our investigations to date are more consistent with the opposite viewpoint since the data obtained from questionnaire items and interviews indicate that the under twenty-six years age group often express a lower desire for increased participation than their older colleagues. Similarly younger people feel less well able to convey their views across to management. Whilst we must beware of assuming a causal relationship here, nevertheless it may be that an increase in the actual or perceived involvement level may be obtained if management were to place more emphasis on formal and informal communications with the younger employees.

The third aspect of individual differences in participation is concerned with the influence of personality variables on the desire for and effectiveness of participation. Whilst results so far obtained indicate that participation has positive effects on attitudes and performance, we also want to know whether these results vary with personality characteristics. Vroom's study (1960) demonstrated a positive relationship between high need for independence on the one hand and more favourable work attitudes and increased production on the other. The same researcher also established that equalitarians would operate more favourably than authoritarians in a participative industrial climate. Our own studies have not substantiated our hypothesis that extraverts would exhibit a greater desire for participation. It may be that more interesting results will be obtained from our current research using scales of Internal/External control (Rotter, 1966) and Bureaucratic Orientation (Gordon, 1970). Additionally, more refined analysis which controls for the effect of factors such as age and social class may throw more light on the part played by personality characteristics on participation.

The question here, clearly, is how far towards the right-hand side of the continuum will the mean have established itself in the utopian participative system? Indeed, will it record an overall demand for workers' control? We do not believe that this will be the case. We suggest that the participation needs of employees within the foreseeable future may be seen to rest in two areas, namely

1. A desire for more say in the running of their own particular job, either as individuals or as members of a work group.
2. Confidence that they are well represented by competent and informed colleagues who will have their views fully considered by managements as a basis for action.

SUMMARY

Research into the structures, functioning and effects of workers' participation in management has proceeded on several different, but complementary, levels. At one end of the scale researchers have been concerned with observation and assessment, sometimes in comparative terms, of existing organizational reality. For such research, we have derived several useful conceptual frameworks which help us to define more specifically the notion of 'participation', while on a more practical level the studies have helped to show the likely necessary precursors for success of various schemes in different organizational environments.

An equally important stream of research has evolved at a more rigorous, experimental level, and has involved manipulation of human and situational parameters in controlled situations and determination of the effects of such manipulation. Such research has taken place in a wide range of settings, ranging from the laboratory to actual workplace experimentation.

These two approaches represent the bulk of research on workers' participation. A third approach, somewhat neglected until recently, has examined workers' attitudes to various types of participation in relation to their organizational environment and their background, since the ability and willingness of workers to participate is obviously a necessary prerequisite for the success of any 'democratizing' programme.

FURTHER READING

The references cited in this chapter constitute only a small element of the growing literature in the area of participation. A general overview of the participation systems employed by a range of British industries is given by R. Sawtell in *Sharing Our Industrial Future* (The Industrial Society, 1968). F. E. Emery and E. Thorsrud's *Form and Content in Industrial Democracy* (Tavistock, 1969) presents a discussion of the role and functions of employee representatives on some Norwegian boards in addition to an examination of participation models and experiences in Yugoslavia, West Germany and Great Britain. M. Patchen's *Participation, Achievement and Involvement on the Job* (Prentice-Hall, 1970) is an empirically based consideration of the role of achievement motivation as a determining factor of employee involvement in their jobs.

Theoretical treatments of participation are considered by E. Rhenman in *Industrial Democracy and Industrial Management*

(Tavistock, 1968) and C. Pateman in *Participation and Democratic Theory* (Cambridge University Press, 1970) the latter being a consideration of industrial participation as one facet of a modern theory of democracy.

16
Inter-Group Relations and Negotiating Behaviour

Geoffrey Stephenson

Several earlier chapters have touched upon the relationships which develop between groups of different kinds, and these relationships are now examined in detail. The focus is on conflicts between unions and management, but relevant information obtained by experimental social psychologists in other fields is also used. Much disagreement within organizations is resolved by means of negotiations carried our by group representatives, and Dr Stephenson gives this process special attention. He describes research into group perceptual processes as well as presenting some theoretical accounts of the behaviour of negotiators.

Negotiating has been increasingly studied by psychologists, both in real life situations and in the laboratory. Underlying a great deal of this work are assumptions about the quality of relations between the groups whose representatives meet at the bargaining table. For example, managements and unions have some conflicting interests, and it is often assumed that representatives of such groups will reflect this conflict in their relations with one another. Acting on this assumption, some work on negotiating has sought ways of making negotiators emotionally independent of their groups, free to convert the dispute into a mere problem to be solved. Negotiators cannot, however, readily escape the conflict between their own needs and the needs of the parties whom they represent. It is a basic problem, and makes the negotiating situation peculiarly fascinating for the social psychologist. Because of this, it is essential that in learning about negotiating behaviour, we examine carefully the relations between the groups represented by the negotiators. In this chapter I shall first describe briefly a research tradition in the psychological study of intergroup relations which has inspired much of the recent work on negotiating behaviour. We shall then turn to look more directly at this behaviour.

COMPETITION IN INTER-GROUP RELATIONS

There is a tendency, endemic in social relationships, to compare critically our fortunes, our abilities and prestige with those of other people. It is reasonable to expect that this individual competitive tendency is greatly enhanced when representatives of one group interact with representatives of another group, for representatives of a group enjoy the additional incentive of recognition and acceptance by their fellows in the event of a creditable performance. Individual *and* group prestige are both at stake. Ferguson and Kelley (1964) had eleven pairs of groups of from three to six students of business administration set to work on a constructional task, an architectural planning task and a story-writing task. Each pair of groups worked in a separate room, and a different (non-participant) subject was taken from each group for each task. At the completion of each task both the non-participant and participant members rated their own and the group's products, and were asked to give reasons for their ratings. The conditions of the experiment deliberately minimized competition between the groups. It was stressed that the groups were strictly temporary and were formed purely for the present investigation of group performance.

With what results? Considerable bias was shown by both participant and non-participant subjects, when rating their own and other group products. A bias in favour of own group was evident even in those cases where one or other group's product was obviously superior; and it was consistent across all three tasks. Using the average of the two groups' ratings as a measure of the 'true' worth of a product, 71 per cent of the participants and 73 per cent of the non-participants showed bias in favour of their own group.

Given the conditions of the experiment, the most plausible explanation of the results is in terms of attachment to own group. Such attachment leads one, presumably without awareness, to overvalue its products in comparison with those of other groups. This explanation is enhanced by the finding that persons high on 'morale' produced the greatest bias. Competition intrudes into relations between groups as a by-product of attachment to our own groups. Disloyalty is perceived if we do not show a marked preference for our own group and its products. As the investigators say: '. . . the seeds of inter-group conflict are exceedingly easy to lay'.

Experimental demonstrations of the development of inter-group hostilities between groups of adults

When competition is engendered between two groups, Sherif's (1966) analysis of inter-group behaviour and conflict suggests the emergence of (1) stereotyped conceptions in favour of own group, which contrast with derogatory stereotypes of the other group; (2) as a consequence of the first effect, prejudiced perceptions and judgements in favour of our own group, and to the disadvantage of the other group, and (3) changes in own group structure which will increase the chances of success in the inter-group conflict. Sherif's schoolboy experiments amply confirmed these expectations. A number of investigators (Blake and Mouton, 1961a, 1961b, 1961c, 1962; Mouton and Blake, 1963; Bass and Dunteman, 1963) have since demonstrated an essentially similar course of events using adults in an industrial setting. In the experiments by these workers, we usually find three stages imposed by the experimenters. First, there is a stage of *ingroup formation.* Groups of adults meet, usually in the context of a management training course, to study and evaluate their own decision making. Two or more days are devoted to this part of the exercise. Next comes the stage of *creating the inter-group competition.* This is effected by assigning problems to groups, and announcing some procedure by which 'winning' and 'losing' groups will be determined. The third stage involves a *comparison of group positions.* Judgements are obtained from individual members of their own and other groups' solutions. Opportunities for negotiations between representatives may be given.

Stereotyping is particularly well illustrated by the Bass and Dunteman experiment. They created four matched groups of supervisors and engineers from a petrochemical refinery. After three days' 'in-group development' a competition between two 'alliances' was announced. Two groups were to combine against the two remaining groups, in formulating a plan describing the criteria for judging a 'development group'. Subjects were required to rank the four groups according to 'how good each group was' at four stages. There were no differences between the evaluations of allies and competitors at the outset, but the mere announcement of a competition was sufficient to initiate a re-orientation: evaluations of allies significantly increased and evaluations of competitors plummeted. For victors the final ranks remained in the order of: self>allies>opponents. For the losers, a shameless *volte face* occurred, and they reported the extraordinary order, self>opponents>allies. Desertion of allies – whilst maintaining a high self estimate – was their paradoxical concession to reality.

Prejudiced perceptions and judgements follow naturally from the stereotyping. Ferguson and Kelley showed that even in the absence of overt competition, groups over-valued their own product, and underestimated the worth of other group products. This effect is much more dramatic when groups are in actual competition. Blake and Mouton (1962) found that 92 per cent of the 410 industrialists taking part in their inter-group competition rated their own group product higher than any other, whilst only 3 per cent thought their own group product inferior.

The competitive inter-group relationship determines the groups' views of one another. How are relationships within any one group affected? In what way does the inter-group relationship impinge on intra-group relations? Blake and Mouton (1961b) address themselves to this issue, following Sherif's lead. Sherif had shown that inter-group competition induced greater cohesiveness in the groups concerned, and the emergence of a more aggressive leadership. Blake and Mouton have some evidence that group cohesiveness does, indeed, increase in adult groups, following the introduction of competition. Julian, Bishop and Fiedler (1966) showed that competing army squads became more cohesive than non-competing squads, and even showed evidence of increased personal adjustment. The effects on inter-squad relations were not reported, although it is noted that the efficiency of the overall unit was not, apparently, impaired! Blake and Mouton (1961c) demonstrated that the most salient perceived characteristics of the elected negotiating representatives were procedural and intellectual skills. The representative was not seen to possess social tact; rather, he was seen as one who 'dominates and imposes his will on the majority'. In one experiment, when negotiating which solution was the better, those formidable characters – acting in pairs – laboured on into absolute deadlock on thirty-two out of thirty-three occasions. It seems that they had every reason to be so intransigent, for the groups extended no mercy to those who led them to defeat. When a neutral judge determined the winner, or when one representative was secretly instructed by the experimenter to yield up his claim, on returning to his group the defeated representative was greeted with dismay and distrust; he lost his previous influence with the group, as did other previously high status members of the group. In effect, the losing group's clear-cut role structure was eroded, and new leaders emerged. In contrast, representatives of victorious groups were given a hero's welcome and assumed their old influential role. In objective ratings by subjects of group atmosphere both before and after the negotiation, 'fighting', 'competitiveness' and 'flight' virtually disappeared in the victorious group, but increased to a significant extent in the defeated group, to the detriment of constructive group activity.

These important experiments demonstrate how the inter-group relationship constrains individual perceptions and judgements, and determines relationships within groups in a way calculated to achieve inter-group goals. Two recent experiments (Rabbie and Horwitz, 1969; Tajfel, 1970) have returned to this theme, asking what the minimum conditions are for inter-group bias to occur. Is merely the different labelling of two groups sufficient to induce mutual prejudice? Rabbie and Horwitz demonstrate that it is not sufficient. Arbitrary division of persons into groups does not produce bias. What Lewin (1948) calles 'interdependence of fate' is lacking in such a case. Similar experiences in the past, or merely anticipated, seem necessary to induce a number of people to decide in their own favour and against the interests of another group. Such 'common fate' may be readily induced, however. In Tajfel's experiments the mere knowledge that a friend, whose precise identity was not known, had different artistic tastes from one's own, led to financial discrimination against him and in favour of a friend (again whose precise identity was unknown) whose tastes were similar. Those alternatives were chosen which would maximize the difference between what 'similar' and 'dissimilar' friends received – even though this might mean less for the 'ingroup', and certainly less for one's friends as a whole!

This quixotic loyalty leads Tajfel to the conclusion that social categorization is sufficient in itself to produce the intergroup effects described by previous investigators.

Intergroup conflict in industry

The studies I have described bear directly on the work situation, for competition affects relations between work groups, and it characterizes relations between managements and unions. In this section I shall briefly explore the implications of this fact.

Work group relationships

Cash posting, most of it, is just mechanical, but station work is a responsible job. You have to deal with customers and with the stores, and if you don't do something right, someone is going to suffer. Of course that's true of cash posting, too, but there are a lot more things that a station clerk has to do. It's a more responsible job, and yet the station clerks get just the same pay as the cash posters. It seems that they ought to get just a few dollars more to show that the job is more important.

These words were spoken, of course, by a 'station' or 'ledger clerk', and they highlight a problem that recurs incessantly in studies of industrial relationships – that of 'differentials'. According to the ledger clerk's perceptions of the situation, they needed a token rise in pay – 'a few dollars more to show that the job is more important'. In absolute terms, their pay was good and they were happy to acknowledge that they would not do better elsewhere. That was not the point. They were working alongside another group of women receiving the same pay who performed, in their eyes, a less responsible, less worrying job, and who also happened, by and large, to be younger and less experienced than themselves. The ledger clerks were not absolutely deprived, but relative to the cash posters, they were unjustly treated.

Industrial work groups are in competition for pay with other groups of workers in the same plant, and will in certain circumstances regard themselves as in competition with other groups at a local, national, or even international level. The experimental work I have reviewed suggests that it is extremely unlikely that any two groups will agree on the relative merits of the work they do, of their qualifications and abilities. Homans (1961), from whom the example of the ledger clerks is taken, describes clearly the consequences of such disagreements. Disagreements about relative skill, age, experience etc. are concerned with the 'investments' that a person contributes to a relationship – in this case, with his employer. Disagreements about pay, embarrassing duties, the worry of a responsible job, and the like, are about the relative 'rewards' and 'costs' in the relationship: from these two factors the 'profits' in a relationship may be computed. People demand, says Homans, that the ratio of 'profits' to 'investments' should be 'just', 'fair' or 'equitable'. 'Justice' is defined in terms of the equation:

$$\frac{\text{One's own rewards} - \text{costs (profits)}}{\text{One's own investments}} = \frac{\text{The other's rewards} - \text{costs (profits)}}{\text{The other's investments}}$$

An employer will be expected to maintain this relationship between two persons, or groups of persons. The ledger clerks, according to the way they perceived matters, had greater investments than the cash posters and thus deserved greater profits. Far from having higher profits, all told they were worse off. They had the same pay (rewards), and greater costs – worry and temporary 'demotion' for example. The consequence of such injustice is anger, which may find expression in various activities designed to redress injustice. If increasing own profits by, for example, obtaining a pay rise, is not feasible, an alternative strategy might be to lose interest in the job or to take fewer responsibilities. This has the merit of balancing the equation by reducing own costs. It may be possible to attempt an assault on other's profits, and in the last resort it is possible to alter one's perceptions of own and other's investments to 'justify' the *status quo*: or, of course, one may leave the job altogether. Patchen (1961) and Pym (1969) have provided data that is consistent with different aspects of this account. Patchen demonstrated that satisfaction with own earnings in comparison with the earnings of another, depends on the relative 'investments' of the two persons or groups. Men who were satisfied with a specific wage comparison justified it mainly in terms of an agreement between relative wage standing and standing on such attributes as education, skill, seniority, age and experience. Pym (1969) shows the progressive disenchantment of groups of non-graduate engineers whose progress in their firms contrasts unfavourably with groups of comparably qualified graduate engineers. The non-graduates progressively lost interest in their jobs and took on less responsibility, in contrast with the graduates who shouldered greater burdens with time.

Sayles (1958) showed that exaggerated and invidious comparisons between competing groups lay behind the bulk of the grievances in the automobile plants he studied. All the economic goals pursued by work groups – protection in the event of technological change, more overtime, higher hourly rates etc. – all have a comparative aspect. The fact that an improvement for one work group is a relative loss for another ensured that different groups' perceptions of each others' relevant attributes rarely coincided. Deriding another group's abilities and responsibilities is as effective as exaggerating one's own in determining management's perception of the justice of any claim, and this fact was not lost on the more powerful 'strategic' groups in particular. These groups, confident of their critical position in the plant and well-organized, strove hard to achieve and maintain high status. Essentially, 'distributive justice' was their aim. Exaggeration of own investments and denigration of another group's investments was the essence of the game, and it was played with zest. Group patterns of behaviour and group self-images did not remain constant over time, however. The active, forceful leadership characteristic of 'strategic' groups is less appropriate after it has been thoroughly successful. Then the group's status is raised and further competition is ruled out for lack of competitors. Such groups subsequently assume the more complacent attitudes and leadership of what Sayles calls the 'conservative' groups, who could, by all accounts, afford an attitude of *noblesse oblige*:

We consistently heard that highly paid occupational (conservative) groups had more 'reasonable', 'intelligent', 'worthwhile', well founded' grievances. Even assuming that many of these evaluations are invalid, such opinions cannot help influencing management reaction to their grievances. For a case originating in a low-status department, the executive frequently begins with the preconception: 'This is undoubtedly another foolish grievance with no basis in fact'. In contrast, in a high-status department, the first impression is often, 'There must be something to this if they are raising a complaint'.

This brief consideration of relations between industrial work groups is illuminated by the experimental work previously considered. Effective competition for limited resources invites comparisons between different groups that are destined to be exaggerated and vindictive. Agreement on what constitutes a 'just' claim is ruled out because perceptions of relative 'rewards', 'costs' and 'investments' vary between groups. Inter-group competition will persist, but many factors, of which Sayles has discerned some of the more important, influence where the group lines will be drawn. This offers some hope that we may be able to minimize the more harmful personal and social effects of competition between groups.

Union–management relationships. Competition between work groups underpins much of present-day union–management conflict, by its provision of a constant flow of grievances which have as their basis the perception of unjust relationships between groups. It is up to management to maintain a state of 'distributive justice', but faced with the frequently opposed perceptions by different groups of the important variables – the skills needed for two different jobs, for example – this is not a simple task. When union membership cuts across group lines these problems become fiendishly complicated. But there is, of course, a more enduring, economic and political basis for conflict between managements and unions. There is an opposition of interests that makes conflict inevitable and desirable so long as the opposition is genuine or realistic. Realistic conflict (see Mack and Snyder, 1957) rightly determines the direction of social change. It helps set group boundaries and clarifies group goals and norms; it may in certain circumstances reduce tension and increase overall integration of groups (North, Koch and Zinnes, 1960). The difficulty is that realistic conflict between groups produces prejudiced, hostile relationships between individual members of those groups. This generates a thoroughly unrealistic conflict, the basis of which is not necessarily evident to the participants. This secondary conflict may overlay and substitute for the genuine conflict of interests which stays as unresolved as ever. In this circumstance meetings between the two sides, for whatever benign purpose, serve merely as occasions for a further exchange of hostilities across group lines. Harbison and Coleman (1951) describe the standard 'peaceful' industrial relationship as one of 'armed truce'. At best, management feels that unions and collective bargaining are necessary evils in modern society, and unions believe their main job is to dispute managerial actions. Fundamental disagreements over the scope of collective bargaining and rivalry between management and unions for the loyalty of workers characterize this type of relationship. Energies are mobilized for continual assaults on the other parties' power positions, for it is openly recognized that settlements of major differences will be made on the basis of the relative power positions of the two sides. Much rarer – at the other end of the scale – is 'union-management cooperation'. Through joint action, the two parties seek to reduce production costs, increase efficiency and improve the competitive position of the firm. But such instances occur only in exceptional circumstances, and it is undoubtedly true that the competitive end of the scale is more characteristic of union-management relationships, and that individual attitudes of managers and union officials towards each other are determined by this: being more distrustful than trusting, conditioned more by contempt than respect.

These attitudes are not based on experience, but reflect group stereotypes that are widely shared and imbibed at an early age by children. In a study of schoolchildren Haire and Morrison (1957) found that the critical factor determining how they perceived representatives of such groups was socio-economic status, this factor increasing in importance with age. High-income groups of children judged a union man to be significantly more lazy, stupid, greedy, communistic and useless, than did low-income children. The low-income groups thought he was very much more industrious, skilled, intelligent, enterprising and, interestingly enough, more submissive, than did the high-income groups. A 'boss' to the low-income children was 'one who gives orders', and to the high-income children, more of a 'leader, head, important'. All told, the results of this study revealed a class consciousness and split in attitudes between members of high and low income groups that does not encourage an optimistic approach to social policy in this area. There is an urgent need for up-to-date work here if we are to understand, let alone reconcile, the unceasingly partisan stances adopted not merely by the chief protagonists, but by the public at large.

Active involvement in union–management relationships might be expected to modify the stereotypes typified by the children in Haire and Morrison's study, to take account of the particular relationship between the parties. An ingenious experiment by Haire (1968) confirmed this expectation. The subjects were 184 negotiators from both sides of industry. In one part of the experiment the managers and the union representatives were introduced via photographs and written descriptions to a 'Mr B' – an ordinary, middle-aged, reasonably well-dressed man, with no marked expression on his face. Managers who thought Mr B was a fellow-manager, described him as especially 'conscientious', 'dependable', 'conservative', 'industrious' and 'sincere'. Those managers who understood this same person to be 'Secretary-Treasurer of his Union' saw a very different set of qualities emanating from the identical expressionless face. To them he was particularly 'active', 'argumentative', 'aggressive', 'opinionated', 'outspoken' and 'persistent'. Perhaps these two descriptions reflect the managers' conception of the union-management relationship: solid virtue under fierce, unreasoning, relentless attack! The union men did not differentiate so markedly between the two guises, and their description of the management facsimile bordered on the patronizing. The union representatives were, however, allied with management in their emphasis on the more dynamic, aggressive character of the union stereotype – albeit for rather different reasons.

Characterizing the negotiating relationship

One would expect the activities of representatives at the bargaining table to be vigorously geared to establishing an advantage over the opposing side and ruthlessly exploiting it, for the bulk of official union-management negotiations involves conflict of interest – in which what one party wins the other loses. This inevitably commits bargainers to what Walton and McKersie (1965) call *distributive bargaining* – 'dividing the cake'. The spirit in which this process is customarily engaged is illustrated by the fact that, according to Walton and McKersie, the principal aim of distributive bargainers is not to argue their Party's case, but to destroy their Opponent's – in their words, to modify the Opponent's 'subjective expected utility' in a favourable direction. The attempt must also be made to mislead Opponent about Party's case so that Opponent cannot effectively mount a similar campaign. The initial tactics – designed to assess and change Opponent's aims by disorienting him – are reminiscent of the football pitch: man-to-man marking is adopted in observing Opponent's team; members of one's own team are rotated to this end and personal abuse is frequent; the most telling thrusts are directed at the least well coached members of Opponent's team; impatience and frustration are deliberately exaggerated; and as a particularly testing tactic one may even appeal to the referee by threatening to call in the mediator. This is no amateur game. Other principal aims in distributive bargaining, for which equally devious and hard-line tactics are prescribed, are to modify the opponent's estimates of the costs to each of a strike, or sanctions etc. in the event of failure to agree, and to alter Opponent's estimates of the probability that a given outcome will prove acceptable or not. Assuming the validity of this description of the process of distributive bargaining (there are other ways in which cakes may be divided, or football matches played) as an account of what tends to occur in practice, we may well ask, in view of the work we have examined above, how it is that negotiations do ever get concluded, and why it is that acrimony and bitterness between the two sides is not even more in evidence. Walton and McKersie provide at least part of the answer in their delineation of three other sub-processes, or goals, in bargaining encounters in industry.

Integrative bargaining occurs when members of opposing sides recognize their shared interests and goals. It is a problem-solving process, which 'identifies, enlarges, and acts upon the common interests of the parties'. Although Walton and McKersie do not present it in these terms, integrative bargaining is an alternative, cooperative approach to bargaining, in which agenda items are perceived as 'common problems' rather than 'divisive issues', as in distributive bargaining. 'One often wonders,' state Walton and McKersie, 'why under similar circumstances some negotiations produce innovative solutions and others produce deadlock and conflict'. The main problem seems to be one of the perception of common interests in the first place. For example, managements are often under severe pressure to achieve short-term results, and find it impossible to take other than a short-term, competitive view of the situation. Another sub-process which may modify the competitive workings of the distributive bargaining sub-process is what Walton and McKersie call *attitudinal structuring*. This describes behaviours 'designed to change attitudes and relationships'. The main point about this sub-process is that it recognizes that negotiating parties have an interest in maintaining a stable relationship within which business may be properly conducted. Especially in plant-level negotiations where the relationship between the teams is a continuing one, the chief negotiators have a vested interest in maintaining the good-will of their opposing members to insure that the relationship between the parties – of whatever character – does not break down. The problems of the chief negotiators are further exacerbated by the necessity for a fourth sub-process which Walton and McKersie term *intra-organizational bargaining*. This term recognizes that chief negotiators are responsible for the performance of a team of individuals, representing different unions, or sections within a firm. The interests of these individuals may conflict, as was shown earlier in the section describing relations between work-groups. Their activities in bargaining, however, must be coordinated, and this poses severe problems, especially for the chief union negotiator. Walton and McKersie define this sub-process as 'the system of behaviours which brings the expectations of the principals into alignment with those of the chief negotiator'. Chief negotiators are well aware of the problems their opposing numbers face in this respect. In one instance I observed, the management negotiator deliberately did not exploit differences of opinion in the opposing side, beyond making a light-hearted jest. To have done so would have weakened the opposing chief's position to a degree that would have jeopardized agreement between the teams, besides undermining the close relationship between the two leaders. This demonstrates neatly how the sub-processes may impinge on one another. An emphasis on distributive bargaining would have prescribed that the management negotiator take full advantage of the conflict in the union team.

Walton and McKersie have drawn attention to the diverse activities of negotiators. They do not merely mediate a competition between opposed factions. Other shared goals – to solve common problems, to maintain their preferred relationship, to unite factions within their own teams – modify their competitive orientation. Morley and Stephenson (1970a and b) express this rather differently in their distinction between inter-party and interpersonal aspects of bargaining. Negotiators must come to terms with the demands of *representing* their parties on the one hand, and *maintaining a personal relationship* with their opposite numbers on the other. This second aspect is crucial to the pursuit of goals implicit in Walton and McKersie's concepts of the sub-processes of integrative bargaining, attitudinal structuring and intra-organizational bargaining, if not to the fulfilment of the distributive bargaining process itself. 'Collusion' between chief negotiators need not refer only to one kind of union-management relationship at the cooperative extreme of a competition – cooperative continuum – as suggested by Walton and McKersie – but to an attempt to deal with the conflict between inter-party and interpersonal expectations. In one such situation we encountered the representative and interpersonal aspects of the negotiating relationship were kept apart, quite explicitly, by the chief negotiators. Personal considerations – primarily their respective 'intra-organizational' goals – moved them to negotiate secretly, in advance, the course that the 'public' negotiation would take. The latter was thereby stage-managed to satisfy to the full the demands of inter-party competition without detriment to other, personally-mediated goals. The representatives could act out their respective roles boldly, fearing no damage to their relationship.

EXPERIMENTAL WORK ON NEGOTIATING BEHAVIOUR

Introduction

By 'negotiation' I refer to occasions in which representatives of two or more parties interact in an explicit attempt to reach a jointly acceptable position on a divisive issue. This is what may usefully be called a *formal* negotiation. Such occasions can be distinguished from informal discussions in which individuals debate an issue, or come to terms, each on his own behalf, not as a representative. How is it possible to create formal negotiations in the laboratory? McGrath (1966, p. 118) has argued that thoroughly realistic experimental work may be conducted on formal negotiations, the only artificiality being the occasion for the negotiation. Morley (1971) in a discussion of McGrath's argument, distinguishes between *simulations*, and *simulation games*. The most important characteristic of a simulation is that subjects should be genuine representatives, or members, of a party to the negotiations. This ensures genuine commitment to the party's aims. Another essential characteristic is that the issues being negotiated should be of *importance* to the parties and their representatives, and that, thirdly, the conflict of interest between the parties should occur *independently* of the experimental setting. The issue, in other words, must be a genuinely divisive one in real life. The remaining two criteria are concerned with the quality of interaction between the representatives, and they rule out consideration of 'games' of the Prisoner's Dilemma (see Kelley, 1965; Deutsch and Krauss, 1962) or economic bargaining (Fouraker and Siegel, 1963) variety. One affirms that the laboratory setting must permit full verbal communication between representatives, and the other prescribes that the issues must be sufficiently complex to allow subjects to adopt a problem-solving, 'creative' approach to their resolution.

McGrath's own experiments have been simulations of this kind, but other researchers have followed what Morley calls the 'simulation game' paradigm. The simulation game relaxes the requirements of the first three criteria because of the practical difficulties involved and the limitations it places on the experimental manipulations to be employed. The two final criteria are, however, not set aside. The procedure has been to ask subjects to play a role as a representative of some real group in a negotiation with fellow subjects playing similar roles. Background information to a dispute is provided, and this is the major constraint on their otherwise spontaneous performances. Greater realism is sometimes obtained by selecting subjects for particular roles according to their expressed attitude and beliefs on relevant topics, e.g. by assigning left-wing students to Union roles in a management-union simulation game. In fact most subjects in such experiments become strongly identified with their role, whatever their initial attitudes, and the resolution of the issue with an opponent is a meaningful, if sometimes harrowing, experience.

The experimental work on inter-group behaviour suggests a number of quite explicit hypotheses about the course that negotiations between representatives will follow in different circumstances. For example, it would be expected that the more competitive the relationship, the more difficult it will be to obtain agreement; the less acceptable will be the solution to any one party and the less 'creative' will be the solution. These effects stem from the increased commitment of negotiators to their parties' goals, the increased mutual misunderstanding between negotiators and the negotiators' increased fear of rejection by their parties in the event of 'failure', which heightened competition between groups entails. Perhaps the unfortunate effects of competition would be lessened if certain steps were taken. It might be possible in some way to decrease the commitment of negotiators to their parties' goals, or to increase in some way a negotiator's understanding of the other party's position. Alternatively, the negotiators' freedom of manoeuvre may be strengthened, or steps taken to increase the salience of aims which are shared. Experimental laboratory research, although comparatively meagre to date, has thrown considerable light on the effectiveness of measures which bear directly on such stratagems. Two issues have received particular attention, and I shall describe their treatment in some detail. The first concerns the pre-experience and perceptual set of negotiators, the second concerns the composition of teams. Other equally compelling issues have received only perfunctory attention and I will not discuss them in detail. Interested readers are referred to Pruitt and Johnson (1970) on the role of the mediator, to McGrath (1966) and Druckman (1967) for data on personality factors, and to Johnson and Lewicki (1969) for an interesting comparison of the the effects of two types of 'superordinate' or shared, unifying goals, on the outcomes of simulated disputes.

Pre-experience of negotiators

Bass (1966) and Druckman (1967, 1968) employed the 'simulation game' technique in the negotiation of a union-management 'package deal' covering nine or more diverse issues, e.g. the Hospital and Medical Plan (with the union demanding that the company pay the full cost, and the Company offering only one-quarter) and the Night Shift Differential (with the Company rejecting a five cents increase to ten cents per hour). For each of the nine issues the Company's offer and the Union's demand constituted the two extremes on a bargaining range. Subjects negotiated a settlement-point for each issue in pairs, after having undergone one of a number of alternative pre-negotiation sessions. The major concern was with the effect of encouraging negotiating teams to plan their detailed strategy in advance, compared with the effect on subsequent negotiations of requiring negotiators to study the issues dispassionately either with members of their own team, or with opposing team members. Druckman's (1968) experiment was the best-controlled of these studies, and his results indicated that enforced study for forty minutes, whether with own, or opposing group members, had the effect of reducing the time taken to complete the contract. Bargainers moved farther from their initial positions and closer to the opponent's position after study than after strategy-planning, whilst there was no difference between the strategy group and a control group of no pre-experience bargainers with respect to any of these measures. It seems that the study experience inclined the negotiators to perceive the situation as more of a problem-solving enterprise than was the case with the 'strategists', whose initially win-lose orientation was encouraged by the implicitly competitive instructions. Bass's work confirms this general superiority of study over strategy in facilitating agreement and in addition provides some evidence of the greater effectiveness of bilateral rather than unilateral pre-experience. One interesting problem in Bass's work that merits further investigation is the impact of a deadline on the ease with which negotiations are concluded. There was some indication that setting a deadline increased competitiveness and hindered effective negotiation.

Composition of teams

If teams are to succeed in competitive games they must employ a common strategy. In any case, it is evident, as Evan and McDougall (1967) assert, that unanimity in a negotiating team has been highly regarded by negotiators. Disagreement on one side, it is supposed, will be exploited ruthlessly by a competitively oriented and united opposition. The problem is that unanimity itself is likely to increase further the intransigent spirit of both sides as it becomes increasingly clear that the other side is as stubborn and bloody-minded as one's own. This is hardly in the long-term interests of the parties, particularly in the field of industrial relations, where, as Evan and McDougall point out, social pressures and the common economic interests of the parties generally promote a high rate of *some* conflict resolution, higher than, for example, in the international realm. Mere compromise, or victory for one of the parties, which the employment of the unanimity principle by both sides encourages, is poor reward for the grand expenditure of effort by all concerned. Evan and McDougall propose that an alternative 'principle of dissent' may serve to move negotiators away from game-like competition and towards a more cooperative approach characteristic of debates. By the 'principle of dissent' the authors mean the 'airing of *intra*-organizational differences'. Persuading their subjects to air differences with fellow-negotiators on the same side required some ingenuity on the part of the investigators (Evan and McDougall, 1967), for the natural tendency is for a team to close ranks in the presence of the adversary, as the inter-group research demonstrated. Their solution was to establish from the start a conflict of interest within each negotiating team whenever the *dissensus* strategy was required. On the management side one subject played the role of a cost-conscious assistant vice-president of production who took an extreme position on the automation issue under dispute. His partner in the two-man management team played the role of an assistant vice-president of personnel whose major concern was harmonious worker-management relations, and who took an appropriately moderate stand. On the union side one representative took an extreme view of the issue because some of his worker members were to be displaced by the proposed automation. His fellow-negotiator took a moderate position because the craftsmen he represented were not affected by the projected programme. When *consensus* was required, the representatives of a management or union team had identical constituency interests.

How did dissensus and consensus affect the outcomes of the negotiations? The first result, contradicting both the authors' expectations and commonsense alike, showed no differences between the consensus, dissensus and a third 'mixed' (one team showing consensus, the other dissensus) condition on the ease with which agreement was reached. There were, however, marked differences in the *quality* of the settlements. Agreements classified as 'creative' or 'integrative' were more likely to occur in the dissensus condition than in either the consensus or mixed condition. There was no statistically significant evidence that the side adopting a dissensus strategy was dominated by their consensus opposition in the mixed condition, although the results do tend in that direction. The results of this very interesting experiment do, indeed, suggest that permitting an expression of internal disagreement by both sides initiates a less competitive approach to bargaining. However, there is some evidence, overall, that if only one side adopts a policy of dissensus, the outcome is less satisfactory than when the sides combine on a policy of consensus.

McGrath (1966) and Vidmar and McGrath (1965) explored the ramifications of playing the opposing role, using the simulation technique. It is difficult for members of competing groups to understand or evaluate objectively the position of the opposed group. In one of McGrath's experiments the student subjects were members of two opposed organizations with different policies concerning 'residence houses'; open political conflict had occurred over this issue. Thus, as in all of McGrath's experiments, the subjects were members of real-life, opposed groups and were given 'position papers' defining the values, goals and position on various issues, of their particular organizations. These were signed by high ranking members of the appropriate organization. Payment was made to the subjects on the basis of the acceptability of the settlement to these persons. A 'creative' solution, highly acceptable to leaders of both organizations and to a neutral third party, would merit the highest payments to both subjects. Least profitable for *both* representatives would be an outcome satisfactory to only one side, i.e. a 'victory' for one side. McGrath studied two experimental conditions – the *standard* in which a member of the Fraternity faction negotiated with a member of the Independent organization; and the *cross-assigned* in which two fraternity representatives 'negotiated' a solution acceptable to both sides, one subject adopting his real-life Fraternity role, the other the opposed Independent role. McGrath found that, in fact, the cross-assigned groups were distinctly more effective than the standard groups. Their solutions tended to be acceptable to both sides and to merit a high ranking from neutral judges. There was no evidence at all of bias towards the Fraternity position in the cross-assigned groups, and their solutions were generally more imaginative and constructive than the solutions of the standard groups. This happy outcome was, however, achieved at some cost to their personal relationship. Whereas in the standard groups the negotiators liked each other more at the close of the negotiation, members of the cross-assigned groups, despite their splendid solutions, finished up rather disliking each other. For them, the exercise was not a comfortable business. Similarly, whereas in the standard groups, respect for the other party's position increased on both sides, in the cross-assigned groups only those Fraternity men arguing the Independent case came to change, more favourably, their view of the Independent case. The Fraternity men in their natural role lost respect for the Independent case. Arguing a position alien to one's own has, of course, been shown to be an effective way of revising attitudes (Zimbardo and Ebbeson, 1969).

McGrath's experiments are particularly important because he used representatives of real-life groups to debate personally meaningful issues. In the light of this fact it is especially interesting that mutual sympathy and understanding between negotiators increased in the standard groups. Antipathy is not the inevitable outcome of contact between representatives of opposed factions as the inter-group research described earlier would suggest. McGrath has evidence that in the standard group there was more concern with establishing an effective rapport than in the cross-assigned groups, where concentration on the task predominated. Opposed negotiators in a real-life setting, like the negotiators in this experiment, do have a vested interest in producing mutually acceptable, if not necessarily constructive, agreements. They may be expected to collude at the personal level in pursuit of this shared goal. Experiments of this kind are especially valuable in elucidating the conditions under which satisfactory personal relationships emerge between representatives of opposed factions.

Communication systems

The reconciliation of the representative and personal aspects of the negotiating relationship has been a recurrent theme in this discussion. Agreements between parties are negotiated by people, and the quality of the personal relationship between negotiators of opposite sides is a critical factor in determining the style and outcome of negotiations. A quotation from Harold Macmillan's memoirs illustrates in an amusing way just how futile negotiations may be when conditions prevail against the development of any kind of rapport between opposed representatives. He describes his feelings at the July 1955 'summit' conference as follows:

The room in which we met filled me with horror the moment we entered it. The protagonists were sitting at tables drawn up in a rectangle; the space between them was about the size of a small boxing ring. But this arena was itself surrounded by rows of benches and seats which were provided, presumably, for the advisers, but seemed to be occupied by a crowd of interested onlookers. The walls were decorated with vast, somewhat confused, frescoes depicting the end of the world, or the Battle of the Titans, or the Rape of the Sabines, or a mixture of all three. I could conceive of no arrangement less likely to lead to intimate or useful negotiations. The whole formal part of the conference was bound to degenerate into a series of set orations. It was only when the Heads of Government or Foreign Ministers met in a small room outside in a restricted meeting that any serious discussion could take place. (Macmillan, 1969).

Formality – seating arrangements, the presence of advisers, having an audience, and so on – prevailed against the development of a personal relationship between negotiators and hindered effective negotiation. Formality encourages representative behaviour – 'set orations' – and discourages empathic understanding between negotiators. Morley and Stephenson (1970a and b) use the term 'communication system' to refer to such external conditions which influence the balance between the representative and personal aspects of the negotiating process. When the communication system (size of group, seating arrangements, procedural roles, etc.) favours formality, then the representative aspect is encouraged and the behaviour of negotiators is constrained by commitment to their own groups. When informality prevails, then the development of a personal empathic relationship is facilitated. The strength of commitment to own group and the degree of empathy between negotiators will affect directly the perception and evaluation of both one's own Party's aspirations and the desires and devices of the Opposition. In turn such perceptions and judgements will decisively influence the kind of offers that are made, and the response to them.

Morley and Stephenson (1969, 1970a, 1970b) established different communication systems for a simulation game. In one condition, for example, negotiators were obliged to communicate using a head-phone and microphone combination – the 'telephone' condition. Other teams negotiated 'face-to-face'. In addition, the extent to which negotiators were free to interrupt each other was varied. Some groups were 'constrained', others were 'free' – to interrupt. The 'telephone' and 'constrained' conditions are 'formal' because – like the physical separation Macmillan described – they militate against spontaneous interaction by reducing the number of social cues available to the negotiators.

How will the negotiator's performance be affected by differences in 'formality'? Will the outcome of a negotiation be affected? In the experiments Morley and Stephenson asked pairs of students to read the background to an industrial dispute involving the introduction of a new wage agreement. Some specimen arguments were provided from each side, giving an initially stronger case either to the management representative or to the union representative. Subjects were aware that the merits of the case were in the direction intended. Specific *target* and *resistance* points for each side established a *negative settlement range*: that is, no wage was minimally acceptable to both sides at the outset. Given that one party always had the stronger case, the main hypothesis of the study was that victories for the party with the stronger case would occur most frequently in the more formal conditions. The effect of formality is, essentially, to depersonalize the relationship between negotiators and to encourage single-minded concentration on representing their cases. Hence the relative merits of the cases are more likely to become apparent, and 'irrational' outcomes are less likely for that reason to occur. Moreover, there will be a tendency for the representative with the stronger case to play down his advantage in the more personalized, informal condition. Whereas the 'interparty' exchange will be governed by the merits of the case, 'interpersonal' exchange will be influenced by considerations of 'reciprocity'. A marked deviation from a straightforward, equitable compromise solution will be perceived as somewhat 'unjust' in the more informal situations. Such considerations are less likely to come to the fore over the telephone where the embarrassment of the 'loser' cannot be perceived so clearly. The results confirmed the authors' expectations. For example, when the management had the stronger case, 75 per cent of the agreements were victories for management over the telephone, compared with a mere 12·5 per cent in the face-to-face conditions. Similarly, when negotiators were not free to interrupt each other, victories for management were more likely. Parallel results occurred when the union was given the stronger case. In that instance, it was the union negotiators who secured victories in the formal conditions, but not in the informal conditions. A subsequent experiment by Stephenson and Henley (1971) looked at the effect of a television link compared with the face-to-face and telephone conditions. The results suggest that the physical presence of the other negotiator is a crucial factor. Victories for the party with the stronger case were more likely to occur in the face-to-face than in either the telephone or television conditions. The practical implications of these experiments are discussed in detail by Morley and Stephenson (1970a) and Kingston (1970). In this respect the work of Vitz and Kite (1970) is also of interest.

Successful negotiations and negotiating skill

Ann Douglas (1957) described with zest and considerable insight the way in which deadlocked industrial disputes were successfully settled at the final stage of governmental mediation in the USA. It was apparent to her that the interplay of representative and personal interests was the central problem facing negotiators. Initially, the delegates seemed hell bent on disagreement, emphasizing the deep and irreconcilable gulf between their positions. Indeed, says Douglas, representatives in private may 'pine for a stiffer competitive challenge against which to pit their prowess'. Yet agreement does come, and it comes, according to Douglas, only when the conflict between parties is starkly emphasized at the outset and thoroughly explored subsequently. The aim of the first stage is to 'establish the bargaining range' within which the representatives will have to do business, and it is unhelpful if at this time the full extent of their disagreement is blurred by well-intentioned but nonetheless foolish attempts to secure agreement. The principal characteristic of the next stage of successful negotiations was 'reconnoitering the bargaining range'. During this stage the party allegiance of representatives was much less in evidence. Interaction was more spontaneous, as the negotiators sought, tacitly and warily, for signs of agreement. A degree of sympathy between the sides ensured that indiscretions and false moves – more likely to occur in the freer atmosphere of this stage – were not exploited by the opposition. The third and final stage – 'precipitating the decision-making crisis' – heralds something of a return to inter-party debate as offers are made and sides consult privately to assess them. This orderly sequence characterizes successful negotiations and is adopted more or less as a matter of policy by skilled negotiators – according to Douglas.

Douglas's conclusions have been partially confirmed by other investigators. For example, Landsberger (1955) studied twelve disputes referred to a mediation agency in the USA, using Interaction Process Analysis to analyse the content of the negotiations. Landsberger did find that successful negotiations followed an orderly sequence, corresponding roughly to the 'phase sequence' delineated by Bales and Strodtbeck (1951) from a study of problem-solving groups. He found that successful groups were initially high on 'orientation' – giving and asking for information. 'Evaluation' – giving and seeking opinions and feelings on proposed solutions – predominated in the middle third of the discussion, to be succeeded by 'control' in which definite proposals were made for general acceptance. This aspect of his results coincides with Douglas's description of the ideal sequence. 'Orientation' in the context of a negotiation is close to the idea of 'establishing the bargaining range', 'evaluation' corresponds to 'reconnoitering' the range, and 'control' is required to 'precipitate' the decision-making crisis. Landsberger's results deviate from Douglas's when Bales's 'socio-emotional' categories are considered. 'Tension' and 'tension release', 'antagonism' and 'solidarity' typically show a progressive increase during problem-solving discussions. Landsberger found this to be true of his successful negotiations, but discovered in particular that the more the negotiators showed *antagonism*, the less likely was a negotiation to be successful. In particular, it was important that antagonism be not in evidence in the *initial* stages of the negotiation. This certainly seems to be inconsistent with Douglas's statement that in the initial stages of successful negotiations attacks on the other party's position are 'not infrequently derisive and venomous'.

The work of McGrath and his associates lends credence to the view that antagonism between negotiators in the early stages of a negotiation is particularly harmful. McGrath and Julian (1963) analysed the content of both successful and unsuccessful negotiations, 'success' being determined from ratings of the outcomes by the leaders of the organizations represented by the negotiators and by neutral judges. Overall the results supported Douglas's contention that 'representative' behaviour in the early stages – long speeches setting forth the group position – is succeeded by more frequent, spontaneous interaction in the later stages. However, there were something like twice as many hostile critical observations initiated by negotiators in unsuccessful groups as in successful groups – in all phases of the negotiation; and there was an even greater discrepancy in the same direction for 'negative' responses. This latter result was especially characteristic of the early stages of the negotiations. Attempts to control the group also varied with success, not in absolute terms, but in relation to time. Structuring of group activities was markedly high in the final, pre-writing-up stage of negotiating by successful representatives. McGrath and Julian suggest, reasonably enough, that the chairman's role may be particularly important with respect to the timing and positioning of the various activities.

There is reason to suppose from these results that one approach to the problem of negotiating skill is via the detailed analysis of the performance of those negotiating groups which are successful. The evidence accumulated so far suggests that successful negotiating stems from the character of the personal relationships established by the negotiators in the group. Morley and Stephenson's experiments showed how critically the development of a more intimate relationship may affect outcomes. Douglas's studies indicate that negotiators must be sufficiently mature, and confident in the other's essentially cooperative orientation not to mistake hard-hitting party tactics for personal hostility. Landsberger and McGrath have both demonstrated how the expression of interpersonal hostility may damage the prospects of a successful outcome to the discussions. McGrath (1966) found that no one mediator could consistently bring about satisfactory outcomes in different groups, and that a number of ostensibly crucial personality characteristics – including various cognitive measures – could not predict successful performance. The character of the interaction, however, *can* predict successful performance, and the hallmark would seem to be a mutual determination not to allow inter-party conflict to create inter-personal hostility. Given this resolve an orderly progression through the stages necessary for successful problem-solving may be effected. The importance of pre-experience, personality, communication systems and other extraneous factors lies, perhaps, in the effect they have on personal relationships within the negotiating group. This conclusion is tentative because our knowledge of what actually happens in negotiations is still meagre. There are few analyses of real-life negotiations, and the content of most experimental negotiations remains unexamined. The exceptions are not satisfactory. An extensive, detailed analysis of strategy and tactics in formal negotiating is crucial if the phasing of satisfactory negotiations is to be understood. No such analysis has yet been concluded.

SUMMARY

This chapter describes how psychologists have started to study formal negotiating, both in the laboratory and in industry. Experimental studies of inter-group relations have informed much of this work, and a description of these studies opens the chapter. Their application to the problem of relations between work-groups and between managements and unions follows, and the stage is set for the consideration of negotiating.

Formal negotiating is of especial interest to the social psychologist because it dramatizes a conflict that is inherent in many social situations. At different times we are acting as members, or 'representatives' of groups, besides expressing our individual needs. A man will be variously representing his family, his country, his occupational group, his club, his political party, or whatever, as he interacts both formally and informally with others whose interests are 'opposed'. This conflict is vividly represented in formal negotiating and studies of its resolution elucidate not merely an important practical problem in many spheres, but a basic issue in social life generally.

FURTHER READING

The work described in this chapter is mostly contained in journal articles or unpublished reports, and readers especially interested in a particular topic will need to follow up the references given in the text. Of the books cited M. Sherif, *Group Conflict and Co-operation* (Routlege & Kegan Paul, 1966) is a readable general introduction to the psychology of social conflict and inter-group relations. R. E. Walton and R. B. McKersie's *A Behavioral Theory of Labor Negotiation* (McGraw-Hill, 1965) remains the most compelling analysis of management–union negotiating behaviour, and is essential further reading on that topic. A clear description of the British system of industrial relations is contained in the Donovan *Report of the Royal Commission on Trade Unions and Employers' Associations 1965–1968* (HMSO, 1968).

17
Organizations as Psychological Environments

Roy Payne and Derek Pugh

The early chapters of this book were particularly concerned with the behaviour of individual people, and at that stage only limited attention was paid to the organization in which this behaviour was set. In a very rough way it may be said that later chapters have become progressively more concerned with social and technological features, and the present, final contribution is devoted entirely to this topic. The authors illustrate the major ways in which organizations differ from each other, and they sketch out some of the psychological consequences of these differences. Questions of size, horizontal and vertical divisions and degrees of centralization or decentralization are some of the issues which are covered. Professor Pugh has carried out a great deal of important research into organizational behaviour, and Mr Payne also has extensive experience in this and other fields.

The purpose of this chapter is to locate man in the context of the organization as a whole. As Kahn *et al.* (1964) say: 'Organizations are reducible to individual human acts; yet they are lawful and in part understandable only at the level of collective behaviour.' Whilst that may be obvious, it is just as relevant and just as obvious that some of those individual human acts are only understandable when related to the social environment in which they occur. The question is, what kinds of environments do work organizations create and why, and what is their effect on behaviour?

This area of research has in recent years acquired its own labels: organizational psychology (see books with that title by Schein, 1965; and Bass, 1965), and organizational behaviour (see Scott 1967; and Pugh, 1966 and 1969). The latter term seems more likely to continue in use due to its non-discipline-based content. This can be seen to be important from Pugh's (1969) definition of organizational behaviour:

Organizational Behaviour is the study of the structure and functioning of organizations and the behaviour of groups and individuals within them. It is an emerging, inter-disciplinary quasi-independent science, drawing primarily on the disciplines of psychology and sociology, but also on economics, operational research and production engineering (p. 345).

Its difference in emphasis from traditional industrial psychology is reflected in the fact that organizational activity is regarded as an object of study in its own right rather than as a setting in which to apply accepted psychological knowledge.

It is not to be imagined that this journey into what used to be regarded as the sociological hinterland developed out of a need for some epistemic stimulation. It was a response to a scientific need. The attempts of social and industrial psychologists in the 1950s and 1960s to explain the behaviour of small industrial work groups, and such phenomena as job satisfaction and job performance proved less than completely successful. It became clear that some of the variance was probably attributable to factors in the wider organization, hence the latter became an object of study itself. This development is most clearly observed in the work of the social psychologists at the University of Michigan (see Likert, 1961, and 1967; Katz and Kahn, 1966).

A FRAMEWORK FOR CONCEPTUALIZING BEHAVIOUR IN ORGANIZATIONS

Figure 17.1 (pp. 376–7), presents a framework which will help outline the field of study and the interrelationships of its main units of analysis. The major units of analysis are individuals, small groups or teams, departments or major segments of organization and the organization as a whole. Each of these units of analysis is presented as a separate open system, that is, a system which has to have transactions with its environment in order to survive. The system must acquire resources or inputs, convert them by creating a structure and set of processes to do this, and then output them in the form of some product or service. These outputs then become part of the system's environment, hence the feedback loop from the output stage (what we have called evaluated behaviour, just to limit our area of concern) and back to the input stage. Diagrammatically expressed, we have:

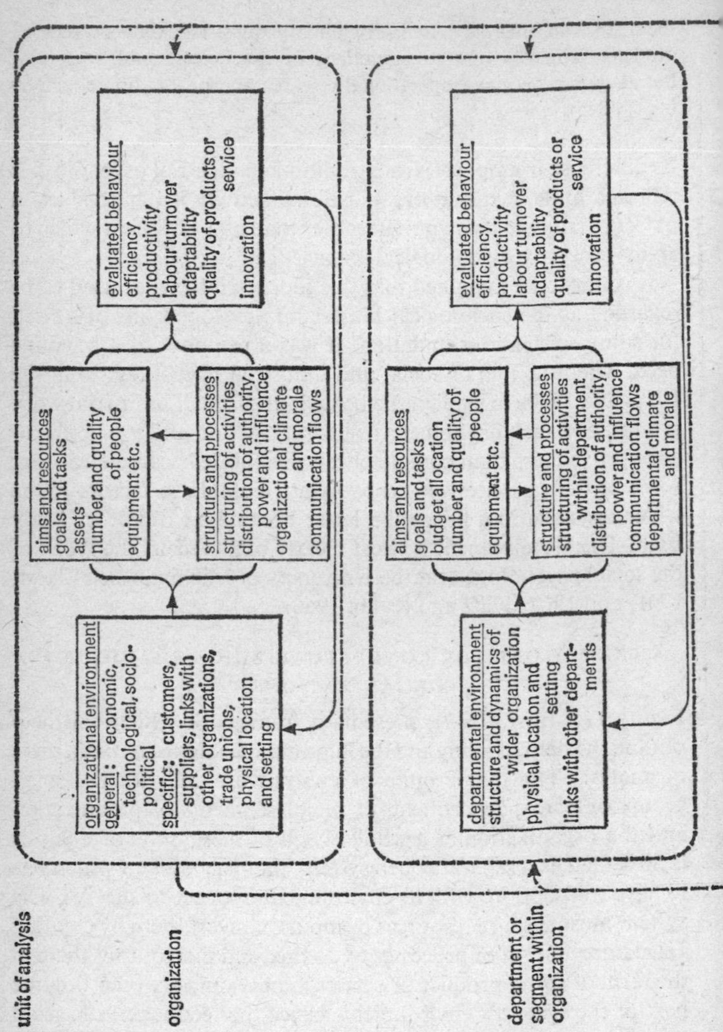

Figure 17.1 A framework for the study of behaviour in organizations

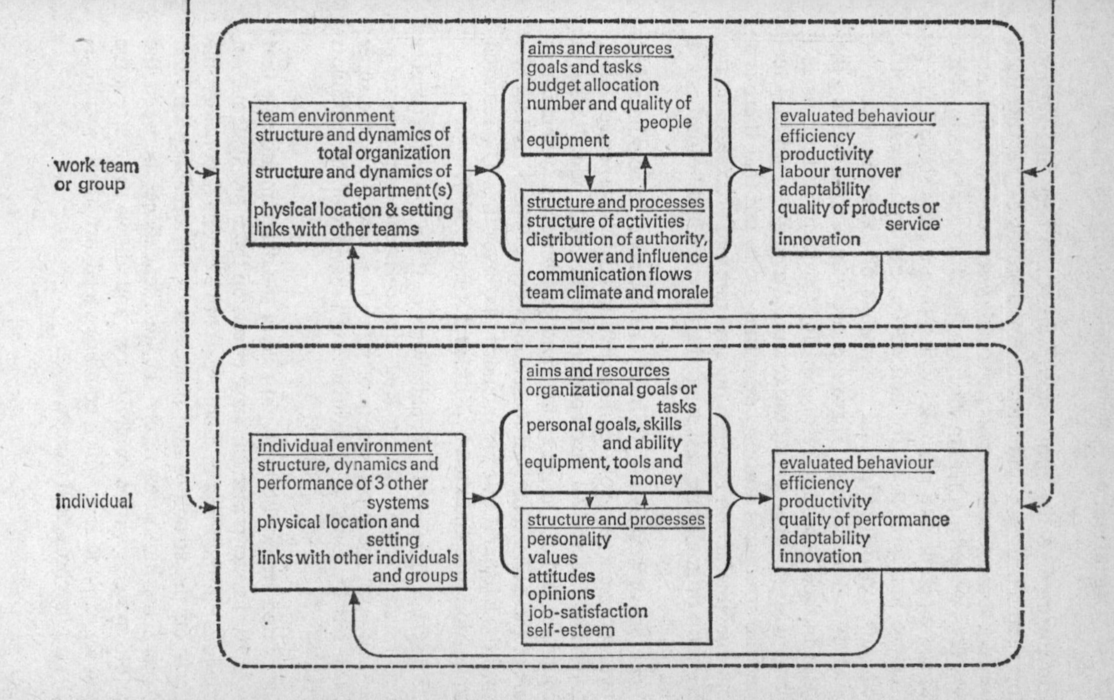
work team
or group
team environment
structure and dynamics of total organization
structure and dynamics of department(s)
physical location & setting
links with other teams
aims and resources
goals and tasks
budget allocation
number and quality of people
equipment
structure and processes
structure of activities
distribution of authority, power and influence
communication flows
team climate and morale
evaluated behaviour
efficiency
productivity
labour turnover
adaptability
quality of products or service
innovation
individual
individual environment
structure, dynamics and performance of 3 other systems
physical location and setting
links with other individuals and groups
aims and resources
organizational goals or tasks
personal goals, skills and ability
equipment, tools and money
structure and processes
personality
values
attitudes
opinions
job-satisfaction
self-esteem
evaluated behaviour
efficiency
productivity
quality of performance
adaptability
innovation

In Figure 17.1 the conversion process has been divided into 'aims and resources', and 'structure and processes' because until there are some people there is no social system or conversion process. Thus we feel justified in starting off with a social system which has some people and purposes which then creates some form of structure and processes to achieve those purposes, given the demands, opportunities and constraints of the environment in which it is functioning. There are two-way arrows linking the boxes marked 'aims and resources' and 'structure and processes', for we wish to suggest that the resources available tend to determine the structures and processes that occur, but that there is a continual interaction between the structure and processes and the definition of goals and tasks and the uses to which resources are put.

The lists of variables in the boxes are not meant to be exhaustive, but to represent some of the major features that have been studied. Hopefully, Figure 17.1 also conveys the fact that individuals and groups are part of a larger system, and that the larger system forms part of the environment of these sub-systems. The dotted arrows down the left-hand side are intended to convey this. The research implication is highlighted by Katz and Kahn (1966):

> The first step (in research) should always be to go to the next higher level of system organization, to study the dependence of the system in question upon the super system of which it is a part, for the super system sets the limits of the variance of behaviour of the dependent systems.

The dotted arrows up the right side of the diagram indicate that lower level systems also can have effects on the supra-systems. An individual in the form of a chief executive can have considerable effects on the structure and processes of the organization as a whole. This illustrates nicely the interdependence between the various systems within organizations and allows us to stress the need for explanations which combine social-structural (sociological) and psychological frameworks.

TYPOLOGIES OF ORGANIZATION

Having stated that our purpose is to examine organizations as work environments, the first essential is to attempt to identify the various types of organizations that exist. Several writers have offered conceptually-based classifications of organizations. The best known are those by Thompson and Tuden (1959), Blau and Scott (1962) and Etzioni (1961). All of these classifications have less than five major types and their limitation is perhaps best illustrated by the fact that all business organizations are included as one type. To be fair, all the typologies allow for mixtures of the main types, and Blau and Scott suggest that their typology could be combined with others. But on their own even the more complex forms say little about the nature and structure of the organization, and they have rarely been used in empirical studies.

For once in social science the British have been the most active in developing empirically-based typologies of organizations. In the 1950s, Joan Woodward carried out a survey of one hundred manufacturing organizations in S.E. Essex. Data were collected about many aspects of organizational structure such as number of employees, number of hierarchical levels and ratio of supervisory personnel. Information about the nature of the production processes was collected and about company performance. The typology developed was based solely on the nature of the production processes or production technology. A ten-category scale of production technology complexity was produced. These ten can be classified into three broad groups without distorting the concept. The simplest group of production processes were named unit and small batch production, indicating that articles were produced one at a time or in fairly small batches. It is important to understand that the units made could be quite complex (e.g. trains, ships and computers), but the production technology itself is simple. The next group is called large batch or mass production and the final group is called process production where, in the most complex production situation, there is literally a continuous flow of liquids, gases or solids being produced, requiring a highly integrated, automated production system.

This has been a very influential study because it established production technology as one of the contenders for being a major determinant of organization structure.[1] Woodward (1965) found that as the production technology became more complex, the number of levels of authority in the management hierarchy increased, as did the ratio of managers and supervisory staff to other personnel. Taking firstline supervisors alone, however, it was the mass-production firms that had the largest number of men per supervisor. It may have been this which indirectly, and only partly, caused the 'human relations' in the mass-production organizations to be poorer than in the other types of organizations. A tantalizing finding which has not been investigated again was that organizations that had structures very different from the median for their technological type were poorer in performance terms.

It was also a performance difference that led Burns and Stalker (1961) to propose another influential typology of organizations. They were investigating a number of manufacturing organizations, amongst which were several electronics firms. One of these in particular was performing very well and it organized itself in a very different way from some of its competitors. Compared to them and other more traditional types of organizations, it had an organismic as opposed to a mechanistic structure. The meaning of these terms is best established by contrasting the two extreme types, though all variations in between these two extreme types are possible.

Mechanistic	*Organismic*
1. Great division of labour and specialist tasks.	The person with the specialist knowledge goes where he is needed.
2. Clear hierarchy of authority.	Authority vested in the person who can deal with the problem *whoever* he is.

1. To be strictly accurate, the researchers at the Tavistock Institute of Human Relations had already proposed the notion of the socio-technical system (see Emery and Trist, 1960) which stressed how social and technological systems needed to complement each other if both of them were to function effectively. At this stage, however (the late 1950s), their work had centred on shop-floor groups only, though the ideas were later related to total organizations (see Rice, A. K. (1963), *The Enterprise and its Environment*; and Miller, E. J., and Rice, A. K. (1967), *Systems of Organization*).

Mechanistic	*Organismic*
3. Precise definition of job duties, rules, etc.	Continual re-definition of individual's jobs as situation requires.
4. Centralization of information and decision-taking.	Information, knowledge may be located *anywhere* in the organizational network.
5. Preponderance of vertical communication.	Preponderance of horizontal communication.

The mechanistic organization is closely similar to Weber's (1947) description of what he regarded as the most perfect form of organization, the ideal bureaucracy.

The important innovation in Burns and Stalker's work is that they related their organizational types to causes in the environment of the organization. The organismic organizations they studied were electronics firms in which both the technology and the market were changing fast and unpredictably. The organismic system, with its lack of defined roles, stress on immediate face to face communication and willingness for technical leadership to predominate over status, was well suited to deal with the problems presented by such an environment. Some of the electronics firms, however, were trying to use a more mechanistic structure and were struggling severely. On the other hand, a highly mechanistic firm producing rayon, with a predictable process type of production for a relatively stable market, was coping well with its environmental demands. The notion of 'the one best way' to organize, advocated by some of the early management thinkers such as F. W. Taylor and Henri Fayol was clearly no longer admissible.[2]

The lessons of this work seem to be that organizations have complex structures made up of a variety of factors (centralization of authority, specification of roles, hierarchical levels, etc.); that these various structural features are likely to derive from factors in the environment, from the kinds of goals the organization is trying to achieve and from the production technology adopted to achieve those goals; and that organizations can vary along all these dimensions so that more adequate comparison or classifica-

2. See chapter 13 and Tillett, Kempner and Wills (1970).

tion of organizations requires a means of measuring these attributes in a dimensional or continuously varying form.

An attempt to deal with some of these problems was made by a group at the University of Aston in Birmingham. The details of the conceptual framework which guided their activities can be found in an article by Pugh *et al.* (1963). For present purposes, we shall concentrate on two sets of variables in the scheme – structural variables and contextual variables. The aim was to find ways of measuring these two sets of variables in a dimensional form and then to see whether certain types of structures were produced by certain types of contexts. The structural and contextual variables are:

Context

Origin and history – whether an organization was privately or publicly founded, and the kinds of changes of ownership, location, etc. it has experienced.

Ownership and control – the kind of ownership (e.g. public or private) and its concentration in a few hands or dispersion into many.

Size – number of employees, net assets, market position, etc.

Charter – the nature and range of goods and services.

Technology – the degree of integration achieved in an organization's work processes.

Interdependence – the extent to which an organization depends on customers, suppliers, trade unions, etc.

Structure

Specialization – the degree to which an organization's activities are divided into specialized roles.

Standardization – the degree to which an organization lays down standard rules and procedures.

Formalization – the degree to which instructions, procedures, etc. are written down.

Centralization – the degree to which the authority to take certain decisions is located at the top of the management hierarchy.

Configuration – the 'shape' of the organization's role structure, e.g. whether the managerial chain of command is long or short, or whether the organization has a large percentage of 'supportive' personnel.

Data were collected by interview with relevant executives in fifty-two organizations which were randomly sampled from all organizations in Birmingham employing over 250 people. All the questions concerned material of the formal, objective variety; for example, 'Does the organization have any specialists concerned solely with the training of employees? How many people are employed on this specialism only? What are the organization's net assets? Is there a despatch note to cover each unit of output?' As far as possible each question was directed at the executive with responsibility for the area in question, and formal confirmatory evidence was requested. For example, the question about despatch notes would normally be asked of the production manager or equivalent, and an actual despatch note could be requested as evidence. In general the attempt made to keep the questions free from ambiguity and interpretation seemed to be successful. Finally, extra information was gathered from other sources; for example, measures of ownership and control, such as an index of individuality of ownership, were compiled from information from public records.

Individual item responses were then arranged into cumulative measures and after demonstrating the scaleability of the variables, structural and contextual variables were factor analysed separately and resulting factors related to each other. The details of these efforts can be found in Pugh *et al.* (1968 and 1969a). On the basis of the first three factors of the structural variables an empirical taxonomy of organizations was possible (Pugh *et al.*, 1969b). The three structural factors and the variables of which they are composed are:

Factor	*Component scales of the factor*
1. *Structuring of activities* – the degree to which the behaviour of employees is defined by dividing work into specialist jobs, laying down routines, procedures and formalizing them by insisting on written records, etc.	Specialization Standardization Formalization

Factor	*Component scales of the factor*
2. *Concentration of authority* – degree to which authority to take decisions is concentrated at the top of the organization, or outside the organization, if it is part of a larger company.	Centralization Degree of autonomy of chief executive
3. *Line control of workflow* – the degree to which control is exercised by line personnel as against its exercise through impersonal procedures.	Number of subordinates per supervisor (few vs many) Degree to which written records of role performance are collected (low vs high)

Organizations can in principle range along each of these three factors to provide a very large number of combinations of scores. However, if we classify organizations as simply high or low, or high, medium or low on each of the three factors, we can produce quite a complex taxonomy or typology, but one which is not too complex to comprehend. Pugh and his colleagues divided organizations into three groups on Factor 1 (structuring of activities: structured, medium, unstructured), and into high or low on the remaining two factors. Thus organizations either have concentrated decision taking or dispersed decision taking, and they are either controlled predominantly by line personnel or by impersonal procedures. Figure 17.2 shows the various possibilities in diagrammatic form and names the types of organizational structures such a classification produces.

The seven types within the taxonomy are:

Full bureaucracy
Nascent full bureaucracy
Workflow bureaucracy
Nascent workflow bureaucracy
Pre-workflow bureaucracy
Personnel bureaucracy
Implicitly structured organization

More detailed descriptions of the types follow, including a brief description of the kinds of contexts in which these structures tend to occur.

The *full bureaucracy*, of which there was only one in the sample, has relatively high scores on both structuring of activities and concentration of authority. The instance in the original study is a government owned factory and thus has a high score on the contextual variable of dependence. It has high scores on both standardization of procedures for dealing with the personnel aspects of selection and promotion, etc., and roles are formalized and defined.

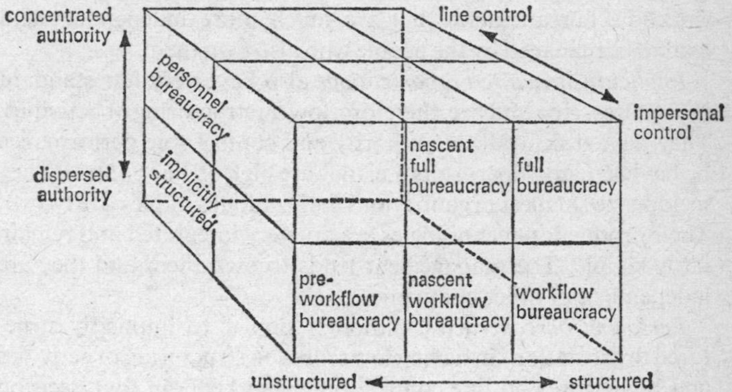

Figure 17.2 A three-dimensional taxonomy of work organization

It is the only organization with the characteristics of both a personnel and a workflow bureaucracy. The existence of this type of organization has been confirmed by another study (Inkson *et al.*, 1969), and the organizations were once again government owned, concerned with railways, electricity supply, etc. The *nascent full bureaucracy* possesses the same characteristics, but not to such a pronounced degree.

Workflow bureaucracies are characterized by high scores on structuring of activities combined with relatively low scores on the remaining two structural factors. Their use of impersonal control mechanisms is shown by the high scores on formalization of recording of role performance, as well as by having a high percentage of people not directly engaged on production, such as supervisors and clerks. This type includes the largest organizations in the sample, which are manufacturing organizations having well integrated, fairly complex production technologies. *Nascent workflow bureaucracies* show the same characteristics to a less pronounced degree and are much smaller. If they grow they will become workflow bureaucracies, hence their nascence.

Pre-workflow bureaucracies have far fewer rules, regulations, standard procedures and their concomitant, paperwork, but they have the typical workflow bureaucracy pattern of decentralized decision taking and control by impersonal procedures rather than by supervisory personnel. They are smaller in size than nascent workflow bureaucracies, but are much more independent and tend to be managed by the people who also own them.

Implicitly structured organizations also have very few standard procedures, etc., and are, therefore, low on structuring of activities. They have decentralized authority and control role performance by having many supervisors, i.e. they are high on line control. They include the smallest organizations in the initial sample of fifty-two. Their production technologies are not very integrated and remain fairly simple. The management tends to own them and they are independent of other companies.

Personnel bureaucracies, although similar to implicitly structured organizations in having low scores on structuring of activities and high scores on line control, differ markedly in that decision taking is highly centralized. This is because they tend to be part of central or local government and these central organizing bodies keep control over decisions that are made. This applies to operating decisions as well as to recruiting and promotion decisions, so that personnel bureaucracies have a high score on a scale called standardization of procedures for selection and advancement. Unlike some of the other types they vary considerably in size, ranging in this sample from 250 to 16,500.

Five of the boxes in Figure 17.2 are empty, because there were no examples of organizations having such profiles amongst the fifty-two studied. This illustrates the fact that this taxonomy of organizations is empirical rather than conceptual as the other typologies were. Indeed, it is a taxonomy rather than a typology because it is empirically derived, and because it is multidimensional. Whilst it might seem that a taxonomy of this complexity is quite a useful start, it is instructive to make a diversion and show how limited the scheme is in the light of changes in organizational structures that have only recently started to occur.

The reader may have noticed that Pugh *et al.* did not describe any of the organizations as unbureaucratic. This is due to the fact that 'every organization of any size is bureaucratized to some degree, or, to put it differently, exhibits more or less stable patterns of behaviour based upon a structure of roles and specialized tasks' (Perrow, 1970). Yet, the logical opposite of being bureaucratized is *not* being bureaucratized, or having very few specialists, rules, regulations and being decentralized etc. Examination of Burns and Stalker's mechanistic-organismic dimension suggests, therefore, that organismic is not the *necessary* opposite of mechanistic. As we shall see more clearly later, organizations with low scores on the dimensions operationalized by Pugh and others are not organismic. But as organismic types of organizations do seem to exist, it suggests that the Pugh *et al.*, measures of organization structure would pick up the bureaucratic aspects of an organismic structure, but not its organismic aspects. Lawrence and Lorsch (1967) report a study looking at the structure and effectiveness of organizations operating in environments of different predictability. The organization that was most successful in dealing with the most unpredictable environment was a plastics factory, which was very differentiated in Lawrence and Lorsch's terms, or specialized in Pugh *et al.* terms; that is, it had specialist departments of sales production and research which were highly differentiated from each other. In order to integrate this diverse group of functions, the organization had developed a special group dealing specifically with integrating the three other groups. Lawrence and Lorsch suggest that this highly differentiated and highly integrated structure was characteristic of organizations dealing successfully with turbulent environments. Whilst the Pugh *et al.* measures would have indicated the degree of differentiation with much greater sophistication than Lawrence and Lorsch, they would not have picked up the degree of integration at all. As organizational forms such as matrix structures (Shull, 1967) and horizontal overlapping group structures (Likert, 1967)[3] are appearing more frequently now, there is obvious room for the development of new measures

3. Both these forms of structure have developed in an attempt to ensure that the hierarchical differentiation that seems indispensable to organizations of any kind does not prevent an adequate amount of horizontal integration.

of organization and the more comprehensive taxonomies that will result from them.

Although the work we have described might seem to imply that organizational structures create relatively homogeneous environments for the individuals working in them, it would be a great mistake to come to that conclusion. Even in a government bureaucracy it is obvious that the head of the Civil Service lives in a very different environment from the lowliest of clerical officers. Thus, level in the hierarchy is a factor which must be considered when investigating the effects of organizational structure on attitudes and behaviour. Another relevant factor might be the routineness of the work performed, and Table 17.1, presents a matrix using level in hierarchy and routineness of work to demonstrate that even within the same structure there are many different psychological environments.

Table 17.1 Predictability or Routineness of Work

		Much routine	*Little routine*
	Upper and middle level managers	Administration accounts production (line)	R & D (staff) but also some production systems
Level in hierarchy	Supervisors and lower level managers	Quality control many production systems	Research, some production, maintenance systems
	Workers or operator level personnel	Mass production workers, clerks	Toolmaking Pattern-making

What is suggested then is that within, say, a workflow bureaucracy the impact of its rules and procedures will be felt less by managers in the R and D department than by managers in the accounts department, just because of the nature of their work. Whilst this may appear reasonably obvious, research hypotheses and empirical data of this complexity are quite rare.

At this point it seems useful to summarize the position. We have shown that it is possible to classify work organizations into at least seven types, and that within each of those types there may be six different environments created by differences in (a) job level and (b) the degree to which work is more or less routine. Potentially, there are on this basis forty-two different work environments. What would now seem logical is that we present research findings about attitudes and behaviour in each of these forty-two environments. Unfortunately, that would require a considerable research effort in itself, and even then the data that would be needed to classify the research on such a basis would not be available in many instances. In some cases there just would not be any data. We shall, therefore, review some of the findings for the main structural variables such as size, job level and centralization, which will at least give some idea of what effects organizational variables can have. The reader should keep in mind, however, the broad diversity of organizational environments we have described, and evaluate the present state of knowledge accordingly.

ORGANIZATIONS, ATTITUDES AND BEHAVIOUR

Effects of organizational size[4]

One of the most studied aspects of organizations is the effect of size. We know that size is strongly related to bureacracy or mechanistic forms of organizations so that larger organizations tend to be more bureaucratic. Pugh *et al.* (1969a) found a correlation of 0·69 between size and the factor 'structuring of activities'. The causal relationships between large organization size and resulting psychological states have been effectively explored by Indik (1965). Bringing in the effects of bureaucratic dimensions as well as of size, he presents the hypothesis that,

> The size of the organization as a variable of *organizational structure* influences member participation *indirectly* through its effect on specific *organizational processes* such as those relating to communication, control, task specialization, and coordination. These processes, in turn, affect *the ties that bind the individual to the organization*, i.e. the degree of attraction among organizational members, the amount of intrinsic job-satisfaction derived by the members, and the degree of bureaucratic inflexibility felt by members. It is these latter variables that directly affect *member behaviour*, i.e. member-participation rates (p. 339).

4. Some aspects of training technology which are related to organizational size are described in chapter 4.

This set of hypotheses was tested out in three different types of organizations: a set of 32 package delivery organizations varying in size from 15 to 61 members: a set of 36 automobile sales dealership organizations which ranged in size from 25 to 132: and in 28 units of a national voluntary organization whose members had the goal of increasing citizen participation in political activities; these varied in size from 101 to 2,989 members. One of the positive attributes of this research design is that within each set of organizations the individual units operated in similar market, technological and union conditions.

On the whole, Indik's hypotheses were upheld. Large size was found to lead to organizational processes which resulted in lower levels of communication and coordination, and increased job specialization. These in turn led to psychological states of dissatisfaction and lowered attraction to other members. The psychological states themselves resulted in people leaving the organization, or to increases in absenteeism, lateness and so on.

The relationships between size and various attitudinal and behavioural indices are more completely summarized by Porter and Lawler (1965) in their review of the effects of various properties of organization on attitudes and behaviour. The research findings are slightly confused by the fact that some investigators have taken total organizations as their unit of study, and others have taken sub-units within organizations as their unit of study. Indik, for example, followed the latter course, each automobile dealership being treated as a separate organization. Porter and Lawler found only two studies that have related total organization size to job-satisfaction. Both studies found that people in larger companies were less satisfied with their jobs. As they point out, however, the evidence is much more conclusive if sub-unit size is taken as the relevant measure. Table 2 of their article summarizes the relationships between sub-unit size and job-satisfaction (negative), sub-unit size and absenteeism (positive), labour turnover (positive), accidents (positive, curvilinear and negative relationships are found), labour disputes (positive), and productivity (negative, curvilinear and zero relationships found). Such findings cast doubt upon the relationship found at total organizational level because it is possible that large organizations have larger sub-units and that this is the crucial factor, not total organizational size. Here is a very good example of why future research needs to be conducted within the total systems sort of framework proposed earlier in Figure 17.1.

The effects of hierarchical level

The general effect of job level on job or need satisfaction is fairly clear. Across most types of companies need satisfaction increases directly as level in the hierarchy increases, and the most significant increases tend to be in those areas of work which satisfy needs for self-actualization (Herzberg *et al.*, 1957; Porter, 1963 and 1964). Porter and Lawler (1965) also review studies which suggest that higher level managers receive more informal communication and are better informed, have less contact with colleagues at the same level, and more with people outside their organization. One thing that is not affected by job level is people's perceptions of the importance that needs have for them. People at all levels of the workforce see Maslow's higher order needs (see chapter 13) as having the same degree of importance for them. That is, even unskilled workers think that it is important that work provides the opportunity to obtain feelings of accomplishment and achievement (Porter, 1963, 1964).

One recent study deals with differences in levels and adds in another area of complexity – namely the multi-dimensionality of alienation and/or job-satisfaction. Bonjean and Grimes (1970) collected information about feelings of alienation from 104 independent businessmen, 108 managers, and 120 workers. Six aspects of alienation were measured: feelings of isolation; feelings of inhabiting a world where no norms of behaviour existed; powerlessness; feelings of anomie; feelings of self-estrangement; and general alienation. The subjects were also asked to describe the organization structures of the companies for which they worked, or which they owned. Ratings were collected for six dimensions of bureaucracy: amount of authority, number of procedures, degree of specialization, degree to which there were written rules, impersonality of relationships and overall or general bureaucracy.

The data in no way support the generalization that bureaucracy leads to alienation. Relationships were found for the blue-collar sample only. And within that sample the authority dimension of bureaucracy was by far the most strongly related to alienation.

Furthermore, the form of alienation most closely related to bureaucratization was self-estrangement. As the authors say, 'The use of a single measure of bureaucracy or alienation would have obscured most of the findings presented here.'

The effects of the interaction between organizational size and hierarchical level

Size, we already know, has a negative effect on satisfaction and various performance indices for blue-collar workers: statistics on absence, accidents and lateness do not tend to be kept for managers, of course. But does size have a different effect on managers? Porter (1963 and 1964) has shown that the effect of size is modified by managerial level. In companies of less than 500, managers at lower and middle levels were more satisfied than managers at the same levels in larger companies. But at the upper-middle and top levels of management, the reverse was true. This may be explained by the findings of Inkson *et al.* (1968). They related the degree of bureaucracy in forty assorted companies to the degree to which the top executives in the companies saw their work roles as being routine vs non-routine, defined-undefined, changing-stable, predictable-unpredictable, etc. They found that top executives in the most bureaucratic organizations saw their jobs as being less routine, less defined, less stable and less predictable. The explanation for this is that the bureaucratic routines that were operated further down the organization effectively freed the senior people to pursue the more unpredictable tasks that faced the company.

The effect of size is also modified by the number of hierarchical levels in the organization. Porter and Lawler (1964) and Porter and Siegal (1964) found that in companies employing less than 5,000 workers, managerial satisfaction was greater in companies having fewer hierarchical levels. For companies employing over 5,000 the relationship was reversed in the first of these two studies, so that in larger companies managers were more satisfied in companies having tall hierarchies. In the second study, no difference was found between companies having tall or flat structures once they employed more than 5,000 people. Whether these effects act differentially at different managerial levels is not explored.

The effects of horizontal divisions at different work levels

The evidence is consistent that line managers obtain more satisfaction than staff managers.[5] This is reflected in the greater turnover that occurs in staff positions too. Traditionally, there is much conflict between line and staff positions (e.g. Dalton, 1950). This is probably because the staff man rarely has the opportunity to make decisions on the basis of his 'expert' knowledge, and because the line man has to 'carry the can' for decisions he takes about situations which have their practical problems and politics that are not always recognized by the staff man. This conflict may have been generated partly by the mechanistic systems that have traditionally been used in industry. Burns and Stalker (1961) found that one of the problems the mechanistic firms could not solve was how to relate effectively to the research scientists they brought in to solve the technological problems they could see they had. The organismic structures would not have this problem because line-staff distinctions would not be built into work roles in the first place. As we have seen already, however, Lawrence and Lorsch (1967) found firms that had used the integrating group as a means of solving this line-staff type of problem. Such a solution may be more generally acceptable to industrial organizations, for Pelz and Andrews (1966) found that industrial research scientists were most effective when their environment provided means for good coordination between the scientists themselves and between the scientists and their production, sales and administrative counterparts, providing that the environment also allowed the scientists the freedom to decide what they would do and how and when they would do it.

As far as horizontal divisions at the blue-collar level are concerned, people in jobs which demand more skill are usually more satisfied with the intrinsic aspects of their work, though they may be less satisfied with extrinsic aspects. Kornhauser (1965) has found that there is a firm relationship between having very unskilled jobs and having poor mental health. He attributes this relationship partly to the debilitating psychological effects of working in

5. A line manager is one whose authority is in the 'mainstream' of an organization (e.g. production in a factory, selling in a retail store). A staff manager has functions which are more clearly advisory – in personnel, work study, accountancy, quality control and so on.

very unstimulating work environments. Lawler (1969) has also shown that jobs which are designed to be more complex lead to improvements in quality in all of the studies he reviewed. This is interpreted to mean that workers are more involved with their work as a result of being able to do a job which is of such a quality that it demands the use of valued skills and abilities, and this leads to increased satisfaction with the intrinsic aspects of work.

The effects of decentralization

One organizational device for further enlarging jobs is to decentralize, so that more people participate in decisions that are relevant to them and their jobs. Although strongly advocated as an efficient mode of organization, empirical studies which have compared the effectiveness of centralized and decentralized structures are few in number. The general trend, however, is to support the decentralized model. Porter and Lawler (1965) quote four studies which showed that executives in decentralized organizations did have more autonomy to take decisions, and that variables such as turnover rate, number of grievances, number of white-collar workers, absenteeism, accident frequency and age of managers were lower in decentralized organizations, though the differences were not large. Morse and Reimer (1956) conducted a field experiment where they persuaded a company to use an authoritarian hierarchically controlled system of supervision in two departments and an autonomous, participative (decentralized) system in another two departments. All departments did similar work. After a period of a year the decentralized department had higher morale and lower labour turnover, but also slightly lower productivity. It is argued, however, that productivity would eventually have fallen in the centralized departments and that the lower morale and higher turnover were indicative of this.

In only one of these four studies was the *degree* of centralization measured. Furthermore, the difference in centralization was the only difference considered, whilst the companies were presumably different in many other ways too. The importance of considering the degree to which any characteristic is possessed, and the intervening effects of other characteristics is revealed by a study we carried out in conjunction with Diana Pheysey (Pheysey, Payne and Pugh, 1971).

The purpose of the study was to see whether differences in organization structure were associated with differences in the structure and climate of work teams at different levels in the managerial hierarchy. Two companies were selected that were similar in size (350–400 employees) and similar in their methods of production, but that were very different in structure. One had many standard procedures, job definitions and lots of written records collected for scheduling and control purposes, was relatively centralized and had five hierarchical levels. The other had few such procedures, was decentralized, but had eight hierarchical levels. Despite this lack of bureaucratic or mechanistic structure, it was certainly not organismic. People's roles had evolved over time and were quite stable and well known to each other, though hardly anything was written down or formalized. The authority structure was a mixture of what Weber (1947) described as traditionalistic and charismatic authority rather than the rational-legal authority of the bureaucratic system, or the 'man with the answer' authority of the organismic system. In terms of the empirical taxonomy described earlier, the former was a workflow bureaucracy and the latter a pre-workflow bureaucracy. Information collected from the members of the line management work teams at the top, middle management and supervisory levels in each company showed that work teams at all levels in the more bureaucratic company saw the work teams themselves as being more formal (bureaucratic). In keeping with the higher levels of centralization in the company as a whole, they also saw themselves as having less autonomy than groups in the less bureaucratic company. Indeed, the group at the lowest level in the less bureaucratic company (i.e. foremen and their immediate superior) saw itself as having more autonomy than the group at the top of the more bureaucratic company (i.e. chief executive and his immediate subordinate). This occurred because this company was a subsidiary and many of its decisions had to be referred to the parent group. On the other hand, groups in the more bureaucratic company were more cohesive, more involved in their group's activities, and more successful in achieving their goals. This finding tends to run counter to common beliefs and to the findings of others who have uncovered some of the dysfunctions of bureaucratic systems. What is important, however, is the *degree* of bureaucracy. Although the workflow bureaucracy was much more bureaucratic than the pre-workflow bureaucracy, it was less bureaucratic than many other workflow bureaucracies. It could be, therefore, that this company had achieved the optimum degree of structure where people's jobs were sufficiently defined for people to be clear on their objectives, and because of the performance data that were collected, to get adequate feedback on performance, whilst still being able to retain the personal contact and involvement which the company's smallish size would permit.

One other important difference was that people in the less bureaucratic company saw their leaders as being psychologically more distant. This occurred despite the fact that this company was very decentralized. The explanation is that it also had more hierarchical levels and this considerable differentiation by status caused this feeling of psychological distance from senior people. Thus the effects of one aspect of organization structure (decentralization) can be counteracted by the effects of another (the status hierarchy). This underlines again the need for future research to concentrate on multi-dimensional descriptions of organizations and the people who work in them.

ORGANIZATIONAL CLIMATE

In the study we have just described we used the idea that work groups had a particular 'climate'. This concept has in recent years been applied to organizations too and it is clearly concerned with the global environment created by an organization. A conference on the topic was held in 1967 and is reported in Taguiri and Litwin (1968). Taguiri defines climate as

> the relatively enduring quality of the internal environment of an organization that (a) is experienced by its members, (b) influences their behaviour, and (c) can be described in terms of the values of a particular set of characteristics (or attributes) of the organization.

In practice it is measured by asking people to describe how they perceive their organizational environment, usually by means of a questionnaire. There are a number of such questionnaires, some of which have been designed for particular types of organizations, such as universities (see Stern, 1970). Campbell *et al.* (1970) have examined most of them and conclude that they measure four main aspects of climate:

1. The degree of autonomy people are given.
2. The degree of structure imposed on work positions.
3. The reward orientation either in terms of individual satisfaction or company achievement.
4. The degree of consideration, warmth and support.

The first two of these seem to be alternative ways of measuring aspects of the organization's structure – namely, degree of decentralization and structuring of work activities respectively. The latter two, however, seem to arise more from the values of the people running the organization, but are obviously important environmental elements.

The 'climate of opinion' amongst social scientists at the moment would probably be that 'good' climates would be high on (1), low on (2), high on (3) and high on (4). There is some evidence to support them; Likert (1967) for instance advocates an open, participative form of organization and produces some evidence to show that organizations adopting such a system do eventually perform well, both economically and socially, in that employees prefer working that way.

Litwin and Stringer (1968) have also carried out some laboratory experiments where they manipulated the climate of their experimental companies by having a stooge as the chief executive, who deliberately created a considerate or an autocratic style and climate. Their studies show that different climates tend to arouse different motivations in terms of McClelland's concepts of Need for Achievement,[6] Need for Affiliation and Need for Power. These differences in aroused motivation are related to differences in group performance and member satisfaction. Their reports of studies of live organizations also show that climates arousing inappropriate motivations for the task situation in hand lead to poor organizational performance.

Climate is obviously an important factor which is likely to affect individuals' satisfactions and organizational performance, but we know little about what creates particular climates and not much

6. See chapter 12, page 273.

more about how a climate affects satisfactions and performance. Nevertheless, it is a concept which will undoubtedly receive much attention in future research.

INDIVIDUAL DIFFERENCES

So far we have talked about such topics as how large size leads to lower satisfaction almost as if everyone in a large company would be dissatisfied. This is obviously not so, and the considerable differences in attitudes and behaviour that people demonstrate in the same environments are of great interest to the psychologist. Some of the factors causing these response differences seem to arise from basic personality factors. Vroom (1960) has shown that people having authoritarian personalities do not like participative styles of leadership. They prefer to work in organizations where they are told what to do clearly and precisely. Cooper and Payne (1967) found that amongst a group of eighty-one female tobacco packers those higher on extraversion, as measured by the Eysenck Personality Inventory, tended to have higher levels of non-permitted absence and more visits to the sick bay. This behaviour was possibly explicable in terms of Eysenck's theory of inhibition, in that the extraverts needed to 'get away' from the fairly boring jobs in order to dispel their high levels of inhibition. Interestingly, too, a year after the study had been completed a much greater proportion of the extraverts had left their jobs, which seems to support the belief that they found their work unstimulating.

Other differences seem to arise from attitudes and values acquired from the wider social environment or from such obvious things as having children to support. It has already been noted in chapter 12 how Turner and Lawrence (1965) discovered that urban blue-collar workers were more satisfied in jobs that were less complex and less demanding, whilst the reverse was true for rural workers. The difference was explained by the contrasting values of the two groups of workers; the rural workers have values associated with the idea of the Protestant ethic. Goldthorpe and his colleagues (1968) also found workers in a Luton car factory who had given up more interesting white-collar jobs for the high salaries. As Goldthorpe expressed it, they were instrumentally oriented to work and did not expect anything more than monetary returns for their labour. But the following quotation from a machine minder's account of his job in Frazer's (1969) second volume of personal accounts of work demonstrates that such work is, to say the least, unpalatable to some people:

Just trying to keep a grip to survive psychologically was difficult enough. The machine dictates simple repetition. It stops, you have to move; no use arguing. A few seconds later, the same thing again. You can't fight a losing battle several hundred times a day and survive. We submit to the repetitiveness and it's no use looking for a gain of significance. Naïvely I kid myself I'm achieving something by completing a roll, and I look for some significance at the end of the shift. There's none, not for us. We continue, changing cones, drudging, withdrawn, labouring animals. Bending over the machine, we stare into the revolving fabric which reflects the blank screen of the mind ... self-hypnotism (p. 93).

One of the more interesting developments in the work on individual differences in organizations is associated with the work on organizational climate. Stern (1970) has developed a personality measure, the Activities Index, which is based on Henry Murray's (1938) Need-Press Theory. He has also constructed a climate measure based on the same needs, and can thus match up personality needs with the perceived degree of press that the environment creates for those needs. He has found that people with strong intellectual needs feel more satisfied and (in some studies only) achieve more in environments which have a strong press in the same need areas. Pervin (1967) has studied ratings of the person and associated aspects of his environment; thus in college environments he has assessments of the faculty, the administration, other students, etc., and finds that where self is perceived differently from the environment people feel less satisfied. These attempts to discover the interactions between people and their environments are exciting developments in the field.

CONCLUSIONS

At the beginning of this essay we asked the question, 'What kinds of environment do work organizations create and why, and what is their effect on behaviour?' We have devoted considerable space to describing the kinds of environments organizations create and some of their effects on the people who work in them. Figure 17.1 provides some indication of why the organizations are what they are. It suggests that some of them have goals to make or do something and that this activity places them in a certain kind of environment. Thus anybody who wants to make electronic equipment places himself in a rapidly changing technological and market environment, and, as the arrow from the box marked Organizational Environment indicates, this has consequences for the structure and processes that the organization adopts. Similarly, organizations operate in varying economic, social and political circumstances which can also provide severe tests of the adequacy of the system to respond to its environment.

One of the strongest forces in the social environment of organizations is man's current philosophy of man, for organizations tend to be designed to cope with the problems presented by any particular philosophy. Schein (1965) suggests that there have been four prevalent philosophies of man, which have their corresponding organizational forms:

Philosophy	*Organizational Form*
Economic Man – man motivated by self-interest.	Mechanistic structure using money as the major incentive and control.
Social Man – man motivated by feelings of belongingness.	Human relations model – bureaucracy with a smile.
Self-actualizing Man – motivated by doing challenging work.	Provide interesting tasks through job rotation, job-enlargement and job enrichment – bureaucracy with an intelligent smile.
Complex Man – man actually motivated by all the above things, as well as being very adaptable.	Man is all the other three philosophies so design organizations to give flexibility and freedom – organismic model.

Bennis (1964) captures the flavour of the current *Zeitgeist*.

Bureaucracy, with its 'surplus repression', was a monumental discovery for harnessing muscle power via guilt and instinctual renunciation. In today's world it is a prosthetic device, no longer useful. For we now require organic-adaptive systems and structures of freedom to permit the expression of play and imagination and to exploit the new pleasure of work.

One of Schein's main points about complex man, however, is that men are individuals and have different needs, personalities and goals. And this is true of organizations. The complex environment our culture creates to-day produces a whole range of environmental niches which require different kinds of organizations to live and thrive in them. Given the present state of knowledge, it seems dangerous to suggest that organic-adaptive structures are the universal panacea, even though they may do universally better than any other *single* form. What seems to be needed is to find what sort of environmental niches there are and which organizational forms do best in them. At the psychological level, the problem is the same: how can we get a good individual-environment fit? That is, what psychological demands and opportunities do different organizational environments offer, and what sort of people will find them comfortable and satisfying environments to inhabit? As this brief survey has shown there is much still to be done to answer these questions as they apply to organizations and individuals, but from a practical and theoretical view they involve some of the most intellectually challenging issues of the day.

SUMMARY

Owing to their variety of purposes and the diversity of available technological and human resources, organizations have developed differences in their structural forms. For the individual this in general means environmental differences, but even within a single organization the psychological environment differs due to variations in job level and in task complexity. Both theory and research suggest that individuals are most effective and well adjusted when the environmental pressures or demands are compatible with their needs, skills, abilities and personality. The practical and theoretical challenge is to match individuals with their environments so that the needs of the person, the organization and society at large are optimally satisfied.

FURTHER READING

Two introductory books which form quite a nice psychological–sociological duet are E. H. Schein's *Organizational Psychology*

(Prentice-Hall, 1965) and C. Perrow's *Organizational Analysis* (Tavistock, 1970). The more psychologically oriented reader wishing to pursue some of the ideas raised in this chapter would do well to obtain the collection of readings edited by L. L. Cummings and W. E. Scott, entitled *Readings in Organizational Behaviour and Human Performance* (Dorsey Press, 1969).

The more sociologically biased reader will probably feel more at home with *Organizations: Structural Behaviour*, volume 1, by J. A. Litterer (Wiley, 1969). The practising manager is recommended D. McGregor's book, *The Professional Manager* (McGraw-Hill, 1967) and *Systems of Organization* by E. J. Miller and A. K. Rice (Tavistock, 1967). If he wishes to actually start changing his organization, he is recommended to read A. S. Judson's book, *A Manager's Guide to Making Changes* (Wiley, 1966).

A single volume which covers some of all the three interest groups mentioned above is *The Handbook of Organizations* by J. G. March (Rand McNally, 1965) but this is both physically and figuratively a heavyweight publication.

References

ACRES, S. E. (1964), 'The 20th century disease', *Canadian Journal of Public Health*, vol. 55, pp. 221–2.

ADAMS, J. F. (ed.) (1965), *Counselling and Guidance, A Summary Review*, Macmillan Co.

ADAMS, J. S. (1963), 'Toward an understanding of inequity', *Journal of Abnormal and Social Psychology*, vol. 67, pp. 422–36.

ADAMS, J. S., and JACOBSEN, P. R. (1964), 'Effects of wage inequities on work quality', *Journal of Abnormal and Social Psychology*, vol. 69, pp. 19–25.

ADAMS, J. S., and ROSENBAUM, W. B. (1962), 'The relationship of worker-productivity to cognitive dissonance about wage inequities', *Journal of Applied Psychology*, vol. 46, pp. 161–4.

ALBRIGHT, L. E., GLENNON, J. R., and SMITH, W. J. (1963), *The Use of Psychological Tests in Industry*, Munksgaard.

ALDERFER, C. P., and MCCORD, C. G. (1970), 'Personal and situational factors in the recruitment interview', *Journal of Applied Psychology*, vol. 54, pp. 377–85.

ALLPORT, G. W. (1935), 'Attitudes', in C. Hutchinson (ed.), *Handbook of Social Psychology*, Clark University Press.

AMERICAN PSYCHOLOGICAL ASSOCIATION (1966), *Technical Recommendations on Tests*, Washington.

ANASTASI, A. (1968), *Psychological Testing*, Macmillan Co., 3rd edn.

ANDERSON, C. W. (1960), 'The relation between speaking times and decision in the employment interview', *Journal of Applied Psychology*, vol. 44, pp. 267–8.

ANDERSON, L. R. (1966), 'Leader behavior, member attitudes and task performance of intercultural discussion groups', *Journal of Social Psychology*, vol. 69, pp. 305–19.

ANDERSON, N. H. (1965), 'Averaging versus adding as a stimulus combination rule in impression formation', *Journal of Experimental Psychology*, vol. 70, pp. 394–400.

ANDERSON, R. C. (1959), 'Learning in discussions: a résumé of the authoritarian-democratic studies', *Harvard Educational Review*, vol. 29, pp. 201–15.

ANDERSON, R. C., FAUST, G. W., RODERICK, M. C., CUNNINGHAM, D. J., and ANDRÉ, T. (eds.) (1969), *Current Research on Instruction*, Prentice-Hall.

ANDREWS, J. D. W. (1967), 'The achievement motive in two types of organization', *Journal of Personality and Social Psychology*, vol. 6, pp. 163–8.

ANNETT, J. (1964), 'The relationship between theories of learning and theories of instruction', *Programmienter Unterricht and Letramaschiner*, Pädagogische Arbeitstelle, Berlin.

ANNETT, J. (1969), *Feedback and Human Behaviour*, Penguin.

ANNETT, J., and DUNCAN, K. D. (1971), *Task Analysis*, Department of Employment Training Information Paper No. 6, HMSO.

ANSTEY, E. (1969), *Staff Reporting and Staff Development*, Allen & Unwin.

ARBOUS, A. G., and KERRICK, J. E. (1951), 'Accident statistics and the concept of accident-proneness', *Journal of the Biometric Society*, vol. 7, pp. 340–429.

ARGYLE, M. (1953), 'The relay assembly test-room in retrospect', *Occupational Psychology*, vol. 27, pp. 98–103.

ARGYLE, M. (1967), *The Psychology of Interpersonal Behaviour*, Penguin.

ARGYLE, M. (1969), *Social Interaction*, Methuen.

ARGYLE, M., GARDNER, G., and CIOFFI, F. (1958), 'Supervisory methods related to productivity, absenteeism, and labour turnover', *Human Relations*, vol. 11, pp. 23–40. Reprinted in V. H. Vroom and L. Deci (eds.), *Management and Motivation*, Penguin, 1970.

ARGYRIS, C. (1957), *Personality and the Organization: The Conflict Between System and the Individual*, Harper & Row.

ARROW, K. J. (1963), 'Utility and expectations in economic behavior', in D. Koch (ed.) *Psychology: A Study of a Science*, McGraw-Hill.

ASCHOFF, J. (1969), 'Desynchronisation and resynchronisation of human circadian rhythm', *Aerospace Medicine*, vol. 40, pp. 844–9.

ASTIN, A. W. (1959), 'Criterion-oriented research', *Educational and Psychological Measurement*, vol. 12, pp. 395–6.

ATKINSON, J. W., and FEATHER, N. T. (eds.) (1966), *A Theory of Achievement Motivation*, Wiley.

AUDLEY, R. J. (1967), 'What makes up a mind?' in *Decision Making*, BBC Publications.

AUDLEY, R. J. (1970), 'Choosing', *Bulletin of the British Psychological Society*, vol. 23, pp. 177–91.

AX, A., and LUBY, E. D. (1961), 'Autonomic responses to sleep deprivation', *Archives of General Psychiatry*, vol. 4, pp. 55–9.

BABCHUK, N., and GOODE, W. J. (1951), 'Work incentives in a self determined group', *American Sociological Review*, vol. 16, pp. 679–86.

BAHRICK, H. P., NOBLE, M. E., and FITTS, P. M. (1954), 'Extra-task performance as a measure of learning a primary task', *Journal of Experimental Psychology*, vol. 48, pp. 298–302.

BALES, R. F. (1950), *Interaction Process Analysis: A Method for the Study of Small Groups*, Addison-Wesley.

BALES, R. F., and SLATER, P. E. (1955), 'Role differentiation in small decision making groups', in T. Parsons and R. F. Bales (eds.), *Family, Socialization and Interaction Process*, Free Press.

BALES, R. F., and STRODTBECK, F. L. (1951), 'Phases in group problem solving', *Journal of Abnormal and Social Psychology*, vol. 46, pp. 485–95.

BALMA, J. (1959), 'The concept of synthetic validity', *Personnel Psychology*, vol. 12, pp. 395–6.

BANKS, J. A. (1963), *Industrial Participation. Theory and Practice: A Case Study*, Liverpool University Press.

BANNISTER, D. (1966), 'A new theory of personality', in B. M. Foss (ed.), *New Horizons in Psychology*, Penguin.

BANNISTER, D., and FRANSELLA, F. (1966), 'A grid test of schizophrenic thought disorder', *British Journal of Social and Clinical Psychology*, vol. 5, pp. 95–102.

BARTLETT, F. C. (1932), *Remembering: A Study in Experimental and Social Psychology*, Cambridge University Press.

BARTLETT, F. C. (1943), 'Fatigue following highly skilled work', *Proceedings of the Royal Society*, vol. 131, pp. 248–57. Reprinted in D. Legge (ed.), *Skills*, Penguin, 1970.

BARTLETT, F. C. (1947), 'The measurement of human skill', *British Medical Journal*, vol. 1, pp. 835–8, 877–80. Reprinted in *Occupational Psychology*, 1948, vol. 22, pp. 83–91.

BARTLETT, F. C. (1951a), *The Mind at Work and Play*, Allen & Unwin.

BARTLETT, F. C. (1951b), 'The bearing of experimental psychology upon human skilled performance', *British Journal of Industrial Medicine*, vol. 8, pp. 209–17.

BARTLETT, F. C. (1958), *Thinking*, Allen & Unwin.

BASS, A. R., FIEDLER, F. E., and KRUEGER, S. (1964), *Personality Correlates of Assumed Similarity (ASO) and Related Scores*, Group Effectiveness Research Laboratory, University of Illinois.

BASS, B. M. (1962), 'Further evidence on the dynamic character of criteria', *Personnel Psychology*, vol. 15, pp. 93–7.

BASS, B. M. (1965), *Organizational Psychology*, Allyn & Bacon.

BASS, B. M. (1966), 'Effect on the subsequent performance of negotiators of studying the issues or planning strategies alone or in groups', *Psychological Monographs: General and Applied*, vol. 80, pp. 1–31.

BASS, B. M., and DUNTEMAN, G. (1963), 'Bias in the evaluation of one's own group, its allies and opponents', *Journal of Conflict Resolution*, vol. 7, pp. 16–20.

BELBIN, R. M. (1953), 'Difficulties of older people in industry', *Occupational Psychology*, vol. 17, pp. 177–90.

BELBIN, E., and BELBIN, R. M. (1968), 'Retraining and the older worker', in D. Pym (ed.), *Industrial Society*, Penguin.

BELBIN, R. M. (1965), *Training Methods*, OECD, Paris.

BELBIN, R. M. (1969), 'Industrial gerontology: origins, issues and applications in Europe', *Industrial Gerontology*, no. 1, pp. 12–25.

BENJAMIN, P. (1970), 'A hierarchical model of a helicopter pilot', *Human Factors*, vol. 12, pp. 361–74.

BENNIS, W. G. (1964), 'The decline of bureaucracy and organizations of the future', in H. Baumgartel, W. G. Bennis and N. R. De (eds.), *Readings in Group Development for Managers and Trainers*, Asia Publishing House, 1967.

BERKOWITZ, M., and BURKHAUSER, R. (1969), 'Unemployment and the middle-aged worker', *Industrial Gerontology*, no. 3, pp. 9–19.

BERLEW, D. E., and HALL, D. T. (1966), 'The socialization of managers: effects of expectations on performance', *Administrative Science Quarterly*, vol. 11, pp. 207–24.

BIEL, W. C. (1962), 'Training programs and devices', in R. M. Gagné (ed.), *Psychological Principles in System Development*, Holt, Rinehart & Winston.

BILODEAU, E. A., and BILODEAU, I. McD. (1969), *Principles of Skill Acquisition*, Academic Press.

BIRD, M. (1969), 'Changes in work behaviour following supervisory training', *Journal of Management Studies*, vol. 6, pp. 331–45.

BIRREN, J. E. (1964), *The Psychology of Ageing*, Prentice-Hall.

BJERNER, B., HOLM, A., and SWENSSON, A. (1955), 'Diurnal variation in mental performance', *British Journal of Industrial Medicine*, vol. 12, pp. 103–10.

BLAKE, M. J. F. (1967), 'Relationship between circadian rhythm of body temperature and intraversion and extraversion', *Nature*, no. 215, pp. 896–7.

BLAKE, M. J. F., and CORCORAN, D. W. J. (1970), 'Introversion-extraversion and circadian rhythm', in W. P. Colquhoun (ed.), *Proceedings of the NATO Symposium on the Effects of Diurnal Rhythm and Loss of Sleep on Human Performance*, English Universities Press.

BLAKE, R. R., and MOUTON, J. S. (1961a), 'Comprehension of own and outgroup positions under inter-group competition', *Journal of Conflict Resolution*, vol. 3, pp. 304–10.

BLAKE, R. R., and MOUTON, J. S. (1961b), 'Reactions to inter-group competition under win–lose conditions', *Management Science*, vol. 7, pp. 420–25.

BLAKE, R. R., and MOUTON, J. S. (1961c), 'Perceived characteristics of elected representatives', *Journal of Abnormal and Social Psychology*, vol. 62, pp. 693–5.

BLAKE, R. R., and MOUTON, J. S. (1962), 'Over-evaluation of own group's product in intergroup competition', *Journal of Abnormal and Social Psychology*, vol. 64, pp. 237–8.

BLAKE, R. R., and MOUTON, J. S. (1964), *The Managerial Grid*, Gulf.

BLAU, P. M., and SCOTT, W. R. (1962), *Formal Organizations: A Comparative Approach*, Routledge & Kegan Paul.

BLOOD, M. R., and HULIN, C. L. (1967), 'Alienation, environmental characteristics and worker responses', *Journal of Applied Psychology*, vol. 51, pp. 284–90.

BLUM, F. H. (1968), *Work and Community*, Routledge & Kegan Paul.

BLUM, M. L., and NAYLOR, J. C. (1968), *Industrial Psychology*, Harper & Row.

BOLSTER, B. I., and SPRINGBETT, B. M. (1961), 'The reaction of interviewers to favorable and unfavorable information', *Journal of Applied Psychology*, vol. 45, pp. 97–103.

BONJEAN, C. M., and GRIMES, M. D. (1970), 'Bureaucracy and alienation: a dimensional approach, *Social Forces*, vol. 48, pp. 365–73.

BONJER, F. H. (1960), 'Physiological aspects of shiftwork', *Proceedings of the 13th International Congress of Occupational Health.*

BORGER, R., and SEABORNE, A. E. M. (1966), *The Psychology of Learning*, Penguin.

BOROW, H. (ed.) (1964), *Man in a World at Work*, Houghton Mifflin.

BOURNE, L. E. (1966), *Human Conceptual Behavior*, Allyn & Bacon.

BRADY, R. H. (1967), 'Computers in top-level decision making', *Harvard Business Review*, vol. 45, pp. 67–76.

BRAYFIELD, A. H., and CROCKETT, W. H. (1955), 'Employee attitudes and employee performance', *Psychological Bulletin*, vol. 52, pp. 396–424.

BROADBENT, D. E. (1954), 'The role of auditory localisation in attention and memory span', *Journal of Experimental Psychology*, vol. 47, pp. 191–6.

BROADBENT, D. E. (1957a), 'Effects of noise on behaviour', in C. M. Harris (ed.), *Handbook of Noise Control*, McGraw-Hill.

BROADBENT, D. E. (1957b), 'Immediate memory and simultaneous stimuli', *Quarterly Journal of Experimental Psychology*, vol. 9, pp. 1–11.

BROADBENT, D. E. (1958), *Perception and Communication*, Pergamon.

BROADBENT, D. E. (1961), 'Non-auditory effects of noise', *Advancement of Science*, vol. 17, pp. 406–9.

BROADBENT, D. E. (1967), 'The word frequency effect and response bias', *Psychological Review*, vol. 74, pp. 1–15.

BROADBENT, D. E. (1971), *Decision and Stress*, Academic Press.

BROADBENT, D. E., and LITTLE, E. A. L. (1960), 'Effects of noise reduction in a work situation', *Occupational Psychology*, vol. 34, pp. 133–8. Reprinted in D. H. Holding (ed.), *Experimental Psychology in Industry*, Penguin, 1969.

BROMLEY, D. B. (1966), *The Psychology of Human Ageing*, Penguin.

BROWN, C. W., and GHISELLI, E. E. (1948), 'Accident proneness among streetcar motormen and motorcoach operators', *Journal of Applied psychology*, vol. 32, pp. 20–23.

BROWN, H. (1957), 'Day and night and three-shift working', *Personnel Management*, vol. 39, pp. 150–56.

BROWN, I. D. (1966a), 'An asymmetrical transfer effect in research on knowledge of performance', *Journal of Applied Psychology*, vol. 50, pp. 118–20.

BROWN, I. D. (1966b), 'Subjective and objective comparisons of successful and unsuccessful trainee drivers', *Ergonomics*, vol. 9, pp. 49–56.

BROWN, I. D., and POULTON, E. C. (1961), 'Measuring the spare "mental capacity" of car drivers by a subsidiary task', *Ergonomics*, vol. 4, pp. 35–40.

BROWN, I. D., TICKNER, A. H., and SIMMONDS, D. C. V. (1969), 'Interference between concurrent tasks of driving and telephoning', *Journal of Applied Psychology*, vol. 53, pp. 419–24.

BROWN, J. A. C. (1954), *The Social Psychology of Industry*, Penguin.

BRUCE, M. M. (1953), 'The prediction of effectiveness as a factory foreman', *Psychological Monographs*, vol. 67, no. 12 (whole no. 62).

BRUNER, J. S., GOODNOW, J. J., and AUSTIN, G. A. (1956), *A Study of Thinking*, Wiley.

BUCKHOUT, R., SHERMAN, H., GOLDSMITH, C. T., and VITALE, P. A. (1963), 'The effects of variations in motion fidelity during training on simulated low altitude flight', US Air Force Report AMRL–TDR–63–108.

BUEHLER, C. (1933), *Der Menschiche Lebenslauf als psychologisches Problem*, Hirzel, Leipzig.

BURKE, R. J., and WILCOX, D. S. (1969), 'Characteristics of effective employee performance review and development interviews', *Personnel Psychology*, vol. 22, pp. 291–305.

BURNS, T. (1957), 'Management in action', *Operational Research Quarterly*, vol. 8, pp. 45–60.

BURNS, T., and STALKER, G. M. (1961), *The Management of Innovation*, Tavistock.

BUROS, O. K. (1938, 1941, 1953, 1959, 1965), *The Mental Measurements Yearbook*, Gryphon Press.

BURSILL, A. E. (1958), 'The restriction of peripheral vision during exposure to hot and humid conditions, *Quarterly Journal of Experimental Psychology*, vol. 10, pp. 113–29.

BURT, C. (1949), 'The structure of the mind', *British Journal of Educational Psychology*, vol. 19, pp. 100–111.

CAMPBELL, J. P., and DUNNETTE, M. D. (1968), 'Effectiveness of T-group experience in management training and development', *Psychological Bulletin*, vol. 70, pp. 73–104.

CAMPBELL, J. P., DUNNETTE, M. D., LAWLER, E. E., and WEICK, K. E. (1970), *Managerial Behavior, Performance and Effectiveness*, McGraw-Hill.

CAREY, A. (1967), 'The Hawthorne Studies: a radical criticism', *American Sociological Review*, vol. 32, pp. 403–16.

CARKHUFF, R. R. (1967), 'Do we have a theory of vocational choice?', *The Personnel and Guidance Journal*, vol. 46, pp. 335–45.

CARLSON, R. E. (1967a), 'Selection interview decisions: the relative influence of appearance and factual written information on an interviewer's final rating', *Journal of Applied Psychology*, vol. 51, pp. 461–8.

CARLSON, R. E. (1967b), 'Selection interview decisions: the effect of interviewer experience, relative quota situation, and applicant sample on interviewer decisions', *Personnel Psychology*, vol. 20, pp. 259–80.

CARLSON, R. E. (1968), 'Employment decisions: effect of mode of applicant presentation on some outcome measures', *Personnel Psychology*, vol. 21, pp. 193–207.

CARLSON, R. E. (1969), 'Relative influence of a photograph versus factual written information on an interviewer's employment decision', *Personnel Psychology*, vol. 22, pp. 45–56.

CARLSON, R. E. (1970), 'Effect of applicant sample on ratings of valid information in an employment setting', *Journal of Applied Psychology*, vol. 54, pp. 217–22.

CARLSON, R. E., and MAYFIELD, E. C. (1967), 'Evaluating interview and employment application data', *Personnel Psychology*, vol. 20, pp. 441–60.

CARLSON, R. E., SCHWAB, D. P., and HENEMAN, H. G. (1970), 'Agreement among styles of selection interviewing', *Journal of Industrial Psychology*, vol. 5, pp. 8–17.

CARTER, L. F. (1953), 'Leadership and small group behavior', in M. Sherif and M. O. Wilson (eds.), *Group Relations at the Crossroads*, Harper & Row.

CARTWRIGHT, D., and ZANDER, A. (1970), *Group Dynamics*, Tavistock, 3rd edn.

CASTLE, P. F. C. (1956), 'Accidents, absence and withdrawal from the work situation', *Human Relations*, vol. 9, pp. 223–33.

CATTELL, R. B., SAUNDERS, D. R., and STICE, G. F. (1953), 'The dimensions of syntality in small groups', *Human Relations*, vol. 6, pp. 331–56.

CAVANAGH, P., and JONES, C. (1970), 'Further trends in programmes in print in the United Kingdom', *Programmed Learning and Educational Technology*, vol. 7, pp. 56–62.

CHAMBERS, E. G. (1951), *Psychology and the Industrial Worker*, Cambridge University Press.

CHAPANIS, A. (1960), 'Human engineering', in C. D. Flagle, W. H. Huggins and R. H. Roy (eds.), *Operations Research and System Engineering*, Johns Hopkins Press.

CHAPANIS, A. (1965), 'On the allocation of functions between men and machines', *Occupational Psychology*, vol. 39, pp. 1–11.

CHAPANIS, A. (1967), 'The relevance of laboratory studies to practical situations', *Ergonomics*, vol. 10, pp. 557–77.

CHAPANIS, A., GARNER, W. R., and MORGAN, C. T. (1949), *Applied Experimental Psychology*, Wiley.

CHERNS, A. B. (1962), 'Accidents at work', in A. T. Welford, M. Argyle, D. V. Glass and J. W. Morris (eds.), *Society: Problems and Methods of Study*, Routledge & Kegan Paul.

CHILES, W. D., ALLUISI, E. A., and ADAMS, O. S. (1968), 'Work schedules and performance during confinement', *Human Factors*, vol. 10, pp. 143–95.

CHOWN, S. (1958), 'The formation of occupational choice among grammar school pupils', *Occupational Psychology*, vol. 32, pp. 171–82.

CLARKSON, G. P. E. (1962), *Portfolio Selection: A Simulation of Trust Investment*, Prentice-Hall.

CLARKSON, G. P. E. (1968), 'Decision making in small groups: a simulation study', *Behavioral Science*, vol. 13, pp. 288–305.

COCH, L., and FRENCH, J. R. P. (1948), 'Overcoming resistance to change', *Human Relations*, vol. 1, pp. 512–32.

COLLINS, B. E., and GUETZKOW, H. S. (1964), *A Social Psychology of Group Processes for Decision Making*, Wiley.

COLLINS, B. E., and RAVEN, B. H. (1969), 'Group structure: attraction, coalitions, communications and power', in G. Lindzey and E. Aronson (eds.), *Handbook of Social Psychology*, vol. 4, Addison-Wesley.

COLQUHOUN, W. P., BLAKE, M. J. F., and EDWARDS, R. S. (1968a), 'Experimental studies of shift work I: a comparison of "rotating" and "stabilised" 4-hour shift systems', *Ergonomics*, vol. 11, pp. 437–53.

COLQUHOUN, W. P., BLAKE, M. J. F., and EDWARDS, R. S. (1968b), 'Experimental studies of shift work II: stabilised 8-hour shift systems', *Ergonomics*, vol. 11, pp. 527–46.

COLQUHOUN, W. P., BLAKE, M. J. F., and EDWARDS, R. S. (1969), 'Experimental studies of shift work III: stabilised 12-hour shift systems', *Ergonomics*, vol. 12, pp. 865–82.

COMMITTEE OF ENQUIRY ON DECIMAL CURRENCY (1963), *Report of the Committee of Enquiry on Decimal Currency*, Cmnd 2145, HMSO.

CONRAD, R. (1960), 'Letter-sorting machines – paced, lagged or unpaced?' *Ergonomics*, vol. 3, pp. 149–57.

COOPER, R., and PAYNE, R. (1967), 'Extraversion and some aspects of work behaviour', *Personnel Psychology*, vol. 20, pp. 45–57.

COPEMAN, G., LUIJK, H., and HANIKA, F. DE P. (1963), *How the Executive Spends His Time*, Business Publications.

CORCORAN, D. W. J. (1965), 'Personality and the inverted-U relationship', *British Journal of Psychology*, vol. 52, pp. 267–73.

COULSON, J. E. (1962), *Programmed Learning and Computer-Based Instruction*, US Office of Naval Research.

CRAIK, K. J. W. (1947), 'Theory of the human operator in control systems. The operator as an engineering system', *British Journal of Psychology*, vol. 38, pp. 56–61. Reprinted in D. Legge (ed.), *Skills*, Penguin, 1970.

CRISSY, W. J. E. (1952), 'The employment interview – research areas, methods and results', *Personnel Psychology*, vol. 5, pp. 73–85.

CRITES, J. O. (1969), *Vocational Psychology*, McGraw-Hill.

CRONBACH, L. J. (1966), *Essentials of Psychological Testing*, Harper & Row.

CRONBACH, L. J., and GLESER, G. C. (1965), *Psychological Tests and Personnel Decisions*, University of Illinois Press, 2nd edn.

CROSSMAN, E. R. F. W. (1959), 'A theory of the acquisition of speed skill', *Ergonomics*, vol. 2, pp. 153–66. Reprinted in D. Legge (ed.), *Skills*, Penguin, 1970.

CUBBON, A. (1969), 'Hawthorne talk in context', *Occupational Psychology*, vol. 43, pp. 111–28.

CUMMINGS, L. L., and SCOTT, W. E. (1969), *Readings in Organizational Behavior and Human Performance*, Irwin.

CYERT, R. M., and MARCH, J. G. (1963a), *A Behavioral Theory of the Firm*, Prentice-Hall.

CYERT, R. M., and MARCH, J. G. (1963b), 'A specific price and output model', in R. M. Cyert and J. G. March, *A Behavioral Theory of the Firm*, Prentice-Hall.

DALTON, M. (1950), 'Conflicts between staff and line managerial officers', *American Sociological Review*, vol. 15, pp. 342–51. Reprinted in T. Burns (ed.), *Industrial Man*, Penguin, 1969.

DAVIS, D. R. (1948), *Pilot Error*, Air Ministry Report AP3139A, HMSO.

DAVIS, L. E. (1966), 'The design of jobs', *Industrial Relations*, vol. 6, pp. 21–45.

DAVIS, R. (1957), 'The human operator as a single channel information system', *Quarterly Journal of Experimental Psychology*, vol. 9, pp. 119–29.

DAWS, P. P. (1968), *A Good Start in Life*, Cambridge Careers Research and Advisory Centre.

DEESE, J., and HULSE, S. H. (1967), *The Psychology of Learning*, McGraw-Hill.

DEUTSCH, M., and KRAUSS, R. (1962), 'Studies of interpersonal bargaining', *Journal of Conflict Resolution*, vol. 6, pp. 52–76.

DION, K. L., BARON, R. S., and MILLER, N. (1971), 'Why do groups make riskier decisions than individuals?', in L. Berkowitz (ed.), *Advances in Experimental Social Psychology*, vol. 5, Academic Press.

DIRKEN, J. M. (1966), 'Industrial shift work: decrease in well-being and specific effects', *Ergonomics*, vol. 9, pp. 115–24.

DODD, B. (1967), *Programmed Instruction for Industrial Training*, Heinemann.

DOUGLAS, A. (1957), 'The peaceful settlement of industrial and intergroup disputes', *Journal of Conflict Resolution*, vol. 1, pp. 69–81.

DRENTH, P. J. D. (1968), *De Psychologische Test*, Van Logehum Slaterus, Arnhem.

DREW, G. C. (1963), 'The study of accidents', *Bulletin of the British Psychological Society*, vol. 16, no. 52, pp. 1–10.

DREW, G. C., COLQUHOUN, W. P., and LONG, H. A. (1959), 'Effect of small doses of alcohol on a skill resembling driving', Medical Research Council, Memorandum no. 38, HMSO.

DRUCKER, P. F. (1966), *The Effective Executive*, Harper & Row.

DRUCKMAN, D. (1967), 'Dogmatism, prenegotiation experience, and simulated group representation as determinants of dyadic behavior in a bargaining situation', *Journal of Personality and Social Psychology*, vol. 6, pp. 279–90.

DRUCKMAN, D. (1968), 'Prenegotiation experience and dyadic conflict resolution in a bargaining situation', *Journal of Experimental Social Psychology*, vol. 4, pp. 367–83.

DUNCAN, S. (1969), 'Non-verbal communication', *Psychological Bulletin*, vol. 72, pp. 118–37.

DUNN, J. G. (1970), 'Skills analysis used for the investigation of accident risk in power saw operation', AP Note 21, Applied Psychology Department, University of Aston.

DUNNETTE, M. D. (1963a), 'A note on *the* criterion', *Journal of Applied Psychology*, vol. 47, pp. 251–4.

DUNNETTE, M. D. (1963b), 'A modified model for test validation and selection research', *Journal of Applied Psychology*, vol. 47, pp. 317–23.

DUNNETTE, M. D. (1966), *Personnel Selection and Placement*, Wadsworth.

EDWARDS, A. L. (1954), *Edwards' Personal Preference Schedule*, Psychological Corporation.

EDWARDS, W. (1954), 'The theory of decision making', *Psychological Bulletin*, vol. 51, pp. 380–417.

EDWARDS, W., and TVERSKY, A. (eds.) (1967), *Decision Making*, Penguin.

EDWARDS, W., LINDMAN, H., and PHILLIPS, L. D. (1965), 'Emerging technologies for making decisions', in *New Directions in Psychology II*, Holt, Rinehart & Winston.

ELITHORN, A., JAGOE, J. R., and LEE, D. N. (1966), 'Simulation of a perceptual problem solving skill', *Nature*, no. 211, pp. 1029–31.

EMERY, F. E. (1966), *The Democratisation of the Work Place*, Tavistock.

EMERY, F. E. (ed.) (1969), *Systems Thinking*, Penguin.

EMERY, F. E., and THORSRUD, E. (1969), *Form and Content in Industrial Democracy*, Tavistock.

EMERY, F. E. and TRIST, E. L. (1960), 'Socio-technical systems', in C. W. Churchman and M. Verhulst (eds.), *Management Science, Models and Techniques*, vol. 2, Pergamon. Reprinted in F. E. Emery (ed.), *Systems Thinking*, Penguin, 1962.

ENGLISH, H. B. (1942), 'How psychology can facilitate military training – a concrete example', *Journal of Applied Psychology*, vol. 26, pp. 3–7.

ERIKSEN, C. W., and LAPPIN, J. S. (1967), 'Selective attention and very short-term recognition memory for nonsense forms', *Journal of Experimental Psychology*, vol. 73, pp. 358–64.

ERIKSON, E. H. (1950), *Childhood and Society*, Norton.

ETZIONI, A. (1961), *A Comparative Analysis of Complex Organizations*, Free Press.

EVAN, W. M., and MACDOUGAL, J. A. (1967), 'Interorganizational conflict: a labor-management bargaining experiment', *Journal of Conflict Resolution*, vol 9, pp. 398–413.

FARMER, E. (1938), 'Critical notice', *British Journal of Psychology*, vol. 28, pp. 350–53.

FARMER, E., and CHAMBERS, E. G. (1926), 'A psychological study of individual differences in accident rate', Industrial Health Research Board, Report no. 38, HMSO.

FARMER, E., and CHAMBERS, E. G. (1929), 'A study of personal qualities in accident proneness and proficiency', Industrial Health Research Board, Report no. 55, HMSO.

FARMER, E., and CHAMBERS, E. G. (1939), 'A study of accident proneness among motor drivers', Industrial Health Research Board, Report no. 84, HMSO.

FARMER, E., CHAMBERS, E. G., and KIRK, F. J. (1933), 'Test for accident proneness', Industrial Health Research Board, Report no. 63, H M S O.

FARR, W. (1865), *Twenty-Eighth Annual Report of the Registrar General of Births, Deaths and Marriages in England*, HMSO.

FEAR, R. (1958), *The Evaluation Interview*, McGraw-Hill.

FERGUSON, C. K., and KELLEY, H. H. (1964), 'Significant factors in overevaluation of own-group's product', *Journal of Abnormal and Social Psychology*, vol. 69, pp. 223–8.

FEURZEIG, W., MUNTER, B., SWETS, J., and BREEN, M. (1964), 'Computer-aided teaching in medical diagnosis', *Journal of Medical Education*, vol. 39, pp. 746–54.

FIEDLER, F. E. (1967), *A Theory of Leadership Effectiveness*, McGraw-Hill.

FISHBEIN, M. (ed.) (1967), *Readings in Attitude Theory and Measurement*, Wiley.

FISHBEIN, M., LANDY, E., and HATCH, G. (1969), 'Some determinants of an individual's esteem for his least preferred co-worker', *Human Relations*, vol. 22, pp. 173–88.

FITTS, P. M. (1951), 'Engineering psychology and equipment design', in S. S. Stevens (ed.), *Handbook of Experimental Psychology*, Wiley.

FITTS, P. M. (ed.) (1951), *Human Engineering for Effective Air Navigation and Traffic Control System*, National Research Council.

FITTS, P. M. (1954), 'The information capacity of the human motor system in controlling the amplitude of movement', *Journal of Experimental Psychology*, vol. 47, pp. 381–91.

FITTS, P. M., and JONES, R. E. (1947), 'Pilot error experiences in operating aircraft controls and psychological aspects of instrument display'. Reprinted in H. W. Sinaiko (ed.), *Selected Papers on Human Factors in the Design and Use of Control Systems*, Dover, 1961.

FITTS, P. M., and LEONARD, J. A. (1957), *Stimulus Correlates of Visual Pattern Recognition – A Probability Approach*, Final Report on Contract NONR – 495(02), US Office of Naval Research.

FITTS, P. M., and POSNER, M. I. (1967), *Human Performance*, Brooks Cole.

FLAGLE, C. D., HUGGINS, W. H., and ROY, R. H. (1960), *Operations Research and System Engineering*, Johns Hopkins Press.

FLANDERS, A., POMERANZ, R., and WOODWARD, J. (1968), *Experiment in Industrial Democracy*, Faber.

FLANNAGAN, J. C. (1954), 'The critical incident technique', *Psychological Bulletin*, vol. 51, pp. 327–58.

FLEISHMAN, E. A. (1953a), 'The description of supervisory behavior', *Journal of Applied Psychology*, vol. 37, pp. 1–6.

FLEISHMAN, E. A. (1953b), 'Leadership climate, human relations training and supervisory behavior', *Personnel Psychology*, vol. 6, pp. 205–22.

FLEISHMAN, E. A. (1954), 'Dimensional analysis of psychomotor abilities', *Journal of Experimental Psychology*, vol. 48, pp. 437–54.

FLEISHMAN, E. A. (ed.) (1967), *Studies in Personnel and Industrial Psychology*, Dorsey Press.

FLEISHMAN, E. A. (1969), *Manual for Leadership Opinion Questionnaire*, Science Research Associates.

FLEISHMAN, E. A., and HARRIS, E. F. (1962), 'Patterns of leadership behavior related to employee grievances and turnover', *Personnel Psychology*, vol. 15, pp. 43–56.

FLEISHMAN, E. A., and PETERS, D. R. (1962), 'Interpersonal values, leadership attitudes, and "managerial success"', *Personnel Psychology*, vol. 15, pp. 127–44.

FOGEL, L. J. (1963), *Biotechnology*, Prentice-Hall.

FOURAKER, L. E., and SIEGEL, S. (1963), *Bargaining Behavior*, McGraw-Hill.

FRAZER, R. (1969), *Work: Twenty Personal Accounts*, vol. 2, Penguin.

FRENCH, E. G. (1958), 'Development of a measure of complex motivation', in J. W. Atkinson (ed.), *Motives in Fantasy, Action and Society*, Van Nostrand.

FRENCH, J. R. P., KAY, E., and MEYER, H. H. (1966), 'Participation and the appraisal system', *Human Relations*, vol. 19, pp. 3–20.

FRENCH, J. W. (1951), 'The description of aptitude and achievement tests in terms of rotated factors', *Psychometric Monographs*, no. 5.

FROGGATT, P., and SMILEY, J. A. (1964), 'The concept of accident proneness: A review', *British Journal of Industrial Medicine*, vol. 21, pp. 1–12.

FUCHS, A. H. (1962), 'The progression-regression hypothesis in perceptual-motor skill learning', *Journal of Experimental Psychology*, vol. 63, pp. 177–82.

GAGNÉ, R. M. (ed.) (1962), *Psychological Principles of System Development*, Holt, Rinehart & Winston.

GARVEY, W. D. (1960), 'A comparison of the effects of training and secondary tasks on tracking behavior', *Journal of Applied Psychology*, vol. 44, pp. 370–75.

GARVEY, W. D., and TAYLOR, F. V. (1959), 'Interactions among operator variables, system dynamics, and task-induced stress', *Journal of Applied Psychology*, vol. 43, pp. 79–85.

GAVRILESCU, N., PAPNOTE, M., VAIDA, I., MIHAILA, I., CARSTOCEA, L., LUCHIAN, O., and POPESCO, P. (1966), 'Control-board shift work turning every two days', *Proceedings of the XV International Congress of Occupational Medicine*, vol. 4, pp. 103–6.

GELATT, H. B. (1962), 'Decision-making: a conceptual frame of reference for counseling', *Journal of Counseling Psychology*, vol. 9, pp. 240–45.

GERSHEFSKY, G. (1969), 'Building a corporate financial model', *Harvard Business Review*, vol. 47, pp. 61–72.

GHISELLI, E. E. (1966), *The Validity of Occupational Aptitude Tests*, Wiley.

GHISELLI, E. E., and HAIRE, M. (1960), 'The validation of selection tests in the light of the dynamic character of criteria', *Personnel Psychology*, vol. 12, pp. 418–20.

GIBB, C. A. (ed.), (1969), *Leadership*, Penguin.

GIBB, C. A. (1969), 'Leadership', in G. Lindzey and E. Aronson (eds.), *Handbook of Social Psychology*, vol. 4, Addison-Wesley.

GILPATRICK, E. G. (1966), *Structural Unemployment and Aggregate Demands: A Study of Unemployment and Employment in the United States 1948–1964*, Johns Hopkins Press.

GINZBERG, E., GINSBURG, S. W., AXELARD, S., and HERMA, J. L. (1951), *Occupational Choice. An Approach to a General Theory*, Columbia University Press.

GLASER, R. (ed.) (1965), *Training Research and Education*, Wiley.

GLOBERSON, A. (1970), 'Spheres and levels of employee participation in organisations (elements of a conceptual model)', *British Journal of Industrial Relations*, vol. 8, pp. 252–62.

GOFFMAN, E. (1956), *The Presentation of Self in Everyday Life*, Social Sciences Research Centre; Allen Lane The Penguin Press, 1969.

GOLDBERG, L. R. (1970), 'Man versus model of man: a rationale, plus some evidence for a method of improving on clinical inferences', *Psychological Bulletin*, vol. 73, pp. 422–32.

GOLDTHORPE, J. H., LOCKWOOD, D., BECHHOFER, F., and PLATT, J. (1968), *The Affluent Worker*, Cambridge University Press.

GORDON, C., and GERGEN, K. G. (eds.) (1968), *The Self in Social Interaction*, Wiley.

GORDON, L. V. (1970), 'Measurement of bureaucratic orientation', *Personnel Psychology*, vol. 23, pp. 1–11.

GORDON, M. S. (1959), 'The older worker and hiring practices', *Monthly Labor Review*, vol. 82, pp. 1198–205.

GOUGH, H. G. (1957), *California Psychological Inventory*, Consulting Psychologists' Press.

GRAEN, G. B. (1967), 'Work motivation: the behavioral effects of job content and job context factors in an employment situation', unpublished doctoral dissertation, University of Minnesota.

GRAHAM, W. (1968), 'Description of leader behavior and evaluation of leaders as a function of LPC', *Personnel Psychology*, vol. 21, pp. 457–64.

GRANT, D. L., and BRAY, D. W. (1969), 'Contributions of the interview to assessment of management potential', *Journal of Applied Psychology*, vol. 53, pp. 24–34.

GRANT, D. L., KATOVSKY, W., and BRAY, D. W. (1967), 'Contributions of projective techniques to assessment of managerial potential', *Journal of Applied Psychology*, vol. 51, pp. 226–32.

GREEN, B. F., and ANDERSON, L. K. (1956), 'Colour coding in a visual search task', *Journal of Experimental Psychology*, vol. 51, pp. 19–24.

GREEN, D. M., and SWETS, J. F. (1966), *Signal Detection Theory and Psychophysics*, Wiley.

DE GREENE, K. S. (1961), *Systems Psychology*, McGraw-Hill.

GREENWOOD, M., and WOODS, H. M. (1919), 'The incidence of industrial accidents upon individuals with special reference to multiple accidents', Industrial Health Research Board, Report no. 4, HMSO.

GREENWOOD, M., and YULE, C. V. (1920), 'An enquiry into the nature of frequency distributions of repeated accidents', *Journal of the Royal Statistical Society*, vol. 83, p. 255.

GREINER, L. E., LEITCH, D. P., and BARNES, L. B. (1970), 'Putting judgment back into decisions', *Harvard Business Review*, vol. 48, pp. 59–67.

GRIEW, S. (1958), 'A study of accidents in relation to occupation and age', *Ergonomics*, vol. 2, pp. 17–23.

GRIEW, S. (1959), 'Methodological problems in industrial ageing research', *Occupational Psychology*, vol. 33, pp. 36–45.

GRIEW, S. (1964), *Job Redesign*, Paris, OECD.

GRIEW, S. (1969), *Adaptation of Jobs for the Disabled*, Geneva International Labour Office.

GRIFFIN, C. H. (1959), 'Application of motion and time-analysis to dexterity tests', *Personnel Psychology*, vol. 12, pp. 418–20.

GROOT, DE A. D. (1961), *Methodologie*, Mouton, The Hague.

GUILFORD, J. P. (1956), *Fundamental Statistics in Psychology and Education*, McGraw-Hill, 2nd edn.

GUILFORD, J. P. (1957), *The Nature of Human Intelligence*, McGraw-Hill.

GUILFORD, J. P. (1959), *Personality*, McGraw-Hill.

GUION, R. M. (1965), *Personnel Testing*, McGraw-Hill.

GULLIKSEN, H. (1950), *Theory of Mental Tests*, Wiley.

HAIRE, M. (1967), 'The incentive character of pay', in E. Andrews (ed.), *Managerial Compensation*, Foundation for Research on Human Behavior.

HAIRE, M. (1968), 'Role-perceptions in labor-management relations: an experimental approach', in H. Toch and H. C. Smith (eds.), *Social Perception*, Van Nostrand.

HAIRE, M., and MORRISON, F. (1957), 'School children's perceptions of labor and management', *Journal of Social Psychology*, vol. 46, pp. 179–97.

HAKEL, M. D., DOBMEYER, T. W., and DUNNETTE, M. D. (1970), 'Relative importance of three content dimensions in overall suitability ratings of job applicants' resumés', *Journal of Applied Psychology*, vol. 54, pp. 65–71.

HAKEL, M. D., HOLLMANN, T. D., and DUNNETTE, M. D. (1970), 'Accuracy of interviewers, certified public accountants and students in identifying the interests of accountants', *Journal of Applied Psychology*, vol. 54, pp. 115–19.

HAKEL, M. D., OHNESORGE, J. P., and DUNNETTE, M. D. (1970), 'Interviewer evaluations of job applicants' resumés as a function of the qualifications of the immediately preceding applicants', *Journal of Applied Psychology*, vol. 54, pp. 27–30.

HALE, D. (1970), 'Speed/accuracy interaction in human performance', Report to Social Science Research Council, Applied Psychology Department, University of Aston.

HALL, C. S., and LINDZEY, G. (1957), *Theories of Personality*, Wiley.

HALPIN, A. W. (1957), 'The leader behavior and effectiveness of aircraft commanders', in R. M. Stogdill and A. E. Coons (eds.), *Leader Behavior: Its Description and Measurement*, Bureau of Business Research.

HALPIN, A. W., and WINER, B. J. (1957), 'A factorial study of the leader behavior description', in R. M. Stogdill and A. E. Coons (eds.), *Leader Behavior: Its Description and Measurement*, Bureau of Business Research.

HAMMERTON, M. (1967), 'Simulators for training', *Electronics and Power*, vol. 13, pp. 8–10.

HARBISON, S. H., and COLEMAN, J. R. (1951), *Goals and Strategy in Collective Bargaining*, Harper & Row.

HARELL, T. W., and HARELL, M. S. (1945), 'Army general classification test scores for civilian occupations', *Education and Psychological Measurement*, vol. 5, pp. 229–39.

HARRIS, E. F., and FLEISHMAN, E. A. (1955), 'Human relations training and the stability of leadership patterns', *Journal of Applied Psychology*, vol. 39, pp. 20–25.

HAVIGHURST, R. J., BOWMAN, P. H., LIDDLE, G. P., MATTHEWS, C. V., and PIERCE, J. V. (1962), *Growing up in River City*, Wiley.

HAYTHORN, W. A., COUCH, D. H., HAEFNER, D., LANGHAM, P., and CARTER, L. (1956), 'The behavior of authoritarian and equalitarian personalities in groups', *Human Relations*, vol. 9, pp. 57–74.

HEISS, R. (1963), *Handbuch der Psychologie, Band 6, Psychologische Diagnostik*, Verlag für Psychologie, Göttingen.

HERON, A., and CHOWN, S. (1960), 'Semi-skilled and over 40', *Occupational Psychology*, vol. 34, pp. 264–74.

HERZBERG, F. (1966), *Work and the Nature of Man*, World Publishing Company.

HERZBERG, F., MAUSNER, B., PETERSON, R., and CAPWELL, D. (1957), *Job Attitudes: Review of Research and Opinion*, Psychological Service of Pittsburgh.

HERZBERG, F., MAUSNER, B., and SNYDERMAN, G. (1959), *The Motivation to Work*, Wiley.

HICKSON, D. J. (1961), 'Motives of workpeople who restrict their output', *Occupational Psychology*, vol. 35, pp. 111–21.

HILL, J. M. M., and TRIST, E. L. (1953), 'A consideration of industrial accidents as a means of withdrawal from the work situation', *Human Relations*, vol. 6, pp. 357–80.

HILL, J. M. M., and TRIST, E. L. (1962), *Industrial Accidents, Sickness and other Absences*, Tavistock.

HILTON, T. L. (1962), 'Career decision-making', *Journal of Counseling Psychology*, vol. 9, pp. 291–8.

HINTON, B. L. (1968), 'An empirical investigation of the Herzberg methodology and two factor theory', *Organizational Behavior and Human Performance*, vol. 3, pp. 286–309.

HOCKEY, G. R. J. (1970a), 'Changes in attention allocation in a multi-component task under loss of sleep', *British Journal of Psychology*, vol. 61, pp. 473–80.

HOCKEY, G. R. J. (1970b), 'Signal probability and spatial location as possible bases for increased selectivity in noise', *Quarterly Journal of Experimental Psychology*, vol. 22, pp. 37–42.

HOFSTEE, W. K. B. (1969), 'Individuele verschillen en averechtse toepassing', *Nederlands Tidjschrift voor Psychologie*, vol. 24, pp. 482–93.

HOLDING, D. H. (1965), *Principles of Training*, Pergamon.

HOLDING, D. H. (ed.) (1970), *Experimental Psychology in Industry*, Penguin.

HOLLAND, J. L. (1966), *The Psychology of Vocational Choice: A Theory of Personality Types and Environmental Models*, Ginn.

HOLLANDER, E. P. (1961), 'Emergent leadership and social influence', in L. Petrullo and B. M. Bass (eds.), *Leadership and Interpersonal Behavior*, Holt, Rinehart & Winston. Reprinted in C. A. Gibb (ed.), *Leadership*, Penguin, 1969.

HOLTER, H. (1965), 'Attitudes towards employee participation in company decision making processes', *Human Relations*, vol. 18, pp. 297–321.

HOMANS, G. C. (1961), *Social Behavior: Its Elementary Forms*, Routledge & Kegal Paul.

HOPSON, B., and HAYES, J. (1968), *The Theory and Practice of Vocational Guidance*, Pergamon Press.

HORST, P. (1962), 'The logic of personnel selection and classification', in R. M. Gagné (ed.), *Psychological Principles in System Development*, Holt, Rinehart & Winston.

HORST, P. (1966), *Psychological Measurement and Prediction*, Wadsworth.

HOUSE, R. J., and WIGDOR, L. A. (1968), 'Herzberg's dual factor theory of job satisfaction and motivation. A review of evidence and a criticism', *Personnel Psychology*, vol. 20, pp. 369–89.

HUMPHREYS, L. G. (1962), 'The organization of human abilities', *American Psychologist*, vol. 17, pp. 475–83.

HUNT, E. (1962), *Concept Learning: An Information Processing Problem*, Wiley.

HURLEY, J. R. (1955), 'The Iowa Picture Interpretation Test: a multiple choice variation of the TAT', *Journal of Consulting Psychology*, vol. 19, pp. 372–6.

INDIK, B. P. (1965), 'Organizational size and member participation', *Human Relations*, vol. 18, pp. 339–50.

INKSON, J., HICKSON, D. J., and PUGH, D. S. (1968), 'Administrative reduction of variance in organization and behaviour: a comparative study', paper presented to Annual Conference of British Psychological Society.

INKSON, J., HICKSON, D. J., and PUGH, D. S. (1970), 'Organization context and structure: an abbreviated replication', *Administrative Science Quarterly*, vol. 15, pp. 318–29.

JACKSON, J. M. (1953), 'The effects of changing the leadership of small work groups', *Human Relations*, vol. 6, pp. 25–44.

JAHODA, M., and WARREN, N. (eds.) (1960), *Attitudes*, Penguin.

JANIS, I. (1958), *Psychological Stress*, Wiley.

JOHNSON, D. W., and LEWICKI, R. J. (1969), 'The initiation of superordinate goals', *Journal of Applied Behavioral Science*, vol. 5, pp. 9–24.

JORDAN, N. (1963), 'Allocation of functions between man and machines in automated systems', *Journal of Applied Psychology*, vol. 47, pp. 161–5.

Journal of the Association for Programmed Learning and Educational Technology, vol. 5, no. 1.

JUDSON, A. S. (1966), *A Manager's Guide to Making Changes*, Wiley.

JULIAN, J. W., BISHOP, D. W., and FIEDLER, F. E. (1966), 'Quasitherapeutic effects of intergroup competition', *Journal of Personality and Social Psychology*, vol. 3, pp. 321–7.

KALDOR, D. R., and ZYTOWSKI, D. G. (1969), 'A maximising model of occupational decision making', *Personnel and Guidance Journal*, vol. 47, pp. 781–8.

KAHN, H. R. (1964), *Repercussions of Redundancy*, Allen & Unwin.

KAHN, R. L., and QUINN, R. P. (1969), *Role Stress – A Framework for Analysis*, University of Michigan.

KAHN, R. L., WOLFE, D., QUINN, R., SNOEK, J., and ROSENTHAL, R. (1964), *Organizational Stress: Studies in Role Conflict and Ambiguity*, Wiley.

KAHNEMAN, D., and GHISELLI, E. E. (1962), 'Validity and nonlinear heteroscedastic models', *Personnel Psychology*, vol. 15, pp. 1–12.

KANNELL, C. F., and KAHN, R. L. (1968), 'Interviewing', in G. Lindzey and E. Aronson (eds.), *Handbook of Social Psychology*, vol. 2, Addison-Wesley.

KATZ, D., and KAHN, R. L. (1966), *The Social Psychology of Organizations*, Wiley.

KATZ, E. (1957), 'The two-step flow of communication', *Public Opinion Quarterly*, vol. 21, pp. 61–78.

KATZELL, R. A., BARRETT, R. S., and PARKER, T. C. (1961), 'Job satisfaction, job performance, and situational characteristics', *Journal of Applied Psychology*, vol. 45, pp. 65–72.

KAY, E., MEYER, H. H., and FRENCH, J. R. P. (1965), 'Effects of threat in a performance appraisal interview', *Journal of Applied Psychology*, vol. 49, 311–17.

KAY, H., DODD, B., and SIME, M. E. (1968), *Teaching Machines and Programmed Instruction*, Penguin.

KEATING, G. F., and BOX, A. (1960), *Accidents, Sickness and Absence Records: A Comparative Study of Two Matched Groups*, British Iron and Steel Research Association.

KELLEY, H. H. (1965), 'Experimental studies of threats in interpersonal negotiations', *Journal of Conflict Resolution*, vol. 9, pp. 79–105.

KELLY, G. (1955), *The Psychology of Personal Constructs*, Norton.

KELVIN, P. (1970), *The Bases of Social Behaviour*, Holt, Rinehart & Winston.

KIDD, J. S. (1962), 'Human tasks and equipment design', in R. M. Gagné (ed.), *Psychological Principles of System Development*, Holt, Rinehart & Winston.

KEPNER, C. H., and TREGOE, B. B. (1965), *The Rational Manager*, McGraw-Hill.

KING, N. (1970), 'Clarification and evaluation of the two-factor theory of job satisfaction', *Psychological Bulletin*, vol. 74, pp. 18–31.

KINGSTON, N. (1970), 'Management research', *Management Abstracts*, vol. 10, pp. 32–5.

KLEEMEIER, R. W. (ed.) (1961), *Ageing and Leisure*, Oxford University Press.

KLEIN, N. K. E., BRUNER, H., HOLTMANN, H., REHME, H., STOLZE, J., STEINHOFF, W. D., and WEGMAN, H. M. (1970), 'Circadian rhythms of pilots' efficiency and effects of multiple time zone travel', *Aerospace Medicine*, vol. 41, pp. 125–32.

KLEINMUNTZ, B. (1967), *Concepts and the Structure of Memory*, Wiley.

KLEITMAN, N. (1963), *Sleep and Wakefulness*, University of Chicago Press, 2nd edn.

KLEITMAN, N., and JACKSON, D. P. (1950), 'Body temperature and performance under different routines', *Journal of Applied Physiology*, vol. 3, pp. 309–28.

KLINGER, E. (1966), 'Fantasy need achievement as a motivational construct', *Psychological Bulletin*, vol. 66, pp. 291–308.

KOGAN, N., and WALLACH, M. A. (1964), *Risk Taking: A Study in Cognition and Personality*, Holt, Rinehart & Winston.

KOGAN, N., and WALLACH, M. A. (1967), 'Risk taking as a function of the situation, the person, and the group', in G. Mandler, P. Mussen, N. Kogan and M. Wallach, *New Directions in Psychology*, no. 3, Holt, Rinehart & Winston.

KORMAN, A. K. (1966), '"Consideration", "initiating structure", and organizational criteria – a review', *Personnel Psychology*, vol. 19, pp. 349–61.

KORMAN, A. K. (1970), 'Toward a hypothesis of work behavior', *Journal of Applied Psychology*, vol. 54, pp. 31–41.

KORNHAUSER, A. (1965), *Mental Health of the Industrial Worker*, Wiley. Abridged in V. H. Vroom and E. L. Deci (eds.), *Management and Motivation*, Penguin, 1970.

KOSSORIS, M. (1948), 'Absenteeism and injury experiences of older workers', *Monthly Labour Review*, vol. 67, pp. 16–19.

KREPS, J. M. (1963), *Employment, Income and Retirement Problems of the Aged*, Duke University Press.

KREPS, J. M. (1967), 'Job performance and job opportunity: a note', *Gerontologist*, vol. 7, pp. 24–7.

KREPS, J. M. (1969), 'Ageing and financial management', in M. W. Riley, J. W. Riley and M. E. Johnson (eds.), *Ageing and Society*, vol. 2, *Ageing and the Professions*, Russell Sage Foundation.

LANDSBERGER, H. A. (1955), 'Interaction process analysis of the mediation of labor-management disputes', *Journal of Abnormal and Social Psychology*, vol. 51, pp. 552–9.

LANER, S., and SELL, R. G. (1960), 'An experiment on the effect of specially designed safety posters', *Occupational Psychology*, vol. 34, pp. 153–69.

LaPiere, R. T. (1934), 'Attitudes versus actions', *Social Forces*, vol. 13, pp. 230–37.

Lawler, E. E. (1969), 'Job design and employee motivation', *Personnel Psychology*, vol. 22, pp. 426–35. Reprinted in V. H. Vroom and E. L. Deci (eds.), *Management and Motivation*, Penguin, 1970.

Lawler, E. E. (1970), 'Job attitudes and employee motivation: theory, research and practice', *Personnel Psychology*, vol. 23, pp. 223–37.

Lawrence, P., and Lorsch, J. (1967), *Organization and Environment*, Harvard Business School.

Lawshe, C. H. (1952), 'Employee selection', *Personnel Psychology*, vol. 5, pp. 31–4.

Lawshe, C. H., and Schucker, R. E. (1959), 'The relative efficiency of four test weighting methods in multiple prediction', *Educational and Psychological Measurement*, vol. 19, pp. 103–14.

Lawshe, C. H., and Steinberg, M. D. (1955), 'A study in synthetic validity: exploratory investigation of clerical jobs', *Personnel Psychology*, vol. 8, pp. 291–301.

Lazarsfeld, P., Berelson, B., and Gaudet, H. (1948), *The People's Choice*, Columbia University Press.

Lazarus, R. S., Deese, J., and Osler, S. F. (1952), 'The effects of psychological stress upon performance', *Psychological Bulletin*, vol. 49, pp. 293–317.

Leavitt, H. J. (1951), 'Some effects of certain communication patterns on group performance', *Journal of Abnormal and Social Psychology*, vol. 46, pp. 38–50.

Legge, D. (ed.) (1970), *Skills*, Penguin.

Leonard, J. A. (1959), MRC Applied Psychology Research Report, no. 326/59.

Lesieur, F. (1958), *The Scanlon Plan*, Wiley.

Lewin, K. (1948), *Resolving Social Conflicts*, Harper & Row.

Lewin, K., Lippitt, R., and White, R. K. (1939), 'Patterns of aggressive behavior in experimentally created social climates', *Journal of Social Psychology*, vol. 10, pp. 271–99.

Lieberman, S. (1956), 'The effect of changes in role on the attitudes of occupants', *Human Relations*, vol. 9, pp. 485–502.

Lienert, G. A. (1961), *Testaufbau und Testanalyse*, Julius Beltz, Weinheim.

Life Insurance Agency Management Association (1968), 'Career guidance in the life insurance agency', *Personnel Psychology*, vol. 21, pp. 1–21.

Likert, R. (1961), *New Patterns of Management*, McGraw-Hill.

Likert, R. (1967), *The Human Organization: Its Management and Value*, McGraw-Hill.

LINDQUIST, E. F. (ed.) (1951), *Educational Measurement*, American Council on Education.

LINDZEY, G., and ARONSON, E. (eds.) (1968–69), *Handbook of Social Psychology*, vols. 1–5, Addison-Wesley.

LITTERER, J. A. (1969), *Organizations: Structural Behavior*, vol. 1, Wiley.

LITWIN, G. H., and STRINGER, R. A. (1968), *Motivation and Organizational Climate*, Harvard Business School.

LOBBAN, M. C. (1965), 'Time, light and diurnal rhythm', in O. E. Edholm and A. L. Bacharach (eds.), *The Physiology of Human Survival*, Academic Press.

LOCKE, E. A. (1970), 'Toward a theory of task motivation and incentives', *Organizational Behavior and Human Performance*, vol. 3, pp. 157–89.

LODAHL, T. W., and PORTER, L. W. (1961), 'Psychometric score patterns, social characteristics and productivity of small industrial work groups', *Journal of Applied Psychology*, vol. 45, pp. 73–9.

LOEVINGER, J. (1951), 'Objective tests as instruments of psychological theory', *Psychological Reports*, vol. 3, pp. 635–94.

LORD, F. M., and NOVICK, M. R. (1968), *Statistical Theories of Mental Test Scores*, Addison-Wesley.

LOVELL, V. R. (1967), 'The human use of personality tests: a dissenting view', *American Psychologist*, vol. 22, pp. 383–93.

LOWIN, A., and CRAIG, J. R. (1968), 'The influence of level of performance on managerial style: an experimental object-lesson in the ambiguity of correlational data', *Organizational Behavior and Human Performance*, vol. 3, pp. 440–58.

LOWIN, A., HRAPCHAK, W. J., and KAVANAGH, M. J. (1969), 'Consideration and initiating structure: an experimental investigation of leadership traits', *Administrative Science Quarterly*, vol. 14, pp. 238–53.

LUCE, R. D., and RAIFFA, H. (1957), *Games and Decisions*, Wiley.

McCLELLAND, D. C. (1958), 'Methods of measuring human motivation', in J. W. Atkinson (ed.), *Motives in Fantasy, Action and Society*, Van Nostrand.

McCLELLAND, D. C. (1961), *The Achieving Society*, Van Nostrand.

McCLELLAND, D. C. (1965), 'Achievement motivation can be developed', *Harvard Business Review*, vol. 43, pp. 6–14, 20–23, 178.

McCLELLAND, D. C., and WINTER, D. G. (1969), *Motivating Economic Achievement*, Free Press.

McCLELLAND, D. C., ATKINSON, J. W., CLARK, R. A., and LOWELL, E. L. (1953), *The Achievement Motive*, Appleton-Century-Crofts.

McFarland, R. A., and Moseley, A. L. (1954), *Human Factors in Transportation Safety*, Harvard School of Public Health.

McGrath, J. E. (1966), 'A social psychological approach to the study of negotiation', in R. Bowers (ed.), *Studies on Behavior in Organizations: A Research Symposium*, University of Georgia Press.

McGrath, J. E. (1970), 'Settings, measures and themes: an integrative review of some research on social-psychological factors in stress', in J. E. McGrath (ed.), *Social and Psychological Factors in Stress*, Holt, Rinehart & Winston.

McGrath, J. E., and Julian, J. W. (1963), 'Interaction process and task outcome in experimentally-created negotiation groups', *Journal of Psychological Studies*, vol. 14, pp. 117–38.

McGregor, D. (1957), 'An uneasy look at performance appraisal', *Harvard Business Review*, vol. 35, pp. 89–94.

McGregor, D. (1960), *The Human Side of Enterprise*, McGraw-Hill

McGregor, D. (1967), *The Professional Manager*, McGraw-Hill.

McKenzie, K. O. (1970), 'Risk as a value and risky shift', *Organizational Behavior and Human Performance*, vol. 5, pp. 125–34.

McKenzie, R. E., and Elliott, L. L. (1965), 'Effects of secobarbital and d-emphetamine on performance during a simulated air mission', *Aerospace Medicine*, vol. 36, pp. 774–9.

McMurray, R. N. (1958), 'The case for benevolent autocracy', *Harvard Business Review*, vol. 36, pp. 82–90.

McRuer, D., and Weir, D. H. (1969), 'The theory of manual vehicular control', *Ergonomics*, vol. 12, pp. 599–633.

Mack, R. W., and Snyder, R. C. (1957), 'The analysis of social conflict: toward an overview and synthesis', *Journal of Conflict Resolution*, vol. 1, pp. 212–48.

Mackworth, J. F. (1969), *Vigilance and Habituation*, Penguin.

Mackworth, J. F. (1970), *Vigilance and Attention*, Penguin.

Mackworth, N. H. (1950), 'Researches on the measurement of human performance', Medical Research Council Report no. 268, HMSO.

Macmillan, H. (1969), *Tides of Fortune*, Macmillan.

Macrae, A. (1932), *Talents and Temperament*, Nisbet.

Macrae, A. (1934), *The Case for Vocational Guidance*, Pitman.

Magnusson, R. (1966), *Test Theory*, Addison-Wesley.

Maier, N. R. F. (1958), *The Appraisal Interview: Objectives, Methods and Skills*, Wiley.

Mangham, I., and Cooper, C. L. (1969), 'The impact of T-groups on managerial behaviour', *Journal of Management Studies*, vol. 6, pp. 53–72.

MANIS, M., GLEASON, T. C., and DAWES, R. M. (1966), 'The evaluation of complex social stimuli', *Journal of Personality and Social Psychology*, vol. 3, pp. 404–19.

MANN, L. (1969), *Social Psychology*, Wiley.

MANN, R. D. (1959), 'A review of the relationships between personality and performance in small groups', *Psychological Bulletin*, vol. 56, pp. 241–70. Reprinted in C. A. Gibb (ed.), *Leadership*, Penguin, 1969.

MANNING, W. H., and DUBOIS, P. H. (1958), 'Gain in proficiency as a criterion in test validation', *Journal of Applied Psychology*, vol. 42, pp. 191–4.

MARBACH, G. (1968), *Job Re-Design for Older Workers*, OECD, Paris.

MARCH, J. G. (1965), *The Handbook of Organizations*, Rand-McNally.

DE LA MARE, G. and WALKER, J. (1968), 'Factors influencing the choice of shift rotation', *Occupational Psychology*, vol. 42, pp. 1–21.

MARPLES, D. L. (1967), 'Studies of managers – a fresh start?' *Journal of Management Studies*, vol. 4, pp. 282–99.

MARQUIS, D. J. (1971), 'Information use in technical problem solving', University of London Invited Lecture, January 1971.

MARRIOTT, R. (1957), *Incentive Payment Systems: A Review of Research and Opinion*, Staples Press.

MARROW, A. J., BOWERS, D. G., and SEASHORE, S. E. (1967), *Management by Participation*, Harper & Row.

MASLOW, A. H. (1943), 'A theory of human motivation', *Psychological Review*, vol. 50, pp. 370–96.

MATARAZZO, J. D., WIENS, A. N., JACKSON, R. H., and MANAUGH, T. S. (1970), 'Interviewee speech behaviour under different content conditions', *Journal of Applied Psychology*, vol. 54, pp. 15–26.

MAYFIELD, E. C. (1964), 'The selection interview: a re-evaluation of published research', *Personnel Psychology*, vol. 17, pp. 239–60.

MAYO, E. (1945), *The Social Problems of an Industrial Civilization*, Harvard University Graduate School of Business.

MEDAWAR, P. (1970), *The Art of the Soluble*, Penguin.

MEILI, R. (1961), *Lehrbuch der Psychologischen Diagnostik*, Stuttgart, 4th edn.

MELTON, A. W. (1962), Foreword to R. M. Gagné (ed.), *Psychological Principles of System Development*, Holt, Rinehart & Winston.

MESSICK, D. M. (1967), 'Interdependent decision strategies in zero-sum games: a computer-controlled study', *Behavioral Science*, vol. 12, pp. 33–48.

MEYER, H. H., KAY, E., and FRENCH, J. R. P. (1964), 'Split roles in performance appraisal', *Harvard Business Review*, vol. 43, pp. 124–9. Reprinted in E. A. Fleishman (ed.), *Studies in Personnel and Industrial Psychology*, Dorsey Press, 1967.

MILES, H. H. W. (1954), 'A psychosomatic study of forty-six young men with coronary artery disease', *Psychosomatic Medicine*, vol. 26, pp. 510–41.

MILLER, A. W. (1968), 'Learning theory and vocational decisions', *The Personnel and Guidance Journal*, vol. 47, pp. 18–23.

MILLER, D. C., and FORM, W. H. (1964), *Industrial Sociology*, Harper & Row.

MILLER, E. J., and RICE, A. K. (1967), *Systems of Organisation*, Tavistock.

MILLER, W. W., KAPLAN, R. J., and EDWARDS, W. (1967), 'JUDGE: A value-judgment based tactical command system', *Organizational Behavior and Human Performance*, vol. 2, pp. 329–74.

MILLER, W. W., KAPLAN, R. J., and EDWARDS, W. (1969), 'JUDGE: A laboratory evaluation', *Organizational Behavior and Human Performance*, vol. 4, pp. 97–111.

MILLER, R. B. (1954), 'Psychological considerations in the design of training equipment', US Air Force, WADC Technical Report 54–563.

MINISTRY OF TRANSPORT (1968), *The Highway Code*, HMSO.

MINTZ, A., and BLUM, M. L. (1949), 'A re-examination of the accident-proneness concept', *Journal of Applied Psychology*, vol. 33, pp. 195–211.

MISCHEL, W. (1968), *Personality and Assessment*, Wiley.

MORAY, N. (1959), 'Attention in dichotic listening. Affective cues and the influence of instruction', *Quarterly Journal of Experimental Psychology*, vol. 11, pp. 56–60.

MORAY, N. (1970), *Listening and Attention*, Penguin.

MORLEY, I. E. (1971), *Social Interaction in Experimental Negotiations*, Ph.D. Thesis, University of Nottingham.

MORLEY, I. E., and STEPHENSON, G. M. (1969), 'Interpersonal and inter-party exchange: a laboratory simulation of an industrial dispute at the plant level', *British Journal of Psychology*, vol. 60, pp. 543–5.

MORLEY, I. E., and STEPHENSON, G. M. (1970a), 'Strength of case, communication systems and outcomes of simulated negotiations: some social psychological aspects of bargaining', *Industrial Relations Journal*, vol. 1, pp. 19–29.

MORLEY, I. E., and STEPHENSON, G. M. (1970b), 'Formality in experimental negotiations: a validation study', *British Journal of Psychology*, vol. 61, pp. 383–4.

MORSE, N. C., and REIMER, E. (1956), 'The experimental change of a major organizational variable', *Journal of Abnormal and Social Psychology*, vol. 52, pp. 120–29.

MORSE, N. C., and WEISS, R. S. (1955), 'The function and meaning of work and the job', *American Sociological Review*, vol. 20, pp. 191–8.

MORTON, J. (1968), 'A retest of the response bias explanation of the word-frequency effect', *British Journal of Mathematical and Statistical Psychology*, vol. 21, pp. 21–33.

MOSER, H., DUBIN, W., and SCHELSKY, J. M. (1956), 'A proposed modification of the Roe Occupational Classification', *Journal of Counseling Psychology*, vol. 3, pp. 27–31.

MOTT, P. E. (1965), *Shift Work – The Social, Psychological and Physical Consequences*, University of Michigan Press.

MOUTON, J. S., and BLAKE, R. R. (1963), 'Influence of partially vested interests on judgment', *Journal of Abnormal and Social Psychology*, vol. 66, pp. 276–8.

MURRAY, H. A. (1943), *Thematic Appreciation Test Manual*, Harvard University Press.

MURRELL, K. F. H. (ed.) (1956), *Fitting the Job to the Worker*, OECD, Paris.

MURRELL, K. F. H. (1959), 'Major problems of industrial gerontology', *Journal of Gerontology*, vol. 34, pp. 275–9.

MURRELL, K. F. H. (1962), 'Industrial aspects of ageing', *Ergonomics*, vol. 5, pp. 147–53. Reprinted in D. H. Holding (ed.), *Experimental Psychology in Industry*, Penguin, 1969.

MURRELL, K. F. H. (1965), *Ergonomics: Man in his Working Environment*, Chapman & Hall.

MURRELL, K. F. H., and GRIEW, S. (1958), 'Age structure in the engineering industry: a study of regional effects', *Occupational Psychology*, vol. 32, pp. 86–8.

MURRELL, K. F. H., GRIEW, S., and TUCKER, W. A. (1957), 'Age structure in the engineering industry: a preliminary study', *Occupational Psychology*, vol. 31, pp. 150–68.

MURSTEIN, B. I. (1963), *Theory and Research in Projective Techniques*, Wiley.

NATIONAL BOARD FOR PRICES AND INCOMES (1970), *Hours of Work, Overtime and Shift Working*, Report no. 161, HMSO.

NEALEY, S. M. (1964), 'Determining worker preferences among employee benefit programs', *Journal of Applied Psychology*, vol. 45, pp. 1–10.

NEISSER, U. (1967), *Cognitive Psychology*, Appleton-Century-Crofts.

NEWBOLD, E. M. (1926), 'A contribution to the study of the human factor in causation of accidents', Industrial Health Research Board, Report no. 34, HMSO.

NEWBOLD, E. M. (1927), 'Practical applications of the statistics of repeated events, particularly of industrial accidents', *Journal of the Royal Statistical Society*, vol. 90, pp. 487–547.

NEWELL, A., SHAW, J. C., and SIMON, H. A. (1958), 'The elements of a theory of human problem solving', *Psychological Review*, vol. 65, pp. 151–66.

NEWELL, A., SHAW, J. C., and SIMON, H. A. (1962), 'The process of creative thinking', in H. E. Gruber, G. Terrell and M. Wertheimer (eds.), *Contemporary Approaches to Creative Thinking*, Atherton.

NORTH, R. C., KOCH, J. R., and KINNES, D. A. (1960), 'The integrative functions of conflict', *Journal of Conflict Resolution*, vol. 4, pp. 353–74.

NUNNALLY, J. C. (1967), *Psychometric Theory*, McGraw-Hill.

OPPENHEIM, A. N. (1966), *Questionnaire Design and Attitude Measurement*, Heinemann.

OPSAHL, R. L., and DUNNETTE, M. D. (1966), 'The role of financial compensation in industrial motivation', *Psychological Bulletin*, vol. 63, pp. 94–118.

OSIPOW, S. H. (1968), *Theories of Career Development*, Appleton-Century-Crofts.

PARSONS, F. (1909), *Choosing a Vocation*, Houghton Mifflin.

PATCHEN, M. (1961), 'A conceptual framework and some empirical data regarding comparisons of social rewards', *Sociometry*, vol. 24, pp. 136–56.

PATCHEN, M. (1970), *Participation, Achievement and Involvement on the Job*, Prentice-Hall.

PATEMAN, C. (1970), *Participation and Democratic Theory*, Cambridge University Press.

PAUL, W. J., and ROBERTSON, K. (1970), *Job Enrichment and Employee Motivation*, Gower Press.

PELZ, D. C., and ANDREWS, F. M. (1966), *Scientists in Organizations*, Wiley.

PERROW, C. (1970), *Organizational Analysis*, Tavistock.

PERVIN, L. A. (1967), 'A twenty-college study of student/college interaction using TAPE (Transactional Analysis of Personality and Environment)', *Journal of Educational Psychology*, vol. 58, pp. 290–302.

PETERS, H. J., and HANSEN, J. C. (eds.) (1966), *Vocational Guidance and Career Development*, Macmillan Co.

PETERS, R. S. (1958), *The Concept of Motivation*, Routledge & Kegan Paul.

PHEYSEY, D. C., PAYNE, R. L., and PUGH, D. S. (1971), 'Influence of structure at organizational and group levels', *Administrative Science Quarterly*, vol. 16, pp. 61–73.

PHILLIPS, L., and EDWARDS, W. (1966), 'Conservatism in a simple probability inference task', *Journal of Experimental Psychology*, vol. 72, pp. 346–54. Reprinted in W. Edwards and A. Tversky (eds.), *Decision Making*, Penguin, 1967.

PORTER, L. W. (1961), 'A study of perceived need satisfaction in bottom and middle management jobs', *Journal of Applied Psychology*, vol. 45, pp. 1–10.

PORTER, L. W. (1962), 'Job attitudes in management: I. Perceived deficiencies in need fulfilment as a function of job level', *Journal of Applied Psychology*, vol. 46, pp. 375–84.

PORTER, L. W. (1963), 'Job attitudes in management: II. Perceived importance of needs as a function of job level', *Journal of Applied Psychology*, vol. 47, pp. 141–8.

PORTER, L. W. (1964), *Organizational Patterns of Managerial Job Attitudes*, American Foundation for Management Research.

PORTER, L. W., and LAWLER, E. E. (1965), 'Properties of organization structure in relation to job attitudes and job behaviour', *Psychological Bulletin*, vol. 64, pp. 23–51.

PORTER, L. W., and LAWLER, E. E. (1968), *Managerial Attitudes and Performance*, Irwin.

PORTER, L. W., and SIEGAL, J. (1964), *The Effects of Tall vs Flat Organisation Structures on Managerial Satisfactions – Foreign Countries*, unpublished manuscript referred to in Porter and Lawler (1965).

POULTON, E. C. (1964), 'Identifying the names and dosage of drugs', *Journal of Pharmacy and Pharmacology*, vol. 16, pp. 213–19.

POULTON, E. C. (1965), 'On increasing the sensitivity of measures of performance', *Ergonomics*, vol. 8, pp. 69–76.

POULTON, E. C. (1966), 'Tracking behaviour', in E. A. Bilodeau (ed.), *Acquisition of Skill*, Academic Press.

POULTON, E. C. (1970), *Environment and Human Efficiency*, C. C. Thomas.

POULTON, E. C. (1972), *Tracking Skill and Manual Control*, Academic Press.

POULTON, E. C., and KERSLAKE, D. MCK. (1965), 'Initial stimulating effect of warmth upon perceptual efficiency', *Aerospace Medicine*, vol. 36, pp. 29–32.

PRITCHARD, R. D. (1969), 'Equity theory: a review and critique', *Organizational Behavior and Human Performance*, vol. 4, pp. 176–211.

PRUITT, D. G., and JOHNSON, D. F. (1970), 'Mediation as an aid to face-saving in negotiation', *Journal of Personality and Social Psychology*, vol. 14, pp. 239–46.

PUGH, D. S. (1966), 'Modern organization theory: psychological study', *Psychological Bulletin*, vol. 66, pp. 235–51.

PUGH, D. S. (1969), 'Organization theory: An approach from psychology', *Human Relations*, vol. 22, pp. 345–54.

PUGH, D. S., HICKSON, D. J., HININGS, C. R., MACDONALD, K. M., TURNER, C., and LUPTON, T. (1963), 'A conceptual scheme for organizational analysis', *Administrative Science Quarterly*, vol. 8, pp. 289–315.

PUGH, D. S., HICKSON, D. J., HININGS, C. R., and TURNER, C. (1968), 'The dimensions of organisation structure', *Administrative Science Quarterly*. vol. 13 pp. 65–105.

PUGH, D. S., HICKSON, D. J., HININGS, C. R., and TURNER, C. (1969a), 'The context of organisation structures', *Administrative Science Quarterly*, vol. 14, pp. 91–114.

PUGH, D. S., HICKSON, D. J., and HININGS, C. R. (1969b), 'An empirical taxonomy of structures of work organizations', *Administrative Science Quarterly*, vol. 14, pp. 115–26.

PYM, D. (1969), 'Education and the employment opportunities of engineers', *British Journal of Industrial Relations*, vol. 7, pp. 42–51.

QUENAULT, S. W. (1967), 'Driver-behaviour – safe and unsafe drivers', Ministry of Transport Road Research Laboratory Report LR70.

QUENAULT, S. W. (1968a), 'Driver-behaviour – safe and unsafe drivers – II', Ministry of Transport Road Research Laboratory Report LR146.

QUENAULT, S. W. (1968b), 'Development of the method of systematic observation of driver behaviour', Ministry of Transport Road Research Laboratory Report LR213.

QUINN, R. P., and KAHN, R. L. (1967), 'Organizational psychology', *Annual Review of Psychology*, vol. 18, pp. 437–66.

RABBIE, J. M., and HORWITZ, M. (1969), 'Arousal of ingroup-outgroup bias by a chance win or loss', *Journal of Personality and Social Psychology*, vol. 13, pp. 269–77.

RABBITT, P. M. H. (1966), 'Identification of some stimuli embedded among others', *Proceedings of the 18th International Congress of Psychology*, Amsterdam, North Holland Publishing Company.

RAFFLE, A., and SELL, R. G. (1970), 'The Victoria Line-operational aspects', *Applied Ergonomics*, vol. 1, pp. 113–20.

RAMONDT, J. J. (1968), *Verantwoordel ijkheid in het werk*, Alphen Aan De Rijn.

RAPOPORT, AMNON (1966), 'A study of human control in a stochastic multistage decision task', *Behavioral Science*, vol. 11, pp. 18–32.

RAPOPORT, AMNON (1967), 'Variables affecting decisions in a multistage inventory task', *Behavioral Science*, vol. 12, pp. 194–204.

RAPOPORT, AMNON (1969), 'Optimal and suboptimal decisions in perceptual problem-solving tasks', *Behavioral Science*, vol. 14, pp. 453–66.

RAPOPORT, ANATOL (1966), *Two-Person Game Theory – The Essential Ideas*, The University of Michigan.

RECHTSCHAFFEN, J., HAURI, P., and ZEITLIN, M. (1966), 'Auditory awakening thresholds in REM and NREM sleep stages', *Perceptual and Motor Skills*, vol. 22, pp. 927–42.

REDDIN, W. J. (1970), *Managerial Effectiveness*, McGraw-Hill.

REUCHLIN, M. (1969), *Methodes d'Analyse Factorielle à l'Usage des Psychologues*, Presses Universitaires de France.

RHENMAN, E. (1968), *Industrial Democracy and Industrial Management*, Tavistock.

RICE, A. K. (1963), *The Enterprise and its Environment*, Tavistock.

RIGNEY, J. W. (1966), 'Training corrective maintenance performance on electronic equipment with CAI terminals', Report 51, Electronics Personnel Research Group, University of Southern California.

RILEY, M. W., and FONER, A. (eds.) (1968), *Ageing and Society*, vol. 1, *An Inventory of Research Findings*, Russell Sage Foundation.

RILEY, M. W., RILEY, J. W., and JOHNSON, M. E. (eds.) (1969), *Ageing and Society*, vol. 2, *Ageing and the Professions*, Russell Sage Foundation.

ROADMAN, H. E. (1964), 'An industrial use of peer ratings', *Journal of Applied Psychology*, vol. 48, pp. 211–14.

ROE, A. (1957), 'Early determinants of vocational choice', *Journal of Counseling Psychology*, vol. 4, pp. 212–17.

ROE, A., and SIEGELMAN, M. (1964), *The Origin of Interests*, American Personnel and Guidance Association.

ROETHLISBERGER, F. J., and DICKSON, W. J. (1939), *Management and the Worker – An Account of a Research Program Conducted by the Western Electric Company, Hawthorne Works, Chicago*, Harvard University Press.

ROGERS, E. M. (1960), *Diffusion of Innovation*, Free Press.

ROMISZOWSKI, A. J. (1967), 'A survey of the use of programmed learning by industry during 1966', *Programmed Learning and Educational Technology*, vol. 4, pp. 210–15.

RONAN, W. W., and PRIEN, E. P. (1966), *Toward a Criterion Theory*, Richarden Foundation.

ROSENBERG, S. (1968), 'Mathematical models of social behavior', in G. Lindzey and E. Aronson (eds.), *Handbook of Social Psychology*, vol. 1, Addison-Wesley.

ROSS, I. C., and ZANDER, A. (1957), 'Need satisfaction and employee turnover', *Personnel Psychology*, vol. 10, pp. 327–38.

ROTTER, J. B. (1966), 'Generalised expectancies for internal vs external control of reinforcement', *Psychological Monographs*, no. 80, pp. 1–28.

ROWE, K. H. (1964), 'An appraisal of appraisals', *Journal of Management Studies*, vol. 1, pp. 1–15.

ROWE, P. M. (1963), 'Individual differences in selection decisions', *Journal of Applied Psychology*, vol. 47, pp. 304–7.

ROWE, P. M. (1967), 'Order effects in assessment decisions', *Journal of Applied Psychology*, vol. 51, pp. 170–73.

ROYAL COMMISSION ON TRADE UNIONS AND EMPLOYERS' ASSOCIATIONS (1968), *Report of the Royal Commission on Trade Unions and Employers' Association, 1965–68* (Chairman: Lord Donovan), HMSO.

ROZEBOOM, W. W. (1966), *Foundations of the Theory of Prediction*, Dorsey Press.

RULON, P. J., TIEDEMAN, D. V., TATSUOKA, M. M., and LANGMUIR, C. R. (1967), *Multivariate Statistics for Personnel Classification*, Wiley.

RUSSEK, H. I. (1965), 'Stress, tobacco and coronary heart disease in North American professional groups', *Journal of American Medical Association*, vol. 192, pp. 189–94.

RUTENFRANZ, J., ASCHOFF, J., and MANN, H. (1970), 'The influence of a cumulative sleep deficit and length of preceding sleep period on multiple choice reaction time at different times of night', in W. P. Colquhoun (ed.), *Proceedings of the NATO Symposium on the Effects of Diurnal Rhythm and Loss of Sleep on Human Performance*, English Universities Press.

SALES, S. (1966), 'Supervisory style and productivity: a review', *Personnel Psychology*, vol. 19, pp. 275–86.

SAMPLE, J., and WILSON, T. (1965), 'Leader behavior, group productivity and rating of least preferred co-worker', *Journal of Personality and Social Psychology*, vol. 1, pp. 266–70.

Sanford, F. H. (1950), *Authoritarianism and Leadership*, Institute for Research in Human Relations.

Sargant, W. (1957), *Battle for the Mind*, Heinemann.

Sawtell, R. (1968), *Sharing our Industrial Future*, Industrial Society.

Sayeki, Y. (1969), 'Information seeking for object identification', *Organizational Behavior and Human Performance*, vol. 4, pp. 267–83.

Sayles, L. R. (1958), *Behavior of Industrial Work Groups*, Wiley.

Schachter, S., Ellertson, N., McBride, D., and Gregory, D. (1951), 'An experimental study of cohesiveness and productivity', *Human Relations*, vol. 4, pp. 229–38.

Schein, E. H. (1965), *Organizational Psychology*, Prentice-Hall.

Saben, S. (1967), 'Occupational mobility of employed workers', *Monthly Labor Review*, vol. 90, pp. 31–8.

Sadie, J. L. (1955), 'Discrimination against older workers in perspective', *Proceedings of the World Economic Conference*, United Nations Publications.

Sadler, P. J. (1968), 'Executive leadership', in D. Pym (ed.), *Industrial Society*, Penguin.

Sadler, P. J. (1970), 'Leadership style, confidence in management and job satisfaction', *Journal of Applied Behavioral Science*, vol. 6, pp. 3–19.

Schroder, H. M., Driver, M. J., and Streufert, S. (1967), *Human Information Processing*, Holt, Rinehart & Winston.

Schultz, D. T. (1969), 'The human subject in psychological research', *Psychological Bulletin*, vol. 72, pp. 214–28.

Scott, W. G. (1967), *Organizational Theory: A Behavioral Analysis for Management*, Irwin.

Seashore, S. (1954), *Group Cohesiveness in the Industrial Work Group*, Institute for Social Research.

Selvin, H. C. (1960), *The Effects of Leadership*, Free Press.

Sergean, R. (1971), *Managing Shiftwork*, Gower Press.

Seymour, W. D. (1954), *Industrial Training for Manual Operations*, Pitman.

Seymour, W. D. (1966), *Industrial Skills*, Pitman.

Seymour, W. D. (1968), *Skills Analysis Training*, Pitman.

Shaw, A. G. (1952), *The Purpose and Practice of Motion Study*, Harlequin Press.

Shaw, M. E., and Blum, J. M. (1966), 'Effects of leadership style upon group performance as a function of task structure', *Journal of Personality and Social Psychology*, vol. 3, pp. 238–42.

SHEPPARD, H. L., and BELITSKY, H. A. (1966), *The Job Hunt*, Johns Hopkins Press.

SHEPPARD, H. L. (1969a), 'The relevance of age to worker behavior in the labor market', *Industrial Gerontology*, no. 1, pp. 1–11.

SHEPPARD, H. L. (1969b), 'Ageing and manpower development', in M. W. Riley, J. W. Riley and M. E. Johnson (eds.), *Ageing and Society*, vol. 2, *Ageing and the Professions*, Russell Sage Foundation.

SHEPPARD, H. L. (1970) (ed.), *Industrial Gerontology*, Shenkman.

SHERIF, M. (1966), *Group Conflict and Co-operation*, Routledge & Kegan Paul.

SHOUKSMITH, G. (1968), *Assessment through Interviewing*, Pergamon.

SHUH, A. J. (1969), 'The predictability of employee tenure', *Personnel Psychology*, vol. 20, pp. 132–52.

SHULL, F. (1967), *Matrix Structure and Project Authority for Optimizing Organizational Capacity*, Business Research Bureau, Southern Illinois University.

SIDNEY, E., and BROWN, M. (1961), *The Skills of Interviewing*, Tavistock.

SIMON, H. A. (1955), 'A behavioral model of rational choice', *Quarterly Journal of Economics*, vol. 69, pp. 99–118.

SIMON, H. A. (1956), 'Rational choice and the structure of the environment', *Psychological Review*, vol. 63, pp. 129–38.

SIMON, H. A. (1960), *The New Science of Management Decision*, Harper & Row.

SINGLETON, W. T. (1960), 'An experimental investigation of speed controls for sewing machines', *Ergonomics*, vol. 3, pp. 365–75.

SINGLETON, W. T. (1967), 'The systems prototype and his design problems', in W. T. Singleton, R. S. Easterby and D. Whitfield (eds.), *The Human Operator in Complex Systems*, Taylor & Francis.

SINGLETON, W. T. (1969), 'Psychological limiting factors in human performance', in A. R. Meetham and R. A. Hudson (eds.), *Encyclopaedia of Linguistics, Information and Control*, Pergamon.

SINGLETON, W. T. (1970), *Introduction to Ergonomics*, Geneva World Health Organization.

SINGLETON, W. T., EASTERBY, R. S., and WHITFIELD, D. (eds.) (1967), *The Human Operator in Complex Systems*, Taylor & Francis.

SINGLETON, W. T., FOX, J. G., and WHITFIELD, D. (eds.) (1970), *The Measurement of Man at Work*, Taylor & Francis.

SKINNER, E. W. (1969), 'Relationships between leadership behavior patterns and organizational-situational variables', *Personnel Psychology*, vol. 22, pp. 489–94.

SLOVIC, P. (1969), 'Analysing the expert judge: a descriptive study of a stockbroker's decision process', *Journal of Applied Psychology*, vol. 53, pp. 255–63.

SMITH, R. D. (1968), 'Heuristic simulation of psychological decision processes', *Journal of Applied Psychology*, vol. 52, pp. 325–30.

SOBEL, I., and WILCOCK, R. C. (1966), *Placement Techniques*, OECD, Paris.

SOMMER, R. (1967), 'Small group ecology', *Psychological Bulletin*, vol. 67, pp. 145–52.

SPEARMAN, C. (1927), *The Abilities of Man, their Nature and Measurement*, Macmillan.

SPENCE K. W. (1959), 'The relation of learning theory to the technology of education', *Harvard Educational Review*, vol. 29, pp. 84–95.

SPERLING, G. (1960), 'The information available in brief visual presentations', *Psychological Monographs*, vol. 74, no. 11 (whole no. 498).

SPRINGBETT, B. M. (1958), 'Factors affecting the final decision in the employment interview', *Canadian Journal of Psychology*, vol. 12, pp. 13–22.

STAGER, P. (1967), 'Conceptual level as a composition variable in small-group decision making', *Journal of Personality and Social Psychology*, vol. 5, pp. 152–61. Reprinted in P. B. Warr (ed.), *Thought and Personality*, Penguin, 1970.

STAGNER, R. (1950), 'Psychological aspects of industrial conflict: II. Motivation', *Personnel Psychology*, vol. 3, pp. 1–16.

STAGNER, R. (1969), 'Corporate decision making: an empirical study', *Journal of Applied Psychology*, vol. 53, pp. 1–13.

STANTON, E. S. (1960), 'Company policies and supervisors' attitudes towards supervision', *Journal of Applied Psychology*, vol. 44, pp. 22–6.

STEDERY, A. C., and KAY, E. (1966), 'The effects of goal difficulty on performance', General Electric Company Technical Report.

STERN, G. G. (1970), *People in Context: Measuring Person-Environment Congruence in Education and Industry*, Wiley.

STEWART, R. (1965), 'Reactions to appraisal interviews', *Journal of Management Studies*, vol. 2, pp. 83–99.

STEWART, R. (1970), *Managers and their Jobs*, Pan.

STEWART, R. (1971), *How Computers Affect Management*, Macmillan.

STEWART, R., and WHITE, M. (1971), 'The classification of the effects of computer systems on management', *Journal of Management Studies*, in press.

STOCKFORD, L., and BISSELL, H. W. (1949), 'Factors involved in establishing a merit-rating scale', *Personnel*, vol. 26, pp. 94–116. Reprinted in E. A. Fleishman (ed.), *Studies in Personnel and Industrial Psychology*, Dorsey Press, 1967.

STOGDILL, R. M., and SHARTLE, C. L. (1948), 'Methods of determining patterns of leadership behavior in relation to organization structure and objectives', *Journal of Applied Psychology*, vol. 32, pp. 286–91.

STRAUSS, G. (1955), 'Group dynamics and intergroup relations', in W. H. Whyte (ed.), *Money and Motivation*, Harper & Row.

STRONG, E. K. (1955), *Vocational Interests Eighteen Years after College*, University of Minnesota Press.

SUPER, D. E., and OVERSTREET, P. L. (1960), *The Vocational Maturity of Ninth-Grade Boys*, Teachers College, Bureau of Publications, Columbia University.

SUPER, D. E., STARISHEVSKY, R., MATLIN, N., and JORDAAN, J. P. (1963), *Career Development: Self-Concept Theory*, Princeton College Entrance Examination Board.

SURRY, J. (1968), *Industrial Accident Research: A Human Engineering Appraisal*, University of Toronto Press.

SWAIN, A. D. (1963), 'A method for performing a human factors reliability analysis', Sandia Corporation Monograph 685, Washington Department of Commerce.

SWETS, J. A., MILLMAN, S. H., FLETCHER, W. E., and GREEN, D. M. (1962), 'Learning to identify non-verbal sounds. An application of a computer as a teaching machine', *Journal of the Acoustical Society of America*, vol. 34, pp. 928–35.

SYDIAHA, D. (1961), 'Bales' interaction process analysis of personnel selection interviews', *Journal of Applied Psychology*, vol. 45, pp. 393–401.

TAGUIRI, R., and LITWIN, G. H. (1968), *Organizational Climate: Exploration of a Concept*, Harvard Business School.

TAJFEL, H. (1970), 'Experiments in intergroup discrimination', *Scientific American*, no. 223, pp. 96–102.

TANNENBAUM, R., and SCHMIDT, W. H. (1958), 'How to choose a leadership pattern', *Harvard Business Review*, vol. 36, pp. 95–101.

TAYLOR, F. V. (1960), 'Four basic ideas in engineering psychology', *American Psychologist*, vol. 15, pp. 643–9. Reprinted in D. H. Holding (ed.), *Experimental Psychology in Industry*, Penguin, 1969.

TAYLOR, F. V. (1963), 'Human engineering and psychology', in S. Koch (ed.), *Psychology: A Study of a Science*, vol. 5, McGraw-Hill.

TAYLOR, P. J. (1967), 'Shift and day work', *British Journal of Industrial Medicine*, vol. 24, pp. 93–102.

THIIS-EVENSEN, E. (1967), 'Shift work and health', *Industrial Medicine*, vol. 27, pp. 493–7.

THOMPSON, J. D., and TUDEN, A. (1959), 'Comparative studies in administration', abridged in H. J. Leavitt and L. Pondy (eds.), *Readings in Managerial Psychology*, University of Chicago Press, 1964.

THOMSON, R. (1968), *The Pelican History of Psychology*, Penguin.

THORNDIKE, R. L. (1949), *Personnel Selection*, Wiley.

THURLEY, K. E., and HAMBLIN, A. C. (1963), *The Supervisor and his Job*, HMSO.

THURSTONE, L. L. (1930), 'Primary mental abilities', *Psychometric Monographs*, no. 1.

THURSTONE, L. L. (1931), *Reliability and Validity of Tests*, University of Michigan Press.

TIEDEMAN, D. V., and O'HARA, R. P. (1963), *Career Development: Choice and Adjustment*, Princeton College Entrance Examination Board.

TIFFIN, J., and MCCORMICK, E. J. (1966), *Industrial Psychology*, Allen & Unwin, 3rd edn.

TILLETT, A., KEMPNER, T., and WILLS, G. (eds.) (1970), *Management Thinkers*, Penguin.

TONGE, H. (1961), *A Heuristic Program for Assembly Line Balancing*, Prentice-Hall.

TOOPS, H. A. (1944), 'The criterion', *Educational and Psychological Measurement*, vol. 4, pp. 271–98.

TRAVERS, R. W. (1951), 'Rational hypotheses in construction of tests', *Educational and Psychological Measurement*, vol. 11, pp. 128–35.

TREISMAN, A. (1960), 'Contextual cues in selective listening', *Quarterly Journal of Experimental Psychology*, vol. 12, pp. 242–8.

TRIST, E. L., and BAMFORTH, K. W. (1951), 'Some social and psychological consequences of the longwall method of coal-getting', *Human Relations*, vol. 4, pp. 1–38.

TUNE, G. S. (1969), 'Sleep and wakefulness in a group of shift workers', *British Journal of Industrial Medicine*, vol. 26, pp. 54–8.

TURNER, A. N., and LAWRENCE, P. R. (1965), *Industrial Jobs and the Worker*, Harvard University Press.

TYLER, L. E. (1964), 'Work and individual differences', in H. Borow (ed.), *Man in a World at Work*, Houghton Mifflin.

ULRICH, L., and TRUMBO, D. (1965), 'The selection interview since 1949', *Psychological Bulletin*, vol. 63, pp. 100–116. Reprinted in E. A. Fleishman (ed.), *Studies in Personnel and Industrial Psychology*, Dorsey Press, 1967.

UNITED NATIONS DEPARTMENT OF ECONOMICS AND SOCIAL AFFAIRS (1956), *The Ageing of Populations and its Economic and Social Significance*, United Nations.

VAN LOON, J. H. (1963), 'The diurnal rhythm of body temperature in night workers', *Ergonomics*, vol. 6, pp. 267–73.

VAN ZELST, R. H. (1952), 'Sociometrically selected work teams increase production', *Personnel Psychology*, vol. 5, pp. 175–85.

VERNON, P. E. (1950), *The Structure of Human Abilities*, University of London Press.

VERNON, P. E. (1956), *The Measurement of Abilities*, University of London Press.

VERNON, P. E. (1963), *Personality Measurement*, Methuen.

VERNON, P. E., and PARRY, J. B. (1949), *Personnel Selection in British Armed Forces*, London University Press.

VIDMAR, N. J., and MCGRATH, J. E. (1965), 'Role assignment and attitudinal commitment as factors in negotiation', Technical Report no. 3, Department of Psychology University of Illinois.

VITELES M. S. (1953), *Motivation and Morale in Industry*, Norton.

VITZ, P. C., and KITE, W. R. (1970), 'Factors affecting conflict and negotiation within an alliance', *Journal of Experimental Social Psychology*, vol. 6, pp. 233–47.

VOSS, R. B. (1961), 'A description of the astronaut's task in Project Mercury', *Human Factors*, vol. 3, pp. 149–65.

VROOM, V. H. (1960), *Some Personality Determinants of the Effects of Participation*, Prentice-Hall.

VROOM, V. H. (1964), *Work and Motivation*, Wiley.

VROOM, V. H. (1969), 'Industrial social psychology', in G. Lindzey and E. Aronson (eds.), *Handbook of Social Psychology*, vol. 5, Addison-Wesley.

VROOM, V. H., and MANN, F. C. (1960), 'Leader authoritarianism and employee attitudes', *Personnel Psychology*, vol. 13, pp. 125–40.

VROOM, V. H., and DECI, E. L. (eds.) (1970), *Management and Motivation*, Penguin.

WALD, R. M., and DOTY, R. A. (1954), 'The top executive: a first-hand profile', *Harvard Business Review*, vol. 32, pp. 45–54.

WALKER, J. (1970), 'A review of the literature on the human problems of shift work', in National Board for Prices and Incomes, *Hours of Work, Overtime and Shift Working*, Report no. 161, HMSO.

WALKER, K. F. (1967), 'Workers' participation in management', *International Institute for Labour Studies Bulletin*, vol. 2, pp. 1–62.

WALKER, K. F. (1970), 'Workers' participation in management: concepts and reality', delivered to the Second World Congress of the International Industrial Relations Association.

WALL, T. D., STEPHENSON, G. M., and SKIDMORE, C. (1971), 'Ego involvement and Herzberg's two-factor theory of job satisfaction: an experimental field study', *British Journal of Social and Clinical Psychology*, vol. 10, pp. 123–31.

WALLACH, M. A., and KOGAN, N. (1961), 'Aspects of judgment and decision making: interrelationships and changes with age', *Behavioral Science*, vol. 6, pp. 23–36.

WALLIS, D., DUNCAN, K. D., and KNIGHT, M. A. G. (1966), *Programmed Instruction in the British Armed Forces*, HMSO.

WALTON, R. E., and MCKERSIE, R. B. (1965), *A Behavioral Theory of Labor Negotiations*, McGraw-Hill.

WARR, P. B. (ed.) (1970), *Thought and Personality*, Penguin.

WARR, P. B., and BIRD, M. W. (1967), 'Assessing the training needs of foremen', *Journal of Management Studies*, vol. 4, pp. 332–53.

WARR, P. B., and COFFMAN, T. L. (1969), 'Affirmation and denial in the structure of inference rules', *Journal of Verbal Learning and Verbal Behavior*, vol. 8, pp. 705–12.

WARR, P. B., and COFFMAN, T. L. (1970), 'Personality, involvement and extremity of judgment', *British Journal of Social and Clinical Psychology*, vol. 9, pp. 108–21.

WARR, P. B., and HAYCOCK, V. (1970), 'Scales for a British personality differential', *British Journal of Social and Clinical Psychology*, vol. 9, pp. 328–37.

WARR, P. B., and KNAPPER, C. (1968), *The Perception of People and Events*, Wiley.

WARR, P. B., and ROUTLEDGE, T. (1969), 'An opinion scale for the study of managers' job satisfaction', *Occupational Psychology*, vol. 43, pp. 95–109.

WARR, P. B., and SMITH, J. S. (1970), 'Combining information about people: comparisons between six models', *Journal of Personality and Social Psychology*, vol. 16, pp. 55–65.

WARR, P. B., BIRD, M., and RACKHAM, N. (1970), *Evaluation of Management Training*, Gower Press.

WARR, P. B., SCHRODER, H. M., and BLACKMAN, S. (1969), 'The structure of political judgment', *British Journal of Social and Clinical Psychology*, vol. 8, pp. 32–43.

WEBB, W. B., and AGNEW, H. W. (1967), 'Sleep cycling within twenty four hour periods', *Journal of Experimental Psychology*, vol. 74, pp. 158–60.

WEBBER, R. A. (1970), 'Perception of interactions between superiors and subordinates', *Human Relations*, vol. 23, pp. 235–48.

WEBER, M. (1947), *The Theory of Social and Economic Organization*, Free Press.

WEBSTER, E. C. (1964), *Decision Making in the Employment Interview*, Applied Psychology Centre, McGill University.

WEDDERBURN, A. A. I. (1967), 'Social factors in satisfaction with swiftly rotating shifts', *Occupational Psychology*, vol. 41, pp. 85–107.

WEINSTEIN, M. S. (1969), 'Achievement motivation and risk preference', *Journal of Personality and Social Psychology*, vol. 39, pp. 294–300.

WEITZ, J., and NUCKOLS, R. C. (1955), 'Job satisfaction and job survival', *Journal of Applied Psychology*, vol. 39, pp. 294–300.

WELFORD, A. T. (1958), *Ageing and Human Skill*, Oxford University Press.

WELFORD, A. T. (1962), 'On changes in performance with age', *Lancet*, (Part 1), pp. 335–9. Reprinted in D. H. Holding (ed.), *Experimental Psychology in Industry*, Penguin, 1969.

WELFORD, A. T. (1967), 'Single channel operation in the brain', *Acta Psychologica*, vol. 27, pp. 5–22.

WELFORD, A. T. (1968), *Fundamentals of Skill*, Methuen.

WHITFIELD, D. (1967), 'Human skill as a determinant of allocation of function', in W. T. Singleton, R. S. Easterby and D. Whitfield (eds.), *The Human Operator in Complex Systems*, Taylor & Francis.

WHITFIELD, D. (1970), 'A pilot survey of human factors aspects of power reactor safety and control', Report EDU01, Applied Psychology Department, University of Aston.

WHYTE, W. F. (1948), *Human Relations in the Restaurant Industry*, McGraw-Hill.

WHYTE, W. F. (1955), *Money and Motivation: An Analysis of Incentives in Industry*, Harper & Row.

WICKELGREN, W. A. (1964), 'Size of rehearsal group and short term memory', *Journal of Experimental Psychology*, vol. 68, pp. 413–19.

WICKERT, F. R. (1951), 'Turnover and employees' feelings of ego-involvement in the day-to-day operations of a company', *Personnel Psychology*, vol. 4, pp. 185–97.

Wildebois, V. G. J. M. Van Der (1968), *Werkstructarering als organisatieontwikkeling*, Eindhoven, N.V., Philips' Industries.

Wilkinson, R. T. (1958), 'The effects of sleep loss on performance', MRC Applied Psychology Research Unit, Report no. 323/58.

Wilkinson, R. T. (1961), 'Interaction of lack of sleep with knowledge of results, repeated testing and individual differences', *Journal of Experimental Psychology*, vol. 62, pp. 263–71.

Wilkinson, R. T. (1963), 'Interaction of noise with knowledge of results and sleep deprivation', *Journal of Experimental Psychology*, vol. 66, pp. 332–7.

Wilkinson, R. T. (1965), 'Sleep deprivation', in O. G. Edholm and A. L. Bacharach (eds.), *The Physiology of Human Survival*, Academic Press.

Wilkinson, R. T. (1969), 'Sleep deprivation: performance tests for partial and selective sleep deprivation', in L. A. Abt and B. F. Reiss (eds.), *Progress in Clinical Psychology*, vol. 7, Grune.

Wilkinson, R. T. (1970), 'Sleep deprivation – a review', in W. P. Colquhoun (ed.), *Proceedings of the NATO Symposium on the Effects of Diurnal Rhythm and Loss of Sleep on Human Performance*, English Universities Press.

Wilkinson, R. T., and Edwards, R. S. (1968), 'Stable hours and varied work as aids to efficiency', *Psychonomic Science*, vol. 13, pp. 205–6.

Wilkinson, R. T., Fox, R. H., Goldsmith, R., Hampton, I. F. G., and Lewis, H. E. (1964), 'Psychological and physiological responses to raised body temperatures', *Journal of Applied Physiology*, vol. 19, pp. 287–91.

Williams, W. L., and Whitmore, P. G. (1959), 'The development and use of a performance test as a basis for comparing technicians with and without field experience of the Nike Ajax IFC Maintenance Technician', Human Resources Research Office Technical Report 52.

Wirtz, W. W. (1965), *The Older American Worker: Age Discrimination in Employment*, US Government Printing Office.

Wolf, M. G. (1970), 'Need gratification theory: a theoretical reformulation of job satisfaction/dissatisfaction and job motivation', *Journal of Applied Psychology*, vol. 54, pp. 89–94.

Woods, P., and Hartley, J. R. (1970), 'Some learning models for arithmetic tasks and their use in computer based learning', unpublished report from the Research Councils' Computer Based Learning Project, Leeds.

WOODWARD, J. (1965), *Industrial Organization: Theory and Practice*, Oxford University Press.

WRIGHT, D. S., TAYLOR, A., DAVIES, D. R., SLUCKIN, W., LEE, S. G. M., and REASON, J. T. (1970), *Introducing Psychology: An Experimental Approach*, Penguin.

WRIGHT, P., HULL, A. J., and CONRAD, R. (1969), 'Performance tests with non-circular coins', *Ergonomics*, vol. 12, pp. 1–10.

YOUNG, L. R. (1969), 'On adaptive manual control', *Ergonomics*, vol. 12, pp. 635–75.

YUKL, G. (1970), 'Leader LPC scores: attitude dimensions and behavioral correlates', *Journal of Social Psychology*, vol. 80, pp. 207–12.

ZILLER, R. C. (1957), 'Vocational choice and utility for risk', *Journal of Counseling Psychology*, vol. 4, pp. 61–4.

ZIMBARDO, P. G., and EBBESON, E. B. (1969), *Influencing Attitudes and Changing Behavior*, Addison-Wesley.

Acknowledgements

Acknowledgement is due to the following for permission to use figures in this volume.

Figure 2.1, *Ergonomics*, P. Colquhoun, R. S. Edwards and M. J. S. Blake; Figure 2.2, University of Chicago Press and N. Kleitman; Figures 2.3 and 2.4, *Psychonomic Science*; Figure 2.5, *Ergonomics*, P. Colquhoun, R. S. Edwards and M. J. S. Blake; Figure 2.6, *Aerospace Medicine*, N. K. Klein, H. Bonner, H. Holtmann, H. Rehme, J. Stolze, W. D. Stanhoss and H. D. Wegman; Figure 2.8, National Institute of Industrial Psychology, G. de la Mare and J. Walker; Figure 10.1, John Wiley & Sons Ltd; Figure 11.1, Holt, Rinehart & Winston Inc.; Figure 11.2, *Nature*, A. Elithorn, J. R. Jagoe and D. M. Lee; Figure 11.4, Prentice-Hall, Inc., Richard M. Cyert and James G. March; Figure 12.3, McGraw-Hill Book Company and F. E. Fiedler.

Author Index

Subject Index